The Geography of Scientific Collaboration

Science is increasingly defined by multidimensional collaborative networks. Despite the unprecedented growth of scientific collaboration around the globe–the collaborative turn–geography still matters for the cognitive enterprise. This book explores how geography conditions scientific collaboration and how collaboration affects the spatiality of science.

This book offers a complex analysis of the spatial aspects of scientific collaboration, addressing the topic at a number of levels: individual, organizational, urban, regional, national, and international. Spatial patterns of scientific collaboration are analysed along with their determinants and consequences. By combining a vast array of approaches, concepts, and methodologies, the volume offers a comprehensive theoretical framework for the geography of scientific collaboration. The examples of scientific collaboration policy discussed in the book are taken from the European Union, the United States, and China. Through a number of case studies the authors analyse the background, development and evaluation of these policies.

This book will be of interest to researchers in diverse disciplines such as regional studies, scientometrics, R&D policy, socio-economic geography and network analysis. It will also be of interest to policymakers, and to managers of research organisations.

Agnieszka Olechnicka is an assistant professor and director at the Centre for European Regional and Local Studies (EUROREG), University of Warsaw, Poland. She is the secretary of the Polish Section of Regional Studies Association.

Adam Ploszaj is an assistant professor at the University of Warsaw, Poland. Adam frequently advises national and international institutions—including the European Commission, World Bank, and UNDP—on regional development and research policy.

Dorota Celińska-Janowicz holds the position of counsellor for student affairs and assistant professor at the Centre for European Regional and Local Studies (EUROREG), University of Warsaw, Poland. She is also the treasurer of the Polish Section of Regional Studies Association.

Routledge Advances in Regional Economics, Science and Policy

21 Post-Metropolitan Territories and Urban Space
Edited by Alessandro Balducci, Valeria Fedeli and Francesco Curci

22 Big Data for Regional Science
Edited by Laurie A. Schintler and Zhenhua Chen

23 The Spatial and Economic Transformation of Mountain Regions
Landscapes as Commodities
Manfred Perlik

24 Neoliberalism and Urban Development in Latin America
The Case of Santiago
Edited by Camillo Boano and Francisco Vergara-Perucich

25 Rural Housing and Economic Development
Edited by Don E. Albrecht, Scott Loveridge, Stephan Goetz and Rachel Welborn

26 Creative Ageing Cities
Place Design with Older People in Asian Cities
Edited Keng Hua CHONG and Mihye CHO

27 Competitiveness and Knowledge
An International Comparison of Traditional Firms
Knut Ingar Westeren, Hanas Cader, Maria de Fátima Sales, Jan Ole Similä and Jefferson Staduto

28 Gastronomy and Local Development
The Quality of Products, Places and Experiences
Edited by Nicola Bellini, Cécile Clergeau and Olivier Etcheverria

29 The Geography of Scientific Collaboration
Agnieszka Olechnicka, Adam Płoszaj and Dorota Celińska-Janowicz

For more information about this series, please visit www.routledge.com/series/RAIRESP

The Geography of Scientific Collaboration

Agnieszka Olechnicka, Adam Ploszaj
and Dorota Celińska-Janowicz

LONDON AND NEW YORK

First published 2019
by Routledge
2 Park Square, Milton Park, Abingdon, Oxon OX14 4RN

and by Routledge
711 Third Avenue, New York, NY 10017

Routledge is an imprint of the Taylor & Francis Group, an informa business

© 2019 Agnieszka Olechnicka, Adam Ploszaj and Dorota Celińska-Janowicz

The right of Agnieszka Olechnicka, Adam Ploszaj and Dorota Celińska-Janowicz to be identified as authors of this work has been asserted by them in accordance with sections 77 and 78 of the Copyright, Designs and Patents Act 1988.

All rights reserved. No part of this book may be reprinted or reproduced or utilised in any form or by any electronic, mechanical, or other means, now known or hereafter invented, including photocopying and recording, or in any information storage or retrieval system, without permission in writing from the publishers.

Trademark notice: Product or corporate names may be trademarks or registered trademarks, and are used only for identification and explanation without intent to infringe.

British Library Cataloguing-in-Publication Data
A catalogue record for this book is available from the British Library

Library of Congress Cataloging-in-Publication Data
Names: Olechnicka, Agnieszka, author. | Ploszaj, Adam, author. | Celinska-Janowicz, Dorota, author.
Title: The geography of scientific collaboration / Agnieszka Olechnicka, Adam Ploszaj, and Dorota Celinska-Janowicz.
Description: Abingdon, Oxon ; New York, NY : Routledge, 2019. | Series: Routledge advances in regional economics, science and policy ; 29 | Includes bibliographical references and index.
Identifiers: LCCN 2018028640| ISBN 9781138203334 (hardback) | ISBN 9781315471921 (pdf) | ISBN 9781315471914 (epub) | ISBN 9781315471907 (mobi)
Subjects: LCSH: Science--International cooperation. | Communication in science.
Classification: LCC Q172.5.I5 O44 2019 | DDC 507.2–dc23
LC record available at https://lccn.loc.gov/2018028640

ISBN: 978-1-138-20333-4 (hbk)
ISBN: 978-1-315-47193-8 (ebk)

Typeset in Bembo
by Integra Software Services Pvt. Ltd.

Contents

List of illustrations vii
Acknowledgements viii

Introduction 1

1 Places and spaces of science 4
   1.1 Science takes place 4
   1.2 From little science spots to the global geography of science 6
   1.3 Driving forces of the geography of science 16

2 Scientists working together 27
   2.1 Before the fourth age of research 28
   2.2 The collaborative turn 34
   2.3 What is scientific collaboration? 40
   2.4 Why do scientists collaborate? 45
   2.5 The collaboration life cycle and its challenges 52

3 Measuring scholarly collaboration in space 61
   3.1 Collaborative data: sources and approaches 61
   3.2 The reward triangle and research collaboration studies 64
   3.3 Spatial scientometric measures 66
   3.4 Methodological issues 72

4 Spatial patterns of scientific collaboration 77
   4.1 Internationalisation 78
   4.2 The global scientific network 89
   4.3 Patterns of collaboration and research performance 96
   4.4 The logic of centre and periphery 102

5 Theoretical approaches to scientific collaboration from a spatial perspective 107
5.1 Explaining the growth of collaboration 107
5.2 Explaining patterns of scientific collaboration 111
5.3 Explaining the impacts of scientific collaboration 120

6 Scientific collaboration policy 133
6.1 Policy through science and for science 133
6.2 Policy shift towards collaboration 135
6.3 Europe: towards the European Research Area 137
6.4 The United States: collaborative culture 145
6.5 China: (r)evolution in science policy 154
6.6 Tools for scientific collaboration policy 163

7 Conclusions 176
7.1 Research collaboration and the geography of science 176
7.2 Future geographies of scientific collaboration 178
7.3 Towards smart policies for scientific collaboration 181

References 185
Index 222

Illustrations

Figures

1.1	Interweaving relationships between places and spaces of science	7
1.2	Scientific papers indexed in Web of Science, 2000–2009	16
1.3	Workplaces of leading scientists, 16th–19th centuries	25
2.1	Collaboration modes	43
4.1	Share of internationally co-authored articles, 1970–2013	80
4.2	Share of internationally co-authored articles in 2013	84
4.3	Research output and internationalisation at country level: articles (left) and patents (right)	85
4.4	International cooperation in patents—share of patents with foreign co-inventors in 2013	87
4.5	Internationally co-authored articles in the US in 2013	88
4.6	Share of internationally co-authored articles in European regions in the period of 2007–2013	90
4.7	Research output and internationalisation in US states and EU NUTS 2 regions (left), and NUTS 2 regions within selected EU countries (right), 2007–2013	91
4.8	The network of internationally co-authored articles in 1980	93
4.9	The network of internationally co-authored articles in 1990	94
4.10	The network of internationally co-authored articles in 2000	95
4.11	The network of internationally co-authored articles in 2013	96
4.12	Scientific collaboration among global macro-regions in 2013 and its evolution since 2000	97
4.13	World network of interurban scientific co-authorships in 2000	98
4.14	World network of interurban scientific co-authorships in 2013	99
4.15	The citation impact of scientific production and the extent of international collaboration (2003–2012)	101
4.16	Normalised mean citations of papers in which scholars from a given country play the role of corresponding or non-corresponding authors (2000–2013)	104

Table

2.1	Selected definitions of scientific collaboration	42

Acknowledgements

This collaborative book on the spatial aspects of research collaboration has its origins in a serendipitous temporal co-location. In 2008, aimlessly roaming the offices of EUROREG at the University of Warsaw, Adam stopped in front of the screen filled by a large spreadsheet. It was Agnieszka's computer, on which she was parsing massive co-authorship data. It soon emerged that we had complementary backgrounds, matching skills, and overlapping research interests. Our collaboration gradually developed and eventually resulted in the idea for this volume. While drafting the synopsis, it became apparent that we needed more comprehensive expertise in geography. In this way, Dorota joined the team.

In a sense, the making of this book had a self-referential flavour. To a large degree, our collaboration was based on spatial proximity. However, we encountered periods of temporal geographical separation when we had to rely on interactions mediated by information and communication technologies. Furthermore, the book would not have been possible without countless fruitful exchanges with our colleagues around the globe, both spatially close and distant.

We are particularly grateful to all those who read parts of the draft and shared their critical insights, brilliant ideas, and heart-warming encouragements: Katy Börner (Indiana University Bloomington), Thomas F. Gieryn (Indiana University Bloomington), Grzegorz Gorzelak (University of Warsaw), Noriko Hara (Indiana University Bloomington), Emanuel Kulczycki (Adam Mickiewicz University), David N. Livingstone (Queen's University Belfast), and Ewa Zegler-Poleska (Indiana University Bloomington).

A number of magnificent colleagues provided us with information on national science policies: Jiří Blažek (Charles University in Prague), Roberta Capello (Polytechnic University of Milan), Andrea Caragliu (Polytechnic University of Milan), David Charles (University of Strathclyde), Marcin Dąbrowski (Delft University of Technology), Leszek Dolega (University of Liverpool), Piotr Dutkiewicz (Carlton University), Martin Ferry (University of Strathclyde), Balazs Lengyel (Hungarian Academy of Sciences), Moritz Lennert (Free University of Brussels), Marion Maisonobe (Paris-Est University and University of Toulouse-Jean Jaurès), David Marek (Technology Centre of the Academy of Sciences of the Czech Republic), Ben Martin (University of Sussex), Olga Mrinska (European Bank for Reconstruction and Development),

Maria Prezioso (University of Rome Tor Vergata), Ryszard Rózga-Luter (Mexico Metropolitan Autonomous University), Frédéric Santamaria (Paris Diderot University), André Spithoven (Ghent University), Yutao Sun (Dalian University of Technology and University of Nottingham), Josselin Tallec (University of Toulouse-Jean Jaurès), Attila Varga (University of Pécs), Ting Yan (China University of Political Science and Law), Sabine Zillmer (Spatial Foresight, Luxembourg), and Arno Van Der Zwet (University of Strathclyde).

Also, we would like to thank the ResearchGate users who contributed to the discussion about the book: Carlos Henrique Brito Cruz (University of Campinas), Jerry Decker (no active affiliation), Geoff Edwards (Griffith University), Brigid Freeman (University of Melbourne), Robert G. Healy (Duke University), Merle Jacob (Lund University), James F. Peters (University of Manitoba), William Sheridan (Infometrica), Darly Henriques da Silva (Brazilian National Council for Scientific and Technological Development), and K. Brad Wray (Aarhus University). We hope that we will be able to meet off-line one day.

Marion Maisonobe (Paris-Est University and University of Toulouse-Jean Jaurès) and Laurent Jégou (University of Toulouse-Jean Jaurès) graciously provided figures 16-18 displayed in Chapter 4. We are grateful for your courtesy.

The positive feedback of the three anonymous Routledge reviewers have been of great help in the refinement of the initial book idea. We also appreciate the professional assistance of the Routledge editors, Elanor Best, Anna Cuthbert, Ananth Ganesan, Robert Langham, Lisa Lavelle, Natalie Tomlinson, and our copy editors: Lucy Bindulska and Lori Goshert.

Funding for this work came from the Polish National Science Centre (project no.: 2011/03/B/HS4/05737), the grant provided by the vice-rector for Research and International Relations of the University of Warsaw, and the resources of the Centre for European Regional and Local Studies (EUROREG) at the University of Warsaw.

Special gratitude should be given to Katy Börner and Pnina Fichman for hosting Adam at the Indiana University Bloomington in 2016. The excellent working environment that you kindly offered proved critical for this book project and beyond.

Our closely co-located colleagues from the Centre for European Regional and Local Studies (EUROREG) at the University of Warsaw should be acknowledged for their continuous support, sincere encouragement, and occasional jokes about the never-ending book project.

Finally, we thank our families for their patience and love.

Introduction

In 1980, Stanley Presser opened a paper in Social Studies of Science with a somewhat alarming phrase: "The dramatic growth of collaborative research over the last few decades has been clearly documented" (p. 95). Since Presser published his article, the average number of co-authors of scientific papers has doubled, the percentage of international collaborative publications has increased fivefold, and the mean distance between collaborating scholars is no longer measured in hundreds, but in thousands of kilometres. If 40 years ago the growth of scientific collaboration was dramatic, what adjective should we use today? Yes, science has always been a collective activity—a social system within which the intersubjective understanding of the world has been crafted and negotiated. But today's science is saturated with collaboration on an unprecedented scale. Multilevel and multimodal networks increasingly condition and shape the contemporary cognitive enterprise. This collaborative turn not only alters the ways science is organised, managed, and performed but also enables new research objectives, accelerates knowledge production, and challenges practices of establishing the epistemic validity of science.

At the same time, in the contemporary technology-dependent and innovation-obsessed world, science occupies an emphasised place. And this is not only a symbolic zone in our imagination. Scientific inquiry takes place at very tangible coordinates: public and private laboratories, university campuses, research libraries, and remote research facilities, to name but a few. The spatial location of scientific activity may seem trivial in contrast to the universal validity of science. But make no mistake, geography matters. On the one hand, the specific conditions of places influence the quantity and quality of scientific activity and its outputs and impacts. On the other hand, the presence of the science sector affects the economic and social development of neighbourhoods, towns, cities, regions, and whole nations.

The juxtaposition of these two broad topics laid the foundation of our study. We started with straightforward questions of how geography conditions scientific collaboration and how collaboration affects the spatiality of science. As we explored the subject, more intriguing questions emerged. Specifically, there is a tension between the seemingly disruptive capacity of the collaborative turn and the persistence of social, economic, and spatial structures of science. Even though scientific enterprise has become increasingly collaborative, networked, and internationalised, it also remains substantially hierarchical. Those hierarchies largely reflect organisational, national, and international disparities ingrained in the pre–collaborative-turn era. At the same time, the rise of new scientific hubs cannot be fully understood without accounting for collaborative networks. In this entangled system, scientific collaboration seems to play a disruptive—as defined by Schumpeter (1942) and Christensen (1997)—and simultaneously a stabilising role.

The other intriguing tension is between proximity and distance. Despite the development of transportation and communication technologies that have overhauled traditional time-space limits and greatly facilitated scientific collaboration on a global scale, proximate collaborative links tend to outnumber distant relations. Spatial closeness constantly matters for the formation of research collaboration. Meanwhile, distant collaborations bring the promise of bolder results and impacts. The combination of diverse capacities—more likely in broader networks—seems to promote the expansion of the knowledge frontier. What, then, is the role of spatial proximity and distance in scientific collaboration? How should science policy respond to the proximity-distance dilemma?

Challenges imposed on science policy by the massive growth of research collaboration go well beyond the above-stated problem. Traditionally, collaboration-oriented science policy was aimed at intensifying collaboration. But since research collaboration has become semi-ubiquitous, the traditional approach is no longer adequate. The key issue is not how to increase collaboration, but rather how collaborative networks should be managed, how to evaluate their benefits and costs, and how to respond to the direct and indirect consequences of collaboration. The increasingly central role of collaboration in scientific enterprise implies the gradual amalgamation of science policy and scientific collaboration policies. Thus, understanding the processes and patterns of scientific collaboration becomes indispensable for crafting science policies in the collaborative-turn era.

Before proceeding, it is essential to distinguish between the geography of scientific collaboration—the research domain that we outline in this volume—and the geography of science. The relation between the two can be seen through the lens of the concept of knowledge stocks and flows (Machlup, 1979). While the geography of science is preoccupied with the location of research activities, the geography of scientific collaboration focuses on flows between those places. Certainly, the two approaches cannot be separated. On the one hand, the localisation of research centres forms a playing field for scientific flows: after all, links do not exist without nodes. On the other hand, flows in the form of scholarly collaboration constitute a significant factor for the progress and impact of scientific places. In a certain sense, "these places are not meaningful in themselves but only as nodes of these networks" (Castells & Ince, 2003, p. 57). Ultimately, spatial hubs of research collaboration fundamentally overlap with centres of scientific production and excellence.

In what follows, we deliberately seek a balance between broad and narrow approaches. First of all, we use a broad, open definition of scientific collaboration: the act of working together to achieve common scientific objectives. This tactic allows us to capture the phenomena in all its complexity and to avoid futile definitional considerations. Simultaneously, we limit our focus to relations among scientists and within science. As a result, we almost entirely pass by the issue of science-industry and science-business relations (already discussed at length by many great authors). Lastly, our theoretical approach is broad. Because there is no definite theory of scientific collaboration from a territorial perspective, we had wide latitude in testing a great variety of concepts, ideas, and frameworks developed within various intellectual schools, scientific fields, and research paradigms. In doing so, we were able to map the emerging theory of the geography of scientific collaboration.

Our journey through the places and spaces of scientific collaboration has seven stages. The first two chapters pave the way for the remaining parts of the volume. To discuss the spatial aspects of research collaboration we need to understand the driving forces of the geography of science (Chapter 1) and the processes that govern collaboration on the level of individuals, teams, and organisations, as well as the historical developments that led to the contemporary collaborative turn in science (Chapter 2). In Chapter 3 we overview data sources, measures, and methodological considerations for spatial studies of research collaboration. Chapter 4 depicts and scrutinises the spatial patterns of scientific collaboration at several territorial levels. We focus on the internationalisation of science, the evolution of global scientific networks, the geographical patterns of collaboration-performance nexus, and the centre-periphery logic of the geography of scientific collaboration. Chapter 5 provides explanations of the driving forces and processes that condition research collaboration in space. Here we outline the theoretical framework for the geography of scientific collaboration. Chapter 6 reviews research collaboration policies. It consists of policy case studies—set in Europe, the United States, and China—as well as a comprehensive catalogue of tools for scientific collaboration policy. The book closes with conclusions that summarise our key insights, reflect on possible future trajectories of the geography of scientific collaboration, and discuss challenges for science policy in the collaborative-turn era.

1 Places and spaces of science

Science, like every human activity, literally takes place. It goes without saying that space matters for scientific enterprise. Yet "There is something strange about science", as David N. Livingstone notes in *Putting Science in its Place*, his fundamental work on geographies of scientific knowledge. He points out that scientific inquiry always takes place somewhere, often in highly specific sites, and at the same time knowledge produced in these places has universal value and ubiquitous qualities.[1] Thus "Scientific findings [...] are both local and global; they are both particular and universal; they are both provincial and transcendental" (2003, p. xi). We suggest that this paradoxical conundrum can be solved by distinguishing—even if somewhat artificially—places and spaces of science. The former relate to particular locations and geographical territories, the latter to the abstract, intangible realm of knowledge. This distinction is analysed in the first part of the chapter. We then discuss selected types of science places and their relation to the development of modern science. Afterwards, we present the global variations of scientific activities. The closing part of the chapter addresses the mechanisms and driving forces underlying the geography of science.

1.1 Science takes place

Let us consider two types of scientific journey: one through physical *places* and the other in the realm of immaterial *spaces*. For centuries, people have travelled to remote places to discover new knowledge. The theory of evolution would not be what it is without Charles Darwin's (1809–1882) five-year round-the-world expedition, which he elaborately described in his acclaimed *The Voyage of the Beagle* (1839). Another scientific giant, Alexander von Humboldt (1769–1859), also reaped exceptional gains from long travels. His five-year Latin American trip enabled him to bring into being modern physical geography, plant geography, and meteorology (Wulf, 2015). The 20th century saw humanity reaching the Moon and sending probes further into the solar system. Now, at the beginning of the 21st century, the physical movement of scholars is also vital, though more in the form of professional mobility and brain circulation than adventurous exploration (Naylor & Ryan, 2010).

However, more and more research endeavour goes on in the endless space of information that humanity has generated and is generating every single second. These expeditions into the digital wilderness—the Big Data Jungle—may seem less exciting. Nonetheless, they can certainly prove incredibly revealing. Scientific voyages into intangible spaces occurred long before those in virtual realms and, in fact, form the bedrock of science. For the sake of brevity we need only mention Plato's (5th and 4th century BC) investigations into the world of ideas (universal truths) and Karl Popper's (1902–1994) theory of three worlds, where the third world contains "objective knowledge" created by people (Jarvie, Milford, & Miller, 2006).

Places produce frames within which scientific endeavour takes place. Various sites constitute core science infrastructure: laboratories, observatories, libraries, archives, university campuses, botanical gardens, agricultural experiment stations, research hospitals, corporate research parks, field sites, and remote research stations, to name only the most obvious. Moreover, particular localities tend to foster intellectual and creative work. Oxford and Cambridge in the UK, Cambridge in Massachusetts, Silicon Valley in California, and Sophia Antipolis in France are immediately associated with science and technology. Larger territorial entities, such as regions or countries, can also be recognised as science places since their state of scientific advancement varies significantly and can be attributed to their individual history, geography, culture, society, politics, and economy.

On the other hand, science spaces reflect the relations between terms, notions, ideas, theories, paradigms, scientific disciplines, and fields. This space of relationships is fundamental for science, which can be understood as an inquiry into how and why phenomena interrelate. Moreover, knowledge as such can be seen as the meaningful organisation of information. Without entering the philosophical debate looming over the two previous statements,[2] let us direct our voyage into spaces of science towards a down-to-earth object: a library catalogue drawer. Library classifications stand as a spectacular example of how relationships in the scientific space can be made visible. When, in 1876, Melvil Dewey (1851–1931) proposed his hierarchical Dewey Decimal Classification (DDC), he brought about a major advance in knowledge management. The DDC helped to shelve books thematically instead of putting them in the order of acquisition, which had been the common practice for centuries. More importantly, it also made it possible to implement an easy-to-navigate, thematic library catalogue—a tool that significantly improved information access and administration.[3]

Much in the same way, classifications, catalogues, ontologies, and other attempts to organise the growing amount of data and information captured meaningful relations in the scientific space and influenced progress in scientific knowledge (Wright, 2007). Linnaean taxonomy, developed in 1735 by Swedish scholar Carl Linnaeus (1707–1778), facilitated biological research, making communication between naturalists easier. The periodic table of chemical elements, published in 1869 by Russian chemist Dmitrij Mendeleev (1834–1907), represented a magnificent milestone, as it foresaw the existence of elements that had not yet been discovered. Different attempts to capture science spaces are embodied in "science maps": usually non-geospatial visualisations, also called infographics or information visualisations. During the 20th century, science maps slowly became more and more popular. At the beginning of the 21st century, largely because of easy access to computing power and the appropriate software, science maps proliferated and permeated a broad spectrum of applications, from mapping scholarly genealogies, co-authorships, citations, and co-citations, through analysing relations between scientific fields, concepts, and paradigms, to showing under-researched topics or forecasting new research fronts (Börner, 2010, 2015).

The concept of science spaces also relates to communities of scholars. Be it the 17th-century Invisible College—a precursor to the Royal Society of London. Be it the famous Republic of Letters in the Age of Enlightenment— an international community based on the circulation of handwritten letters, but also printed materials. Be it the New Invisible College—global science networks facilitated by the development of information technology (Wagner, 2008). This type of science space brings us back to the question of the relations between spaces and places of science. Scientific communities are simultaneously spatial and non-spatial. They can be purely virtual, but the individuals involved in them occupy real places somewhere in the world. Therefore, it is possible to produce a spatial map of the Republic of Letters (Chang et al., 2009) or online scholarly communities. To shed some more light on the relations between places and spaces of science, we can recall an antebellum drawing by Paul Otlet (1868–1944)—the Belgian visionary and great-grandfather of the internet (Day, 2001; Wright, 2014). His imaginary vision of relationships between the world and scientific knowledge corresponds to our space-place distinction (see Figure 1.1). From this perspective, scholars, their tools, and infrastructures occupy distinct, physical places. Simultaneously, they operate in the space of interrelated ideas.

Certainly, places and spaces of science are inextricably connected. At the same time, they differ considerably. Places are defined, particular, and physical. Spaces are abstract, ubiquitous, and nonmaterial. But, beyond a shadow of a doubt, both spaces and places are vital for the emergence and sustenance of science, its diffusion, and our understanding of these processes. While acknowledging the importance of science spaces, we will now put them aside and focus in this chapter—and the whole book—on places of science.

1.2 From little science spots to the global geography of science

The Cambridge History of Science, vol. 3: Early Modern Science dedicates more than 130 pages to analysing the role of markets, piazzas, villages, homes, households, libraries, classrooms, courts, cabinets, workshops, academies, anatomy theatres, botanical gardens, natural history collections, laboratories, sites of military science and technology, coffeehouses, and printshops. In the period from 1490 to 1730, the diversity of science places was already striking. Today, this landscape can only be more complex. While it is always risky to paint with

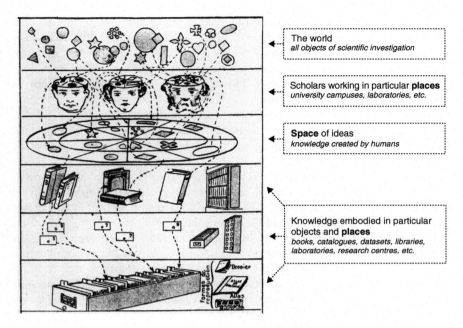

Figure 1.1 Interweaving relationships between places and spaces of science
Source: Drawing on the left from Otlet, 1934, p. 41; schema on the right—conception and design by Adam Ploszaj.

a broad brush, we would argue that for the sake of placing scientific collaboration, we are justified in focusing only on selected science places, namely the laboratory, library and other humanities-related sites, and the university campus. This close-up view of science in places is then complemented by a panoramic view from a distance: the global geography of science.

1.2.1 The laboratory

The laboratory is unquestionably the most iconic place of contemporary science. First, modern science would not have become what it is today without laboratories. As Louis Pasteur (1822–1895), French chemist, microbiologist, and vaccination pioneer, allegedly put it, "Without laboratories men of science are soldiers without arms". Second, the image of a laboratory sticks firmly in the collective imagination and popular culture.

The term laboratory encompasses a very diverse set of sites. Medical laboratories usually do not resemble metallurgical or industrial applied research labs. Wet laboratories used by chemists and biologists necessarily differ from computer labs, where "wet" is not the most welcome condition. Furthermore, we use the term for both high-security, restricted-access facilities (e.g., those dealing with biohazards or radioactivity), as well as much more open sites. Some laboratories take the form of colossal structures, like cyclotrons or radiotelescopes; others fit into a small office space. All these different places are perceived as similar, not based on their appearance, but on the function they serve. Archetypally, the laboratory is a place where scientists carry out their observations and experiments. However, from time to time, the term is also used in relation to units that have little to do with observations, experiments, or specialised apparatuses, but which rather resemble typical offices, where people work on their computers, read, write, meet, and discuss. Consequently, the broader definition of laboratory simply describes a place where scholarly work is done.

The laboratory is not merely a container for scientific work. It has institutional power that plays an essential role in the social construction of scientific knowledge (Latour & Woolgar, 1986). The idea that scientific facts are not discovered, but rather invented or constructed in a laboratory, might be difficult to come to terms with. Indeed, the Latourian approach has been heavily criticised as deeply relativistic (Boghossian, 2006). However, this line of thought convincingly shows how the image of a laboratory is used to build the credibility of knowledge produced by scientists. David N. Livingstone's analysis of the basement laboratory of the first modern chemist, Robert Boyle (1627–1691), finishes with the remark that:

> In order to achieve the status of "knowledge," claims had to be produced in the right place and had to be validated by the right public. *Where* science was conducted—in what physical and social space—was thus a crucial ingredient in establishing whether an assertion was warranted
> (2003, p. 23).

The symbolic authority of the laboratory has also been used to legitimate incipient sciences, e.g., psychology at the turn of the 19th into the 20th century. As James Capshew observed, "In the early years of the discipline, the laboratory was invested with an almost talismanic power and viewed as a sacred space where scientific knowledge was created" (1992, p 132). This facet of places of science—i.e., establishing the credibility of scientific claims—is captured by the term "truth-spot", coined by Thomas Gieryn (2018). Interestingly, it is not only a laboratory that can constitute a truth-spot, but also field sites or experimental farms (Gieryn, 2002). However, the laboratory remains the key truth-spot for modern science.

The naissance and transformations of the laboratory closely relate to the development of modern science. The notion of the laboratory is rooted in the tradition of alchemy (Hannaway, 1986). This protoscientific grandmother of chemistry consisted of somewhat obscure attempts to find the philosopher's stone, transform readily available substances into gold, or produce an elixir of immortality. The alchemist's workshop can be imagined through Terry Pratchett's (1948–2015) literary lens as a "room, heavily outfitted with the usual badly ventilated furnaces, rows of bubbling crucibles, and one stuffed alligator. Things floated in jars. The air smelled of a limited life expectancy" (1993, p. 122). Early modern laboratories resembled artisan workshops, and a furnace for (proto)chemical operations constituted its essential equipment (Shapin, 1988). During the 17th century, along with the formation of modern science, the laboratory steadily evolved into "one of the hallmarks of the new science – the site where theories and hypotheses were purportedly tested by experiment and from which new discoveries and useful knowledge emerged" (Smith, 2006, p. 293). The rise of the modern laboratory goes hand in hand with the naissance of modern science.

The second turning point was reached in the middle of the 20th century when little science became big science (Price, 1963). Big science is characterised by large-scale projects, very often international and involving many researchers, and is, last but not least, considerably expensive. For instance, Forbes estimated that the total cost of finding the Higgs boson ran at about $13.25 billion (Knapp, 2012). The laboratory played a central role in the transition from little to big science. Michael Hiltzik argues that the birth of big science can be represented by the invention of a cyclotron (a type of particle accelerator) made in 1934 by Ernest Orlando Lawrence (1901–1958) (Hiltzik, 2015). Big science needed big laboratories and was willing to pay enormous sums of money to build and run them. Furthermore, the rise of large-scale research infrastructure enabled further advances of big science and led to developments that formed present-day technology, economy, and society. The most telling example here is the origin of the contemporary digital revolution. The development of computers and the internet was profoundly rooted in the World War II and Cold War large-scale military technology research, including the Manhattan Project, which produced the first nuclear weapons (Agar, 2012; Akera, 2007; Wolfe, 2013). The world-changing, simple, and elegant concept of the World Wide Web (WWW) is also directly connected to big science. Tim Berners-Lee designed the WWW to facilitate information management at CERN (European Organization for Nuclear Research)—a large complex of high-energy physics laboratories located near Geneva, Switzerland (Berners-Lee & Fischetti, 1999).

The evolution of laboratories, from alchemists' dens to the present-day clean rooms, corporate research complexes, colossal underground cyclotrons, and the International Space Station, exemplifies changes in science itself, as well as its role in the economy and society. Today, enormous research facilities can be seen as the greatest achievements of our civilisation. The aforementioned CERN houses the Large Hadron Collider, a ring 27 kilometres in circumference, placed a hundred metres underground. At the time of completion of this book, it remains the most expensive scientific instrument ever built and, unsurprisingly, it is also very costly to operate. The whole CERN complex annually uses as much electricity as 300 thousand homes in the United Kingdom ("Powering CERN", n.d.). The enormous cost of the largest contemporary research facilities means that they are hardly affordable by a single country, and thus international cooperation appears to be the only reasonable choice.

Moreover, these cutting-edge laboratories lie almost exclusively in the most advanced and affluent nations. The interesting exception here is Chile—a country which enjoys very favourable conditions for astronomical observations. Since the 1960s, dozens of telescopes have been erected there. It has been estimated that by 2020 Chile will have 70 percent of the total surface area of the world's telescopes (Matthews, 2012). However, Chilean astronomers have limited access to this excellent infrastructure which is almost entirely owned by international consortia. Despite the significant growth of astronomy in Chile in recent decades, its relations with foreign science remain largely locked in the centre-periphery dependency model (Barandiaran, 2015). The Chilean example bluntly shows how big science, with its large machinery and high costs, reproduces disparities in scientific potential on a global scale.

1.2.2 Humanities in their place

The discourse on science places is dominated by sites where natural, medical, and technical sciences are cultivated. But humanities scholars also have their unique places. Research libraries, special archives, and collections are still favourable (Michael, 2016)—if not essential—spots for many humanities scholars, pre-eminently those engaged in historical research. The library has long been the crucial institution and site for the sciences—notably not only humanities—and as Albert Einstein (1879–1955) put it, "The only thing that you absolutely have to know is the location of the library". After all, knowledge produced by scientists has to be stored, preserved, and ready to share. And for many centuries, the library has been seen as "the intellectual central power plant of the college or university" (Klauder & Wise, 1929, p. 70). The rise of digital humanities (Burdick, Drucker, Lunenfeld, Presner, & Schnapp, 2012) and the growing online availability of scanned resources from the past (e.g., www.europeana.eu, the European Union digital platform for cultural heritage), has not resulted in the disappearance of libraries and archives. After all, not every little thing has been scanned and made available on the internet (at least not yet). Moreover—at least for a fraction of academics—immediate communing with a forerunner's works in historic libraries creates a specific atmosphere favourable for intellectual reflection. The smell of old manuscripts and the rustle of parchment-bound volumes fire the imagination; being surrounded by valuable artefacts and reading handwritten notes can be inspiring.

Access to research resources sometimes goes hand in hand with a unique climate or even genius loci. That might be the case of Villa I Tatti, a historic manor with formal garden and estate located near Florence in Italy. Since 1961 Villa I Tatti has been home to The Harvard University Center for Italian Renaissance Studies. The villa—along with its extensive collection of books, photos, and works of art—was presented to Harvard by its alumnus, the celebrated art historian and perseverant collector Bernard Berenson (1865–1959) (Weaver, 1997). Through the years, I Tatti has welcomed over one thousand scholars of the Renaissance. Many of them have enjoyed full-year research fellowships in this near-utopian environment. One of these lucky people, Claudia Chierichini, testifies: "It's a wonderful place [...] a community of scholars of the Italian Renaissance from several different disciplines. However, this environment allows us to transcend those disciplinary boundaries" (Mitchell, 2009, para. 8). Her reference to the concept of community is telling. Being in a specific place with an exceptional group of scholars forms an excellent opportunity to develop a unique scientific community. It also shows how physical proximity, communication, and collaboration in science are inextricably related.

1.2.3 The university and its campus

Without a doubt, the university has become the most important setting of contemporary science. Almost all of the Nobel Prize laureates, at the time they won the award, were affiliated with a university. Universities are responsible for the lion's share of scientific publications and play an important role in developing basic research that might eventually result in revolutionary innovations. The physical setting of universities can therefore be seen as the most important science place of our times. As Brian Edwards in his *University Architecture* puts it, "Few students and academics today would not recognise the university as a distinctive place with its own blend of buildings, spaces and landscaped gardens. The campus, as we increasingly refer to this environment, has a flavour all of its own" (2000, p. vii). However, the spatial aspect of the university as a place of scientific activity is not as obvious as one might think at first glance. Universities are complex institutions and their campuses contain various types of buildings, infrastructures, and landscapes not necessarily related to science (such as sports grounds or student facilities).

The complex nature of the university—and its campus—is mirrored in the concept of its three roles. The university is primarily seen as a higher education institution. Teaching and learning are university's first—and classic—role (Lawton Smith, 2006; Wissema, 2009), and this is reflected in the provenance of the term. The word "university" originates from the Latin phrase *universitas magistrorum et scholarium*, which means "community of teachers and scholars". The second role of the university is research. As German-Swiss philosopher Karl Jaspers (1883–1969) put it, "The university is a community of scholars and students engaged in the task of seeking truth" (1959, p. 1). At the beginning of the 21st century, the words of the German-Swiss philosopher may seem somewhat exalted, if not naïve. It is hard to see the hordes of undergraduates circulating through campuses as seeking for truth. However, Jaspers' words still have something important to say, i.e., that education and research at universities should be united. Many believe that conducting scientific research at a university remains indispensable for high-quality teaching and effective learning (Brew, 2006; Griffiths, 2004; Verburgh, Elen, & Lindblom-Ylänne, 2007). Despite this, not all higher education institutions focus on research. In the United States, out of 4,664 post-secondary institutions active in 2015, only 335 (7%) are classified as research universities (also known as doctoral universities).[4] This does not necessarily mean that colleges not classified as research universities are not active in research at all, but certainly, most of them concentrate on providing professional education rather than on conducting world-class research.

The third role of the university, or the third mission as it is referred to at times, has only been recognised in recent years. The notion originated from the observation that universities constitute an important part of local and regional economies, not only as sources of skilled labour and scientific expertise, but also as employers and consumers of goods and services, as well as investors (Arbo & Benneworth, 2007; Drucker & Goldstein, 2007; Goddard & Vallance, 2011). In many towns and cities, the university is the largest employer and the most precious economic resource. It goes without saying that Cambridge and Oxford are unimaginable without their universities. Although we can easily point out many towns dominated by their academic population in Europe, it is in the United States that more than three hundred college towns[5] form a distinctive academic archipelago (Gumprecht, 2008). However, the notion of the third role goes much further than viewing the university as a mere source of funds for the local economy (Trippl, Sinozic, & Lawton Smith, 2015; Uyarra, 2010). Universities are often enablers or even leaders of regional economic development, being a crucial element of the regional innovation system (Gunasekara, 2006a; Mowery & Sampat, 2005). They are sources of spin-offs, spin-outs, and start-ups, and they transfer knowledge to local enterprises (Breznitz & Feldman, 2012; Rothaermel, Agung, & Jiang, 2007). Universities also collaborate with local governments and communities in designing and implementing knowledge-based policies; they are sources of social innovations, form a creative milieu (Benneworth & Hospers, 2007; Gertler & Vinodrai, 2005), reshape spatial development and urbanisation processes (Wiewel & Perry, 2015), serve local communities, and, last but not least, serve as hotspots of sports and the arts (Bridges, 2006). Many universities house art museums or galleries, and those with music conservatories offer public concerts, frequently for no charge. For example, Jacobs School of Music of Indiana University in Bloomington in the early 2010s offered more than 1,100 performances a year, including fully staged operas.

All three roles of the university are reflected in the spatial shape of the institution. The scenic design for the first role includes lecture halls, seminar rooms, auditoriums, teaching laboratories, graduate and undergraduate halls, reading rooms, group work areas, and sport and recreational infrastructure. The second role is performed in laboratories, workshops, libraries (including research libraries, rare book collections, and archives), and faculty rooms. Some universities have their own sky observatories, research stations, experimental farms, or art museums. The third role is played in technology transfer centres, university research parks, academic incubators, and also in many places used primarily for teaching or research, but accessible to the local community.

Some of these places are clearly multifunctional and can serve as a stage for more than one role, for example, the laboratory, where students learn while participating in their professors' research. Among these various types of spaces, some are centuries old (the library or lecture hall) and have evolved substantially over time (Pevsner, 1976), while others are relatively new, e.g., academic incubators with co-working areas, community centres, or IT rooms. In effect, the physical dimension of a contemporary university has become very complex, composed of many types of buildings and auxiliary infrastructure and areas. Large universities are almost like small cities. Moreover, research-related buildings are not necessarily the most impressive or attractive structures. A good example here are large stadiums and other sports venues that sprung up mainly at North American universities as a result of the enormous commercialisation of college sports (Gaul, 2015; Weigel, 2015).

The architecture and urbanistics of universities is a fascinating topic described in many books. Most frequently these are monographs of a given institution, where the scientific and historical glory of the described alma mater is celebrated. Another approach is to focus on a particular city, where one or numerous universities are located (Wiewel & Perry, 2015). A notable example here is the work of Sharon Haar, *The City as Campus: Urbanism and Higher Education in Chicago* (2011), in which she demonstrates how the university interacts with its urban context. Yet the most relevant works, in light of this study, review the development of university architecture in the historical perspective (Coulson, Roberts, & Taylor, 2011, 2015; Forgan, 1989). Interestingly, these books typically see the university as a mainly educational institution. The discussion of spatial arrangements and architectural features refers mostly to teaching and learning and, to some extent, to recreation, accommodation, and other auxiliary infrastructure and areas, while the second and third roles of the university are somewhat overlooked. This pattern can be found in the classical *College Architecture in America* (Klauder & Wise, 1929), the more contemporary *Campus: an American Planning Tradition* (Turner, 1984), and recent works by Coulson et al. (2011, 2015) and Calvo-Sotelo (2011). However, a new approach is becoming more and more visible as the second and third roles gain greater attention. For instance, Brian Edwards' *University Architecture* (2000) included a 14-page chapter (in a 164-page monograph) on laboratories and research buildings. A decade later, Katy Lee in her *University Architecture* (2011) devoted a quarter of its pages to the presentation of 12 examples of research and laboratory facilities. Taking into account that the first role of universities dominates the architectural discourse relating to them, it may come as no surprise to see growing discussions on planning spaces for creative and efficient learning (Boys, 2011), but far less attention is paid to ideas on designing spaces for enhancing specifically research-related environments (Galison & Thompson, 1999). On the other hand, there is a lot of interest in the places shared by all three roles of the university—physical environments that facilitate social contact, such as meeting places, cafeterias, common areas, dining halls, seminar rooms, and increasingly multipurpose libraries (Törnqvist, 2011).

Finally, universities can be seen as multi-level actors linking global, local, and national domains. The growing importance of the third role of the

14 *Places and spaces of science*

institution results in local engagement. At the same time, universities operate in an increasingly competitive international environment where rivalry for students, world-class lecturers, financial resources, prestige, and attention is the norm. Successful universities are increasingly "both globally competitive and locally engaged" (Goddard, Kempton, & Vallance, 2013, p. 43).

1.2.4 The spiky world of science

Scientific activity is spread unevenly across geographic space. This was true in previous centuries and continues to be the case in today's globalised world. Disparities in global scientific production reflect the socio-economic diversification of regions, countries, and continents. Despite the hopes that globalisation and digital technologies would flatten the world, it remains uneven and spiky. Thomas L. Friedman in his provocatively titled book *The World is Flat* (2005) argued that globalisation and technological development make historical and geographical divisions increasingly irrelevant. To which Richard Florida replied that globalisation has indeed changed a lot, but it has not levelled the global divides, and hence "The World is Spiky" (2005). The dispute between the two is just one of the latest flare-ups in a recurring debate on the death of geography or distance (Cairncross, 1997) and the rebuttal of this idea (Morgan, 2004; Olson & Olson, 2000).

Economic disparities form, indeed, a weighty factor behind the spiky world map of science. Wealthy countries can sponsor more scientific research and attract brilliant scholars. Consequently, their ability to produce more scientific output rises. In 2013 high-income countries—as defined by the World Bank—published 1,192 scientific papers per million inhabitants (the World Bank uses data from the Science Citation Index and Social Sciences Citation Index).[6] At the same time, in low-income countries scholars published only 6.5 journal articles per million inhabitants. Make no mistake, differences between countries are even greater. The highest number of scientific papers per million inhabitants is enjoyed by: Switzerland (2,603), Denmark (2,223), Australia (2,068), Sweden (2,017), Singapore (1,974), and Norway (1,940). Three scientific global powerhouses—the United Kingdom, the United States, and Germany—do not rank so high but, nevertheless, exceed the world average, scoring respectively 1,518, 1,304, and 1,231. At the other end of the spectrum, we find countries with literally zero published papers captured by globally recognised sources. These are usually small island nations, such as Aruba or the Turks and Caicos Islands. However, we can also point out several populous countries with scientific activity measured by published papers close to zero, for example, the Democratic Republic of Congo with 0.2 articles per million inhabitants, Chad with 0.5, Somalia with 0.6, Myanmar with 0.7, and Afghanistan with 0.9.

Not surprisingly, Nobel Prize awards are also very unevenly distributed among countries. The vast majority of awards can be attributed to the US. However, the movement of laureates and changes of state borders since the prize inauguration in 1901 make it difficult to calculate the exact number of awards per country. Numerous Nobel Prize winners lived and worked in their lifetimes in different places. Many of the winners ended up in leading scientific institutions in the US or the UK. A sound example is Marie Sklodowska-Curie (1867–1934)—a double Nobel laureate in physics (1903) and chemistry (1911). She was born in Warsaw, the current capital of Poland, but at that time the city lay in Russian Empire territory (following the partition of Poland in the 18th century). In 1891, Sklodowska-Curie, aged 24, went to study in Paris, where her career developed quickly, and she became the first woman professor at the University of Paris. At the time of announcing the awards, she was evidently more linked professionally to France than to Poland. Thus, which country should be associated with Sklodowska-Curie's two awards: Poland, France, or the no-longer-existing Russian Empire? A simple solution to the problem was proposed by BBC editors ("Which country has the best brains?", 2010). Prizes can be allocated to the country or countries included in the winner's biography on the official website of the Nobel Prize committee (www.nobelprize.org). Where the website mentions multiple countries in relation to a prize winner (country of birth, country of citizenship, country of residence at the time of award), each of those countries is credited as having won the award.

Following this methodology, we find that for 1901–2015 prizes in the sciences (chemistry, physics, physiology-medicine, and economics, i.e., excluding prizes in literature and the peace award), the United States holds the most privileged position, with 321 laureates. The United Kingdom secures the second place, although with a significantly lower number of laureates: 99. The third place is occupied by Germany, with 89. Then comes France (36), Japan (21), Switzerland (20), and Canada (20). Thus, the predominance of the US overwhelms. However, if we count the European Union as one entity (28 countries, as of 2015), we find that its score comes close to that of the US. It shows that almost all of the Nobel Prizes in the sciences go either to Europe or to North America, and almost none go to the rest of the world. Only about one percent of Nobel laureates in the sciences can be attributed to Africa. Latin America scores similarly low. Australia and New Zealand can be allocated around two percent of laureates. The position of Asia remains notably higher, with about seven percent of awards, although here one country—Japan—is responsible for half of the continent's achievement.

A closer look at the world map of science reveals that besides international disparities, the spiky scientific landscape also dominates nationally. This is no surprise when we take into account that scientific establishments—universities, research centres, etc.—usually concentrate in cities and metropolitan areas, as well as in specialised spots, such as college towns or localities where laboratories, observatories, and other unique research infrastructure are based. High-resolution, local-level analysis of the number of publications from the Web of Science shows sharp scientific peaks, clustered in archipelagos (above all in Europe, the US, and Eastern China), surrounded by vast scholarly deserts (see Figure 1.2). A very similar pattern shows up in the global distribution of the scores obtained in

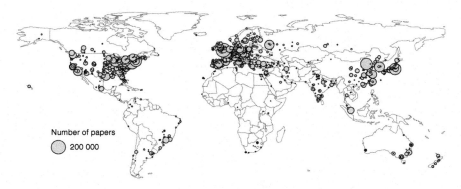

Figure 1.2 Scientific papers indexed in Web of Science, 2000–2009
Source: Conception and design by Adam Ploszaj, based on data from Mazloumian, Helbing, Lozano, Light, & Börner, 2013.

university rankings (Jöns & Hoyler, 2013), as well as inventions measured by patents (OECD, 2010).

The picture gets even more acute when the impact of publications is taken into account. Analysis of how many citations a particular location receives in relation to the number of citations it gives to other locations—ratio of in-coming to out-going citations—exhibits the greatest knowledge sources and sinks. On the global scale, only a few clusters of such defined knowledge sources emerge. These are above all the east and west coasts of the US, England, the Netherlands, Germany (mostly southwest), Switzerland, and Japan (Mazloumian et al., 2013).

The spiky global landscape of science stays very stable in the short run, but in the longer term it slowly evolves. Over the course of three decades, from 1981 to 2011, a gradual global shift in science can be tracked. The decline of the former Union of Soviet Socialist Republics (USSR) and the loss of North America's relative position have been accompanied by a steady growth of scientific activities in the Asia-Pacific region—in recent years fuelled mainly by China. Overall, a slight trend towards deconcentration of scientific activities has emerged (Grossetti et al., 2014). However, the observed changes are largely quantitative, as measured by the number of scientific publications, and much less qualitative, as measured by received citations, which can be taken as a proxy for scientific impact (Radosevic & Yoruk, 2014). This clearly shows the persistence of the global centre-periphery hierarchy in science (Schott, 1998), especially when we focus on scientific excellence and cutting-edge research.

1.3 Driving forces of the geography of science

A broad spectrum of factors and processes underpins the spatial distribution of science. The following part of the chapter discusses the most important ones.

These factors can be spread along a necessity-possibility axis—some make science possible and others make its development indispensable for society. Policy plays the role of a stand-alone factor, although different policies can also be placed on the necessity-possibility axis. In the long run, additional circumstances and processes grow in force—a discussion of the logic of long-term (r)evolutions in the geography of science closes the chapter. But let us start with two perspectives on the connection between science and place.

1.3.1 Science as a cause and as an effect

The relationship between science and places can be seen from two angles. The first perspective investigates the influence of particular spatial settings on the development of science. The second approach looks at scientific research as a factor of socio-economic change in specific places: towns, cities, regions, and countries. The former handles scientific activities as an effect, the latter as a cause. In the real world, these two facets are closely intertwined. Scientific discovery has the potential to generate wealth that can be invested in further development of research. This process is captured by the concept of circular cumulative causation developed by Swedish economist Gunnar Myrdal (1957). In the long run, over multiple cycles, influences can accumulate, in a positive or negative way. This is metaphorically referred to as the Matthew effect: "the rich get richer and the poor get poorer" (Merton, 1973). In consequence, the differences in spatial distribution of scientific activities might not simply persist, but even increase over time.

The supposed relation, or at least co-occurrence, of scientific progress and socio-economic development has caught the attention of scholars, as well as politicians. The recipe for arranging successful places for research endeavour and the commercialisation of its products has become a holy grail for science policy and broader development policy. Investigations of the most successful science and technology places—such as Silicon Valley, Route 186, or Third Italy—often seek to answer the conundrum: What was in the air, and can we bottle it? The very question led Eric Weiner, the New York Times bestselling author (yes! The topic is so hot that it appeals to the general readership), to scrutinise such unlike places as Hangzhou in China, Florence in Italy, Edinburgh in Scotland, Calcutta in India, Vienna in Austria, and Silicon Valley in California, US. These different places share one unique feature: each of them was an unquestionable centre of scientific, technological, or cultural development in a specific period of time in the past, starting from ancient Athens, through 12th–13th-century Hangzhou (Lin'an), Renaissance Florence, Scottish Enlightenment in Edinburgh, 19th-century Calcutta, Vienna from the age of Wolfgang Amadeus Mozart (1756–1791) to the age of Sigmund Freud (1856–1939), up to the contemporary Silicon Valley.

So what is the magic formula for establishing a successful, cutting-edge intellectual hot spot? Apparently, no simple answer has been found yet, if there is a definitive answer to the question at all. The circumstances that shape the success of a given place are quite clear. However, at the same time, the set of factors varies substantially from case to case and cannot be summarised into a simple formula, applicable everywhere and anytime (Weiner, 2016). In contrast, we can give a fair number of examples where policies aiming to boost growth based on science and technology have failed spectacularly: from underperforming USSR science towns (Josephson, 1997) to failed science parks in the US (Luger & Goldstein, 1991; Kefalides, 1991; Wallsten, 2004), Greece (Bakouros, Mardas, & Varsakelis, 2002), India (Phan, Siegel, & Wright, 2005), Poland (Najwyższa Izba Kontroli, 2013), and the UK (Massey, Quintas, & Wield, 1992).

1.3.2 Between possibility and necessity

Cultivating science is not necessary for the survival of the individual or society. In a sense, science stands as a surplus human activity. One ancient belief says that the birth and development of science was possible only because people had free time and resources to leave aside their daily routines, such as hunting, gathering, and—later in history—farming. This thesis surely seems simplistic, if not close to trivial, but ultimately, without surplus food and some spare time, Plato's *Symposium* would not have been possible, just as probably the whole of ancient philosophy. Jumping a few centuries forward, a similar argument can be applied to the development of early universities. John Kenneth Hyde formulated it as follows: "The spontaneous universities of Italy were formed in large, growing cities, distinguished, I think, by fat agricultural regions, with a food surplus which meant that relatively cheap living was possible for an idle student population" (1988, p. 14). In short, economic growth made possible the emergence of medieval universities, and ultimately the whole Renaissance. Jumping on a few centuries once again, to Victorian Britain, we witness a period when scientific advancement, technological invention, and economic development became not only inseparable from, but also admired by, society—according to David N. Livingstone, visitors to the Natural History Museum, which opened in 1881 in London, respectfully removed their hats when entering the cathedral-like edifice (2003, p. 39).

Today, the connection between economic development and science seems obvious. This belief is well grounded in the significant correlation between GDP per capita and the scientific production measured by scholarly papers, as well as patents (Vinkler, 2008; Al & Taşkın, 2015). However, in this case the "chicken or the egg" causality dilemma remains unsolved. Fortunately, this book sets much more modest goals than solving this conundrum. For our purposes, it is sufficient to observe that in the era of big science (since around World War II), where large-scale projects have become the norm, substantial economic resources seem to be a necessary, but not sufficient, condition for scientific development (Galison & Hevly, 1992). This situation resonates with the growth of collaboration in science (but that is another story—see Chapter 2).

Access to resources makes science in certain places more possible than in others. Meanwhile, in some places the need for new discoveries might be more urgent. This idea is captured by the old English-language proverb: necessity is the mother of invention. Harold Dorn (1991) used the argument of necessity to explain the development of science in ancient Egypt and Mesopotamia. Specifically, he argues that in arid and semi-arid places hydraulic engineering projects were a must for the survival and progress of society. Planning, implementation, and sustainment of irrigation and water-control projects was only possible with centralised societies and bureaucratic organisation. Once established, strong, centralised states facilitated further development of scientific and technological progress. For example, in Babylonia:

> we can see the solution of quadratic equations as necessitated by the problems of deploying labour, while linear equations were solved to determine the division of fields and the calculation of volumes was applied to the construction of a hydraulic infrastructure
>
> (Shortland, 1993, p. 130).

This approach can be easily criticised as too deterministic, reducing the development of science and technology to such factors as climate, soil, or topography, and overlooking social and cultural factors (Kenzer, 1992). However, in a broad sense, the claim is sound. Surely, a whole diapason of inventions resulted from necessity.

Hard factors—such as a healthy economy and access to resources—can be seen as a necessary condition for the development of science. But very likely, this condition is not sufficient. Here, intangible factors—specific features of institutions, society, and culture—make the difference. At the beginning of the 21st century, the most well-known concept in this stream of thought is unarguably the theory of the creative class formed by Richard Florida (2002). The creative class lives—of course—in creative places or, more precisely, in creative cities. The class is attracted and reproduced by places characterised by the presence of the three Ts, namely talent, technology, and tolerance. Talent refers to gifted people. Technology denotes a high level of technical and organisational sophistication. Tolerance means that different lifestyles are largely accepted, if not celebrated. The third T makes a crucial point in Florida's theory (as the two former are already largely accepted and profoundly analysed). It has also attracted the attention of the lay public, as Florida measured the level of tolerance by the so-called gay index, understood as the regional proportion of homosexuals. He argues that creativity needs freedom, openness, and a safe social space for experiments—safe enough to accommodate innovation "that is outside of the range of existing practice" (Schumpeter, 1947, p. 50). This conclusion sounds fully in line with traditional ideas of freedom of science and academic autonomy.

Florida's 3T theory belongs to the broad stream of concepts that appreciate the role of intangible factors in regional development. In the context of science places, the notion of a creative milieu is especially noteworthy. According to Charles Landry

20 *Places and spaces of science*

> A creative milieu is a place [...] that contains the necessary preconditions in terms of hard and soft infrastructure to generate a flow of ideas [...]. Such a milieu is a physical setting [...] where face to face interaction creates new ideas
>
> (2008, p. 133).

This excerpt contains two vital messages. First, to explain the creativity of places we have to consider both tangible and intangible factors (e.g., infrastructure and skills). Second, creativity needs interaction between people, a flow of ideas, and mutual inspiration. The role of a collaborative environment is further underlined by Gunnar Törnqvist, an early creative milieu theorist, who in turn coined the sister-notion of scientific milieu. He argues that "Successful research settings are typified by fluent communication and lively information sharing, both internal and external" (2011, p. 171). The importance of external links for prosperous scientific milieus shows that the geography of science cannot be fully understood without the geography of scientific collaboration.

The creative milieu has one more intriguing property. "It suffers from structural instability, like a river that enters a period of instability in its middle course" (Hall, 2000, p. 644). The chaotic nature of a creative milieu periodically forces—or enables—scholars to leave their comfort zones and venture into new ideas or shift longstanding paradigms. A similar approach focusing on instability—although applied on a much broader global scale—led Mark Zachary Taylor to put forward the hypothesis of creative insecurity. He convincingly argues that countries for which external threats outweigh domestic tensions have higher innovation rates than countries where internal tensions prevail (Taylor, 2016). Certainly, being innovative may be inhibited by an unstable domestic situation. But exposure to external competition is likely to elicit creativity. This statement brings us back to our initial focus on the necessity factor in the development of science.

1.3.3 Science and policy

Necessity often takes the form of a science policy. A notable example is a whole mass of scientific and technological developments that resulted from the need for precise determination of a ship's position at sea. This need was institutionalised by the British government in a system of longitude rewards (see Chapter 6.1) (Dunn & Higgitt, 2014). Similarly, in the Cold War era (1947–1991) the rapid progress of science and technology can be labelled as necessity-driven. The arms race between the Soviet Union and the United States (and some other countries) needed cutting-edge science, including space science and exploration (Wolfe, 2013). Cold War science and technology policy, combined with industrial and defence policies, has left a major imprint on the geography of science, both in the West and the Communist bloc. To a large extent, the Cold War produced the Silicon Valley in the US

(O'Mara, 2005)—an iconic area of the knowledge-based economy. It hosts the headquarters and the research labs of dozens of global high-tech companies (Adobe, Apple, Cisco, Facebook, Google-Alphabet, HP, Intel, Lockheed Martin, Netflix, Nvidia, Oracle, Tesla Motors, Visa, and Yahoo!, to name only a few major ones) as well as numerous universities and colleges, including the world-class Stanford University and the University of California, Berkeley (since 2003 occupying second, third, or at least fourth place in the Academic Ranking of World Universities).

Similarly, in the Soviet Union the spatial development of scientific institutions was unprecedented. In 1965 the newspaper *Ekonomicheskaya Gazeta* (Economic Gazette) proclaimed:

> In our country, where the development of science has become one of the determining factors of social progress [...] a completely new approach to the planning of scientific research and even inventions is needed. One of the clearest examples of such an approach is the creation of huge scientific complexes—real cities of science—built with one goal: to make them vanguards of the advance into the unknown
>
> (Nekhamkin, 1965).

A few years later an article in the scientific journal *Priroda* (Nature) remarked, "The degree of success in choosing locations for the new scientific centres will have an effect on their subsequent fate" (Belyayev, 1973). The new science cities (*naukogrady*) in the USSR were often located in remote areas—deep into Siberia, the Urals, or the Far East—to ensure security. Many of them had the status of closed cities, and their existence was kept secret because of the military focus of the research conducted there.

The most illustrious example of a Soviet science city is Akademgorodok, located near Novosibirsk, in the middle of the Siberian birch forest,[7] where the annual average temperature hardly reaches 2 °C (35 °F). The "little academic village" was founded in 1957 on the decision of Nikita Khrushchev—then leader of the USSR—as part of a great vision to turn Siberia into a communist paradise. At its peak, Akademgorodok was home to 65,000 scientists, including their families, and world-class research was carried out there. In 1994, Manuel Castells and Peter Hall described Akademgorodok as the boldest experiment of founding a new town as an instrument of science-based economic development. But the experiment went wrong:

> The Akademgorodok experiment failed as a regional development project, as an instrument of technological modernization, and as an attempt to create a scientific complex. The quality of the research in its institutes was very high, simply because of the quality of the scientists who went to work there. But little added value resulted from the spatial proximity between the institutes
>
> (1994, p. 56).

Another reason why the Soviet Silicon Valley did not materialise was due to the weak relations of Akademgorodok with industry, and its spatial and institutional isolation, which hindered the emergence of added value from collaborative networks. However, the story of Akademgorodok has not yet ended and in new Russia an old dream is being dreamed again. With support from Moscow and better embedment in the global economy, a new plan has emerged to revive Akademgorodok—this time as a Siberian Silicon Forest (Wainwright, 2016).

The story of Akademgorodok shows the importance of policy in shaping the geography of science. Be it Soviet-style creation ex nihilo decreed by the overlord. Be it via an evidence-based participatory decision-making process. Political will can change the spatial organisation of science. Most often, policy aims to create a new scientific hotspot or to enlarge and strengthen existing institutions. But politics can also play the villain. Competition between nations, organisations, individuals, and other entities can be fierce. Take, for example, the curious history of the University of Wroclaw, Poland. Before the Second World War it was the German Universität Breslau—as the city lay in Germany. The Leopoldina—as it was initially named—was founded in 1702. However, the first attempt to establish a university in Breslau was made as early as 1505 by the town council and King Vladislaus II (1471–1516). Eventually the king's request was rejected by Pope Julius II (1443–1513). Rumour has it that the decision was forced by the scholars from Jagiellonian University in Krakow (established in 1364), who wanted to thwart the competition in their catchment area (Reinkens, 1861).

Of course, the effects of political decisions are not guaranteed. In extreme cases—when a new science spot is created in a remote area or when it is weakly embedded in the regional economy—there is a risk of building a "cathedral in the desert". Impressive but expensive ventures create insufficient output and, in the end, are not very useful. Identifying the success and failure factors of such initiatives is one of the most fascinating topics at the intersection of development policy and regional studies. However, for our purposes it is enough to point out policy as a factor underlying the uneven distribution of science and technology centres: a factor that operates between the Scylla of possible and the Charybdis of necessary, sometimes—albeit unwittingly—trying to make the impossible possible.

1.3.4 Between Cardwell's Law and the logic of longue durée

The geography of science evolves constantly. In the long term, scientific leadership moves from one place to another, be it a city, a region, a nation, or a continent. This is captured by the notion of Cardwell's Law.[8] It states that no society has maintained high creativity for more than a short historical period. Over the centuries, shifts of scientific excellence have followed the rises and falls of great civilisations and societies, in very broad terms, from Asia, through Europe, to North America. In recent years, we have witnessed the emergence of a new scientific powerhouse in China. This growth, unprecedented in scale, was not expected. A 1977 article published in *Social Studies of Science* concluded, "It should be noted that the People's Republic of China's (PRC) contribution to the Asian science effort as measured by research publications is practically non-existent. In 1973, the PRC had only one publication which was covered by the SCI" (Frame, Narin, & Carpenter, 1977, p. 506). Four decades later, the number of Chinese papers in SCI exceeded 270,000. Only the US could boast a better result—circa 350,000. Furthermore, China is predicted to overtake the US on R&D spending by 2020 (Casassus, 2014).

Yet, if we look closer at Cardwell's Law, we find that the devil is in the details. The vision of a single creativity torch that is "too hot to hold for long" and, thus, "each individual society carried it for a short time" (Mokyr, 1994, p. 564) serves as an artful metaphor and powerful canvas for telling the history of science. Nonetheless, it requires an uncomfortable assumption that in a given time only one society or place can be the most creative. This thesis might work well for previous centuries, but at the beginning of the 21st century it seems to lose its power. The first reason is the growing importance of collaboration in science (see Chapter 2). Some of the most exciting recent discoveries might not have been possible without vast international collaboration, in extreme instances engaging not hundreds but thousands of researchers, such as the Human Genome Project (McElheny, 2010) or the detection of gravitational waves (Twilley, 2016).

The second rationale stems from the new paradigm of socio-economic development—the knowledge-based economy—that points to science, technology, and innovation as crucial factors for economic growth. The acceptance of this idea is so widespread that almost all countries (leaving aside those struggling with basic problems such as hunger, water shortages, or natural disasters) dedicate at least some resources to expanding their science and technology potential (Taylor, 2016). And even if we agree that, at the beginning of the third millennium, the US is a global leader in science and technology, we can point out numerous countries with a world-class research sector and a high position in science and technology rankings. Without any doubt, countries like Germany, Switzerland, Sweden, the Netherlands, Japan, Israel, and the UK belong to the global scientific premier league. And the current landscape of world science is unimaginable without them. To some extent, the US holds the global leader position owing to its size (of population and economy). But, if we weight scientific indicators by population or GDP, it becomes clear that in some smaller countries scientific saturation is at a much higher level than in the US. All in all, it seems that the logic of the contemporary global scientific race does not resemble the Olympic Podium, with only one spot being reserved for the champion.

At the same time, the geography of science is amazingly stable. Certain places have been on the cutting edge of science for decades or even centuries. The University of Oxford, founded in 1096, and the University of Cambridge,

1209, have for hundreds of years had a great influence on the development of science. Today they still sit at the top of the global academic rankings. Moreover, their host cities enjoy well-developed, high-tech industry, closely related to the universities (however, Cambridge outperforms Oxford in this case, see Castells & Hall, 1994). Oxbridge—as Oxford and Cambridge are sometimes jointly referred to—was at the forefront of science well before the UK took the scientific leadership as a country, and it still is, even after the leadership was handed over to the US. This example proves the importance of spatial scale—in this case city vs. country—as well as the significance of temporal scale. From the millennial perspective, Oxbridge is just a baton pass in the scientific relay race ruled by Cardwell's Law. From the centennial perspective, it serves as a fine example of the long-lasting phenomenon. These developments are driven by the logic of the *longue durée*, the term coined by the prominent French historian Fernand Braudel. The notion refers to the processes embedded in long-term historical structures evolving over centuries rather than decades or years (Braudel, 1958). The phenomena governed by the longue durée remain persistent and can be very unreceptive to policy influences. Several well-known cases of regional development disparities aptly illustrate this. Southern Italy, Eastern Germany, Eastern Poland, and Appalachia in the US continue to be significantly less developed economically than other parts of these countries, despite intensive and continuous developmental support from central governments (Gorzelak, 2010). This might come as bad news for policy makers promising to convert the local or regional economy into one more knowledge-based, as well as for heads of aspiring universities, keen to jump up a few places in the academic rankings.

In the academic world age matters, at least to some extent. An analysis of the *Times Higher Education* World University Rankings suggests that older universities tend to reach a higher rank than newer institutions. However, the correlation, although significant, is rather weak (Grove, 2016). Indeed, old age does not guarantee a high place in the rankings. The University of Bologna, the oldest higher-education institution in the world—established in 1088—secured only 208th place in the 2016 QS World University Rankings. The relationship between age and the quality, achievements, and reputation of universities is much more complex than simple linear correlation. Internal factors, such as accumulated resources, knowledge, and symbolic capital (reputation), interrelate with external circumstances such as the socio-economic context and the level of financing available from national sources. In addition, path dependency phenomena are apparently at play here. Once an organisation has accumulated capital and a reputation, it holds a competitive advantage. But should it suffer a decline, then regaining its previous position may prove difficult.

Neither the longue durée nor Cardwell's Law can fully explain the historical evolution of the geography of science. It is rather a semi-random mixture of them both, a combination of stability and (un)expected shifts. Let us look at the series of four maps depicting the workplaces of leading scientists in Europe from the 16th to the 19th century (see Figure 1.3). We can easily spot the

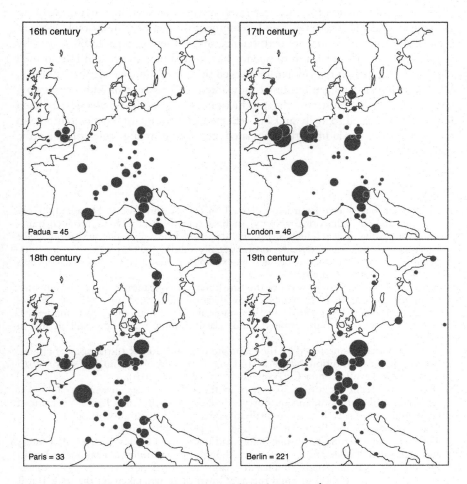

Figure 1.3 Workplaces of leading scientists, 16th–19th centuries*

* Workplace symbols proportional to places with the most career stops in each century. Source: Taylor, Hoyler, & Evans, 2008, p. 400.

emergence of new centres (St. Petersburg, Stockholm, and Uppsala in the 17th century, or Berlin in the 18th century) and the decline of old ones (Padua— from stand-alone hub in the 16th century to putative loss of importance in the 19th century), but we can also get a sense of their longevity, some lasting only for two (Leiden from the 17th to 18th century) or three centuries (Bologna from the 16th to 18th century), with others enduring for the whole of the period covered (Paris and London).

* * *

Places and spaces matter for science. From human-scale working environments to global geographical structures, the development of science is inseparable from its socio-economic and spatial context; science shapes these settings and is shaped by them. The rise and expansion of science has created new places and transformed old ones. The birth of the laboratory marked the rise of modern science. Similarly, large-scale research infrastructures accompanied the naissance of 20th-century big science. Over the centuries, the production of scientific knowledge has been highly concentrated spatially and has reflected global disparities, hierarchies, and transformations, including those related to the growing role of scientific collaboration.

Notes

1 In a similar way, Pierre Bourdieu reflected on science and history. He asked, "How is it possible for a historical activity, such as scientific activity, to produce trans-historical truths, independent of history, detached from all bonds with both place and time and therefore eternally and universally valid?" (2004, p. 1).
2 Science and knowledge can be seen as examples of essentially contested concepts that defy universal definition.
3 Although Dewey's system was not the first library classification—this achievement is attributed to the Paris Bookseller's classification developed in 1845 by Jacques Charles Brunet (1780–1867)—it has undoubtedly been the most influential. Dewey's system not only inspired other classifications, but is also still in use in many libraries.
4 The classification is prepared by the Carnegie Classification of Institutions of Higher Education, an institution based at Indiana University Bloomington since 2015 (Indiana University Center for Postsecondary Research, 2016).
5 Blake Gumprecht identified 305 cities in the US as college towns in 2000. He analysed enrolment—students in four-year colleges constituted at least 20 percent of the population—as well as some qualitative criteria (see: Gumprecht, 2008).
6 Data from the World Bank database: http://data.worldbank.org/
7 The picturesque setting in pristine nature had unexpected inconveniences. As Castells and Hall splendidly describe, "the area, although only 15 miles (25 kilometres) from Novosibirsk, was absolutely uninhabited, allowing for a new settlement in totally virgin land. The decision to build the new town there was taken on the spot. But it turned out that there was a good reason why the area was empty. The beautiful forest, during springtime, was full of tree-leeches whose bite provokes meningitis. Because spring is the only good weather period, this circumstance effectively makes the forest useless for recreation. When Lavrentiev heard of the problem, after the decision to locate the city had been made, he remained adamant: scientists would take care of the problem, he argued, meaning that they would spray the forest with insecticides. They did. But in the process they also wiped out most of the birds, to the point that they had to stop the treatment. The insects came back en masse and have remained ever since. It was somehow representative of the hard realities that would attend the creation of a scientific utopia in the 'academic little village'" (1994, p. 44).
8 The notion of Cardwell's Law was coined by Joel Mokyr (1990) based on Donald S.L. Cardwell's observations included in his well-researched *Turning points in Western technology* (1972).

2 Scientists working together

Nicolas Bourbaki was one of the greatest mathematicians of the 20th century. His multivolume 7.7 thousand page treatise *Éléments de mathématique* (Elements of Mathematics) formed the foundation of modern mathematics. The contemporary concept of mathematical proof originated from his works. They also stimulated the emergence of "New Math" in the educational system of the US and other nations (Aczel, 2006). Almost all of Bourbaki's works are single-authored. From the bibliometric perspective, this would imply that he worked mostly alone and had limited professional relations with other scientists. This interpretation sounds all the more reasonable because mathematics is one of the scientific fields where collaboration is less frequent (Wuchty, Jones, & Uzzi, 2007). So why mention Bourbaki in the context of scientific collaboration? The reason is simple: Nicolas Bourbaki represents one of the most extraordinary examples of collaboration, not only in mathematics, but in science overall.

A veil of mystery hangs over Bourbaki's life. We know that his scientific activity started in France before World War II (1939–1945), but it is not clear if he is still alive (Mashaal, 2006). His story can be traced back to 1934 when two young French mathematicians, André Weil (1906–1998) and Henri Cartan (1904–2008), were struggling with teaching calculus at the University of Strasbourg. When the existing textbooks failed to meet their expectations, they had no choice but to draft a new reader in mathematical analysis. The task seemed challenging. Therefore, Weil and Cartan invited their colleagues from École Normale Supérieure de Paris to help with the writing. In this way, Nicolas Bourbaki—a team of closely collaborating mathematicians—was born. The inspiration for this scientific mystification was a spoof lecture given in 1923 for École Normale freshmen by a third-year student, Raoul Husson (1901–1967). Husson, pretending to be a guest lecturer, gave a nonsensical lecture, ending with the extravagant "Bourbaki's Theorem", all presented in a sophisticated way.

The Bourbaki group, with changing composition, worked for about half a century, meeting regularly for intensive workshops. Its founders decided to work collectively and without any individual acknowledgements. They renounced individual benefits, such as credit and recognition, remaining anonymous members of the team for the sake of science (Borel, 1998; Richer, 2013). This approach may seem eccentric in the era of publish-or-perish pressure and the rocketing competition for attention, acclaim, and grants that are frequently awarded to applicants with the longest publication sections in their CVs.

Bourbaki's story shows how scientific collaboration can be unexpected and elude simple classification. It also raises a number of questions that will be addressed in this chapter: What is scientific collaboration? Why do scientists collaborate? How does collaboration work?

2.1 Before the fourth age of research

Collaboration is not a new practice in scientific enterprise. Let us take the example of the world's first scientific journal, *Philosophical Transactions*. In its inaugural 1665 edition, along with several single-authored articles, a few collaborative papers also appeared (Beaver & Rosen, 1978). Clearly, the naissance of modern academic publishing and the co-authorship of scholarly papers are inextricably connected. But scientific collaboration can be traced even further back in the past. The discussions of ancient philosophers depicted in Plato's dialogue are in essence not very different from contemporary academic debates (though modern scholarly symposia differ from the ancient Symposium in the probability of wine consumption).

Even if scholars did work together through the ages, scientific collaboration was not the norm, as it is today. Practices of collaboration, along with its intensity and role in scientific endeavour, have evolved in the course of history. Based on this evolution of scientific collaboration, Jonathan Adams attempted to distinguish four ages in the global history of science: individual, institutional, national, and international. The first age lasted until the 19th century. It was the age of the individual, marked by such names as Isaac Newton (1643–1727), Gottfried Wilhelm Leibniz (1646–1716), and Charles Darwin (1809–1882). Indeed, before the 19th century, the state of development in science did not induce scientific collaboration on a large scale. Over time, the development of learned societies, scholarly journals, and scientific infrastructure facilitated the professionalisation of science, gradually transforming it into Adams' second age of research—the age of the institution, followed by the third age, of the national research enterprise (such as mission-led Research Councils in the UK). These changes prompted scientific collaboration, leading to the fourth era of research—the age of international research networks (Adams, 2013). The growth of large-scale scientific collaborations, national and international, has also resulted from and enabled the rise of big science (Price, 1963). In the following section of the chapter we will describe the state of scientific collaboration before the fourth age of research, with particular focus on the first signs of the future collaborative turn: the rise of distant collaborative networks and learned societies, the earliest global research project, and the first international scientific congress.

2.1.1 The age of the individual

Before the fourth age of research, a single scholar was the key figure in the practice of science. Collaboration was rare, as is evidenced by the fact that during the first centuries of scientific publishing multiple authorship was very uncommon. Beaver and Rosen (1978), in their analysis of a sample of about 10 percent of all scientific articles published between 1665 and 1800, found that only 2.2 percent of papers had more than one author. This individual skew was so strong that, even in the middle of the 20th century, when joint work in science was becoming increasingly popular, it was not seen as a condition for success. In 1947, Albert Einstein wrote in his *Atomic War or Peace*, "One can organize to apply a discovery already made, but not to make one. Only a free individual can make a discovery. [...] Can you imagine an organization of scientists making the discoveries of Charles Darwin?" (1994, p. 133). This perspective reserved the greatest discoveries for outstanding individuals working alone—the lonely geniuses. It might have been true in Darwin's time, although even the inventor of the evolution theory was not entirely working solo: he co-authored a paper with Alfred Russel Wallace (1823–1913). Albert Einstein also profited from a kind of collaborative process. Although Einstein described how he "lived in solitude in the country and noticed how the monotony of a quiet life stimulates the creative mind" (1983, p. 29), he was not entirely isolated. For instance, in 1912 his friend Marcel Grossmann (1878–1936) brought him inspiration when Einstein was looking for a mathematical approach to general relativity, suggesting that Riemannian geometry (a branch of differential geometry) might be useful in this case (Galenson, 2012). The key idea of the age of the individual is not that there was no scientific collaboration at all, rather that collaboration was far less frequent, less intensive, and less acknowledged.

In the age of the individual, appreciation of the single scholar—reinforced by Romanticism's cult of genius—was accompanied by a habit of overlooking the contribution of a genius's collaborators. Certainly, acknowledging the contributions of collaborators was not always in line with contemporary customs. The 17th-century Anglo-Irish chemist Robert Boyle (1627–1691)—one of the fathers of the modern experimental scientific method—published his work under his name only, despite it being the result of joint work. One of Boyle's collaborators, Denis Papin (1647–1713)—French physicist, mathematician and inventor—ran experiments and also designed some of them, built scientific instruments, and even wrote publications presenting the results as Boyle's sole authorship. Although today this behaviour would be judged as ethically unacceptable, in the 17th century it did not arouse indignation. Boyle took all responsibility for what was claimed in his publications and was in charge of all the activities that took place in his laboratory. That is why, in the age of the individual scientist, all the credit and recognition was assigned to Boyle (Shapin, 1994). Today, the principal investigator also takes the main responsibility, but the contribution of assistants, researchers, and even students is usually properly acknowledged.

2.1.2 Learned societies and academies

Institutionalisation in the form of scientific societies and academies marked a milestone in the process of creating modern science. Simultaneously, it showed the importance of collaboration in science, as societies and academies provided organisational space for knowledge exchange. The first scientific societies emerged in the mid-15th century on the Apennine Peninsula. Accademia Pontaniana, founded in 1443 in Naples by the poet Antonio Beccadelli (1394–1471) and patronised by Alfonso V of Aragon (1396–1458), is one of the earliest examples and it is still operating. Around the turn of the 16th century, privately patronised scientific associations spread across Europe. Among the most famous are the Bessarion's Academy in Rome and the Platonic Academy in Florence. Between 1500 and 1800 in Europe about 2,500 learned societies were established.[1] In 1652 the Leopoldina—since 2008 operating under the name of the German National Academy of Sciences—was founded in Schweinfurt by four physicians: Johann Laurentius Bausch (1605–1665), Johann Michael Fehr (1610–1688), Georg Balthasar Metzger (1623–1687), and Georg Balthasar Wholfarth (1607–1674). Eight years later, the London Royal Society was initiated as a College for the Promoting of Physico-Mathematical Experimental Learning, aimed at holding weekly discussions about science and running experiments. Since 1665 the society has published one of the first scientific journals: *Philosophical Transactions*, originally called *Philosophical Transactions: Giving some Accompt of the present Undertakings, Studies and Labours of the Ingenious in many considerable parts of the World*. In 1666, Louis XIV (1638–1715) founded the French Academy of Sciences as part of the French government, although it was expected to be apolitical (Conner, 2005). Over the centuries, scientific societies and academies were established all over the world.

Apart from formalised societies and academies, less organised scholarly communities built the ground for professional scientific collaborative structures. One example could be the experimentalist network that grew up around the French mathematician and philosopher Marin Mersenne (1588–1648). It was part of the pan-European informal Torricellian network, one of the first international experimental scientist communities. The group gathered researchers around a mercury barometer invented by Evangelista Torricelli (1608–1647) in 1643. The barometer was a key element which served to link the group members by inspiring them to conduct various physical experiments. These ranged from the repetition and improvement of Torricelli's first experiments by Blaise Pascal (1623–1662) and Pierre Petit (1594–1677) in 1646 (following a description of the experiment received from Mersenne), through Otto von Guericke's (1602–1686) construction of a vacuum pump in 1654, to the pneumatic engine invented in 1659 by Robert Boyle (Wootton, 2015). The Torricelli barometer experimental community exemplified the dyad that is essential to science, namely the coexistence of collaboration and competition—or coopetition, as this phenomenon is sometimes referred to (Merton, 1973; Hull, 1988; Walley, 2007).

These early scientific networks, societies, and academies demonstrated that collaboration between scientists can be beneficial for individual researchers and science as a whole. The contribution of scholarly communities to the institutionalisation of science was that they gave firm evidence to support the conviction that the exchange of knowledge could lead to more rapid progress. This idea was similar to Francis Bacon's (1561–1626) perspective on science as a progressive, collective, collaborative, and long-range enterprise (Conner, 2005). However, it should be noted that early scientific societies and academies were not intentionally established in order to support collaboration. In its early days, the Royal Society was focused predominantly on individual scientists who demonstrated experiments to a curious public. Collaborative publications, such as encyclopaedias, the tradition of which dates back to Roman times, were rather the result of combining works of many individual authors than the product of collective teamwork (Beaver & Rosen, 1978). Thus, although in the history of science numerous examples of collaboration can be found, the real age of international research networks (Adams, 2013), when collaboration became an inherent, unavoidable, and recognised element of scientific inquiry, is a rather recent phenomenon.

2.1.3 *The republic of letters*

Until the 19th century, letters were the only distant communication method available for scholars, not counting time-consuming and often risky journeys. The intensive circulation of post in the late 17th and 18th centuries created an almost global scientific community: The Republic of Letters. The exchange of hand-written mail in the scientific community was incredibly intensive. Voltaire's (1694–1778) correspondence alone consists of 19 thousand letters and it is estimated that an additional 9–10 thousand of his missives were not passed down (Edelstein et al., 2010). The German polymath Gottfried Wilhelm Leibniz (1646–1716) built up a network of circa 400 correspondents, not only Europeans, but also Chinese mandarins. Meanwhile, the Rome-based Jesuit Athanasius Kircher (1602–1680) wrote to some 760 correspondents in Europe and overseas (Harris, 2006). Circulating letters helped to exchange knowledge, ideas, and experimental results, discuss contentious issues, share inspirations, and establish a common understanding (Kronick, 2001; Wootton, 2015).

Like today, in early scientific networks some scholars played the role of hubs, enabling the flow of ideas and knowledge between larger numbers of individuals. The polymath Samuel Hartlib (1600–1662), whose network of contacts created the foundation for the Royal Society of London, and Henry Oldenburg (1619–1677), the designer of the scientific peer review system,[2] could both serve as examples of scientific gatekeepers (Knight, 1976). Although today the single scientist's role in knowledge dissemination seems to be diminishing, in 16th and 17th-century Europe—during Adams' first age of research—progress in science and the integration of the scientific community depended heavily on the activity of eminent scholars. The above-mentioned scientific activity of Mersenne perfectly exemplifies the role of a scholarly communication hub. In 1635, Mersenne established the informal, private Académie Parisienne. The institution, in which more than 100 astronomers, mathematicians and natural philosophers shared their ideas and research, laid the foundations for the establishment of the French Academy of Sciences (Sergescu, 1948). Mersenne also organised weekly meetings in his Paris home and was engaged in regular, extensive correspondence with, inter alia, French philosopher René Descartes (1596–1650), Italian astronomer Galileo Galilei (1564–1642), French mathematician and inventor Blaise Pascal (1623–1662), and French lawyer and mathematician Pierre de Fermat (1607–1665). Moreover, Fermat's mutual friendship with Mersenne enabled communication among a group of French experimenters scattered across the country who, between 1646 and 1648, were concurrently working on vacuum experiments (Shea, 2003; Wootton, 2015).

2.1.4 The first global research project

Contemporary science is inconceivable without large-scale international projects involving hundreds of researchers. Similarly, some of the important milestones in science made in previous centuries would not have been achieved without scholars cooperating, in spite of the lack of contemporary transport and communication technologies. The transits of Venus across the Sun in 1761 and 1769 provided the perfect occasion for the first global scientific collaboration (Leverington, 2003). The British royal astronomer Edmond Halley (1656–1742) initiated the series of simultaneous astronomical observations of these events well in advance, in 1716. The exercise engaged about 250 astronomers from different countries who intended to ascertain the distance between the Earth and the Sun and, on that basis, using trigonometry and Kepler's laws of planetary motion, to calculate the size of the solar system. The project, prepared and run by European scientific societies, received substantial financial and organisational support from certain monarchs. For instance, Catherine the Great (1729–1796) sent observation teams across the Russian Empire, Christian VII of Denmark (1749–1808) sent Hungarian astronomers to the extreme northeastern part of Norway, and the British conducted transit observations in North America and Tahiti during James Cook's (1728–1779) *Endeavour* expedition (Wulf, 2012).

The astronomers, equipped with bulky and fragile instruments, travelled to various places which were frequently extremely wild, remote, and inaccessible, such as Tobolsk in Siberia, Madagascar, Mauritius, and Sumatra. Some of them did not reach the observation point in time—not least because of travel constraints resulting from the Seven Years' War (1756–1763). Others saw nothing because of cloudy skies at the time of transit. Extreme bad luck accompanied French astronomer Guillaume Le Gentil (1725–1792), who spent eight years travelling in an attempt to observe either of the transits but missed both. And yet, in the end, the project was successful. After years spent on data gathering and calculations, researchers came out with an excellent result (149.51–156.95 million miles), very close to the actual distance between the Earth and the Sun (149.60 million miles) (Wulf, 2012). None of the collaborating astronomers could have achieved the results alone, without jointly planning the observation process and sharing data. The Venus transit observation proves that worldwide collaboration was possible even without the advanced communication tools which we enjoy today.

2.1.5 The rise of international conferences and congresses

In the present day, international gatherings are the bread and butter of the scientific profession. But it was not always the case. During the time of the Republic of Letters, scientists from distant places rarely met in large numbers. International scientific meetings did not gain momentum until the middle of the 19th century, when the development of railways and steamships facilitated long-distance travel. Indeed, developments in transportation and communication technologies have greatly influenced all kinds of long-distance collaboration, not only in science.

The importance of the rise of international meetings for science development cannot be overestimated. William Bynum, in his *A Little History of Science* (2012), gives a very convincing example of a chemists' gathering in 1860. Leading chemists from eleven European countries, accompanied by one colleague from as far as Mexico, met for three days in Karlsruhe in Germany. The event was organised by three Germans: August Kekulé (1829–1896), Adolphe Wurtz (1817–1884), and Karl Weltzien (1813–1870). They set the aim for the meeting: to agree on a common vocabulary, notation, and understanding of some basic concepts such as atoms and molecules (Leicester, 1956). Although the delegates did not reach a firm consensus, the congress was a milestone in the development of modern chemistry. The gathering not only laid the cornerstone for the global chemist association—The International Union of Pure and Applied Chemistry (Ihde, 1961)—but, and more importantly, it directly inspired some breakthrough developments in chemistry. Dmitrij Mendeleev (1834–1907)—one of the meeting's participants—was genuinely inspired by Sicilian scholar Stanislao Cannizzaro (1826–1910) and his 1858 paper distributed during the convention. In the paper Cannizzaro argued that relative atomic weights could be useful for cataloguing and understanding the nature of the elements. Mendeleev followed this path and created his groundbreaking periodic table, where the elements are indeed ordered by their relative atomic weight.

The 1860 Karlsruhe chemists' congress is considered the first professional international gathering. Further congresses followed soon and played an important role in the formation of contemporary science, including the rise of big science, which relies on and stimulates international scientific collaboration. However, the meaning of international scientific meetings could also be seen in a broader perspective. As William Bynum argues, "They also announced to the world a belief widely shared by the scientific community: that science itself was objective and international, and above religion and politics, which often divided people and set whole nations at war with one another" (2012, pp. 178–179).

2.2 The collaborative turn

A significant increase in scientific collaboration has been noticeable since the beginning of the 20th century, but it is in the last few decades that we have witnessed its exceptional acceleration and intensification all over the world and in all scientific disciplines. And now, before our very eyes, a collaborative turn is taking place in the modes of scientific production. This collaborative revolution indicates something deeper than a growth in the number of collaborative papers, international projects, co-patents, and joint events, or the growing use of shared facilities and equipment. The collaborative turn represents a substantial change in the making of science. Collaboration changes science not only quantitatively, but also qualitatively. Many scientific achievements simply cannot arise from individual effort and, thus, large-scale collaboration makes the impossible possible. But before we discuss the outcomes of the collaborative turn, let us scrutinise its anatomy.

2.2.1 The anatomy of the collaborative turn

Derek John de Solla Price—the father of scientometrics—reported that in 1900 over 80 percent of all papers in the periodical index *Chemical Abstracts* were single-authored, and almost all the rest had no more than two authors. He noticed that by 1960 the share of multiple-authorship papers had increased to 60 percent, and the pace of this increase was even greater for papers with a higher number of authors (Price, 1963). Cronin gave further evidence of the rise in scientific collaboration. He noticed that between 1955 and 1999 the average number of authors per paper in the Science Citation Index (SCI) rose from 1.83 to 3.90 (Cronin, 2001). Leydersdorf and Wagner (2008) confirmed these findings. They estimated that in just 15 years—between 1990 and 2005—the share of internationally co-authored papers in the SCI increased from 10.1 to 23.3 percent. Even in a less collaborative field of science, namely mathematics, the percentage of co-authored papers increased. While during the whole 19th century the share was at a stable and very low level (about 1–2 percent), a rapid rise was observed between 1900 and 1930, and in 1980 the rate was almost 50 percent (Wagner-Döbler, 2001).

The collaborative turn is manifested by the increasing size of research teams and scientific collaboration networks, as well as by the proliferation of collaboration crossing institutional, sectoral, national, and disciplinary borders (Doré et al., 1996; Georghiou, 1998; Glänzel, 2001). For example, between 1975 and 2005 multi-university collaboration among the major US universities was the fastest-growing type of authorship collaboration (Jones, Wuchty, & Uzzi, 2008). Furthermore, an increase in teamwork has occurred in all fields of science (Wagner, 2008; Ma, Li, & Chen, 2014). In the Web of Science the share of multi-authored papers in the natural and medical sciences increased between 1900 and 2011 from 13 percent to 93 percent, and in the social sciences and humanities from 3 to 62 percent. Additionally, in both groups of sciences, multi-authored and multi-institutional papers constituted the majority of papers published in 2011 (Larivière, Gingras, Sugimoto, & Tsou, 2015). Between 1955 and 2000, the average number of authors per paper in the Web of Science database in science and engineering almost doubled, from 1.9 to 3.5. With regard to inventions, there was an increase from 1.7 applicants per patent in 1975 to 2.3 in 2000. At the same time, the share of social science articles written by more than one author grew from 17.5 to 51.5 percent. The share of multi-authored papers in the arts and humanities still remains relatively low (less than 10 percent in 2000) but, in these fields too, the trend towards greater collaboration is visible (Wuchty et al., 2007).

The collaborative turn can be tracked by other means than merely the publication outcomes of scientific activity. For example, multiple laureates of the Nobel Prize in physics, chemistry, and physiology (medicine) have become much more commonplace since the Second World War. The mean number of laureates calculated for the 20-year intervals increased from around 1.5 in the mid-1940s to 2.5 in the 21st century in all three categories mentioned.[3] We should bear in mind that the Nobel Prize cannot be awarded to more than three individuals. This tight condition is against the collaboration trend in contemporary science, and its legitimacy has been openly questioned (Casadevall & Fang, 2013). If the Nobel Committee would like to reward the detection of gravitational waves, announced by the Advanced LIGO team in 2016, it would be a real dilemma as to who should get the prize. The team includes hundreds of researchers from all over the world. The 16-page article presenting the discovery, published in the journal *Physical Review Letters*, contains an alphabetical list of over one thousand authors spread over three pages.

The collaborative turn increasingly affects members of the scientific community, no matter their position and experience. For centuries, the privilege of working with other researchers was reserved for the most prominent scholars (Beaver & Rosen, 1978). In the last few decades, teamwork has not only intensified within the scientific elite, but has also become more widespread in the whole scientific community. Today, co-working with partners from all over the world has become an everyday reality for top scientists and for researchers in non-elite institutions, as well as scientists from countries that a few decades ago were absent from the global scientific collaboration network (Schubert & Sooryamoorthy, 2010).

2.2.2 The roots of the collaborative turn

The collaborative turn is deeply rooted in globalisation processes. International integration and high interdependence among societies, facilitated by the liberalisation of capital, commodity, and people flows, as well as the incredible technological leap in recent decades have influenced scholars' behaviour and have caused the scientific community to become tightly linked as never before. The increased role of international organisations, multinational corporations included, has changed the way in which knowledge is created and disseminated. Science policies have significantly reinforced these spontaneous processes. Various incentives and measures implemented by states and regions foster collaboration as a way of lifting research to a higher level (Katz & Martin, 1997; Sonnenwald, 2007). These changes influence the collaborative behaviour of individuals, from academics settled at universities to researchers based in enterprise laboratories.

Significant progress in transport and communication has facilitated the rise of collaboration on a global scale. Due to technological advancements in the last few decades we have witnessed a substantial drop in travel and communication costs, accompanied by an unprecedented decrease in journey times. The dense flight network enables scientists to cover a distance of thousands of kilometres in just a few hours, and attend a conference or a project meeting on a one-day trip basis, without draining their travel budget. A 2016 study showed that the introduction of new, low-fare airline routes in the US significantly increased scientific collaboration, with the greatest impact made on the collaborative behaviour of early-career scholars, who usually have fewer resources than established professors (Catalini, Fons-Rosen, & Gaulé, 2016). The reduction of travel costs means that shipping costs of sending, for example, samples in experimental research are also substantially less. Furthermore, in many cases the need for short-term relocation of people has been significantly reduced, since modern information and communications technologies (ICTs) enable instant and affordable communication from and to any location.

E-working in science has become a standard nowadays, at least in less infrastructure-dependent disciplines. This is also because scientists are interested in the research opportunities that are dispersed worldwide. Traditional working spaces are redundant since many scholars are constantly on the go, and broadband internet connections enable them to stay online wherever they are with the use of a portable virtual office, equipped with ever more sophisticated devices. ICTs facilitate fast, low-cost, and secure transfer of large amounts of data, and allow for joint research irrespective of the partners' location. Email communication does not require synchrony, which is especially important when partners live in different time zones or have very tight schedules (as many scientists do). Geographically dispersed collaborations and projects with a large number of partners particularly benefit from these facilitating factors (Stokols, Misra, Moser, Hall, & Taylor, 2008).

In fact, ICTs assist both research activities, such as exchanging data or discussion, and project management (Bos et al., 2007). Here, basic tools such as email or online video calls are complemented by more advanced technological features such as shared file-hosting platforms and calendars, or online meeting planners (Barjak, 2006; Sonnenwald, 2007; Walsh & Maloney, 2007). Noticeably, although still at a very early stage of development, social networking sites for scientists, such as ResearchGate, Academia, or Mendeley, are gradually gaining interest among scholars. Like all social media tools, these portals can be used to foster collaboration between their users, especially at the initial stages of the process (Van Noorden, 2014). It is also worth emphasising that the positive impact of ICTs on research collaboration is conditioned by the compatibility between new tools and existing practices (Duque et al., 2005).

Despite all the advantages of ICTs, face-to-face interaction is still important, or even essential, in establishing and conducting fruitful collaboration. This can apply not only to intensive integrated collaboration, but also joint work based on relatively independent complementary tasks (Vasileiadou & Vliegenthart, 2009). For many researchers, contact through the internet complements rather than substitutes for traditional face-to-face communication (Koku, Nazer, & Wellman, 2001). As already mentioned, since joint research is something more than just exchanging data or results, interpersonal chemistry, trust, and mutual understanding are necessary for successful collaboration (Hara, Solomon, Kim, & Sonnenwald, 2003; Laudel, 2001; Numprasertchai & Igel, 2005). And these might be difficult to develop using internet-mediated communication alone. Vicens and Bourne describe this in a very outright way:

> Nothing new here, it is the same as for friendship and marriage. Communication is always better face-to-face if possible, for example by travelling to meet your collaborators, or by scheduling discussion related to your collaborations during conferences that the people involved will attend. Synchronous communication by telephone or video teleconferencing is preferred over asynchronous collaboration by e-mail
>
> (2007, p. 336).

Apart from new technologies, collaboration in science is made significantly easier by the new lingua franca of our age: English. Through the centuries of scientific history several languages have been used for international communication, with Latin, French, and German as examples. However, since the 1930s, the role of English has been constantly increasing, marginalising other languages. The proliferation of English might be seen as the fruition of the dream of a "Paradise lost, a moment of universal comity before the descent of Babel" (Gordin, 2015, p. 24) that was supposed to have been realised by Latin. Today, the domination of English is turning into a monopoly, at least in some scientific disciplines. A symbolic date is January 1, 2012, when the *International Code of Nomenclature for algae, fungi and plants*—the set of rules dealing with botanical names—was allowed to include a non-Latin description of candidates of a new species. Of course, the only alternative language to Latin was English. Using a common language has clear advantages for collaboration: it enables scientific communication with partners from different countries, including transfer of knowledge, discussion, and peer review. Nowadays, even if papers are written in other languages, more or less popular, they are almost always supplemented with an English title and abstract. A common language is also crucial in such areas as managing collaborative projects or distributing money, e.g., through international grants with calls announced and applications processed in English.

2.2.3 Outcomes of scientific collaboration

The impetus of the collaborative turn comes from the individual scholars who strive to build a network of collaborators, knowing that collaboration is key to pursuing their scientific careers. Generally, scholars who collaborate intensively publish more, their articles gain more citations, and consequently their personal work is recognised by a wider public (Sonnenwald, 2007). Collaboration's positive effect on the number of scientific papers which an individual scientist can publish results from the advantages of division of labour. In 1966, Price and Beaver explained the mechanism of how collaboration increases publication productivity, starting with the simplifying assumption that the number of articles that a scholar is able to write during his or her academic career can be determined. In the mid-1960s this value was relatively low—on average 0.96 for a five-year period. Therefore, collaboration can be seen as "a method for squeezing papers out of the rather large population of people who have less than a whole paper in them" (p. 1015). The large-scale 2016 study based on Web of Science data found that the number of articles published by early-career researchers (in their first 15 years of publication activity) did not change significantly between 1900 and 2013 if controlled for collaboration. The number of papers per researcher rose, but simultaneously the number of collaborators increased from almost zero at the beginning of the century to between two and seven in 2013 for various scientific fields, excluding the arts and humanities, where co-authorship is still quite rare. If we take co-authorship into account and calculate fractional publication rates, i.e., the ratio of the number of publications and the number of co-authors, it turns out that the number of papers per researcher has not increased but has actually slightly declined in the course of the last century (Fanelli & Larivière, 2016). This shows that co-authoring—and collaboration in general—is a powerful tool for increasing the number of output items, but it does not necessarily translate into the substantially greater ability of a single scholar to produce more new knowledge.

Collaboration can also augment the quality of scientific production, and by this we mean the excellence of research outcomes that actually push forward the frontier of knowledge. Shared responsibility for a precisely limited piece of work makes it possible to achieve better results in time-restricted projects. Collaboration brings into play the advantages of specialisation, complementarity, and synergy effects. By working together, scientists gain access to partners' knowledge, expertise, and skills, giving them new ideas, solutions, and approaches. Furthermore, partners can jointly control the accuracy of their results, detect errors, and comment on the methods selected and techniques applied (Beaver, 2001; Franceschet & Costantini, 2010).

Collaborative publications generally gain more citations than single-authored papers (see Beaver, 2001; Franceschet & Costantini, 2010). There are two main reasons for this. On the one hand, multi-authored publications can be of better quality in terms of their originality, significance, and depth, and are therefore of greater interest to the scientific audience. Consequently, the results are more frequently mentioned in other publications and are thus more visible. On the other hand, the visibility of collaborative papers can also be put down to the advertising factor. Authors bring their papers to the attention of people through formal and informal personal contacts. Therefore, the fact that multi-authored publications are embedded in broader social networks may explain the higher number of citations. In particular, publications with authors from different institutions or countries can expect to have more citations due to this advertising mechanism (Franceschet & Costantini, 2010; Goldfinch, Dale, & DeRouen, 2003). In the case of less developed countries, there is a whole list of other tangible rewards related to collaboration. For example, a study of the local and foreign publication productivity of agricultural scientists in two Philippine locations revealed that participation in collaborative research projects is mainly aimed not at producing papers and citations, but at gaining access to other professional opportunities. Through collaboration, scholars can acquire access to research project offers, domestic and foreign travel opportunities, and financial incentives in the form of additional income, honoraria, and per diems, as well as high prestige in the local scientific community (Ynalvez & Shrum 2011).

2.2.4 Multi-speed collaborative science

The clear and growing trend towards collaborative science is becoming more and more widespread, although not uniform. Researchers' individual characteristics, such as the stage of their career, age, and gender, greatly influence the proclivity for collaboration (Abramo, D'Angelo, & Murgia, 2014; Bozeman & Gaughan, 2011; Jeong, Choi, & Kim, 2011). Above all, collaboration levels are highly diversified across the scientific fields. Despite the fact that the collaborative turn is visible everywhere in the scientific universe, it has altered each of the disciplines differently, and some types of teamwork have grown and spread more rapidly than others. We might say that there are as many collaborative customs as there are scientific fields. Larivière and his collaborators (2015) analysed more than 28 million Web of Science papers from 1900–2011. They concluded that in the 20th century overall, co-authored publications increased in both analysed categories, i.e., natural and medical sciences (NMS), and social sciences and humanities (SSH). However, while the share of single-authored papers in NMS plummeted from 87 to just 7 percent, in SSH it fell less dramatically, from 97 to 38 percent.

A study of co-authorship published in Web of Science in the years 1996–2000 revealed that the average number of authors spanned from 1.06 to 4.39 depending on the scientific field (Wuchty et al., 2007). In some disciplines collaboration is more a matter of choice than necessity, as in the case of theoretical sciences, such as philosophy or history, where co-authorship is rare. On the other hand, in some fields where research requires access to unique resources, the number of co-authors exceeded four. Examples can be seen in clinical experiments, where researchers need to closely collaborate with doctors to obtain biological samples, or in experimental physics, where only some research centres have access to the special instruments or infrastructure required. In general, co-authorship is low in the arts and humanities. In the social sciences, mathematics, and computer science it is moderate, while in the sciences and engineering co-authorship is the most common and the broadest (Francescheta & Costantini, 2010; Wuchty et al., 2007). Furthermore, experimentalists tend to collaborate more with other scientists than theoreticians, regardless of the scientific field (Gordon, 1980; Meadows & O'Connor, 1971; Price, 1963).

These discipline differences in the proclivity to collaborate could be explained by variance in the modes of knowledge production and the nature of work typical for a specific scientific field (Birnholtz, 2007). However, empirical analyses have not been able to identify which disciplinary characteristics play a crucial role in this matter. For example, Wagner (2005) proposed a distinction between four types of scientific fields—data-driven, resource-driven, equipment-driven, and theory-driven—but the results of her study did not show a clear pattern of relations between collaboration propensity and the type of scientific discipline. Furthermore, since most of the studies use co-authorship as a proxy of collaboration, differences between disciplines might also be the result of the authorship contribution rules and conventions typical for a specific scientific field. In some disciplines, it is only the first author that gains significant credit for the publication (Engers, Gans, Grant, & King, 1999; Laband & Tollison, 2000), while in others all project members are listed as authors in alphabetical order.

2.3 What is scientific collaboration?

It is often taken for granted that the concept of scientific collaboration is quite obvious to most people and easily understood. Yet the truth is that under closer scrutiny it remains a challenging and complex phenomenon (Katz & Martin, 1997). For instance, while a joint research project or co-authorship of a scientific paper unquestionably exemplifies scientific collaboration, it is not as clear in the case of discussing research nuances during a conference coffee break. Can we still call this collaboration? Physicist Richard Feynman (1918–1988), the 1965 Nobel Prize laureate, wrote in his autobiography:

> The questions of the students are often the source of new research. They often ask profound questions that I've thought about at times and then given up on, so to speak, for a while. [...] The students may not be able to see the thing I want to answer, or the subtleties I want to think about, but they remind me of a problem by asking questions in the neighbourhood of that problem. It's not so easy to remind yourself of these things
> (2010, pp. 91–92).

The boundary between collaboration and inspiration is blurred. Certainly, when we cite Richard Feynman we do not collaborate with him, even if we owe him a great deal of inspiration. But things get more complicated if we consider receiving enlightening comments on our manuscript from anonymous peer reviewers. We cannot cite them or list them as co-authors, but have they not consciously worked with us and influenced the outcome of our efforts?

2.3.1 Defining a fuzzy concept

The *Oxford English Dictionary* defines collaboration as "the act of working with another person or group of people to create or produce something" ("Collaboration", n.d.). Applying this approach to science, we can see scientific collaboration as the act of scholars working together to make something. This something can be almost anything, from a well-defined research proposal, a presentation abstract, or a journal paper, to concepts less easy to grasp, such as new knowledge or advancement of science and technology. Two main components of scientific collaboration arise here. First, the collaborative process needs two or more collaborating sides: units, people, or groups of people. Second, collaborating parties act to achieve a particular goal, to do something that would not be possible without collaboration, or would be significantly more difficult to achieve. The latter is crucial for the understanding of collaboration in science. The common goal component differentiates collaboration from other forms of interaction in science.

Not surprisingly, many attempts to define scientific collaboration focus on the shared goal or common outcomes of the process. Katz and Martin define scientific collaboration as "the working together of researchers to achieve the common goal of producing new scientific knowledge" (1997, p. 7). Similarly, Laudel underlines the significance of shared goals as the main factor driving joint work. She defines scientific collaboration as "a system of research activities by several actors related in a functional way and coordinated to attain a research goal corresponding with these actors' research goals or interests" (2002, p. 5). Ynalvez and Shrum share this view when they describe collaboration as "the interaction of two or more scientists in a project with a specific goal or objective, attained by sharing knowledge, skills or resources" (2009, p. 872). Meanwhile Schrage (1995) takes a broader stance and points to shared understanding as an outcome of scientific collaboration.

In some definitions, the common goal component remains implicit. This is the case in the broad definition coined by Patel. According to him, scientific collaboration is "a process of functional interdependence between scholars in their attempt to coordinate skills, tools and rewards" (1973, p. 80). The definition appears to make no direct reference to a common goal, but we can argue that effective coordination is not possible without shared outcomes in mind, even if they are as abstract as advancement of the sciences. Similarly, the definition proposed by Melin and Persson (1996), which focuses on communication and sharing of competences and other resources (see Table 2.1), includes an implicit assumption that collaboration can produce efficiencies in these areas—and it is this efficiency of scientific production that can be seen as the common goal of collaborators.

2.3.2 Weak and strong collaboration

Collaboration modes vary across different scientific disciplines and people, as well as stages of research. Scientists can divide work and combine individual contributions in a number of ways, depending on the specificity of the task, relations

Table 2.1 Selected definitions of scientific collaboration

Scientific collaboration is...	Source
"a process of functional interdependence between scholars in their attempt to coordinate skills, tools, and rewards"	Patel, 1973, p. 80
"the process of shared creation: two or more individuals with complementary skills interacting to create a shared understanding that none had previously possessed or could have come to on their own"	Schrage, 1995, p. 40
"an intense form of interaction, that allows for effective communication as well as the sharing of competence and other resources"	Melin & Persson, 1996, p. 363
"the working together of researchers to achieve the common goal of producing new scientific knowledge; definition supplemented with the putative criteria for distinguishing 'collaborators' from other researchers"	Katz & Martin, 1997, p. 7
"a system of research activities by several actors related in a functional way and coordinated to attain a research goal corresponding with these actors' research goals or interests"	Laudel, 2002, p. 5
"the interaction of two or more scientists in a project with a specific goal or objective, attained by sharing knowledge, skills or resources"	Ynalvez & Shrum, 2009, p. 872

Source: Own elaboration.

between team members, available resources, and the degree of functional and strategic dependence among researchers. Some tasks can be performed sequentially, some have to be done concurrently, while others are inseparable and thus require joint work (Steiner, 1972; Whitley, 2000). Based on the work of Laudel (2002) we can distinguish two types of collaboration: (1) *strong*—tightly and directly related to the specific research process, and (2) *weak*—loosely associated with the specific research process or independent of it (see Figure 2.1).

Strong modes of collaboration rest upon horizontal specialisation, with various strengths of cooperative bonds as well as a creativity component. There are two main forms of strong collaboration—creative and imitative. Creative collaboration involving the division of tasks is the most intensive and is characterised by a shared research goal and distribution of inventive work. An example could be a research project in an experimental discipline. Each phase of the project requires joint work and intensive interaction, which are essential for achieving final success. Hara et al. (2003) further distinguishes between two detailed subtypes of creative collaboration depending on the intensity of interaction and interdependency between partners. The complementary collaboration subtype requires input from a number of partners who can work to a large extent independently. This type does not require much interaction between partners and is based on the results being put together by the project coordinator. Meanwhile, the integrative

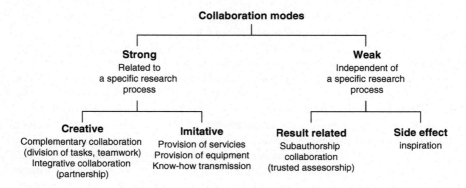

Figure 2.1 Collaboration modes
Source: Own elaboration based on Laudel (2002) and Hara et al. (2003).

collaboration subtype involves more intensive joint work on complex and often interdisciplinary problems involving a large number of interdependent subtasks. Partners have to interact intensively during the whole project, discussing not only the research design and plan, but also solutions to emerging problems and the consequences of partial results, as these may affect further stages in their joint work. This kind of collaboration is based on close working relationships since intensive interaction occurs between all partners, and as a result it generates synergy and provides support for collaborators (Hara et al., 2003).

Secondly, the imitative type of strong collaboration refers to service collaboration and provision of equipment. In such cases, the principal investigator (lead partner) sets the research goal and also performs all the creative work. Other partners' contribution is routine, and they might be called subcontractors. In the experimental sciences, such collaboration may occur when a research designer does not know the method required or does not have access to research equipment, such as large telescopes or telescope arrays. Scientists from all over the world visit observatories that are often remotely located, use the equipment for a specific period of time in order to collect data, and return to their host institutions to analyse the results of the measurements. Wray (2002) underlines that in this form of subcontracting collaboration, all the credit and responsibility rest with the lead partner. He proposed labelling such collaboration as collective but non-collaborative research.

As a separate subtype of imitative strong collaboration, Laudel (2002) distinguished transfer of know-how—procedural knowledge in the form of advice, often as a response to a spontaneous, informal request, for example at a conference. As Subramanyam notes, "a brilliant suggestion made by a scientist during casual conversation may be more valuable in shaping the course and outcome of a research project than weeks of labour-intensive activity of a collaborating scientist in the laboratory" (1983, p. 35).

Weak collaboration modes encompass scholarly activities indirectly associated with a given research process. The first group here falls under the notion of sub-authorship collaboration—or trusted assessorship, as it is called by Mullins (1973). These are comments and remarks made by colleagues acting as friendly critics during the publishing process. Gratitude for this kind of support is manifested in an article's acknowledgements (Patel, 1973). Finally, there is a certain side effect of scientific communication which can be viewed as the weakest mode of scientific collaboration. This is understood to include offshoots such as inspiration or fertilisation of ideas, stimulation of creativity, and unexpected food for thought unrelated to the collaborative task in hand.

Martin and Katz (1997) also distinguish between strong and weak collaboration. However, their approach is slightly different from the above-described classification. It does not use the criterion of dependency on a specific research process. Their definition of strong collaboration takes into account only those scientists who directly contribute to all of the main research tasks. On the contrary, in weak scientific collaboration anyone who provides any input to a particular piece of research may be recognised as a collaborator. In other words, the weak definition of collaboration is much broader and inclusive, incorporating both strong and weak forms of joint work. This simple classification, as Martin and Katz argue, might not work in the case of complex and multidisciplinary research, in which no single researcher could meet the criterion of strong collaboration and be worthy of the title of collaborator.

2.3.3 Formal and informal collaboration settings

The distinction between formal and informal collaboration is important from the organisational and managerial point of view, as managing formal structures varies greatly from handling informal ones. Formal collaboration is based on two-party or multilateral agreements, contracts, or arrangements. They can vary depending on their range level of detail, and duration. This category includes collaboration within research projects conducted by formal consortia, as well as miscellaneous framework agreements signed by scientific institution authorities. In most cases, access to human resources, funds, and infrastructure requires some sort of formalised collaboration. However, some of the formal agreements work more like an umbrella and do not lead to creating any kind of strong collaboration. Hence, formal collaboration does not necessarily mean strong collaboration.

Informal collaboration is based on the direct relations of engaged scholars sharing their research interests. Participation in conferences, seminars, and workshops facilitates informal communication among scholars and creates the foundation for future collaboration. Information and communication technologies, as well as social media tailored for scholars, ease and accelerate informal contacts among researchers. Unofficial scientific contacts are essential, not only in scientific networking, but also in building the mutual trust and understanding that are the foundation of smooth and successful teamwork. The main advantage of informal relations lies in their flexibility and high level of leeway.

Informal collaboration works especially well when partners know and trust each other. During their professional careers, scientists establish many informal collaborations which form a substratum of their social network (Crane, 1972; Maglaughlin & Sonnenwald, 2005). It can serve as a source of inspiration and a reservoir of possible partners for joint research and other activities requiring cooperation, such as inviting speakers for a conference or members of the editorial board of a scientific journal. In social networks, not only are direct relations important, but also those built indirectly through friends of friends. In this case, the person who matches up scholars acts as a bridge in knowledge flows. Based on empirical analysis of co-authorship in biomedical research, physics, and computer science, Newman (2001b) proved that scientists are more likely to produce a joint publication with someone with whom they have a common collaborator than with a randomly chosen partner.

Formal and informal collaborations occur simultaneously. Informal collaboration usually starts a process which, in further phases, may develop into formal cooperation; it gives impetus for the formation of strong collaboration modes (Price & Beaver, 1966; Lambert, 2003). On the other hand, when partners have different interests and goals (as in the case of science-business collaboration), formalisation might be necessary in order to secure partners' interests and avoid conflicts. However, formal arrangement may postpone the start of a project and cause further delays during its lifespan since all necessary amendments and adjustments require additional negotiations and agreements (Katz & Martin, 1997).

2.4 Why do scientists collaborate?

Let us put it simply: scientists collaborate because they benefit from doing so. Collaboration allows them to conduct greater amounts of high-quality research with widely visible results—the desire of many scholars. Multiple motivations come into play here. The scholarly profession is driven by the scientific ethos, the intrinsic desire to gain knowledge, or a dream to make the world a better place. But researchers also have much more prosaic motivations, like a good pay check, career development, and high prestige (Hull, 1988). In the case of an individual scientist, several incentives usually coincide, and not all of them are deliberate. Some are strongly rooted in miscellaneous personal motivations, while others are more external, as when scientists must work with other people to have access to the necessary samples or instruments, or due to the injunction of a superior. In the short term, collaboration may be aimed at gaining access to unique resources (including knowledge), while in the long term, it may be seen as a way to build a scientific career and reputation (Rijnsoever, Hessels, & Vandeberg, 2008; Whitley, 2000).

2.4.1 Specialisation and the division of scientific labour

The umbrella term for the discussion on the motivations of scientific collaboration is "division of scientific work". Collaboration enables scientists to undertake more complex work, and in many cases it is a prerequisite for conducting research, especially that which requires many simultaneous observations, as in the case of the 18th-century Venus transits. A deeper division of labour has been triggered in recent years by the enormous growth of research tasks, the increasingly interdisciplinary nature of research, increasing costs, and limited access to expertise and tacit knowledge (Beaver, 2001; Katz & Martin 1997; The Royal Society, 2011).

Contemporary science is increasingly complex and specialised. As a result, in many scientific disciplines, especially experimental, "No individual scientist can possess all of the knowledge, skills, or time required to make theoretical or applied contributions in more than a very narrow area of research" (Hara et al., 2003, p. 953). The task of expanding the knowledge frontier is increasingly too demanding for a single scholar to cope with alone. The solution is the division of labour. According to Adam Smith, science can benefit from the division of labour because "Each individual becomes more expert in his own peculiar branch, more work is done upon the whole, and the quality of science is considerably increased by it" (1776, p. 8).

The advantages offered by the division of labour provide a powerful basis for scientific collaboration. The concept appears so obvious that it is sometimes overlooked. A good example is James Lovelock, British environmentalist and author of the Gaia hypothesis, which assumes that the Earth is a self-regulating system. He postulates the need for independent scientists that are just as important as large research teams in the scientific progress. Lovelock gives his own example as an autarkic scientist, working alone in his own laboratory, who does not need "immersion in a think-tank to excite ideas". But at the same time, Lovelock admits that

> If there was something very complex that I could not easily make, such as an electron microscope or a new form of mass spectrometer, I considered solving my problem another way, or sought a friend who could sell or donate spare time on his instrument, or could do the job for me
> (2014, para. 12).

He thus acknowledges that collaboration—in this case in the form of division of labour or service provision—is necessary to conduct a research project, even if someone is not a member of a research team.

Division of labour not only enables scientists to do more work in a given time, but also to use partners' knowledge, equipment, and technical skills, and thus save money and time on learning a new method or buying equipment. By sharing work, scientists can conduct increasingly complex research, which enables them to tackle larger and more complicated problems. On the other hand, the division of labour can also lead to diffusion of responsibility. This is especially important in ethically sensitive research areas such as clinical trials, military technologies, or animal experiments (Wray, 2002). Furthermore, collaboration depends on mutual trust that partners will provide reliable contributions. This issue cannot be underestimated, as there is good evidence to suggest that collaborators of unreliable scholars usually suffer in terms of their career development (Mongeon & Larivière, 2015). Clearly, division of labour generates advantages, but it can also trigger costs. The balancing of costs and benefits therefore remains the key to successful collaboration.

2.4.2 Tacticians and buddies

Scientific collaboration involves relationships between people, thus, personal factors may play an important role in this process. Personality and preferable modes of scientific work influence a scientist's proclivity for joint research. Some people prefer to work alone or in small research teams, others feel at home in larger groups. Personal factors also affect the selection of partners and the ability to sustain the collaboration process. Especially vital qualities are mutual trust and understanding, compatible working styles, and the ability to get along (Creamer, 2004; Hara et al., 2003; Maglaughlin & Sonnenwald, 2005). Although in many cases selection of collaborators is a matter of chance or external factors, it can also be a result of an intentional strategy. For some scientists—*taskmasters*—the most important aspect is the reliability of a partner and sticking to a schedule, while for others—*nationalists*—nationality and language proficiency play a crucial role. Experienced researchers often present a *mentor* approach, being motivated to help younger colleagues in their careers, whereas *tacticians* choose partners with skills complementary to their own. Now and then collaboration is forced by the request of the administration (the *follower* strategy). The last type are *buddies* who choose collaborators they have known for a longer time, with whom they have had good previous collaboration experiences, and find fun and entertaining. Of course, individual scientists may display features of two or more collaboration types, and the same scientist can alter the criteria when selecting partners for different activities. This empirically grounded typology shows how diversified motivations can be in the collaborators' selection process, and that it is not always pragmatic effectiveness that plays the decisive role (Bozeman & Corley, 2004).

Science as a social institution is based on the recognition and credit that are awarded to scientists and drive their professional career (Hull, 1988). Recognition and credit usually follow scientific contributions and have a tendency to accumulate. Thus, scholars who have once gained appreciation for their work find it is easier to obtain further recognition in the future and, as a consequence, build their prestige (Merton, 1973). For less recognised scientists, collaboration with established researchers creates a chance to learn and gain professional experience, and it also allows some of the prestige to rub off on them, thereby increasing their visibility. In this situation collaboration with a scientific star is perceived as a manifestation of the scientific community's acceptance and recognition, and as a consequence it increases a researcher's credibility. For younger scientists, it can also be a rite of passage (Hara et al., 2003; Mervis & Normile, 1998).

Doing science with other people can also be fun, or "hard fun"—the notion coined in the MIT Media Lab to describe an attitude towards tasks that are challenging but also very rewarding (Moss, 2011). For some scientists, the source of pleasure could be contact with people with certain personality traits; others place more importance on the professional dimension of such relations, which can satisfy scientific curiosity and intellectual interest (Beaver, 2001). The scholarly profession is very demanding and, since not all scientists achieve success and recognition, it can also be very frustrating. Joint work means that scientists can share their victories, doubts, and failures with other people who are in the same position. Sir Tim Hunt, British biochemist, molecular physiologist, and 2001 Nobel Prize laureate, when asked if he enjoyed collaboration said:

> I've always liked to collaborate with at least one other person on any project that I do, because you need somebody to cheer you up when things are going badly, and you need somebody to celebrate with when you have a small success [...] The public maybe has an idea of the lonely researcher, but in my experiences it has never been that of loneliness, it has been much more togetherness actually. And I like that very much
> (Hunt, n.d.).

2.4.3 Access to facilities and resources

The uniqueness of an expensive scientific infrastructure fosters or even forces collaboration. An extreme case in point involves unique facilities, such as the Large Hadron Collider or the International Space Station. The motivation to collaborate emerges when the costs of equipment exceed the possibilities of the individual researcher, team, or institution. From the economic perspective, access to a shared infrastructure eliminates redundancy of equipment and enhances efficiency. However, in some cases the limited availability of the facilities and equipment results from its location rather than its cost. For example, astronomical observatories require exceptional geographical conditions to achieve the highest quality of observational data. They are usually located at high altitudes, to minimise the negative influence of the Earth's atmosphere, and at a distance from urban areas, to avoid light pollution. Such sites are not available in every country, thus, astronomers and astrophysicists may need to collaborate with colleagues based in places with more favourable conditions where observatories are located, such as Chile or Hawaii.

Another type of unique resource that can be reached through collaboration is data. Their uniqueness may result from the originality of the population they represent (e.g., medical samples in epidemiology), the length of the time series (e.g., long-term panel data in sociology), or the unique and costly method of gathering, with an extreme example being moon rocks collected by the Apollo Missions. In some cases, access to data might be subject to exceptionally liberal legal conditions that allow specific research to be conducted in a given country. Such practices could be ethically controversial when rare data or samples are collected through morally doubtful clinical experiments or methods harmful to the environment (Oldham, 2005). However, the rising competition in global science may encourage such practices. Sleeboom-Faulkner (2013) even argues that in some cases, permissive regulations, e.g., regarding stem cell research, may be an element of a national science development strategy, aimed at attracting foreign collaborators.

Both access to data and the right to use the infrastructure are directly related to the financial aspects of scientific research. The escalating costs of conducting fundamental science activity at the research frontiers is one of the reasons for the recent growth in scientific collaboration (Katz & Martin, 1997). The largest scientific projects can only be conducted within research consortia, concentrating funds from public and private institutions from numerous countries. The most illustrative example of such equipment is the above-mentioned Large Hadron Collider—to date the world's largest and most complex experimental facility— which cost over €3 billion and was possible to build only through the joint efforts of public and private agencies from 56 countries. Another example is the Human Genome Project, the largest biological project in history, aimed at sequencing a human-sized genome. It was coordinated by two US institutions—the National Institute of Health and the Department of Energy—and gathered partners from the UK, France, Germany, and Japan. The 13-year project, launched in 1990, ended up with an overall budget of $2.7 billion (Human Genome Project Information Archive, 1990–2003).

2.4.4 Access to knowledge and expertise

In 2012, about 28,100 peer-reviewed scientific journals published almost 2 million articles, according to the report of the International Association of Scientific, Technical and Medical Publishers (Ware & Mabe, 2015). Even if about half of the papers published in academic journals are read only by the author, the journal's editor, and the referees (Meho, 2007), that still leaves a very large number of about 1 million scientific articles published every year to be digested by scientists. Obviously, this number covers papers from all scientific disciplines, but even if a single research area is considered, the volume of knowledge produced and published every year exceeds the cognitive possibilities of any individual scholar. In the most dynamic disciplines, scientists find it challenging to stay up to date with the latest results, sometimes even in their narrowly defined specialisations. Building networks of collaborators can thus be indispensable as a way of gaining access to expertise and knowledge.

Collaborating scientists can utilise others' competences and obtain the maximum advantage from their specialisation (Hoekman, Frenken, & van Oort, 2009; Katz & Martin, 1997). In particular, collaboration cannot be underestimated in the case of acquiring tacit knowledge, hardly transferable in writing or verbal communication. Direct access to a partner's expertise and tacit knowledge also generates opportunities to learn something new by taking the knowledge, as it were, straight from the horse's mouth. Additional knowledge and expertise not only enables scientists to extend the scope of the research and tackle larger problems, but also helps to foster innovation (Cummings & Kiesler, 2003; Lambert, 2003).

Engaging more people in providing and assuring the accuracy of research results, through collective discussion and verification, increases the quality and probability of success of the whole research project. When more eyes look at the research and its results, flaws can be found more quickly and efficiently, and thus the risk of errors and mistakes diminishes. This additional advantage results from the possibility of immediate intersubjective verification, expressing opinion and criticism (Beaver, 2001; Thagard, 1997).

2.4.5 Growing interdisciplinarity

Today we can witness the proliferation of interdisciplinary research that naturally reinforces collaboration involving representatives of various scientific fields. The 2006 report of the United States National Science Foundation points out that:

> Discovery increasingly requires the expertise of individuals with different perspectives—from different disciplines and often from different nations—working together to accommodate the extraordinary complexity of today's science and engineering challenges. The convergence of disciplines and the cross-fertilization that characterizes contemporary science and engineering have made collaboration a centerpiece of the science and engineering enterprise
>
> (2006. p. 2).

Interdisciplinary collaboration leads to the integration of knowledge from more than one discipline (Klein, 1990; Palmer, 2001; Salter & Hearn 1996). It combines approaches, methods, and paradigms, and thus it can result in cross-fertilisation across disciplines through inspiration from different scientific backgrounds (Bozeman & Corley, 2004; Cummings & Kiesler, 2003). In the long run, interdisciplinary collaboration can also lead to the emergence of new scientific disciplines and research areas, such as bioinformatics, which combines molecular biology with computer science, statistics, and engineering. This kind of collaboration requires intensive flows of resources (mostly intellectual, but also financial and infrastructural) among disciplines. In order to utilise such cooperation, partners have to make an additional effort to build a common understanding with representatives of distinct knowledge domains (Monteiro & Keating, 2009).

The teamwork of representatives from different scientific disciplines can be also called multidisciplinary, although, as Sonnenwald (2007) points out, some authors differentiate inter- and multidisciplinary collaboration: they define the latter as that which adds and uses knowledge from different scientific disciplines, but does not synthesise or integrate it (Bruce, Lyall, Tait, & Williams 2004; Klein, 1990).

Another term discussed in the literature is transdisciplinary collaboration, which involves holistic schemes created by the integration of all knowledge important for a specific problem or issue, as well as actors from different sectors and groups (Klein, 1990; Klein, 2004). In this approach, only transdisciplinary teams go beyond the discipline-specific bases of their members and build a common conceptual framework (Rosenfield, 1992). This kind of collaboration usually applies to the most complex and challenging problems that require not only knowledge from a larger number of scientific disciplines, but also creative and innovative approaches to tackle questions that cannot be answered without such collaboration.

2.4.6 Collaboration in the shadow of publish or perish

Academic publishing is the most important form of dissemination of research results and is the basis of scientific knowledge circulation. Scientific results and concepts have to be shared and distributed in order to be available for other scientists' use. Publishing is thus essential to the progress of science. But it also becomes critical for scientists' professional careers since the quantity and quality of scientific publications add significantly to weightings in the science evaluation systems. In such circumstances, if scientists want to foster their academic careers, they should not only perform high-quality and sound research, but also publish extensively, mainly in the form of papers in highly ranked, peer-reviewed journals. This pressure to publish is concisely described in the expression "publish or perish". Eugene Garfield (1996) tracked the origins of the expression to the 1942 Logan Wilson publication titled *The Academic Man: A Study in the Sociology of a Profession*. We can read there, "The prevailing pragmatism forced upon the academic group is that one must write something and get it into print. Situational imperatives dictate a 'publish or perish' credo within the ranks" (1942, p. 197).

Several reasons explain why the publish or perish strategy fosters scientific collaboration. First, it is easier to publish many co-authored papers, where the individual contributions are fractional, than to publish many single-authored works. Second, collaboration may increase the quality of publications. When a paper is written collectively, the probability of tracing flaws or misstatements is higher and, as a consequence, so is the quality of the paper. Using the tacit knowledge and writing skills of more experienced members of the team also increases the scientific level of the publication. Third, collaboration between less and more established scholars can help the former to break into highly selective journals. In particular, collaboration with a scientific star and placing him or her on the author list can increase the paper's chances for publication in a prestigious journal. Authors may assume that if an article is authored by a prominent scientist, journal editors will mitigate the review criteria for such an article. The editors and reviewers can in turn assume that a well-recognised author can vouch for a paper's content and the credibility of the presented results (Merton, 1973).

This was the case of an infamous article presenting an astonishing new procedure for obtaining the stimulus-triggered acquisition of pluripotency cells.

52 *Scientists working together*

Haruko Obokata and her mentor Charles Vacanti wanted to publish their paper in a top journal. They felt that adding a high-profile scientist as a co-author would significantly increase their chances of acceptance. The choice fell on Teruhiko Wakayama, who gained his fame from being the first to clone a mouse. They submitted the paper to *Nature*, but it was rejected. In turn, a fourth co-author got on board: Yoshiki Sasai (1962–2014), one of Japan's leading developmental biologists. He had the advantage of being on good terms with *Nature*'s editors, and he also "had an instinct for how to frame the findings in the larger conversation about stem cells, embryology, and cell fate" (Goodyear, 2016, p. 51). After revisions, the paper appeared in *Nature*. But the luck did not last long. A few months later the paper was retracted, in a scandalous atmosphere, after major errors and the scientific misconduct of Obokata became evident. As a consequence, Obokata's PhD was revoked. But the highest price was paid by one of her colleagues: Sasai hanged himself from a handrail on the staircase of the laboratory (Goodyear, 2016; Meskus, Marelli, & D'Agostino, 2018). The case exemplifies not only the power of a scientific star in facilitating publishing, but also the risk of fraudulent behaviour or unconscious carelessness that may be induced by skyrocketing competition in the publish or perish environment.

2.5 The collaboration life cycle and its challenges

Scientific collaboration proceeds in stages: foundation, formulation, sustainment, and conclusion (Sonnenwald, 2007). Each step brings specific challenges. Depending on the level of trust among collaborators, these challenges are more or less difficult to solve. Mistrust can hamper collaboration throughout its life cycle—this will be discussed in the initial subchapter. In the subsequent three sections we look more closely at selected key challenges that may occur at the different stages of the collaboration process. Certainly, these challenges can occur, or co-occur, at all stages of collaboration, but the probability of their emerging and causing a damaging outcome changes during the project's lifetime. To keep things simple, the foundation and formulation phases are addressed as a single initial phase, followed by the sustainment and conclusion stages. We will discuss issues related to personal temperament, communication obstacles, competition between collaborators, coordination and management challenges, and finally, authorship recognition concerns.

2.5.1 Trust in collaboration

In the 1920s, Austrian biologist Paul Kammerer (1880–1926) claimed to have proved the theory of Lamarckian inheritance (inheritance of acquired characteristics) by causing the male midwife toad, which lacks pigmented thumb pads, to inherit such bumps (by forcing the toads to mate in water). In 1926, Gladwyn Kingsley Noble (1894–1940) revealed that the pigmented pads were in fact injected with Indian ink. Kammerer suggested that one of his assistants might have done the injection independently. Shortly after, Kammerer committed suicide, most likely as a result of his public humiliation and undermined credibility (Gliboff, 2010; Vargas, 2009). The story perfectly illustrates that trust is a prerequisite of any collaboration and breach of trust may have disastrous consequences.

Trust in scientific collaboration has two dimensions. Affective trust relates to interpersonal bonds among people and is manifested in the feeling of security and perceived strength of a relationship. Cognitive trust is based on judgments of a partner's scientific credibility, competence, and reliability, confirmed by their reputation (Johnson & Grayson, 2005; Sonnenwald, 2003). The increasing scale of scientific collaboration has caused the second dimension to prevail. Collaborating scholars from various institutions, countries, and cultures often have limited possibilities to build mutual trust based on personal relations. Moreover, the level of trust depends on the spatial and social proximity of collaborators. Scientists closer in space and closer socially (e.g., long-term friends) are more likely to establish collaboration (Agrawal, Kapur, & McHale, 2008) and profit from a smooth transition of tacit knowledge (Coleman, 1988).

In professionally managed projects lack of mutual trust can, to some extent, be rectified by explicit collaboration rules, conventional practices, and control procedures that minimise risk and uncertainty. However, one can never rule out unintentional mistakes, measurement errors, or intentional misconduct, which may be made by an individual but affect all the collaborating parties. An illustrative example could be one of the threads of the Korean stem cell scandal, which broke out in 2005. Woo-suk Hwang, a South Korean veterinarian and professor at Seoul National University, reported in 2004 and 2005 in *Science* that he had cloned human embryonic stem cells. When the experiments were revealed as fraudulent, not only was Hwang's credibility undermined, but also that of his collaborators (Strange, 2008; University of Pittsburgh, 2006).

2.5.2 Initiation

Not everyone is lucky enough to work with a spouse, like Marie Skłodowska-Curie, who was awarded a Nobel Prize in 1906 for the joint work with her husband Pierre Curie (1859–1906); or with a companion, like a 1912 Nobel Prize winner, Alexis Carrel (1873–1944), who invented a perfusion pump with his close friend Charles Lindbergh (1902–1974). In the initial stages of collaboration, a positive attitude and personal chemistry seem to be vital. They facilitate the allocation of tasks and responsibilities as well as setting the communication rules and information flow (Maglaughlin & Sonnenwald, 2005; Olson, Olson, & Cooney, 2008). A partner's character, competences, and personal features may be crucial here. Niels Bohr (1885–1962)—one of the fathers of the American atomic bomb and 1922 Nobel Prize winner—highly valued his collaboration with Richard Feynman precisely because of his temperament. Bohr once allegedly said:

> Remember the name of that little fellow in the back over there? He's the only guy who's not afraid of me, and will say when I've got a crazy idea.

So, next time when we want to discuss ideas, we're not going to be able to do it with these guys who say everything is "yes, yes, Dr. Bohr." Get that guy and we'll talk with him first

(Feynman, 2010, p. 71–72).

However, every so often a new collaborator's character turns out to be not as favourable as expected. But if these difficult partners possess unique resources, joint work is desirable, if not essential.

Collaboration demands smooth communication. Therefore, misunderstandings and communication bottlenecks are nightmares for collaborative project managers. Communication obstacles refer chiefly to differences in perception and language barriers that can impede discussion and understanding of visions, goals, and tasks (Jeffrey, 2003; Maglaughlin & Sonnenwald, 2005; Palmer, 2001; Traoré & Landry, 1997; Walsh & Maloney, 2007). Apparent language problems spring from the fact that the scholarly community nowadays communicates in English, while most scientists are from outside the Anglosphere (Hwang, 2012).

Particularly in distant collaborations, communication can be challenging. Exchanges between partners who rely almost fully on interaction via ICT tools can suffer from the lack of non-verbal signals. Indirect communication can consume more time than face-to-face information exchange and can often lead to misinterpretations. Moreover, greater physical distance between partners is often accompanied by larger social differences. Although scientists all over the world share similar scientific values and standards (scientific ethos), cultural differences may affect communication and collaboration. Organisations and individuals, even from the same country, differ in research working modes, management and coordination approaches, priorities, vocabularies, and communication styles. Not surprisingly, scholars situated in historically linked places and sharing similar cultures collaborate more often than those having no common ground (Wagner & Leydesdorff, 2005). Indeed, spatial and non-spatial proximity (social, organisational, economic, etc.) play a major role in forming collaborative links (Ponds, van Oort, & Frenken, 2007).

Interdisciplinary collaboration seems to be the most challenging, because different disciplines may use the same terms with various meanings (Sonnenwald, 2007). A good illustration is the term "map", originating from geography, where it usually refers to a generalised, mathematically defined representation of all or a portion of the planet's surface, including discernible elements of scale, projection, and symbolisation, showing the distribution, state, and relations of various natural and social phenomena. For geographers, a visual presentation which does not meet all the above-mentioned criteria cannot be called a map, although for non-geographers it might look like a map. Today, the word "map" is commonly used to describe diagrams, schemes, or graphs in many scientific disciplines, having very little in common with the original meaning of the term. A few examples include a mind map (a tool to visually organise information), a road map (a plan of action), a brain map (in neuroscience), and a map as a morphism in category theory (in mathematics).

Even when partners come from the same country and represent the same scientific field, communication problems may occur, often resulting from a failure to give full or precise information. Hidden assumptions, taken for granted by partners, might not be the same for all team members. Sometimes they refer to very basic issues, such as units of measurement, which are treated as obvious and thus as something that does not require explicit description. That was the case with the $125 million NASA probe, Mars Climate Orbiter. Its mission failed in 1999 due to a large deviation of the probe from the planned trajectory, caused by differences between the units of measure used by the probe's constructor, NASA (metric system), and the producer of the ground software, Lockheed-Martin (United States customary system) (Hotz, 1999).

2.5.3 Sustainment

The main challenges at the sustainment stage of the collaboration process relate to unexpected perturbations, delays, and tensions between collaborators. The tensions can be triggered—among other things—by increasing competition in a team (Beaver, 2001; Latour, 1987). Competition increases especially at critical points of the project, when team members feel that a breakthrough is coming. One of the researchers interviewed by Atkinson and his colleagues put it this way:

> You can see it every time [...] the one who has the best publication gets the money, so it would be a stupid thing to tell everybody what you have found before you have your paper in press and we always say we collaborate with other people, but if you look at it really objectively, every group does its own thing and in the end they do collaborate, but everybody tries to get the most out of it for their group
> (Atkinson, Batchelor, & Parsons, 1998, p. 269).

To reduce obstacles related to collaboration, especially in large and spatially dispersed teams, efficient management is needed. Even a research team of highly skilled specialists can fail if not well managed. Planning, managing resources, internal and external communication, monitoring, reporting and evaluation, building trust, tuning up, and reconciling different opinions and points of view—all of these aspects require time and effort, and can present difficulties for scholars, who usually do not have a professional management background. Additionally, individuals sometimes have strong, introverted, or conflicting personalities, thus, smooth coordination of the collaboration requires strong leadership (Schiff, 2002; Stokols, Harvey, Gress, Fuqua, & Phillips, 2005). In many projects, especially large ones, professional managers are hired. However, a situation where the manager is not familiar with the idiosyncrasies of scientific inquiry often produces additional costs and may involve the risk of conflict and misunderstanding (see Chompalov, Genuth, & Shrum, 2002). On the other hand, a scholar who simultaneously plays the role of project manager might feel torn between the role of scientist and manager and become frustrated by having to deal with project coordination at the expense of scientific activity.

Delays in a project or lack of satisfactory results can be more difficult to identify and address when larger teams are involved. Changes in the organisational structure of a team or personnel replacements affect the course of the project and may negatively impact on meeting the deadlines and achieving the expected results (Cummings & Kiesler, 2003). Moreover, the more partners involved and the more diverse they are, the more sources of unexpected perturbations and the longer time necessary to diagnose the problem, revisit a project's goals and methods, and reach a new shared understanding. An extreme example might be the International Thermonuclear Experimental Reactor (ITER), aimed at developing the technology of clean nuclear energy produced by fusing atoms (a process similar to what happens on the Sun) and recognised as the largest scientific project to date. ITER, gathering scientists from 35 countries, has cost over €15 billion at the time of this writing. The project has been delayed at least nine years due to—among other things—an extensive design review conducted at the beginning of the project, and the 2011 earthquake in Japan (Gibney, 2014).

Institutional differences can disturb collaboration, even between organisations of the same type, which theoretically are close in terms of organisational distance. A 2005 study of 62 projects of the US National Science Foundation revealed that projects involving a larger number of universities were systematically more problematic in terms of coordination and achieving positive outcomes than projects with principal investigators from fewer universities (Cummings & Kiesler, 2005). Interdisciplinary research, including that carried out within a single institution, can face obstacles related to the organisational structure. Universities are divided into departments, which traditionally conduct research and education limited to one scientific field. The creation of an interdisciplinary research team within the department, or participation in an interdisciplinary project, the aims of which go beyond the department's scientific portfolio, may lead to tensions among co-workers.

Scientific collaboration increasingly goes beyond academia. Partnerships between scientific and business sectors are seen as beneficial for both sides, e.g., by enabling access to facilities and intangible resources, as well as funds, including from sources designated exclusively for business-academia initiatives (Autio, Hameri, & Nordberg, 1996; Lambert, 2003). However, scientific collaboration that crosses sectoral boundaries can be exceptionally challenging since it triggers the need to combine different goals, work modes, and attitudes to disseminating results. Businesses usually focus on pragmatic and immediate solutions with direct commercial application, while academics prefer to work with a longer-term perspective (Mathiassen, 2002). Moreover, companies tend to be reluctant to widely disclose the research outcomes, while this remains essential for an academic's professional career. This divergence of goals may lead to prejudices and conflicts. Collaboration with business can also give rise to doubts and concerns which are harmful to the collaborating scientists' reputations. These concerns relate to the credibility and impartiality of research financed by companies whose profits heavily depend on the inquiry's results (Resnik, 2005).

2.5.4 The first author et al.[4]

The conclusion stage delivers the products of research. Collaboration, especially when the number of partners is large, inevitably means a diffusion of epistemic responsibility. In such projects, it is very difficult to determine the contributions of individuals and thus define the range of their responsibility. This issue becomes especially important when research results are going to be awarded or—at the other extreme—questioned (Merton & Zuckerman, 1973; Wray, 2002). This was the case of Gerald Schatten from Pittsburgh University, who was listed as the last author of some questioned articles on cloned human embryonic stem cells. According to the authorship rules in the biomedical sciences, Schatten was assumed to be the principal investigator and senior author of these publications. In his defence, he claimed that he had worked on the manuscripts but had not been aware that they presented forged results and had had little interaction with most of the research team members, including Hwang Woo-suk, who was accused of fabricating the experiments. As the Investigative Board of Pittsburgh University described it:

> We feel that he did not exercise a sufficiently critical perspective as a scientist. For example, he did not ask what event in Hwang's lab prompted the change in the reporting of some data differently in two successive versions of the same table. In another example, he reported that he was told by Dr. Hwang in the middle of January, 2005 that some contamination of the cells had occurred. Dr. Schatten's reaction was apparently to accept Dr. Hwang's assurance that this problem was a minor nuisance
> (University of Pittsburgh, 2006, p. 7).

Apart from the research misbehaviour in assigning the articles' authorship, the Schatten example shows how much harm can ensue from lack of criticism and precaution in scientific collaboration (Strange, 2008; University of Pittsburgh, 2006).

The choice of a suitable channel for disseminating findings may divide collaborating scholars, especially when it comes to interdisciplinary research. For example, computer scientists prefer conference publications over journal papers, which are the traditional and first-choice dissemination channel for most scientific disciplines. Thus, if a project involves specialists from the computer sciences as well as other disciplines, choosing where to publish research results might provoke a conflict. Scholars may also fall out over issues related to appreciation and recognition of accomplishments. Historically, authorship was attributed to those who made a major contribution to the research and the resulting paper. However, in some disciplines today, research problems are so complex that they require the collaboration of not only dozens, but even hundreds or thousands of people. With the increasing number of authors and the growing role of publications in scientists' professional careers, the need to clarify authorship rules is becoming more evident. Some of the most prestigious journals, such as *Science*, *Nature*, or *Proceedings of the National Academy of Sciences*, introduce explicit rules about authorship, requiring a structured description of each author's contribution before the article can be accepted (Venkatraman, 2010). Some organisations have even introduced their own authorship rules. High-energy physics is a good example (Galison, 2003). The official authorship policy of the ATLAS Collaboration specifies that all ATLAS publications are signed in alphabetical order by all ATLAS members, including engineers and technicians (ATLAS Authorship Policy, 2013). In other disciplines, like the social sciences or arts and humanities, such a practice would be seen as inappropriate and unethical, violating scientific standards and rules which require that the authors of the paper are those who actually worked on the manuscript.

Collaborators have to decide on the content of the authors list. The main area of controversy here is whether a scientist's contribution to the research and writing of the paper was sufficient to warrant a place on the list of authors. Various forms of authorship misappropriations can be distinguished here. For example, an honorary, guest, or gift authorship is granted to a person who has not contributed significantly to the research presented in the article. Meanwhile, ghost authorship takes place when a person who provided significant contribution to the study is not listed as an author (Flanagin et al., 1998; Mowatt et al., 2002).

Moreover, the order of listing authors can also be disputable. In rare instances, the order may be completely unrelated to the research itself, as in the case of Michael P. Hassell and Robert M. May, who determined the authorship order from a 25-game croquet series held at Imperial College Field Station.[5] Authorship ordering rules depend largely on the specific customs of a scientific discipline, thus, multidisciplinary papers create the greatest challenges. However, at least in most of the natural sciences, the typical pattern is that the first author should be the person who has done the most work, the second is the one who contributed the second largest amount of work, etc. The last place in the authorship list is secured for the principal investigator—usually the head of the lab or research group (He, Ding, & Yan, 2012). Still, assessing the levels of contribution is challenging and largely subjective. A 2007 study of 919 authors of 201 articles submitted to a general medical journal found that two-thirds of corresponding authors disagreed with their co-authors regarding the contributions of each author (Ilakovac, Fister, Marusic, & Marusic, 2007). Therefore, it could be argued that the most neutral approach would be to list authors in alphabetical order (Laband & Tollison, 2000; Joseph, Laband, & Patil, 2005). Yet this has its own drawbacks too, as it favours scholars with particular surnames. This is why Georges Aad, a physicist from Fribourg University and CERN, is "the most prominent name in particle physics" (Hotz, 2015, para. 1). In particular, publications with just a few authors are usually recognised by the name of the first author only (Riesenberg & Lundberg, 1990). Readers habitually read and remember only the first name, and the remaining co-authors are "essentially anonymous 'fractional' scientists" (Beaver, 2001, p. 370). This is why the authorship order is not just a matter of a courtesy.

This first-author bias is an aspect of a broader phenomenon that Robert K. Merton called the Matthew effect (Merton, 1968)—a complex pattern of credit misallocation and accumulation of advantage. This effect is visible when a significant difference between the scientific positions and statuses of the article's authors occurs. When a less experienced scientist publishes along with a more experienced one, tenure and evaluation bodies may diversify their assumed contribution to the research and publication, and give disproportionally higher credit to the eminent scientists. This recognition and credit bias may affect early career scientists, less recognised scholars, and women, regardless of their age and experience (Sarsons, 2015). Belittlement of female scientists' contribution and attribution of their work to their male collaborators was described by Margaret W. Rossiter (1993). She called it the Matilda effect (analogously to Merton's Matthew effect), after Matilda Joslyn Gage (1826–1898)—the American women's rights activist and the leader of the National American Woman Suffrage Association.

* * *

Joint research is no longer a distinct form of doing science, but rather a default mode of the process. Research teams are expanding to enormous sizes, hyper-authorship is booming, and international collaboration is proliferating. The rise of mass collaboration in science has been accompanied by the decline of solitary scholars, who are gradually becoming a rare—if not endangered—species. On the one hand, the collaborative turn has resulted from the increasing specialisation, interdisciplinarity, and complexity of contemporary science. On the other, the intensifying collaboration allows for even more specialised, interdisciplinary, and complex research endeavours. Consequently, the collaborative turn is both a sign and a factor of changes in contemporary scholarship.

Notes

1 Most of learned societies did not last to the present day. For example, Academia Secretorum Naturae operated in Naples from 1560 to 1578, when it was closed by order of Pope Gregory XIII under suspicion of sorcery.
2 Henry Oldenberg was the editor of the *Philosophical Transactions of the Royal Society*, the first journal devoted purely to science, established in 1665 in London. He started sending manuscripts submitted to the journal to experts who appraised them before publication.
3 Own elaboration based on http://www.nobelprize.org/
4 Have you ever wondered who the most cited scientist is? It is "Professor et al.", enjoying 2,477,068 citations (at the end of 2016). Her Google Scholar profile includes only 333 publications but, due to their extremely high impact (almost 200 thousand citations of the top paper), her h-index is 333. This astonishing publication portfolio covers papers representing various disciplines from biology, chemistry,

medicine, and physics to language studies, management, and social psychology (Dingemanse, 2016). Moreover, probably accidentally, her name matches the short form of "et alia", which in Latin means "and others", and is used in scientific writing for referencing multi-authored papers (following the name of the first author). These absurd records result from the design and algorithms of Google Scholar, the largest browser of scientific publications. It allows scientists to create profiles with an automatically updated list of publications and citations. In most cases, the profiles are set up by actual scientists, but several are fake, created in order to show deficiencies of the system (e.g., the profile of "A. Author" from the "Department of Citation Analysis, University of University"). Et al's profile, as well as A. Author's, was created by Mark Dingemanse from the Language and Cognition department of the Max Planck Institute for Psycholinguistics. In the middle of 2016, Google Scholar blocked the profile from appearing in the browser's top rankings. The full story can be read on Dingemanse's blog: http://ideophone.org/some-things-you-need-to-know-about-google-scholar/

5   See the footnote in Hassell & May, 1974.

3 Measuring scholarly collaboration in space

The sudden expansion of scientific collaboration has been accompanied by the rapid development of sources and methods applicable to studying research collaboration. Collaboration in science has become a hot topic in the burgeoning field of informetrics, which comprises bibliometrics (statistical analysis of publications), scientometrics (the quantitative study of science, technology, and innovation), and their younger sister webometrics (measurement of the World Wide Web) (Bar-Ilan, 2008; Egghe, 2005). This development would not have been possible without contemporary information and communication technologies that enable efficient storage and manipulation of scientometrics data, as well as contributions from other fields, with network science in the first place (Barabási, 2002; Börner & Scharnhorst, 2009).

Spatial studies of scientific collaboration are based on generic scientometric ideas, sources, and methods. Simultaneously, they are intrinsically interdisciplinary because they add a geographical dimension to scientometrics. This spatial aspect is often of minor importance—particularly in country-level analyses, which usually do not account for the location of, or distance between, collaborators. But, at times, geolocation plays a central role in scholarly collaboration studies. In such cases, cutting-edge approaches are frequently employed that are simultaneously grounded in and lead to advances in social and economic geography, spatial analysis, and regional science.

The following sections review established and novel approaches, sources, and measures for spatially oriented studies in scientific collaboration. Then, the main methodological issues of the field are discussed. Due to space limitations and the breadth of the topic—note that the *Handbook of Bibliometric Indicators*, published in 2016 by Roberto Todeschini and Alberto Baccini, has 483 pages—only selected topics are discussed at length.

3.1 Collaborative data: sources and approaches

The essential information needed to measure scientific collaboration in space is the geolocation of collaborators. The level of location accuracy depends on the aim of the analysis and the data availability. It spans from continents and countries, through regions, cities, and campuses, to inside-building location (see for instance: Lee, Brownstein, Mills, & Kohane, 2010; Maisonobe, Eckert, Grossetti, Jégou, & Milard, 2016; Matthiessen, Schwarz, & Find, 2010). Information on the geolocation of collaborators is obtained from primary and secondary sources. The former takes direct account of collaboration; the latter infers collaborative behaviour from artefacts of scientific work. Primary sources consist of self-reported surveys and interviews (Landry, Traoré, & Godin, 1996; Isabelle & Heslop, 2011; Kwiek, 2017), active and passive participant observation of collaboration practices, surveillance of real and virtual meetings (Hara et al., 2003; Vasileiadou, 2009), mail and email exchanges (Kossinets & Watts, 2006), phone calls (Button et al., 1993), and approaches based on tracking devices: geolocation, co-location, and proximity data gathered from GPS units, mobile phones, RFID networks, and other innovative devices (Cattuto et al., 2010; Eagle, Pentland, & Lazer, 2009). Secondary data sources are based on the outputs of scientific work, mainly in the form of co-authored publications, patents, and conference presentations, or on other information that suggests collaborative processes, such as joint-project data. Secondary data are primarily derived from databases but can also be gathered one by one, for example, from individual publications or researchers' curricula vitae (Costa, da Silva Pedro, & de Macedo, 2013; Lee & Bozeman, 2005).

Both primary and secondary sources have advantages and drawbacks (see for instance: Lee & Bozeman, 2005), but they provide equal and complementary contributions to understanding the phenomenon of scientific collaboration. Information provided in surveys and interviews can significantly supplement quantitative approaches—typically based on secondary data—by assessing the motivations for, challenges of, and peculiarities regarding collaboration (Mirskaya, 1997). This approach makes it possible to understand the social dynamics of knowledge creation as it goes beyond the knowledge encapsulated in the form of a scientific paper or other tangible scientific output. Moreover, in countries with limited sources of secondary data it might be the preferred way to evaluate collaboration, for example, in the cases of the Philippines (Ynalvez & Shrum, 2011) and Kenya (Muriithi, Horner, & Pemberton, 2013). However, the drawbacks of directly obtained data are usually their limited scope, high cost, and lack of comparability.

By and large, spatial studies of scientific collaboration predominately employ secondary data sources. Two proprietary databases dominate the special scientometrics landscape: Web of Science and Scopus. Web of Science (under different names) was originally provided by the Institute for Scientific Information funded by Eugene Garfield in Philadelphia in 1960. The service was acquired by Thomson Reuters in 1992, who subsequently sold it to Clarivate Analytics at the end of 2016. Scopus was founded in 2004 by Elsevier, a large publisher and scientific information provider based in Amsterdam, the Netherlands. Both services provide data on scientific publications derived from indexed journals, conference proceedings, and, recently, academic books.

Apart from comprehensive bibliometric databases, various subject-oriented sources can be mined for scientific collaboration data. MEDLINE, curated by the US National Library of Medicine, provides bibliographic data on life sciences and biomedical topics. The service is freely available through PubMed, an online search engine (Vanni et al., 2014). Correspondingly, open-access INSPIRE-HEP compiles bibliographic data in the field of high-energy physics (Lorigo & Pellacini, 2007), DBLP in a computer science bibliography (Rahm & Thor, 2005), and ADS in astronomy and physics (Chang & Huang, 2013), while the proprietary GEOBASE, operated by Elsevier, gathers bibliographies of geography, ecology, and earth science (Sun & Manson, 2011).

A further source of collaborative data consists of informetric databases covering a single nation or group of countries. Noteworthy examples include the Ibero-American SciELO (De Sordi, Conejero, & Meireles, 2016; Macías-Chapula, 2010) and Redalyc (López, Silva, García-Cepero, Bustamante, & López, 2011), the Brazilian Lattes Platform (Sidone, Haddad, & Mena-Chalco, 2016), the Researcher database provided by Taiwan's National Science Council (Velema, 2012), the Rated Researchers database curated by the National Research Foundation of South Africa (Barnard, Cowan, & Müller, 2012), the Chinese Science Citation Database hosted by Clarivate Analytics as a part of Web of Science (Liang & Zhu, 2002), and the Italian Research Assessment Exercise (Carillo, Papagni, & Sapio, 2013; Franceschet & Costantini, 2010). These sources have been developed mainly, but not only, for the purpose of individual and institutional research performance evaluation. For this reason, some of them, aside from bibliographies, include other information valuable for spatial scientometric exercises, such as data on grants, participation in projects, and academic mobility.

The input for scholarly collaboration analyses can be retrieved from the local archives of research institutions. This has been done using institutional databases such as the Korea Institute of Machinery and Materials database (Jeong et al., 2011) and the database of the University of Salerno in Italy (De Stefano, Giordano, & Vitale, 2011), as well as annual reports of collaborative projects, for example, the analysis of the Center for Embedded Networked Sensing, jointly operated by five universities in California (Pepe, 2011). Notably, a number of papers compare results based on both international and local sources (for the details see: De Stefano, Fuccella, Vitale, & Zaccarin, 2013; Hennemann, Wang, & Liefner, 2011).

The spatial aspects of scholarly collaboration have also been investigated using patent data. Patent-based analyses reflect collaboration in applied science. They are used in innovation or technological development studies of countries and regions and generally portray intersectoral or business-to-business collaboration (Maurseth & Verspagen, 2002). Patent analyses are usually based on data from the European Patent Office (Ejermo & Karlsson, 2006; Hoekman et al., 2009; Maggioni, Nosvelli, & Uberti, 2007; Maurseth & Verspagen, 2002) or the United States Patent and Trademark Office (Zheng, Zhao, Zhang, Chen, & Huang, 2014) and—less frequently—national data sources, for instance, the Chinese Patent Office database (Hong, 2008; Ma, Fang, Pang, & Wang, 2015). These data sources contain primarily contemporary patents, while historical data is rather difficult to deal with (even if digitalised copies have been prepared, the data are barely structured). However, an important step has been made recently[1] with the development of the HistPat online database, which provides geolocalised data, at county level, on US patents from the period 1836–1975 (Petralia, Balland, & Rigby, 2016).

Collaborative programmes and projects provide one more useful source for spatial scientometrics. While analyses regarding subsequent editions of the European Union Framework Programmes (see Chapter 6 for details) prevail in such studies (Gusmão, 2001; Scherngell & Barber, 2009; Ukrainski, Masso, & Kanep, 2014), other initiatives are also studied. Examples include the study based on the Portuguese Foundation for Science and Technology projects (Gama, Barros, & Fernandes, 2018), the US National Science Foundation grants (Cummings & Kiesler, 2005), and the Polish Federation of Engineering Associations-Chief Technical Organization programme (Olechnicka, 2013).

Recently, many alternative data sources and measures, dubbed altmetrics, have been gaining the attention of scholars investigating research collaboration. Promising sources include scholarly blogs, web hyperlinks (Kretschmer, Kretschmer, & Kretschmer, 2007), online reference managers (e.g., CiteULike, Mendeley, and Zotero), scholarly search engines (with the predominant role of Google Scholar, and the comparatively less well-known Microsoft Academic and its predecessor Microsoft Academic Search—see Ortega, 2014), social networking services targeted at the general public (mainly Facebook, LinkedIn, and Twitter), and services designed for scholars (among which the most popular are ResearchGate and Academia.edu). However—to date—altmetrics derived from online tools and environments have tended to supplement traditional sources of collaborative data, particularly with regard to impact and dissemination indicators (Abbasi, Altmann, & Hossain, 2011; Kousha & Thelwall, 2007), rather than allowing for analysis of the spatial aspects of scientific collaboration based on altmetrics alone.

3.2 The reward triangle and research collaboration studies

Among the various sources of collaborative data, the information collected from publications is the most widely used and valuable owing to its broad scope, easy availability, and comparatively low cost. Moreover, the collection of bibliometric data does not interfere with the practices of scientific work and research collaboration. Three complementary types of bibliometric information can be employed to illustrate spatial patterns of scholarly collaboration: authorship, citations, and acknowledgements—the components of the so-called reward triangle as coined by Blaise Cronin and Sherrill Weaver-Wozniak in 1993 (Desrochers, Paul-Hus, & Larivière, 2016).

Co-authorship as the key mechanism of linking scholars is the most palpable, reliable, and universally accepted approximation of scientific collaboration (see: Kumar, 2015; and Chapter 2). Since the late 1970s, the trailblazing Web of Science database has systematically included the full affiliation addresses for all authors of indexed publications. Web of Science and its younger brother Scopus allow researchers to mine the raw data of scholarly journal articles, conference proceedings, books, and book chapters. The mechanism of using these databases is analogous. Each bibliographic record contains detailed information about the authors' affiliations, making it possible to precisely determine the collaborative links in geographic space. Scientific authorship is increasingly complemented by contributorship statements, which are required more and more frequently by journal publishers. From the analytical point of view, contributorship statements provide additional detailed knowledge about the functions that authors have in the reported research and the preparation of the paper (and allow these functions to be correlated with the authorship order). Such contributorship statements can significantly enrich our understanding of the division of labour in knowledge production (Larivière et al., 2016).

Alongside co-authorship, the study of citations offers other means of tracking scholarly collaboration. Firstly, we can distinguish approaches that use citations received by the set of papers affiliated to the given institution or location to find out what kind of authors and readers are linked and how (Bornmann, Stefaner, de Moya Anegón, & Mutz, 2014; Gorraiz, Reiman, & Gumpenberger, 2012; Huang, Tang, & Chen, 2011; Rahm & Thor, 2005). Secondly, there are studies based on the co-occurrence of citations. They investigate networks formed among documents appearing in the reference list of the given paper—so-called co-citations—or among documents that cite the same scientific articles, an approach known as bibliographic coupling. Thirdly, a few studies use a complex approach to citations. For instance, the combination of citations and references of geolocalised papers produces a network of citing and cited places—a "scientific food web" that enables us to identify areas where more knowledge is produced than consumed, and those who tend to consume more than produce (Mazloumian et al., 2013; Zhang, Perra, Gonçalves, Ciulla, & Vespignani, 2013). Whereas co-authorship attempts to investigate collaboration patterns among scholars or organisations, citations, co-citations, and bibliographic coupling predominately depict relations between ideas. The former can be mapped in geographic space, the latter in the space of ideas (as defined in the introductory section of Chapter 1). Citation-based measures are used to identify research fronts. This type of analysis allows us to detect clusters of interrelated scholars, scientific specialisations, and invisible colleges. Studies in this scientometric research stream concentrate on revealing the names of scholars and their science domains, rarely on their geographical locations, although the spatial approach is also sometimes applied (see: Ahlgren, Persson, & Tijssen, 2013; Gmür, 2003; Wallace, Gingras, & Duhon, 2009).

The citation approach is equally relevant for patents. Patent citations are commonly used for depicting knowledge flows among different locations, for instance, regions (Nomaler & Verspagen, 2016) or cities (Rigby, 2015). Furthermore, altmetrics gives increasingly new opportunities for assessing who (and where) is interested in the given piece of scientific output produced in a certain location. Altmetrics provides information—complementary to standard citation analysis—on the fame and impact of research. It enables us to measure how many times a scientific work was viewed, saved, bookmarked, downloaded, mentioned, or discussed in the online media (Haustein, Costas, & Larivière, 2015; Thelwall, Haustein, Larivière, & Sugimoto, 2013; Todeschini & Baccini, 2016). This tactic has been applied, for instance, to track readership within Mendeley—a reference manager and online social network service for researchers (Sud & Thelwall, 2016).

Of the scholarly rewards, acknowledgements are the most demanding to use for studies in scholarly collaboration. The reason for this lies in the usually loosely structured and incomplete data on acknowledgements, difficulties in name disambiguation of acknowledged individuals and organisations, and the varied position of acknowledgements in scientific publications (Desrochers, Paul-Hus, & Pecoskie, 2015). In comparison to co-authorship, acknowledgements are less tangible and also rarely employed in depicting spatial patterns of research collaboration. So far, spatially oriented acknowledgement analyses have referred mostly to university-industry collaboration (see for instance: Morillo, 2016; Wang & Shapira, 2015). The development of this approach was facilitated in 2008 by the introduction of the Funding Text field by the Web of Science, which made the acknowledgement data available on a massive scale and opened up new research possibilities (Paul-Hus, Desrochers, & Costas, 2016). The advantage of using acknowledgements lies in their ability to expand our view on collaboration by going beyond co-authorship (Cronin & Weaver-Wozniak, 1993; Laudel, 2002). Recent advancements in acknowledgement studies show their ability to explain differences in team sizes among disciplines—namely, with regard to the social sciences and humanities, which are less saturated with co-authorships than science—and thus, they might expand our knowledge of patterns of scientific collaboration in various disciplines (Paul-Hus, Mongeon, Sainte-Marie, & Larivière, 2017).

3.3 Spatial scientometric measures

This section surveys selected measures of scientific collaboration.[2] The review has been narrowed to the most important and frequently used spatially related indicators, although the distinction between spatial and non-spatial scientific collaboration measures is not easy to make. We should bear in mind that individual scholars in a given time have their own distinctive spots in space, their unique geolocations. Hence, collaboration between individuals always takes place in space, no matter what the distance, and thus every collaboration measure has a spatial dimension. Even the mean number of authors per publication (the *collaborative index*, as termed by Stephen Majebi Lawani in 1980) can be compared using spatially meaningful units (see for example: Karpagam, Gopalakrishnan, Babu, & Natarajan, 2012). However, the simple proportion of multi-authored papers, referred to as the *degree of collaboration* by Subramanyam in 1983, is more frequently used in spatial scientometrics. Initially, the index was applied to bibliometrics, but it can be generalised as the ratio of collaborative artefacts or events to all artefacts or events of a given kind. It can be written as:

$$DEGREE\ OF\ COLLABORATION = \frac{P_{COLL}}{P_{COLL} + P_{SINGLE}} = 1 - \frac{P_{SINGLE}}{P}$$

where P denotes research artefacts (usually publications or patents) or events (most frequently projects) attributed to a given unit (be it a single scholar, research organisation, region, or country). P_{COLL} and P_{SINGLE} represent, respectively, P involving collaboration or P without collaboration. The analyses presented in section 3.2 of this paper are largely based on the degree of collaboration.

The degree of collaboration is frequently used in scientometrics, mostly due to its simplicity and comprehensibility. An important limitation of the degree of collaboration is that it gives information about the level of scientific collaboration, but it cannot capture the direction of collaboration or its strength. The same is true of the so-called *collaboration coefficient*, a single measure that combines the collaborative index and the degree of collaboration (Ajiferuke, Burell, & Tague, 1988) and the subsequent *modified collaborative coefficient* (Savanur & Srikanth, 2010; see also: Rousseau, 2010).

Accordingly, various indicators—derived from the degree of collaboration— have been proposed to measure the direction of collaboration and its strength. The idea is simple: different types of collaboration can be distinguished and the measures calculated respectively. As a result, we can use the *degree of international collaboration* (sometimes referred to as the *internationalisation degree*), *degree of domestic collaboration*, and many other variations, namely, inter-regional and intra-regional or inter-institutional and intra-institutional collaboration. This approach is frequently applied in spatially oriented scientometric studies, mostly at the global or country level (Gazni, Sugimoto, & Didegah, 2012; Leclerc & Gagné, 1994), but also at the subnational level. For example, in 1996, Canadian scholars Benoit Godin and Marie-Pierre Ippersiel scrutinised the international, intra-regional, and inter-regional collaboration of five regions in Quebec (other examples of regional-level applications of variations on the degree of collaboration include: Chinchilla-Rodríguez, Vargas-Quesada, Hassan-Montero, González-Molina, & Moya-Anegóna, 2010; Hansen, 2013; Olechnicka & Ploszaj, 2010a).

Another approach which can be used to enrich the degree of collaboration is focused on bilateral relations. A bundle of measures is used to evaluate the inclination of a given unit, be it a country, region, or an institution, to collaborate with another unit. Among measures reflecting such bilateral relations, *Salton's cosine, Jaccard's index*, and the *affinity index* are the most popular. Salton's cosine measures the strength of bilateral collaboration by comparing collaboration between i and j (P_{ij})—where P can be joint projects, co-authored publications, or co-patents, and i and j can be organisations, cities, regions or countries—to the square root of the product of total collaborations of i (P_i) and j (P_j):

$$SALTON'S\ COSINE_{ij} = \frac{P_{ij}}{\sqrt{P_i \times P_j}}$$

Jaccard's index is based on an analogous approach, but its denominator is calculated in a different way:

$$JACCARD'S\ INDEX_{ij} = \frac{P_{ij}}{\left(P_i + P_j - P_{ij}\right)}$$

The values of both measures vary from 0 to 1, where 0 means no collaboration between the two analysed units and 1 means that all P involves collaboration in the analysed pair. Due to the mathematical features of the measures, Salton's cosine underestimates the collaboration of smaller entities with larger units. In effect, Jaccard's index is preferable to Salton's cosine in analyses that involve entities of significantly different scale, which is usually the case of studies on international collaboration between countries, e.g., Finland and the US (Luukkonen, Tijssen, Persson, & Sivertsen, 1993). Nevertheless, both measures are frequently applied in spatial scientometrics (see for example: Bolaños-Pizarro, Thijs, & Glänzel, 2010; Glänzel & Schubert, 2001; Glänzel, Schubert, & Czerwon, 1999).

The affinity index is built on a slightly different approach to bilateral relations. While Salton's and Jaccard's indices are essentially symmetric—there is one value of the measure for the pair i and j—the affinity index nearly always produces two different scores for two collaborating entities. The affinity index is defined as:

$$AFFINITY\ INDEX_{ij} = \frac{P_{ij}}{P_{COLL\,i}}$$

This relates the amount of collaboration P (joint projects, co-authored publications, or co-patents) between i and j (most frequently countries) to $P_{COLL\,i}$ (the total collaboration of the given i) with the whole set of units of a given type (for instance international collaboration with the entire world). The index calculated for collaboration between i and j more often than not achieves different values because of various denominators (i.e., a different overall number of collaborations—P_{COLL}). In effect, the index measures asymmetrical collaborative relations. If country i has a higher affinity index than its collaborator j, it suggests that j is a much more important collaborator for i, than i is for j. Examples of studies based on the affinity index include Campbell, Roberge, Haustein, & Archamba, 2013; Costa et al., 2013; Glänzel, 2001; Leclerc & Gagné, 1994; and Nagpaul, 1999.

Even more detailed patterns of scientific collaboration may be uncovered by the tools derived from social network analysis (Wasserman & Faust, 2007). The network approach is frequently used to visualise research collaboration. The availability of user-friendly visualisation tools—e.g., CiteSpace, CitNetExplorer, Science of Science (Sci2) Tool, and VOSviewer (Cobo, López-Herrera, Herrera-Viedma, & Herrera, 2011)—has powered a growing stream of collaborative network visuals on various levels, from individual scholars, through research groups, networks, and organisations, to regional, trans-regional, national, and also supranational levels. Network graphs can at times be difficult to comprehend and analyse—especially if they take the form of a dense "hedgehog"—but various network measures enable us to make sense of even extremely complex systems of relations. On the one hand, network-level metrics inform us about the properties of the overall network. For instance, *network density* measures the proportion between existing direct ties among nodes in a network and the total number of possible ties. Meanwhile, *average path length* indicates the mean number of steps along the shortest paths between all pairs of nodes in the network. Both measures allow us to evaluate how well the nodes in a network are connected. In the context of spatial scientometrics, network density and average path length are frequently used to investigate the evolution of a given network or to compare the overall features of different collaborative networks (see inter alia: Cassi, Corrocher, Malerba, & Vonortas, 2009; Fraunhofer ISI, Idea Consult, & SPRU, 2009; Vonortas, 2013; Zhai, Yan, Shibchurn, & Song, 2014).

On the other hand, node-level metrics measure how an individual node—be it an individual scholar, organisation, region, or country—is embedded in a given network. To this end, centrality measures are the most commonly used in spatial scientometric studies. They enable us to differentiate between nodes' positions in a network in terms of their possible influence over the network, access to the network resources, and control of information flows in the network. The most basic centrality measure is *degree centrality*, defined as the number of direct links that a node has with other nodes in the network:

$$DEGREE\ CENTRALITY_i = \sum_j DIRECT\ LINKS_{ij}$$

Degree centrality is interpreted as the involvement of a given node or its network activity. For instance, in the case of co-authorship networks at the regional level, the degree centrality is defined as the number of co-authorship relations that a region has. Furthermore, degree centrality can be enriched by taking account of the strength of these ties—instead of simply counting the existence of links, they can be weighted based on the number of relations between given nodes, e.g., the number of co-publications between countries. Regions directly connected to many other regions—and in the weighted version, by multiple relations—play the most important role in a network. Degree centrality is simple to calculate and comprehend, but as it concentrates on direct links, it simultaneously omits the global structure of the network. For example, a region might be connected to many others, but if these connections occupy peripheral network positions, they might be less valuable than a single link to the key network player. In other words, the number of a node's connections matters, but the connections of its collaborators can matter more. To address this issue, many centrality measures take account not only of direct ties, but also of indirect connections. Among them is *closeness centrality*, which measures how close, on average, a node is to all other nodes in the network, not only those in immediate proximity. Closeness centrality is defined as:

$$CLOSENESS\ CENTRALITY_i = \frac{V-1}{\sum_j NETWORK\ DISTANCE_{ij}}$$

where V is the number of nodes in the network, and $NETWORK\ DISTANCE_{ij}$ is the number of edges between vertices i and j. Closeness centrality can be interpreted as the connectedness or reachability of a given node. High values of closeness centrality suggest that the given node can easily reach other nodes in the network, either through direct or indirect ties. Thus, it has an advantage based on access to its collaborators' knowledge and resources. The next centrality measure goes even further and tries to capture the power of a node to control flows in the network. *Betweenness centrality* is obtained by determining how often a particular node is found on the shortest path between any pair of nodes (that are not directly connected). It is defined as:

$$BETWEENNESS\ CENTRALITY_i = \sum_{k=1}^{V-1}\sum_{j=k+1}^{V} \frac{\min PATH_{kj}(i)}{\min PATH_{kj}} \, k,j \neq i$$

where $\min PATH_{kj}$ is the number of shortest paths linking nodes k and j, and $\min PATH_{kj}(i)$ is the shortest path between k and j that goes through the node i. A high value of betweenness centrality means that the node is the most probable connector between nodes that are not directly connected. This network position enables the node to control the flow of information. This power can be used either to facilitate the flow of information (in this case the node plays the role of a bridge or knowledge broker) or to tame it (e.g., in order to secure the node's competitive advantage).

Another approach which can be used to capture a node's network position is *eigenvector centrality*. Eigencentrality combines the number of links and their quality. It is based on the idea that a node is more central if connected to other highly central nodes. The eigenvector centrality of a node i can be understood as the sum of the centralities of nodes adjacent to the node i. As such, it is based not only on the centralities of directly connected nodes, but also on the centralities calculated for connections of connections (and so on). Eigenvector centrality is believed to measure a node's importance and its influence over the network. A high value of the measure shows that the node is tightly connected to the most important players in the network.

The four discussed centralities are the most frequently used network measures in scientometric studies, mostly at the individual level (Liu, Bollen, Nelson, & Van de Sompel, 2005; Uddin, Hossain, Abbasi, & Rasmussen, 2012; Vidgen, Henneberg, & Naudé, 2007), but also in more spatially oriented studies concerned with networks of organisations, cities, regions, or countries (for instance: Choi, 2011; Kumar, Rohani, & Ratnavelu, 2014). Notably, node-level measures can be aggregated at the network level in the form of average centralities. In this light, the above-mentioned average path length can be seen as a network-level mean of closeness centralities. This approach to network-level analysis is also frequently encountered in spatial scientometrics (e.g., Franceschet, 2012; Guan & Liu, 2014; Ortega, 2014; Pan, Sinha, Kaski, & Saramäki, 2012).

Next to the most popular centrality measures, others can also be incorporated into the spatial analysis of collaboration in science. The following remarkable approaches can be pointed out: *average ties strength and efficiency* (Abbasi et al., 2011), *load centrality* (De Stefano et al., 2011), *subgraph centrality* (He, Ding, & Ni, 2011), and various community detection algorithms: *leading eigenvector, walktrap, edge betweenness*, and *spinglass* (Rodriguez & Pepe, 2008). A distinctive stream of advanced measures combines network and non-network features to produce comprehensive collaboration indicators. A particularly remarkable example of this approach is the *ego network quality* proposed by Tamás Sebestyén and Attila Varga from University of Pécs in Hungary. Notably, the index was constructed for the purpose of spatial analysis. The ego network quality reflects both the network position and node characteristics (attributes). It takes into account three dimensions of the network of knowledge flows: (1) the knowledge potential of a given node, which is derived from the knowledge stock of its direct and indirect neighbours (knowledge potential of partners), (2) the extent of collaboration among partners calculated as the average number of links in the node neighbourhood (local connectivity), and (3) the structure of the network behind the region's immediate neighbourhood (global embeddedness). The ego network quality is thus based on a similar idea to eigenvector centrality, but it adds node-specific characteristics (Sebestyén & Varga, 2013a, 2013b; Sebestyén, Hau-Horváth, & Varga, 2017).

Another approach to unfolding spatial collaboration patterns—somewhat surprisingly not heavily exploited—relies on studying the physical distance between collaborating scholars, institutions, or various spatial entities. An example might be the bundle of indicators based on the so-called *geographical collaboration distance* (GCD). This is defined as the largest geographical distance between collaborating units, for instance the authors' affiliation addresses included in a particular publication's address list. Based on the concept of the geographical collaboration distance, other measures can be derived, such as the *mean geographical collaboration distance* (average GCD of a set of collaborations, e.g., co-publications) or the percentage of collaborations at a given distance (e.g., percentage of publications with a GCD of more than 5,000 km) (for details see: Waltman, Tijssen, & van Eck, 2011). Moreover, the spatial distance between collaborating units can be comprehended not only as the distance measured along the surface of the earth ("as the crow flies"), between points which are defined by geographical coordinates in terms of latitude and longitude, but also on the basis of accessibility, measured as *transport accessibility* (Andersson & Ejermo, 2005) or on a micro scale as the *walking distance* between researchers in laboratories and offices.

In addition, a more nuanced approach brings into play the concept of functional proximity (or functional distance) among collaborators—by and large individuals—taking into account not only the shortest distance between two scholars but also aspects of the spatial layouts of possible interactions between them. Studies on relations among researchers at the campus or building level proposed—in addition to the physical distance and the walking distance—the *path overlap measure*, calculated as the total length of the overlapping paths of two individuals. Interestingly, examination of the correlations between measures of physical distance and path overlap revealed that they capture complementary aspects of collaboration in space (Kabo, Cotton-Nessler, Hwang, Levenstein, & Owen-Smith, 2014; Kabo, Hwang, Levenstein, & Owen-Smith, 2015).

3.4 Methodological issues

Spatially oriented studies of scholarly collaborations face specific methodological challenges. These issues relate to the dual nature of the field: some of the challenges stem from the scientometric methodology; the others derive from spatial analysis. The scientometric perspective raises questions on: (1) counting collaborators' contributions, (2) quantifying collaborative networks, (3) aggregating individual data at various organisational levels, and (4) accounting for disciplinary differences. The geospatial perspective adds further issues of: (5) geolocalisation, (6) distance measurement, and (7) modifiable spatial units. These seven intertwined issues may modify the results of collaboration analysis and may also affect related studies, for instance those addressing collaboration effects on scientific productivity and impact (see for instance Luukkonen et al., 1993).

The first methodological question is how to quantify the contribution of collaborators. The issue is extensively discussed in the bibliometric tradition, but it equally applies to other scientometric data, mainly patents and projects. For example, if three scholars co-authored a paper (or a patent, or worked together on a project), how should this paper (patent or project) be assigned to each individual? There are two main solutions: full counting and fractional counting (the former is sometimes referred to as whole, standard, normal, complete, or total, while the latter as adjusted or uniform). In the case of the above example, triple co-authorship, the full counting method assigns full credit to each author, while fractional counting assigns only one-third of the credit. In effect, the first method inflates the total sum of articles assigned to individuals, whereas the second method keeps the sum as one. In the full counting method, the credit given to an author does not depend on the number of co-authors. In fractional counting, the number of co-authors is taken into account, but the differences in contributions are not addressed. Consequently, more sophisticated approaches have been proposed (e.g., proportional, geometric, and harmonic counting) to capture the different levels of contribution to a joint work. For instance, the name sequence in the byline can be taken into account, or credit can be assigned only to the first and last co-author (first/last counting). The counting method applied to credit attribution in studies of scholarly collaboration influences its conclusions. In their 2005 article, Sooho Lee and Barry Bozeman revealed that the authorship counting procedure greatly affects scientific productivity measures. In this study, collaboration and publishing productivity were found to be significantly related when the full counting method for ascribing publications to their authors was applied, but the relationship disappeared when fractional counting was used. Similarly, at the country level, the distorting effect of various counting procedures can be observed. Marianne Gauffriau and her team (2007) showed that the full counting scheme boosts the position of more internationally tied countries with a relatively weak science base in relation to those scientifically stronger, yet less internationally connected.

The second methodological issue is how to quantify collaborative links. The reasoning behind this challenge mirrors that behind counting contributions. Coming back to the example of a paper co-authored by three individuals, collaborative relations can be fully or fractionally counted. In the full counting approach, each relation is assigned a full score, while in the fractional method each of the three links is attributed with one-third of the score. The intuition underlying the fractional counting of collaborative relations is that collaboration between two individuals is hardly comparable to collaboration among dozens or hundreds of scholars: the former is expected to be more intensive than the latter. Interestingly, while the quandary regarding whole/fractional counting of publications—and scientometric indicators in general—is addressed every so often in the literature, the application of this approach to bibliometric networks is a relatively new development (see: Leydesdorff & Park, 2017; Perianes-Rodriguez, Waltman, & van Eck, 2016). Another variant on the issue of collaborative links quantification relates to the classification of publications by collaboration type, most frequently, internationally, nationally, locally, institutionally co-authored, or sole-authored. In the so-called hierarchical coding, foreign addresses are looked for first, and papers with at least one such address are identified as international (even if they enlist national, local, or organisational authors). National, local, or organisational papers are then identified correspondingly. The procedure is problematic because an internationally co-authored paper may have more local than international co-authors. In effect, hierarchical coding devalues local and domestic collaboration, and at the same time overestimates international collaboration (2009). An alternative approach is a comprehensive coding. In this case, all of the possible variants are taken into account, e.g., for a simple classification into nationally and internationally co-authored papers, an additional mixed category of papers that have both national and international co-authors can be added. The downside of comprehensive coding is the multiplication of mixed categories that follows from the addition of each basic category. It can result in constructing categories that are too narrow and too difficult to be used in the analyses (such as "papers co-authored locally and internationally, but not organisationally and nationally").

The third issue is how to deal with various organisational levels, particularly in the case of overgeneralised aggregation or imprecise names of organisations as recorded in various data sources. For instance, Li and Willett (2009), in their Chinese study, observed methodological constraints relating to the way in which large, multicomponent scientific organisations are described in the Web of Science. The authors claim that this causes significant distortions in the interpretation of data on collaboration. In fact, the number of national collaborative articles in China is substantially higher than presented by the Web of Science data. This stems from the fact that the authors of many articles work for various units within the Chinese Academy of Sciences, which are also often spatially dispersed.

The fourth challenge concerns the disciplinary differences of scientific collaboration intensity and impact. Various fields of science are altered by collaboration differently. Scholarly disciplines feature distinctive collaborative customs resulting from discipline-specific factors (see for instance: Larivière et al., 2015; Luukkonen, Persson, & Sivertsen, 1992; Wuchty et al., 2007). Paragraph 2.2.4 refers in detail to these issues and provides numerous examples of variations among disciplines and their possible explanations. Next to field-by-field analysis, some more general regularities can be traced based on the collaborative performance of specific disciplines. The differentiating factor may be the level of applicability of the given discipline (Bordons, Gomez, Fernández, Zulueta, & Mendez, 1996; Muriithi et al., 2013) or the level of its advancement in a given country (Pedin, Južnic, Blagus, Sajko, & Stare, 2012). Remarkably, the positive impact of collaboration on productivity and citation levels tends to be weak or absent in the social sciences (Avkiran, 1997; Endenich & Trapp, 2015; Hart, 2007; Hollis, 2001; Leimu & Koricheva, 2005; Medoff, 2003). To account for interdisciplinary differences and to make field comparisons feasible, normalisation procedures of bibliometric indicators are implemented (van Raan, 2005). Nevertheless, the discipline-specific characteristics call for caution in the interpretation of multidisciplinary studies results.

The fifth concern is the geolocalisation of collaborators. To begin with, the precise geolocalisation of scientometric data is a non-trivial, time-consuming task due to the ambiguity and incompleteness of affiliations and addresses included in publications and patents. Although the overall quality of address data in the major scientometric sources has been continuously improving, along with more sophisticated geolocalisation techniques, the intrinsic limitations persist. An address reported with the scholar's affiliation does not necessarily indicate the exact location where the research was conducted. This might be the case of complex research organisations or studies that involve multiple organisations or that require scholars to be mobile. Furthermore, some authors report more than one address. Those double or multiple co-affiliations might result from simultaneous affiliations to different institutions or from academic mobility during the process of a paper's preparation and publishing. In this case, co-affiliations might be mistakenly interpreted as collaboration between individuals. Certainly, a scholar affiliated with multiple organisations can play the role of collaboration broker between them, but the meaning of such a link "is clearly different from a project where multiple researchers from different organisations are involved" (Frenken, Hardeman, & Hoekman, 2009, p. 226).

The ambiguity of geolocalisation translates into the sixth challenge, which is calculating the physical distance between collaborators. When high-resolution data—geolocated at organisation or city level—is not available, a proxy for calculating the distance has to be adopted. For instance, in the case of country-level studies, the geographical distance between collaborators can be computed using either the distances between the capital cities or the weighted average of the distances between the biggest cities of those countries. The city weightings can reflect science-related features, such as research and development (R&D) employment, the number of publications and patents, or general socio-economic indicators, for example population or gross domestic product (Nomaler, Frenken, & Heimeriks, 2013).

Finally, the last issue concerns the aggregation of geolocalised data at different spatial levels and units. This relates to the observation that spatial analyses are sensitive to the way in which considered spatial units are defined. This issue is referred to in geography as the modifiable areal unit problem (Grasland & Madelin, 2006; Openshaw, 1983). Spatial scientometrics deals with various geographical levels: a single address can be aggregated to the level of a neighbourhood, town, city, metropolitan area, region, province, country, or continent, to name only a few. Analyses performed on various levels often give dissimilar results, mainly due to the loss of information at higher levels of aggregation (Patuelli, Vaona, & Grimpe, 2010). Therefore, the choice of the spatial level of analysis for a particular problem remains fundamental. Naturally, researchers are frequently constrained by the availability of data on a given spatial level. Even if scientometric address data can be flexibly aggregated, other relevant data—e.g., R&D expenditures and employment—can be obtained only for predefined entities. These units usually reflect administrative areas, which are not always the most appropriate for spatial scientometrics or easily comparable across countries. It is argued that labour market areas consisting of a central city and its commuting area are most suited to local-level studies (Frenken et al., 2009; Hoekman et al., 2009). If delimitation of adequate functional areas is not available, custom spatial units can be constructed (usually by the aggregation of lower-level areas or analyses of raster data on population density—see: Eckert, Baron, & Jégou, 2013 and Grossetti et al., 2014). Furthermore, comparison across spatial levels can raise a number of questions. Consider a comparative study of international collaboration between the US and European countries. What should be compared: single European countries to the US, the whole of Europe to the US, or individual European countries to individual states of the US? Each of these alternatives gives markedly different results (Kamalski & Plume, 2013).

* * *

Spatial studies of scientific collaboration combine methods and approaches developed within informetrics, and the broadly defined science of science, with spatial sciences. The policy importance and relative novelty of spatial scientometrics have fuelled rapid advancements in data sources, techniques, and methodologies. In consequence, the research field is inherently interdisciplinary, internally diverse, and paradigmatically blurred. Further development of the geography of scientific collaboration increasingly depends on the establishment of a coherent theoretical framework. A well-defined research paradigm is needed to enhance causal inference.

Notes

1 Another impressive development regarding historical sources for the quantitative analysis of scientific collaboration is Electronic Enlightenment—an online collection of correspondence among intellectuals from the early 17th to the mid-19th century. Geolocation of this correspondence has been prepared within the Mapping the Republic of Letters project run by Stanford University (Chang et al., 2009). An interactive visualisation of the geolocalised correspondence network is available at: http://stanford.edu/group/toolingup/rplviz/rplviz.swf
2 The *Handbook of Bibliometric Indicators* by Todeschini and Baccini (2016) offers an exhaustive review of bibliometric indicators.

4 Spatial patterns of scientific collaboration

This chapter develops around four issues: (1) internationalisation of science and its varied dynamics, (2) formation and evolution of global scientific networks, (3) the collaboration-performance nexus in the geography of science, and (4) the centre-periphery logic of the geography of scientific collaboration. Before we go into details, it is worth taking some time to discuss the rationales and assumptions underlying the presented approach.

To begin with, patterns of scientific collaboration can be observed at various spatial levels, from the micro-level of individual scholars, buildings, and campuses, through mezzo-levels of towns, cities, and other subnational entities such as counties, regions, or states, to the macro-level of countries and their groupings. The micro-level—where individuals and organisations get their hands dirty with everyday collaboration—is addressed at length in Chapter 2 and is given suitable attention in Chapters 5 and 6. In this section, we focus primarily on the mezzo and macro levels, as they are the most relevant from the perspective of the global geography of science.

Research collaboration in space constantly evolves. The temporal dimension is especially vital in an era of unprecedented growth in scientific collaboration. The rise of global research collaboration networks—analysed here on country and city levels—provides the ultimate illustration of the collaborative turn in science. However, the dynamics of research internationalisation are unequally spread across the world, and the resulting global network is not horizontal, but shows a clear centre-periphery pattern.

The structural aspect of research networks is accompanied by a functional dimension. Structures formed by scientific collaboration serve particular functions, such as establishing scientific hierarchies or increasing the quantity and quality of scientific enterprise. The geography of science clearly reflects this functional aspect. For instance, the positive impact of collaboration is spatially diversified not only due to the varied intensity of scientific collaboration, but also because of the inherent disparities between collaborators. Hence, the advantages of collaboration are not necessarily evenly distributed among collaborating units. In this chapter, the functional dimension of scientific collaboration is addressed mainly by analysing the relationship between co-authorship and citations.

Last but not least, there are many types of scientific collaboration (see Chapter 2), and these can be measured using various data (see Chapter 3). Consequently, the observed patterns of scientific collaboration depend on the data and methods employed. This chapter draws primarily on bibliometric data sourced from the Web of Science database. However, to enrich and cross-validate the analysis, it is complemented by publication and citation data from the Scopus database, information on patents sourced from OECD, and selected results and conclusions provided by the rich empirical literature on the spatial aspects of scientific collaboration.

4.1 Internationalisation

The growth of international scientific collaboration in the last few decades can be seen as the most remarkable feature of the global geography of science. For centuries, international co-authorship was extremely rare. Even in 1970, internationally co-authored papers constituted only 1.9 percent of articles indexed in Web of Science.[1] Since then, the number has been growing steadily. In 1980, the share of internationally co-authored papers amounted to 4.6%. In the following years, the value almost doubled every decade. It reached 8.9% in 1990 and 16.1% in 2000. Finally, in 2013, almost every fourth publication—23.1%—had authors from more than one country (comparable results are reported by Leydesdorff & Wagner, 2008; Wagner, Park, & Leydesdorff, 2015).

On the national level, the percentage of internationally co-authored articles often significantly exceeds the global average. Values over 50%—which means that more than half(!) of the publications affiliated with a given country are co-authored internationally—are not uncommon. As of 2013, this was the case, for instance, in Switzerland (69%), Belgium (64.7%), Sweden (60.2%), the Netherlands (58.8%), France (56.2%), Germany (53.2%), the United Kingdom (53%), and Canada (50.1%)—to point out only selected countries with large overall scientific output. The remarkable difference between the world average and national averages may seem illogical. Yet the numbers are correct. The inconsistency stems from the nature of the phenomenon, which can be understood as an example of Simpson's paradox (altered trends or averages in aggregated and subdivided data, see Ramanana-Rahary, Zitt, & Rousseau, 2009). Furthermore, we have to bear in mind that collaborative relations are not necessarily bilateral. Of course, internationally co-authored publications result most frequently from collaboration between scholars from two countries (17.8% of the total number of articles published in 2013), and definitely less often from three (3.7%) or four (0.9%). Publications produced by researchers from five or more countries account for 0.7% of global research output as indexed by Web of Science in 2013. The last category may seem tiny—applying to less than one in a hundred publications—but let us think about the quantity of international relations associated with the aforementioned categories. For example, co-authorship among four countries translates into six bilateral relations between countries, in the case of five-country co-authorship we already have ten bilateral relations, and with six-country co-authorship 15, and so on.[2] Hence, even a low number of multi-country publications contributes significantly to the number of bilateral collaborative relations and inflates internationalisation rates.

The dynamics of internationalisation differ among countries (see Figure 4.1). In recent decades, the majority of nations have experienced a steady increase in the percentage of foreign co-authored papers—for instance the US and the UK, Germany, France, Canada, and Italy. Meanwhile, in some other countries the indicator has stagnated, as epitomised by China. In others, after an initial increase, there has been a noticeable decline in internationalisation, as in the case of Iran, Poland, and Romania. Particularly large fluctuations in the internationalisation rate affect countries with a low number of Web of Science–indexed papers in a given period. This explains the spectacular peaks and valleys recorded in South Korea, Singapore, and Saudi Arabia throughout the 1970s and 1980s, in China in the 1970s, and in Egypt, Thailand, and Colombia—with other examples easily noticeable in the charts placed on the following pages.

As a result of diversified paths of internationalisation, the participation of individual countries in global scientific cooperation varies considerably (see Figure 4.2). In the 32 most productive countries—defined as having more than 10,000 articles published in 2013—the degree of internationalisation can be as low as 20.9% in the case of Turkey, 22.5% for India, and 22.9% for Iran. At the other end of the spectrum, internationalisation is seen to reach 69% in Switzerland, 66.6% in Austria, and 64.7% in Belgium. However, the given values are not record-breaking. Many of the less scientifically advanced countries have even higher rates of internationalisation. In the group of countries that published between 5,001 and 10,000 articles in 2013, Saudi Arabia reached a rate of 75.9%. In the group of 1,001–5,000 published papers, Kenya attained an internationalisation rate of 86.7%, which was only narrowly higher than the value for Indonesia, 84.8%. Next, among countries with 101 to 1,000 publications, the internationalisation rate often approaches 100% (e.g., Mongolia—98.6%, Zambia—96.3%, Cambodia—96.1%). Predictably, some countries with a very limited scientific sector (from 10 to 100 papers in 2013) publish only internationally co-authored articles.

Clearly, the highest rates of internationalisation do not apply to the global scientific powerhouses. The two most scientifically productive nations in terms of the number of published papers, the US and China, display relatively modest internationalisation rates of 35.1% and 24.3%, respectively. The explanation of this phenomenon lies in the mass of a particular national science system. On the global scale, there is a strong negative correlation between the number of articles and the degree of their internationalisation (see Figure 4.3). There are two main reasons for this. For countries with the largest science sectors, there are plenty of—and sometimes entirely sufficient—internal possibilities to collaborate, while for the least developed, international collaboration may be the only means of entering the global world of science. For authors from less scientifically advanced areas, due to low endogenous scientific capacities, publishing in the world's top, usually English-language, journals might be difficult. One way to overcome this obstacle is to collaborate with foreign, often more experienced, established, and visible

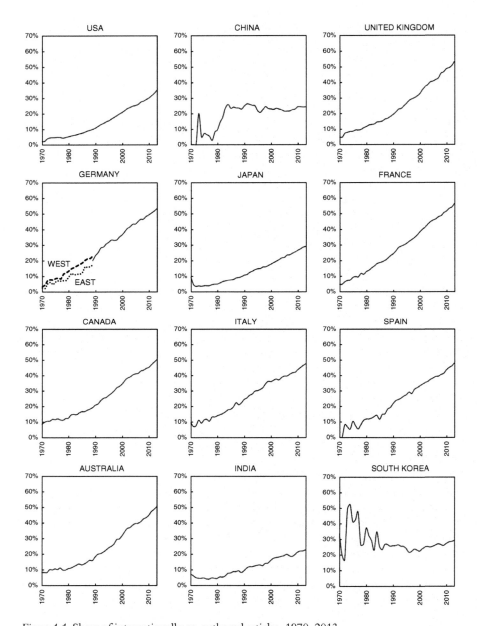

Figure 4.1 Share of internationally co-authored articles, 1970–2013

The figure includes countries with the highest number of articles in 2013, sorted in descending order.
Source: Conception and design by Adam Ploszaj, based on Web of Science data.

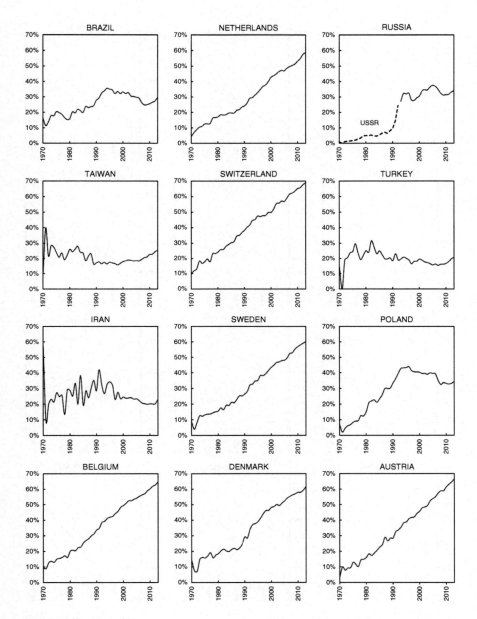

Figure 4.1 (continued)

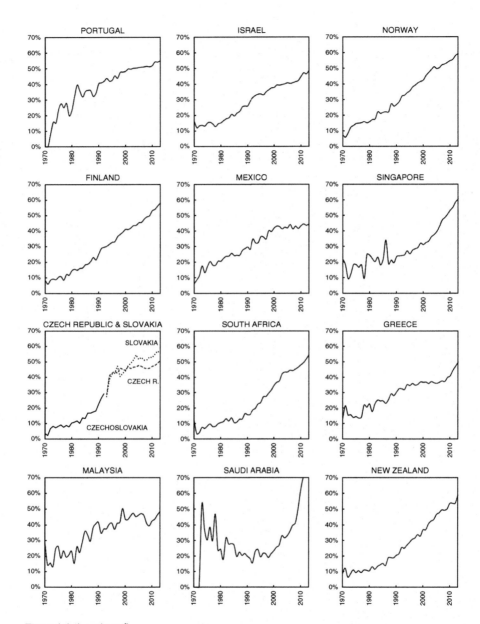

Figure 4.1 (continued)

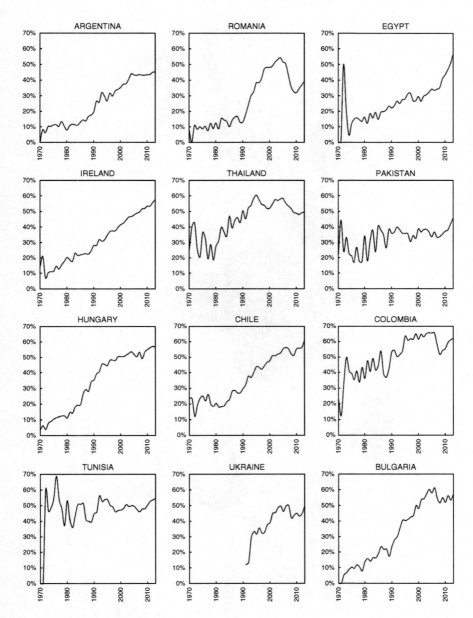

Figure 4.1 (continued)

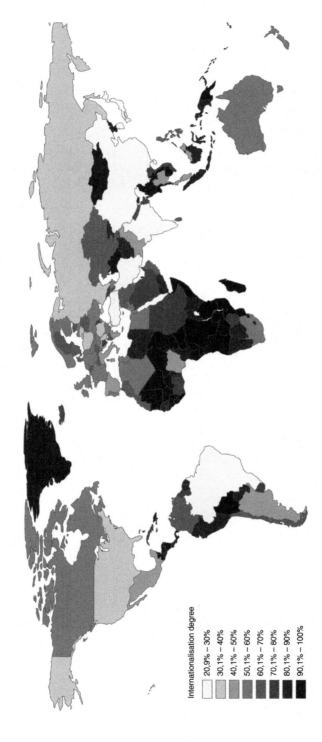

Figure 4.2 Share of internationally co-authored articles in 2013

Source: Conception and design by Adam Ploszaj, based on Web of Science data.

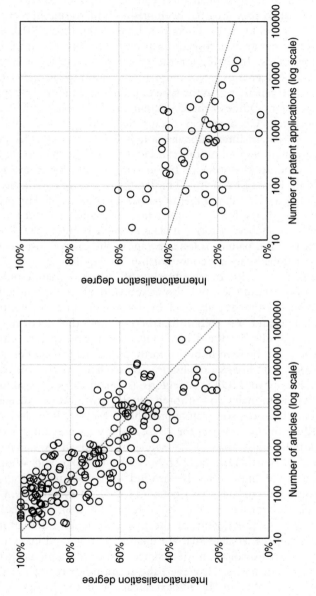

Figure 4.3 Research output and internationalisation at country level: articles (left) and patents (right)
Source: Conception and design by Adam Ploszaj, based on data from Web of Science (left) and OECD (right).

partners from more scientifically advanced countries (Didegah, Thelwall, & Gazni, 2012; Zanotto, Haeffner, & Guimarães, 2016).

Parallel patterns of internationalisation can be found in patenting activities. Firstly, international co-patenting has been gradually increasing in recent decades (see: De Prato & Nepelski, 2014; Frietsch & Jung, 2009; Picci, 2010; Su, 2017). However, the achieved level of foreign co-patenting is lower than in the case of foreign co-publications. In 2013, for the group of countries included in the OECD statistics, the degree of patent internationalisation totalled circa 6.7–8.2%, with the exact value depending on the type of patent application, i.e., applications to the European Patent Office or the US Patent and Trademark Office, or patents filed under the Patent Co-operation Treaty. Secondly, countries differ significantly in terms of patent internationalisation (see Figure 4.4). The percentage of international patent co-applications can be as high as in the Slovak Republic (44–67%), Luxembourg (56–66%), or Indonesia (60–73%), or as low as in Japan (2–3.1%) or South Korea (3.2–3.4%). Thirdly, the degree of patent internationalisation is related to the overall number of patent applications filed by inventors in individual countries. It tends to be higher for small countries and for countries with less developed science sectors (Guellec & de la Potterie, 2001; Lei et al., 2013). Nevertheless, this pattern is less apparent in the case of co-patents than in the case of international scholarly co-authorship (see Figure 4.2).

Spatial diversity in the internationalisation of science is manifested not only in differences among countries, but also at subnational levels, where it reflects regional variations in the overall level of socio-economic development, the distribution of a unique research infrastructure, and the scientific potential accumulated as a result of Braudelian long-term processes (see Chapter 1). Similar regularities can be seen in both North America and Europe, despite the higher overall level of internationalisation of science on the old continent. While in the European NUTS 2 regions (subnational statistical units) the percentage of internationally co-authored articles quite often exceeds 50% or even 60%, in the US no state even approaches 50% (see: Kamalski & Plume, 2013).[3] According to the US data for 2013, the lowest percentages of foreign co-authored articles—less than 30%—were recorded in Arkansas (27.1%), Kentucky (29.2%), North Dakota (29.5%), Idaho (29.6%), and West Virginia (29.7%). In turn, the highest levels—around 40%—occurred in the northeastern and southwestern states: Arizona (39.1%), Maryland (39.5%), New Mexico (39.7%), California (39.9%), New Jersey (40.2%), and Massachusetts (41.4%) (see Figure 4.5). A glance at the map of science internationalisation rates in the US suffices to state that the pattern is not random. Clearly, the high level of internationalisation of science tends to coincide with well-developed research capacities. However, the relationship is not unambiguous, and unexpected variability of the indicator can be noticed, especially in the case of states where a smaller number of articles have been affiliated.

In Europe, the highest rates of internationally co-authored papers occurred predominately in key metropolitan areas and in regions where major universities are located. Internationalisation degrees exceeding 50% were recorded in

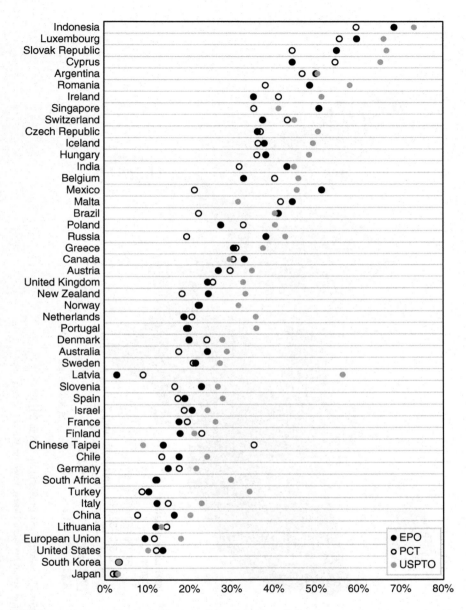

Figure 4.4 International cooperation in patents—share of patents with foreign co-inventors in 2013

EPO—European Patent Office; PTC—Patent Co-operation Treaty; USPTO—United States Patent and Trademark Office.
Source: Conception and design by Adam Ploszaj, based on data from OECD.Stat.

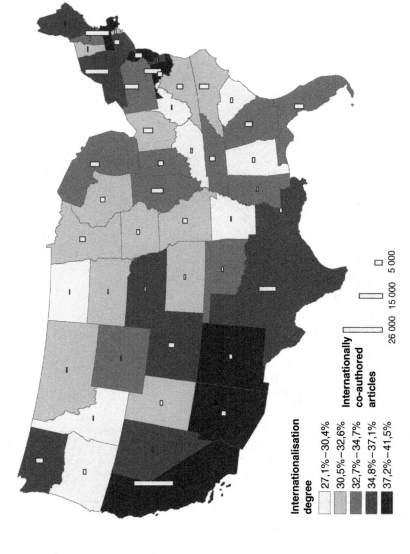

Figure 4.5 Internationally co-authored articles in the US in 2013

Source: Conception and design by Adam Ploszaj, based on Web of Science data.

the NUTS 2 regions of Oxford, Cambridge, London, and Edinburgh in the UK, Dutch Groningen, Belgian Leuven and Louvain-la-Neuve, Zurich and Lausanne in Switzerland, Stockholm and Uppsala in Sweden, Berlin and Munich in Germany, and regions hosting unique research infrastructure, such as Dutch Drenthe with its large radio telescope and Geneva with the CERN headquarters. Moreover, a distinct latitudinal belt of high internationalisation rates can be seen to spread from Barcelona in Spain, through the French southern regions, Switzerland, and Austria, to Bratislava in Slovakia and Budapest in Hungary. Meanwhile, the less scientifically internationalised regions tend to cluster in European economic peripheries. The majority of regions with less than 33% of internationally co-authored articles are located in the eastern flank of the European Union—in Bulgaria, Lithuania, Poland, and Romania (see Figure 4.6).

The previously discussed relationship between the number of publications and internationalisation rates occurring at the cross-country level (Figure 4.3) is also manifested at the subnational level. But, curiously, the direction of the relationship is entirely reversed. For both the US states and European NUTS 2 regions, the number of publications positively correlates with the degree of internationalisation (at the global cross-national level the relationship is negative). In other words, regions and states with higher scientific output also exhibit higher internationalisation rates. The volume of scientific papers has a greater effect on internationalisation in the case of the European NUTS 2 regions than in the case of American states (Figure 4.7 left). For the former, a tenfold increase in the number of papers translates into a circa six percentage point increase in the internationalisation rate. For the latter, the effect is only about 2.8 percentage points. Furthermore, cross-national differences matter considerably in Europe. For the whole set of European regions, the relationship between the number of papers and internationalisation is only weakly linear—Pearson's correlation coefficient equals circa 0.28. The correlation becomes stronger when regions within individual countries are taken into account (Figure 4.7 right). This is the case, for instance, of France (0.48), the UK (0.51), Spain (0.60), Germany (0.61), Poland (0.73), Romania (0.74), and Sweden (0.85) (but not of Italy and the Netherlands, where the correlation is negligible). The analysed phenomenon shows the multilevel nature of the geography of scientific cooperation: the direction of the relationship between the volume of scientific production and the intensity of international research collaboration differs across levels of analysis. At the level of global international comparisons it is clearly negative, while at the subnational level the relationship tends to be positive.

4.2 The global scientific network

The increasing collaboration and internationalisation in science have led to the formation of global scientific networks that connect researchers, organisations, cities, and countries. Worldwide flows of knowledge are decreasingly

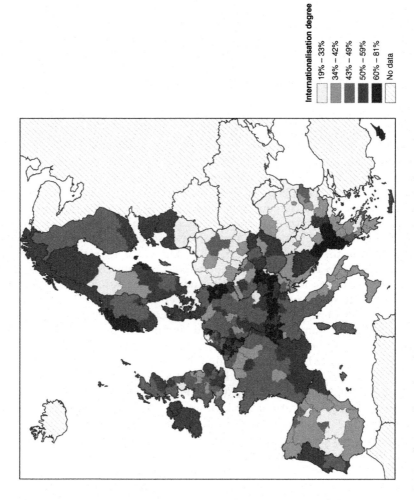

Figure 4.6 Share of internationally co-authored articles in European regions in the period of 2007–2013
Source: Conception and design by Adam Ploszaj, based on Web of Science data.

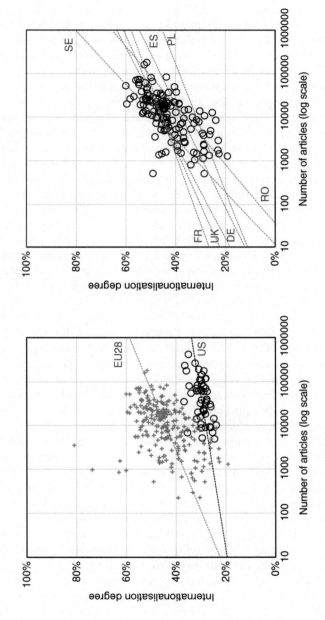

Figure 4.7 Research output and internationalisation in US states and EU NUTS 2 regions (left), and NUTS 2 regions within selected EU countries (right), 2007–2013

Source: Conception and design by Adam Ploszaj, based on Web of Science data.

characterised by pair-wise, bilateral relations and increasingly by the logic of networks. Two countries—or other types of nodes—that have the same number of external scientific connections can occupy radically different positions in the global scientific web because not only should the number of relations be taken into account, but also where they lead. It is the pattern of interlinked components that matters, as well as the position of nodes in the network and the architecture of relationships (Strogatz, 2003).

The contemporary global scientific network is woven around the US. Its central role is largely derived from the superior mass of the US research and development sector. A large number of scholars, research organisations, and scientific undertakings create numerous opportunities for international collaboration and put the US at the centre of the scientific network of nations. For most countries, the US is usually the most important collaborator, at least when we consider the scale of cooperation measured in absolute numbers. On the other hand, the international scientific network is getting denser as more and more of the possible links between countries are actually forged.

Both phenomena are well illustrated by the international co-authorship network of the 30 countries with the highest number of scientific articles indexed in the Web of Science in 2013 (see Figure 4.11). Firstly, the US is undeniably the most important collaboration partner for the remaining 29 countries, with each of them having at least 1,000 papers co-authored with the US. Secondly, all 30 countries are fully interconnected. Of course, the number of collaborative papers in particular pairs of countries differs according to the size of their scientific output (e.g., US-China: 24.6 thousand, France-UK: 6.6, and Japan-Poland: 0.4). But all of the 435 possible collaborative relations among the countries in question are actually realised, with at least 25 co-authored papers for any country-pair in the sample. Moreover, for one-third of the possible collaborative relations, the actual number of co-authored articles exceeds 1,000.

Such a dense network appeared only recently. Figures 4.8–4.11 show its formation. The evolution of the network is characterised by an exponential increase in the absolute numbers of co-authored papers, densification, and the successive entrance of new nodes. In 1980, only 17 country-pairs in the sample had more than 100 co-authored articles.[4] In 1990, the number grew to 73, and a decade later—in 2000—it rose to 238. Finally, in 2013, the number of country-pairs with at least 100 co-authored papers hit 417—which represents 96% of all possible collaborative relations between the 30 most scientifically productive countries. Furthermore, in 1980 there was no single country-to-country relation with 1,000 co-authored papers, in 1990 there were five such cases, in 2000 it rose to 42, and in 2013 as many as 143. This network growth and densification have been accompanied by the evolution of particular nodes' positions in the global collaboration. In this respect, two features should be given particular attention. First, the US constantly occupies a stable position as the central hub of the global scientific collaboration network. Second, China has gained a prominent position in the network in the first decade of the third millennium.

Spatial patterns of scientific collaboration 93

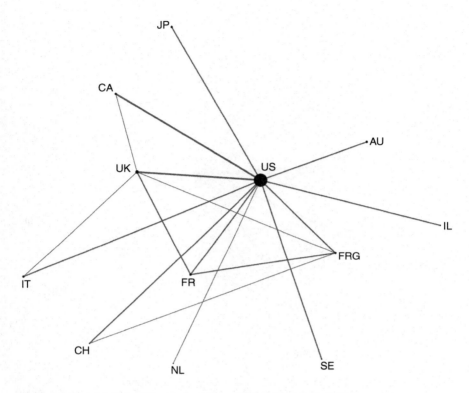

Figure 4.8 The network of internationally co-authored articles in 1980
The size of nodes is proportional to the overall number of articles. Only nodes with at least one edge with 100 or more co-publications are shown. Correspondingly, only edges with 100 or more co-publications are displayed.
Source: Conception and design by Adam Ploszaj, based on Web of Science data.

The unparalleled rise of the Chinese presence in the global scientific network, combined with the significant expansion of India and South Korea, and the already solid position of Japan, has resulted in a great shift of worldwide knowledge flows. Between 2000 and 2013 East Asia became one of the three key macro-regional nodes of the global scientific network (see Figure 4.12). North America and Europe, the other two primary nodes, have also developed their external scientific collaboration. Notably, their bilateral relations have intensified relatively less than their collaboration with East Asia, as well as with secondary nodes—the Maghreb and the Middle East, Latin America, Sub-Saharan Africa, Oceania, and Southeast Asia (see also: Maisonobe, Grossetti, Milard, Eckert, & Jégou, 2016).

Macro-regional analysis gives the basis for one more observation. Treating European countries as one unit of analysis—justified by integration within the

94 *Spatial patterns of scientific collaboration*

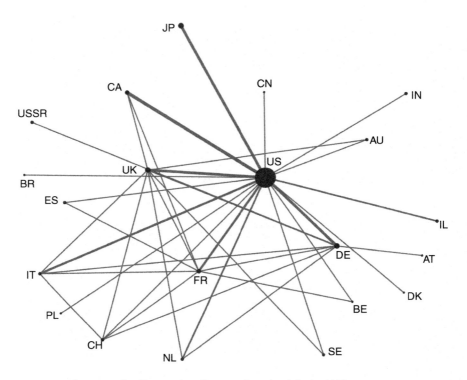

Figure 4.9 The network of internationally co-authored articles in 1990
The size of nodes is proportional to the overall number of articles. Only nodes with at least one edge with 200 or more co-publications are shown. Correspondingly, only edges with 200 or more co-publications are displayed.
Source: Conception and design by Adam Ploszaj, based on Web of Science data.

European Research Area (see Chapter 6)—considerably reshapes the global scientific network. The single European Research Area node becomes comparable with the US, which is responsible for the lion's share of scientific activity in North America. This suggests that the contemporary global scientific network at the country level is not organised around a single core (US), but instead can be characterised as a dual-core system (US-EU). Furthermore, expansion of science in East Asia, especially China, is leading to the development of a triple-core model (US-EU-China).

Countries and global macro-regions are somewhat abstract entities for the analysis of scientific collaboration, even in the context of the geography of science. After all, research activity within individual countries is typically extremely unevenly distributed. Thus, subnational entities—such as regions, towns, and cities—better reflect the real nature of the phenomenon. This more detailed approach demonstrates that the mean distance between collaborating units is

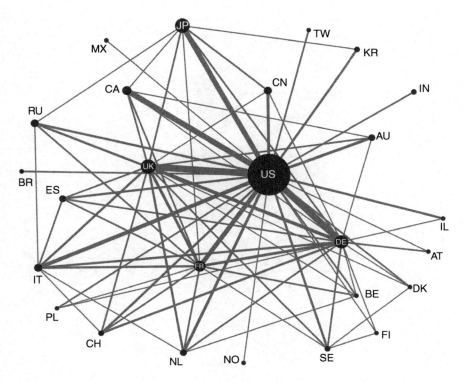

Figure 4.10 The network of internationally co-authored articles in 2000

The size of nodes is proportional to the overall number of articles. Only nodes with at least one edge with 500 or more co-publications are shown. Correspondingly, only edges with 500 or more co-publications are displayed.

Source: Conception and design by Adam Ploszaj, based on Web of Science data.

continuously increasing. Between 1980 and 2009 the average collaboration distance per publication grew from 334 to 1,553 kilometres (Waltman et al., 2011; see also Agrawal, McHale, & Oettl, 2014). Despite this incredible rise in distant collaboration, spatial proximity is of great importance. The likelihood of collaboration decreases as the distance increases. Collaboration with collocated colleagues within the same organisation is obviously more likely than collaboration with scholars from the other side of the globe (see Chapter 5).

The finer spatial granularity reveals the crucial role of a limited number of major research hubs in the global scientific cooperation network, first and foremost the so-called world cities (Matthiessen et al., 2010). Global metropolises such as London, New York, Paris, and Tokyo are not only very well connected to each other, but they also serve as national and macro-regional collaboration gateways. This effect is clearly visible in Figures 4.13 and 4.14, presenting the most essential cities and interurban co-authorship relations in

96 Spatial patterns of scientific collaboration

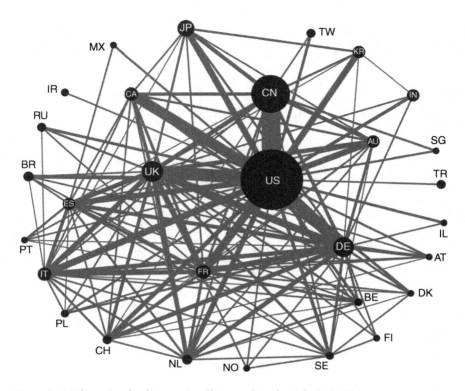

Figure 4.11 The network of internationally co-authored articles in 2013
The size of nodes is proportional to the overall number of articles. Only nodes with at least one edge with 1,000 or more co-publications are shown. Correspondingly, only edges with 1,000 or more co-publications are displayed.
Source: Conception and design by Adam Ploszaj, based on Web of Science data.

2000 and 2013.[5] On both graphs, collaborative relations that cross national borders are almost exclusively those that connect major global metropolises. The vast majority of relations are of an intra-national nature. This demonstrates that, despite the ongoing internationalisation of scientific collaboration, the intra-national dimension remains more important than it might seem (Maisonobe, Eckert et al., 2016). Furthermore, comparison of graphs from 2000 and 2013 confirms the already discussed dynamic entry of China into the global arena of scientific cooperation.

4.3 Patterns of collaboration and research performance

The geography of scientific collaboration simultaneously shapes and is shaped by the geography of scientific performance. The relationship is two-way. On

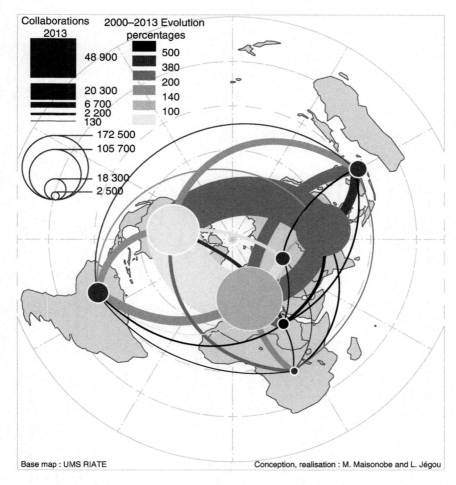

Figure 4.12 Scientific collaboration among global macro-regions in 2013 and its evolution since 2000
Source: Courtesy of Marion Maisonobe and Laurent Jégou.

the one hand, high-performing places of science attract collaborators. On the other, more intensively collaborating sites, hubs of scientific collaboration, outperform less collaborative places. This effect is visible in terms of the expanding quantity of scientific production (Ductor, 2015)—although the quantitative surplus of collaboration tends to diminish or even disappear when fractional counting is applied (Fanelli & Larivière, 2016). More remarkably, collaboration is supposed to enhance the quality of research outputs. Collaborative papers are cited more frequently (Lawani, 1986; Persson,

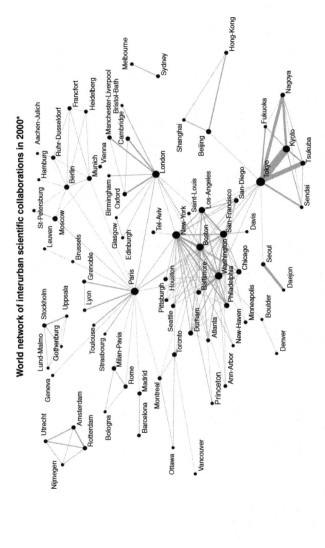

Figure 4.13 World network of interurban scientific co-authorships in 2000

Source: Courtesy of Marion Maisonobe.

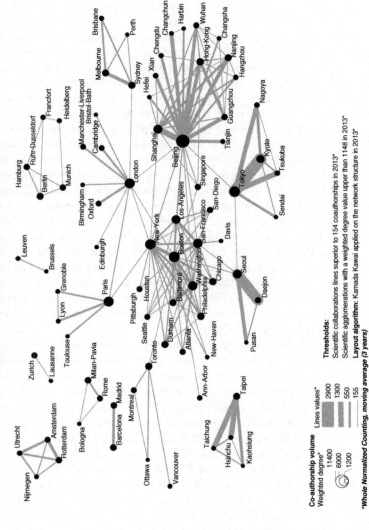

Figure 4.14 World network of interurban scientific co-authorships in 2013

Source: Courtesy of Marion Maisonobe.

Glänzel, & Danell, 2004; Tahamtan, Afshar, & Ahamdzadeh, 2016), are less often rejected from publication (Presser, 1980), and receive more positive peer reviews (Carillo et al., 2013; Franceschet & Costantini, 2010).

Furthermore, the type of collaborative links and the scope of collaboration affect the strength of the impact. In other words, the influence of the collaboration factor is not zero-one but rather gradual. Firstly, links to stronger partners are more valuable than links to less developed ones. Higher citation gains from co-authorship with more developed collaborators, as compared to co-authorship with less developed ones, can be observed on various levels: individual researchers (Pravdić & Oluić-Vuković, 1986), organisations (Ahn, Oh, & Lee, 2014), and countries (Tang & Shapira, 2011). Secondly, more collaboration translates into greater impact. The number of citations received by a publication grows not only with the growing number of co-authors but also with the increasing number of unique organisations, cities, and countries involved in the preparation of a collaborative publication (Hsiehchen, Espinoza, & Hsieh, 2015; Larivière et al., 2015; Pan, Kaski, & Fortunato, 2012). Thirdly, research performance depends not only on the number and characteristics of collaborators but also on their position in the overall collaboration network. At the individual level, it is particularly beneficial to work with various established scholars or groups that are otherwise not too strongly interconnected. In short, higher betweenness centrality corresponds with more significant impact (Ortega, 2014). Parallel effects can be observed at the regional level. For instance, a study of European regions showed that the research productivity of a region is related to the quality of its inter-regional knowledge network, understood as the extent of collaboration among partners, the position of partners in the entire knowledge network, and knowledge accumulated by the partners (Sebestyén & Varga, 2013a).

In the context of the geography of science, the distinction between foreign and domestic collaboration is of particular interest. Internationally co-authored papers tend to receive more citations than papers involving only domestic collaborators. This observation is confirmed by cross-national analyses (e.g., Didegah & Thelwall, 2013; Glänzel et al., 1999; Narin, Stevens, & Whitlow, 1991) as well as by case studies of particular countries, for instance Brazil (Kim, 1999), China (Ma & Guang, 2005; Zhou & Leydesdorff, 2006), South Korea (Leta & Chaimovich, 2002), Poland (Olechnicka & Ploszaj, 2010b), Spain (Bolaños-Pizarro et al., 2010), and the UK (Katz & Hicks, 1997).[6] Moreover, it is suggested that international collaboration is crucial, in particular, for geographically peripheral countries—such as New Zealand—since it creates opportunities for improved visibility of research outputs (Goldfinch et al., 2003).

Superior citation returns to international collaboration—the effect sometimes referred to as the international collaboration premium—imply that higher internationalisation rates translate into greater citation rates. This regularity can be seen in the example of Scopus data for economically advanced countries defined as members of the Organisation for Economic Co-operation and Development (OECD). The greater the percentage of

Spatial patterns of scientific collaboration 101

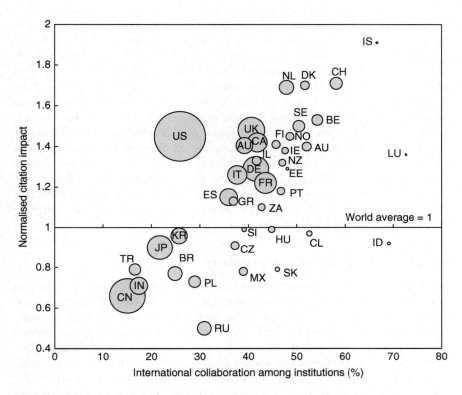

Figure 4.15 The citation impact of scientific production and the extent of international collaboration (2003–2012)
Source: Based on OECD 2015.

internationally co-authored articles, the higher the field-normalised citation impact (see Figure 4.15). In the subgroup of countries that achieved a normalised citation impact above the world average, all but one exceeded the 35% threshold of internationally co-authored publications. The US is the only outlier in this subgroup. The US relative citation impact, 45% higher than the world average, significantly outperforms its internationalisation. The reason for this is twofold. First, the size of the US science system provides enough opportunities to collaborate internally and, as a result, it is less focused on international collaboration (see subchapter 6.4). Second, internationalisation is not the only factor influencing scientific performance, and other variables also have to be taken into account: human capital, established institutions, accumulated knowledge, and research funding (see: King, 2004). The second aspect also applies to the other group of outliers, namely those countries that have a lower citation impact than they should, given their level of internationalisation—for instance, Indonesia, Russia, and Chile.

International collaboration indicates that collaborators are separated by a significant geographic distance, greater than domestic collaborators. This may suggest that not only can the fact of crossing the national border modify the research impact, but perhaps the geographic separation between collaborators also matters. The study by Nomaler, Frenken, and Heimeriks (2013) of international co-authorship networks among European countries provides the evidence for this thesis. It showed that an increase of 1,000 km in the distance between collaborating units leads to a rise in citations by seven to nine percent. In other words, it is beneficial to have remote collaborators because the greater the kilometric distance, the more citation impact the collaborative paper can achieve.[7] On this basis, a noteworthy conclusion can be drawn on the relations between geographic distance, propensity to collaborate, and collaboration impact. Growing spatial distance, on the one hand, reduces the probability of collaboration and, on the other, increases the probability of achieving above-average effects from collaboration.

4.4 The logic of centre and periphery

We would expect that the escalation of international collaboration in science is accompanied by decreasing cross-country disparities in scientific performance. But this is not necessarily the case. The network structure of global scientific collaboration does not imply that horizontal relations among countries prevail. On the contrary, the system can be described as hierarchical. Although horizontal and hierarchical relations coexist in this system, they are not uniformly distributed in the global space. While relations among the most scientifically developed countries are largely horizontal, the relationships between stronger and weaker science players are rather hierarchical. Hereby, the world of science reproduces the global structure of centre and periphery (Schott, 1993; Shils, 1991). This can be further explained in the light of the world-system theory crafted by the influential American intellectual Immanuel Wallerstein (2004). Core and periphery play complementary roles in the global system. The core is at the forefront of socio-economic and technological development, while the periphery provides cheap labour and low-processed resources. In the case of science, this is manifested by the fact that new ideas are generated predominately in the centre and then imitated in the periphery. Furthermore, the world-system is composed not only of core and periphery, but also of semi-periphery. The semi-periphery acts as a periphery to the core and as a core to the periphery. The hierarchy of the global scientific system is thus multi-level (Hwang, 2008). At the same time, the system is segmented into macro-regions within which horizontal relations are dense. Horizontal relations occur especially among core countries, while between core and periphery relations tend towards domination and subordination.

Research collaboration is one of the means that the centre uses—even if unintentionally—to ensure its scientific domination over the periphery (Schott, 1998). This process has various dimensions. First, core countries occupy central positions in the global scientific collaboration network, and therefore they are able to control knowledge flows and thus maintain a competitive advantage. Second, the core sets the rules of the game in the world scientific tournament and establishes the institutional framework in which global science operates (Ben-David, 1984; Schott, 1993). To take part in the game, peripheral countries have no option but to collaborate with the centre. Collaboration with partners from core countries helps them to acquire international financing, catch the attention of the world scientific audience, and publish in leading journals (Paasi, 2015). Third, the core imposes its research agenda on the periphery. The agenda is not necessarily consistent with the needs and wants of the periphery. Less developed countries often serve merely as subcontractors or routine research service providers for core countries (Kreimer, 2007). Four, core countries, due to the availability of resources and accumulated academic prestige, are able to attract talented scholars from peripheral countries. Scientific collaboration enables them to identify such individuals. For peripheral areas, this brain drain remains a serious challenge (Boeri, 2012; Trachana, 2013), even though academic mobility is increasingly portrayed as brain circulation, beneficial for both sending and receiving countries (Saxenian, 2005).

Nonetheless, it is rather the peripheries that strive for joint research and publications with core countries, not the other way round (Schubert & Sooryamoorthy, 2010). As we noticed in the previous subchapter, collaboration with stronger partners boosts scientific performance. But for stronger partners, working with weaker collaborators is less attractive and can even lead to a decrease in performance (Ahn et al., 2014; Glänzel & Schubert, 2001; Glänzel et al., 1999; Pravdić & Oluić-Vuković, 1986). This greater advantage for weaker partners may seem—at first glance—contradictory to the aforementioned centre-periphery hierarchical dominance. But this contradiction is illusory. It turns out that weaker partners' benefits from collaboration with stronger ones depend, ceteris paribus, on what role they play in the given collaboration. This phenomenon is visible when we compare the mean citations of collaborative papers in which authors from different countries perform a leading or complementary role. The leading role is usually played by scientists indicated as corresponding authors (Mattsson, Sundberg, & Laget, 2011), while non-corresponding authors can be seen as complementary partners. In the group of 53 countries that published at least 20,000 articles in years 2000–2013, only eight achieved higher mean citations of their corresponding-author collaborative papers as compared to their non-corresponding author papers. Corresponding-author collaborative papers are particularly beneficial for the US. For Singapore, the UK, Germany, Switzerland, the Netherlands, and France the benefits are smaller but still significant, while in Australia corresponding-author papers receive only slightly more citations than papers in which Australian scholars play a complementary role. For all other countries in the sample it is more valuable—in terms of the citation premium—to act as non-corresponding co-authors (see Figure 4.16). This diversity reflects the core-periphery structure of international relations in science. Core countries

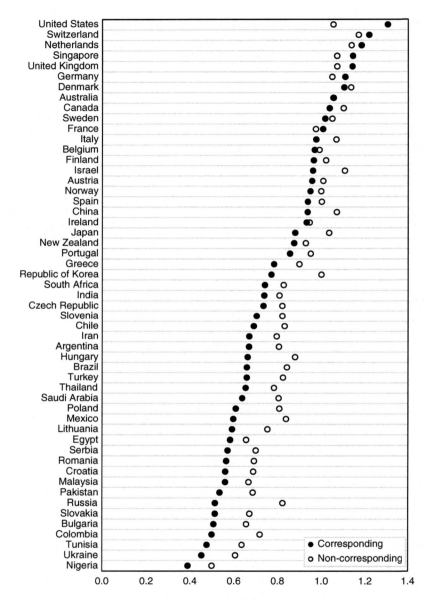

Figure 4.16 Normalised mean citations of papers in which scholars from a given country play the role of corresponding or non-corresponding authors (2000–2013)

To reduce the influence of hyper-authorship, only papers co-authored by scholars from exactly two countries are taken into account. Moreover, we disregarded papers where scholars from two countries simultaneously serve as corresponding co-authors.
Source: Conception and design by Adam Ploszaj, based on Web of Science data.

benefit most from international cooperation when they lead the research, while peripheral countries benefit most from being led.

The core-periphery structure of global science is very stable (Schubert & Sooryamoorthy, 2010). Breaking the vicious cycle of lasting peripheralisation is rarely possible. A negative feedback loop—from low performance, to stagnating or falling funding, then to aggravating brain drain, and in turn to even poorer performance—keeps the periphery in a peripheral position. What is more, some actions taken in the periphery to overcome peripherality reproduce the peripheral logic. For instance, authors publishing in predatory journals are, for the most part, inexperienced researchers from developing countries (Xia et al., 2015). They fall into a trap while trying to meet the expectations of contemporary publish or perish academic culture. Another example is provided by the dubious acquisition of co-affiliated scholars. One of the strategies to overcome peripherality is to bring, even temporarily, prominent scientists from core institutions. This type of collaboration can generally be very positive and beneficial, especially in the long run, due to the diffusion of innovation and spillover effects (see Rogers, 2003). However, it sometimes turns into a caricature or at least raises questions. This was the case of King Abdulaziz University in Jeddah, Saudi Arabia. The university contacted highly cited world-class mathematicians and invited them to serve as adjunct faculty for $72,000 per annum. The contract terms, according to a recruiting letter, assumed that "the mathematicians had to work three weeks a year in Saudi Arabia. The university would fly them there in business class and put them up at a five-star hotel" (O'Neil, 2016, p. 62). In return, scientists had to change their affiliations in the Web of Science database. As a result, King Abdulaziz University has become the institution with the largest number of co-affiliated highly cited scientists and has quickly conquered the global rankings of universities (Pachter, 2014). However, long-term results of such strategies are not at all certain, and in the short-term, it rather undermined the reputation of the university than enhanced its prestige.

On the other hand, the recent examples of Singapore, South Korea and, in particular, China indicate that transfer from periphery to semi-periphery, or even to the core, is possible. Research collaboration is an important ingredient of a successful attempt to catch up with leading scientific countries. Indeed, there are dozens of scientific collaboration tools and measures that can boost the scientific performance of nations (see Chapter 6). However, we cannot expect that the widespread use of these tools will result in the disappearance of scientific peripheries and the global levelling of scientific performance. The structural hierarchy is an immanent feature of global science, as it is in the case of the overall world-system. Despite constant evolution in the positions of countries, there will always be some sort of scientific centre and some sort of scientific periphery.

* * *

Geography is of constant importance for scientific collaboration. Despite the unprecedented intensification of collaborative relations around the globe, the location of collaborators matters. Spatial distance modulates both the propensity to collaborate and the expected impact of collaborative work. Furthermore, places that have accumulated great scientific capacities are better prepared to take part in the collaborative turn and fully profit from its effects. As a result, the geography of scientific collaboration reflects the core-periphery structures embedded in long-term historical processes. The dynamic collaborative turn strengthens—somewhat paradoxically—the persistency of the global distribution of research excellence.

Notes

1 Web of Science data presented in this chapter—unless a different source is indicated—are based on the in-house Web of Science dataset provided by the Network Science Institute and the Cyberinfrastructure for Network Science Center at Indiana University Bloomington. All presented numbers refer strictly to the publication type "article" (book chapters, conference proceedings, reviews, letters, etc. are not taken into account) included in Science Citation Index, Social Sciences Citation Index, and Arts & Humanities Citation Index.
2 For a symmetric network with n nodes (in our case countries), the number of undirected relations between nodes equals $n(n-1)/2$.
3 However, it has to be remembered that the American states and European NUTS 2 regions are not equivalent, and it is even argued that states are more comparable with countries, see, e.g., Kamalski & Plume, 2013.
4 Note that the sample reflects geopolitical changes, i.e., for 1980 two German states are taken into account—the German Democratic Republic (GDR) and the Federal Republic of Germany (FRG)—while for 1980 and 1990 the Union of Soviet Socialist Republics (USSR) is treated as a predecessor of present-day Russia.
5 To ensure decent comparability between 2000 and 2013, displayed nodes (cities) and links (co-authorships) meet identical criteria for both maps. First, only cities with the highest number of collaborations are shown. The visible cities are those which, ranked in descending order, are involved in 55% of all interurban collaborations. Second, only links with the highest number of co-authorships are included. The visible links are those which, ranked in descending order, account for 20% of all interurban collaborations (for the details see: Maisonobe, Eckert, Grossetti, Jégou, & Milard, 2016).
6 However, it should be noted that a limited number of studies negate the significance of the international collaboration premium (Abbasi & Jaafari, 2013; He, 2009; Landry, Traoré, & Godin, 1996).
7 It should be emphasised that the issue of the relationship between citation and physical distance between collaborators is still under-researched. Moreover, some studies attempt to prove the existence of an inverse relationship, at least in the case of intra-organisational research collaboration (Lee et al., 2010).

5 Theoretical approaches to scientific collaboration from a spatial perspective

There is no specific theory of the geography of scientific collaboration. Furthermore, there is no complete, widely accepted theory on research collaboration in general. The increasing importance of scientific collaboration has attracted a lot of attention and stimulated almost countless empirical analyses. At the same time, the theoretical pillar of the discipline can hardly catch up with the deluge of new scientometric data and the increasing enthusiasm among science policymakers for evidence-based knowledge. Make no mistake, a broad spectrum of concepts and theoretical approaches relate to—or can be (re)interpreted as relating to—the geography of scientific collaboration. But usually these are either fragmentary or overgeneralised. Furthermore, their relevance may be diminishing due to the rapidly evolving ways of doing science. Conceivably, the collaborative advantage gained from international collaboration is less significant nowadays than it was a decade or two ago, when scholars collaborated internationally far less frequently. As a result, theories sourced from empirical analyses embedded in a significantly different historical context of scientific collaboration might be incompatible with the contemporary situation. All in all, there is a growing need for a comprehensive conceptual synthesis. An overall theory of scholarly collaboration, properly addressing its spatial dimension, could facilitate the standardisation of the field, the increase of its epistemic validity, and the enhancement of scientometrics research replicability.

This chapter does not pretend to construct a single theory of the geography of scientific collaboration. Its aim is modest: it draws a map of the issues and ideas that such a comprehensive theory should embrace. Four questions occupy central positions in this theoretical territory. Why does scientific collaboration grow? How are spatial patterns of scholarly collaboration shaped? How does collaboration impact research outcomes? What is the role of scientific collaboration in local and regional development? A review of possible answers to these questions is presented in the four following subchapters.

5.1 Explaining the growth of collaboration

The picture of intensifying scientific collaboration on various spatial levels presented in Chapter 4 entails the fundamental question of the causes and factors behind this process. This issue was already touched on in Chapter 2, in which the roots of the collaborative turn and benefits of collaboration for the individual researcher were elaborated. However, the aforementioned discussion focused on the description of key processes and evidence, primarily on the individual level, while little theorising was offered. This section evokes the main theoretical concepts that can be used to explain the unprecedented intensification of spatially embedded research collaboration. The scrutinised concepts and theories are rooted in diverse fields and methodological approaches: economics, sociology (primarily the sociology of science), management and organisation studies (predominantly inter-organisational relations and innovation management), and interdisciplinary science studies. The variety of ideas can be grouped into three categories that jointly explain the contemporary growth of research collaboration: the collaborative advantage, the changing role of research organisations, and the costs of collaboration.

5.1.1 The collaborative advantage

The escalation of scholarly collaboration—in general and in its spatial dimension in particular—lies in the sophistication of contemporary science. The increasing complexity of research questions makes contemporary science more and more problem focused, less discipline oriented. Unsurprisingly in such an environment, the preference is given to collaborative performance rather than individual scientific achievement (Gibbons et al., 1994). The tendency is manifested in a blurring of disciplinary boundaries, the emergence of new fields of science, and the omnipresence of inter-, multi-, and cross-disciplinary research (Nowotny, Scott, & Gibbons, 2003). The interdisciplinary networks of individual scholars, research teams, and scholarly institutions emerge and evolve according to the new scientific challenges. As expected, this results in practices that involve mixtures of institutions—often spatially scattered—such as universities, research centres, spin-offs, laboratories, consultancies, and think tanks. These processes—described by the Mode 2 knowledge production theory as transdisciplinarity and heterogeneity—explain the growth of dynamic inter-institutional collaboration in the socially and territorially dispersed process of knowledge production (Gibbons et al., 1994).

The concept of Mode 2 knowledge production was presented by Michael Gibbons and colleagues in contrast to the traditional way of doing science[1]— purely academic, scholar-oriented, and discipline-based—labelled as Mode 1. The shift towards intensification of collaboration among different institutions in various spatial configurations was also referred to by the concept of open innovation—one of the hottest ideas in the early 21st century, rooted in the theory of innovation management. Open innovation was proposed by Henry William Chesbrough as an alternative and a successor to the close innovation approach,[2] comparable to the introduction of Mode 2 vs. Mode 1 by Gibbons and colleagues. Organisations which operate in the closed innovation formula—typical of large 20th-century corporations—carry out all the

R&D activities on their own: they individually develop, implement, and introduce innovations into the market. In contrast, organisations which have adopted the open innovation approach are porous. They rely on the inflow of knowledge developed elsewhere: R&D produced by other firms or research organisations. At the same time, open innovation companies allow their internally produced knowledge to cross organisational boundaries. They spread new ideas in the form of spin-offs, spin-outs, licencing agreements, technology transfer, or even completely freely, without any direct benefit to themselves (Chesbrough, 2003). Such an approach naturally extends collaboration, both among spatially dispersed individuals and organisations.

The focal point of the open innovation concept is the advantage which organisations can achieve by higher integration with the outside environment through openness to outflows and inflows of information and expertise. Open innovation—like other free-flow concepts: free information (Brand, 1987), free culture (Lessig, 2005), free software (Berry, 2008), and open science (Nielsen, 2011)—is built on the assumption that lack of restrictions in developing someone else's ideas, combined with collaboration in non-hierarchical networks that can be widely distributed spatially, makes it possible to develop solutions that would otherwise be difficult to comprehend, or even not viable to accomplish. In other words, benefits can be achieved from the ordinary division of labour or sharing resources and knowledge, but also—and more importantly—from the synergy effects that emerge in the process of collaboration. The added value of collaboration is perfectly mirrored by the concept of collaborative advantage developed in the field of organisation and management studies. Elisabeth Lank, in her study of inter-institutional relations, defined the collaborative advantage as "the benefits achieved when an organization accomplishes more than it would have independently, by developing effective working relationships with other organizations" (2006, p. 7). This definition can be straightforwardly extended beyond the corporate realm and cover various types of organisations (universities, public research centres, non-profit laboratories), as well as territorial units (cities, regions, countries). Such collaborative advantage at the regional level has been described by Anne Lee Saxenian in her comparative study of Silicon Valley and Boston Route 128. She concluded that "industrial systems built on regional networks are more flexible and technologically dynamic than those in which experimentation and learning are confined to individual firms" (1994, p. 161).

5.1.2 The changing role of research organisations

The growth in scientific collaboration can also be theorised as a result of the changing role of science in contemporary society and the economy. Universities and other research organisations are expected to meet external requirements to a greater extent than ever before. Scholars become more concerned about the expectations of the recipients of their work and more conscious of the economic, social, political, and cultural repercussions of their research endeavours. In consequence, the scope of scientific collaboration expands beyond the academic community's interest. Mode 2 knowledge production refers to this by emphasising the social accountability and reflexivity of science. Social accountability permeates the entire process of knowledge production, which means that challenges targeted by scholars are derived from societal needs or inspired by public interest, as well as the fact that scientific outcomes are assessed in the context of their application. In this respect, the Mode 2 concept relates to the research classification proposed by Donald Stokes. His famous Pasteur's quadrant defines three types of scientific research: pure basic research (exemplified by the work of Neils Bohr), pure applied research (Thomas Edison type), and user-inspired basic research (Louis Pasteur type). The unique feature of the latter is that it combines consideration for the potential use of research results (as in applied research) with the quest for fundamental understanding (as in basic research) (Stokes, 1997).

The changing role of modern academia has attracted a lot of attention and resulted in a number of descriptive and prescriptive theories. This heterogeneous plethora of ideas has, however, at least one leitmotif: intensifying connections between scientific organisations and their local and regional environment. In the mid-1990s, Burton Clark—a classic theorist of the university as an organisation—identified features of the so-called entrepreneurial university, among which enhancing collaboration with the local environment was mentioned next to structural changes, modern management, new funding sources, and promotion of an entrepreneurial culture (Clark, 1998). Another closely related concept—the engaged university—was coined in the framework of the learning region theory (Goldstain, 2010). It underlines the developmental role of the university in the region and stresses the ability of a university to adapt to the regional and local needs (Gunasekara, 2006b). In a similar manner, John Goddard (2013) argued for the civic university, which combines local and global engagement. The changing role of the university, motivated by increasing awareness of the importance of local contexts and features for the process of collective learning and knowledge production, was also referred to as the concept of the Mode 2 university (Harloe & Perry, 2004) by the innovation systems theory (see subchapter 5.3), as well as by many other theoretical attempts (see for instance: Kukliński, 2001; Lawton Smith, 2006; Youtie & Shapira, 2008). All in all, the changing role of universities—and research organisations in general—translates into more links crossing the boundaries of the ivory tower, more inter-organisational cooperation, and, as a result, more spatially distinct patterns of research collaboration.

5.1.3 Costs of collaboration

The benefits from collaboration need to be examined in juxtaposition with the costs and risks of collaborative work—some of them directly associated with the geographical dimension of scientific collaboration. The decision to engage in scholarly collaboration is based on the trade-off between the effort of collaboration and its expected effects (Bikard, Murray, & Gans, 2015). Maintaining too many or too demanding external relations with closer and more distant partners can lead to high costs of collaboration resulting from, among others, information overload, unclear responsibility, and communication constraints of diverse origins. The costs are captured by the notion of coordination costs. Coordination costs are higher in inter-institutional and geographically dispersed collaborative networks than in single-institution projects. The costs are derived from both institutional features (e.g., publication practices, salary scales, performance assessment practices) and geographical characteristics of the collaborating institutions. Spatial separation of collaborating organisations may significantly add to coordination costs. For instance, Cummings and Kiesler noticed that "Geographical distance can slow group communication and consensus making, and a problem at one location may go unnoticed by researchers at the other universities" (2007, p. 1621). Enormous progress in transportation and communication technologies, as well as effective management practices, may substantially reduce coordination costs, although this might be more straightforward for monetary than for non-monetary costs. The former category relates to travelling between different places and virtual communication, while the latter is associated with variances in partners' semantic models, which have to be coordinated in terms of their research background, collaboration portfolio, and territory-dependent factors like institutions, language, and culture (Button et al., 1993).

The concept of coordination costs relates to the broader theory of transaction cost economics. This theory addresses the costs involved in market exchange as a factor that shapes the behaviour of individuals and organisations. Oliver E. Williamson—following the findings of Ronald Coase included in his famous paper "The Nature of the Firm" (1937)—claimed that economic organisations emerge from cost-minimising behaviour, including the strive to reduce transaction costs, in conditions of limited information and opportunism (Williamson, 1991). This way of thinking can be applied to scholarly collaboration. Collaboration occurs when the resources needed for the specific units are less costly to mobilise in the network of relations than on the market (e.g., acquisition of research results) or with the use of internal potential (e.g., by means of the given institutions). This leads to the emergence of a hybrid organisation (or network organisation) which may take the form of various vertically integrated partnerships and agreements. The increasing complexity and monetary costs of contemporary research raise the transactional costs involved, resulting in more collaboration in science. Transaction cost economics also sheds light on the limits of collaboration: at a certain level of coordination costs, collaboration reaches its limit, and it becomes uncompetitive with more hierarchical forms of knowledge acquisition and creation.

5.2 Explaining patterns of scientific collaboration

Scientific collaboration flows unevenly across space. Some places are more likely to become hubs of collaboration; others persistently occupy peripheries of the global scientific web. Some nodes in this network tend to stick together, while others are unlikely to unite. Geography—certainly—plays its role here. But other, non-spatial factors also affect the formation and evolution of collaborative networks in space. This section evokes the most prominent concepts, models, and theories that make sense of the complex spatial patterns of research collaboration.

The review begins with spatial proximity—the rudimentary concept that, actually, explains a great deal of the geography of scientific collaboration. The probability of collaboration between people, organisations, or territories depends on the distance separating them: the lesser the distance, the higher the likelihood of collaboration. The extreme case of spatial proximity is collocation, i.e., being in the same place at the same time, either permanently (working in the same lab, building, or campus) or temporarily (during short visiting scholarships, project meetings, or conferences). Furthermore, proximity is a multifaceted feature, as it not only has a geographical dimension, but also non-spatial aspects: cognitive, cultural, economic, institutional, organisational, social, and technological. By and large, proximity can be imagined as a kind of similarity. Scholars specialising in the same field are cognitively closer than those working in different disciplines. Even spatial proximity can be conceptualised as similarity—for instance, researchers from the same lab are similar in terms of their working environment. This leads to an even more general notion that explains collaboration patterns: homophily, i.e., the tendency to connect with similar others.

Nonetheless, the triad collocation-proximity-homophily does not fully explain the complexity of scientific collaboration patterns. Despite the tendency to work with those located nearby, remote links are not uncommon. A number of explanations can be useful here. First, non-spatial proximities indicate advantages of spatially distant collaborations (e.g., in the case of laboratories working on the same topic but located on different continents). Second, collaboration is often based on complementarity, which means that collaborative links arise between dissimilar individuals or organisations—a tendency called heterophily. Third, nodes in collaboration networks—be they individuals, organisations, cities, regions, or countries—vary in their collaborative attractiveness. Those already well connected are generally preferred, and this is captured by the notion of preferential attachment. Also, those with larger capacities are the most favoured, which is explained by the gravity and node fitness models of collaboration. Finally, the characteristics of scientific fields, or even the unique features of particular research problems or methods, shape spatial patterns of research collaboration. Some scientific domains require organisation of research that is spatially concentrated or distributed in a strictly defined way, while for others geography is largely irrelevant.

5.2.1 Spatial proximity

Spatial proximity is the central category in the geography of scientific collaboration. This concept has been discussed in economic geography since the early 19th century, in the seminal works of Johann Heinrich von Thünen (1826) on the location of urban and agricultural activities, and Alfred Marshall (1890) on industrial districts. In simple words, proximity is a small distance between units, be they individuals, organisations, cities, or countries. What is understood by a "small distance" depends on the scale in which the given phenomena occur and in which the analysis is conducted. On one occasion, a small distance may be measured in kilometres, on others in metres. Very close proximity often equals collocation—a state of being in the same place at the same time.

At the individual level, spatial proximity enables face-to-face communication, which in turn can lead to collaboration. The relation between communication and distance in the workspace is captured by the so-called Allen curve, named after Thomas J. Allen from the MIT Sloan School of Management. In the 1970s, Allen showed that the frequency of communication between individuals in science and engineering organisations drops exponentially with the growing distance between their offices. The study identified the distance of 50 metres as critical for the probability of communication. Distances exceeding 50 metres did not differentiate the probability of communication, whereas distances below this threshold strongly encouraged interactions (Allen, 1977).

Spatial proximity can be thought of as physical or functional. The former is a simple linear distance between the units in question. The latter takes into account relationships among spaces visited by individuals in their daily routines. Lifts, stairwells, mailboxes, print rooms, coffee rooms, and restrooms—among others—create the opportunity to encounter colleagues from outside one's team and, in effect, increase the probability of establishing new collaborations. Consequently, two individuals are more likely to collaborate if their paths cross frequently or largely overlap (Festinger, Schachter, & Back, 1950; Kabo et al., 2014; Kabo et al., 2015).

The concepts of physical and functional spatial proximity can be combined with the notion of collocation. A long-term collocation equals high physical closeness—depending on the scale of an analysis it can be exemplified by working in the same lab, building, or campus. Meanwhile, functional proximity might be based on a short-term collocation. Again, depending on the spatial-temporal scale of an analysis, short-term collocation may refer to rapid encounters in lifts, minutes at workplace cafeteria tables, or substantially longer meetings at conferences or during visiting scholarships. The acknowledgement of the significant role of temporal collocation in stimulating collaboration has led to more pro-collaborative organisational and architectural designs (see: Allen & Henn, 2007). This pursuit has been described, somewhat teasingly, by Diane H. Sonnenwald: "universities should have only one water cooler or coffee machine, so that scientists would meet and get to know each another informally" (2007, p. 656).

All in all, the relation between spatial proximity and collaboration relies on two complementary mechanisms. On the one hand, proximity increases the likelihood of interaction. Those located closer to each other are more likely to meet, communicate, and initiate collaboration. On the other hand, proximity facilitates collaboration by reducing the transactional costs of initiating and conducting joint research. Communication and other interactions became less demanding if the interacting units are nearby or collocated. Therefore, spatially close collaboration is not only more likely to be initiated, but also sustained over a longer period.

5.2.2 Gravity versus distance

If spatial proximity explains a great deal of scientific collaboration, why in some cases do intensive scientific flows link places separated by thousands of kilometres? Chapter 4 showed that the global collaboration network in science is sewn together by the seams between world cities. Some of them, such as New York and Tokyo, are geographically separated, yet the scientific collaboration between them thrives. The proximity approach fails to explain this phenomenon. Other factors are apparently at play. New York and Tokyo collaborate despite the large distance separating them because they have amassed great scientific potential that makes the collaboration possible and attractive. In the complex network theory this phenomenon is referred to as the concept of node fitness. Nodes can vary in their inherent capability of attracting other nodes. The fitter the node, the more links it attracts (Bianconi & Barabási, 2001; Ke, 2013). This largely parallels the earlier and humbler idea: the gravity model. The model assumes that not only does the distance between collaborating units matter, but their masses should also be taken into account.

The socioeconomic gravity model is conceptually based on the well-known universal law of gravitation formulated by Isaac Newton. He realised that the gravitational force between two objects is proportional to their masses and inversely proportional to the square of their distance of separation. Against the background of scientific collaboration gravity, the model can be rephrased as:

$$INTERACTION_{ij} = \alpha \frac{MASS_i^{\beta 1} MASS_j^{\beta 2}}{DISTANCE_{ij}^{\beta 3}}$$

where $INTERACTION_{ij}$ is the intensity of flows (e.g., common projects, co-authorships, co-inventions) between units i and j (countries, cities, organisations, etc.). $MASS$ is the size of interacting units (e.g., number of publications, value of R&D spending, counts of research personnel). $DISTANCE$ is the measure of separation between units i and j. $\beta 1$ and $\beta 2$ are parameters modifying the influence of unit masses. The distinction between $\beta 1$ and $\beta 2$ makes it possible to capture directed flows, which are interactions where a sender and a receiver can be distinguished (citations, researcher mobility, coordinator-partner relations in inter-organisational projects, etc.). In such cases $\beta 1$ can be understood as the potential to generate flows, and $\beta 2$ as the potential to attract them (e.g., citing and being cited). In the case of undirected or reciprocal interactions, when the direction of flows is not determined (co-citation, co-authorship, co-invention, etc.), $\beta 1$ will be equal to $\beta 2$. Furthermore, parameter $\beta 3$ modifies the influence of the distance between i and j (e.g., decreasing rate of interactions with additional unit of distance). Finally, α is the model coefficient.

The gravity model was applied in social science to analyse migration flows as early as the 19th century (Carey, 1867; Ravenstein, 1885). Later, in the 1930s, it was used to examine patterns in retail (Reilly, 1931), and since the 1960s it has helped to portray spatial tendencies in international trade (Anderson, 2010). As might be expected, studies related to the spatial dimension of scientific collaboration have also been using the gravitational approach. The picture is clear: the probability and intensity of research collaboration are negatively related to the geographical distance which separates the units in question and are positively affected by their accumulated research potential (see: Andersson & Persson, 1993; Fischer, Scherngell, & Jansberger, 2006; Hoekman, Frenken, & Tijssen, 2010; Hoekman, Scherngell, Frenken, & Tijssen, 2013; Maggioni et al., 2007; Peri, 2005; Picci, 2010; Plotnikova & Rake, 2014; Ponds et al., 2007; Scherngell & Barber, 2009; Scherngell & Hu, 2011).

5.2.3 Beyond spatial proximity

Neither spatial closeness nor the force of collaborative gravity constitutes a sufficient condition for collaboration. Boschma and Iammarino put it straightforwardly: "it is unclear what a pig farmer can learn from a microchip company even though they are neighbours" (2009, p. 292). Indeed, even close neighbours need a minimal level of collaborative capacity to engage in meaningful cooperation. This capacity can be understood in terms of non-spatial proximities—a concept developed in the second half of the 20th century (Torre & Gilly, 2000). Various forms of non-spatial proximity—and distance—have been suggested: cognitive, cultural, economic, institutional, organisational, social, and technological, to name only those regularly discussed in the literature (see: Knoben & Oerlemans, 2006). In the context of research collaboration, the most prominent approach has been proposed by the aforequoted Dutch economist and geographer Ron Boschma (2005). His analytical framework encompasses five proximities, one geographical and four non-spatial: cognitive, organisational, social, and institutional.

Cognitive proximity is interpreted as similarity in the way actors perceive, understand, and evaluate the world (Wuyts, Colomb, Dutta, & Nooteboom, 2005). In every type of interaction, a minimum level of cognitive proximity—common basic knowledge—is necessary for effective communication. However, the role of cognitive proximity might be particularly important in the case of research collaboration due to the high level of reasoning capacities required to absorb, interpret, and communicate scientific knowledge (Broekel, 2015; Huber, 2012). Some authors focus on a subtype of cognitive proximity, i.e., technological proximity. This encompasses shared experiences and knowledge relating to particular technologies (Knoben & Oerlemans, 2006; Scherngell & Barber, 2009).

Organisational proximity refers to (1) organisational membership, for instance, people in the same organisation or organisations belonging to the same network, and (2) organisational similarity, for example, a university is organisationally closer to other higher education institutions than to any kind of industrial enterprise. The second approach is related to institutional proximity. It can be understood as the similarity of macro-level institutional frameworks that determine the way people's behaviour is coordinated (Ponds et al., 2007). This definition is derived from the understanding of institutions as socially constructed frameworks of political, economic, and social interaction. The rules can be informal, such as customs, traditions, and codes of conduct, or formal, usually identified with laws and other official regulations (North, 1991). The common space of mental models, norms, and procedures (e.g., scientific reward schemes) eases communication and transfer of knowledge (Kirat & Lung, 1999). Thus, in general, collaboration between scientists from the same institutional context, country, region, or sector, flows more smoothly than when it is international or intersectoral (Cassi, Morrison, & Rabellotti, 2015; Ponds et al., 2007; Hoekman et al., 2010).

Social proximity relates to belonging to the same space of social relations based on friendship, kinship, and joint experiences. This proximity is sometimes called personal (Schamp, Rentmeister, & Lo, 2004) or relational (Coenen, Moodysson, & Asheim, 2004). Scientific collaboration benefits from social proximity because it facilitates open communication, durable non-opportunistic relationships, and the exchange of tacit knowledge. Although trust, friendship, and kinship are personal characteristics, studies on the role of social proximity in scholarly collaboration often focus on such relations between organisations or territories—in this case, social proximity is attributed to groups, not to individuals (Autant-Bernard, Billand, Frachisse, & Massard, 2007; Balland, 2012). An example of such an approach is the study of scientific collaboration among European regions conducted by Capello and Caragliu (2018). They defined social proximity as a similarity in the level of regional social capital, measured using survey data from the European Values Study.

The concept of non-spatial proximities is particularly important for the geography of science in the extent to which non-spatial proximities correlate with spatial distance. For instance, social proximity often arises from close spatial proximity or collocation. Institutional proximity can also be associated with physical closeness, since formal and informal institutions are often embedded at national level. Individuals located in a given country operate within the same institutional framework. This means that—as a rule—they are characterised by a high level of institutional proximity. At the same time, in the majority of cases, possible collaborators within the same country are spatially much closer than those from the overseas. This leads to the so-called same (or own) country preference—the tendency to collaborate with individuals within the same country (as well as the same organisation, city, or region). By the same token, neighbouring or nearby countries often share socioeconomic, historical, and cultural backgrounds—in this case spatial and non-spatial proximities are also entangled (Kato & Ando, 2017).

5.2.4 The Goldilocks principle

In many circumstances, the most wanted partners for collaboration are not the closest, neither spatially nor non-spatially. For instance, all interdisciplinary collaborations rely on links between cognitively distant individuals or organisations. Furthermore, it is believed that innovation and creativity ripen in the sun of diversity. The most difficult and demanding problems have a better chance of being solved by multidisciplinary teams, frequently composed of scientists from different countries, representing varied scientific cultures or even other paradigms (Gazni et al., 2012; van Rijnsoever & Hessels, 2011). The engagement of dissimilar partners prevents cognitive lock-in—the situation when the similarity of collaborators' knowledge, skills, and competences is so high that it inhibits innovativeness (Heringa, Horlings, van der Zouwen, van den Besselaar, & van Vierssen, 2014; Nooteboom, Van Haverbeke, Duysters, Gilsing, & van den Oord, 2007; Visser & Boschma, 2004).

This leads to the observation that collaborators do not simply aim to minimalise the distance, but rather to reach a point of equilibrium on the close-distant continuum. The tendency to collaborate with similar others is balanced by the need to unite resources, skills, and efforts with dissimilar ones. The first tendency is known as homophily (love of the same), the second as heterophily (love of the different). The interplay of these two opposing tendencies governs scientific collaboration patterns. It can be seen as an example of the Goldilocks principle: collaborative networks arise between partners that are neither too close nor too far (Fitjar, Huber, & Rodríguez-Pose, 2016), or—more realistically—between units that are close in one dimension and far in the other. For instance, the analysis of 280 collaboration networks in Germany revealed that increasing geographical distance is correlated with increasing cognitive proximity between organisations. Spatially close knowledge contacts—in some cases—tend to be more cognitively diverse, while geographically distant links require higher levels of cognitive closeness (Broekel, 2015). Congruent conclusions stem from the analysis of an information technology cluster located in Cambridge, UK (Huber, 2012), a case study of the Tallinn University of Technology, Estonia (Kuttim, 2016), and the cross-sectional study of interregional research collaboration networks in Europe (Capello & Caragliu, 2018). This implies that different types of proximities in scientific collaboration not only co-occur (as for instance spatial and institutional proximity), but can sometimes substitute each other. In the aforementioned examples, cognitive closeness can be treated as a substitution for physical proximity. Similarly, this kind of substitutive mechanism can be seen in the relation between spatial and organisational proximity. Being a part of the same organisation, even distributed worldwide, not only facilitates collaboration, but can indeed impose collaboration on previously non-collaborating members.

5.2.5 Preferential attachment

While at the level of links between individual nodes—as described in the previous section—some moderating tendencies can be found; at the network level, the opposite, cumulative trends prevail. In research networks, typically, a small fraction of nodes have many links, while the large majority have just a few. The pattern closely resembles the so-called scale-free network: a network characterised by the power-law degree distribution (in contrast to the normal, Gaussian distribution) (Clauset, Shalizi, & Newman, 2009; Newman, 2004).[3] In such networks, the key positions are occupied by a very limited number of hubs directly linked to many other, sparsely connected nodes. In science this role is played by star scientists, world-class research institutions, and—in the spatial perspective—places that concentrate the two previously mentioned.

The star, or the hub-and-spoke, phenomenon in scientific collaboration is well exemplified by Hungarian mathematician Paul Erdős (1913–1996). Erdős, with a publication count of about 1,500, is believed to be the most prolific mathematician known. He was also one of the most collaborative—the list of his co-authors exceeds 500. In recognition of his enormous output, his colleagues created a scientific parlour game of calculating the Erdős number. The measure describes the number of handshakes between a person and the famous mathematician, as measured by the co-authorship of papers. For Erdős the number is 0, for his co-author it is 1, for co-authors of Erdős's co-authors it is 2, etc. (Castro & Grossman, 1999; Goffman, 1969). Apparently, the extensive collaboration network developed by Erdős is an outstanding exception in comparison to the average scholar's collaborative engagement.

But why do scholars like Erdős—and by the same token certain institutions or locations—attract such a disproportionate number of collaborators? Some explanations have been already presented in the above sections. These are, namely, amassed capacities and node fitness: the variables that can be roughly thought of as quantitative and qualitative characteristics of nodes. Meanwhile, the scale-free network theory offers a different explanation, one focused not on a node's attributes, but on its position in the network: the concept of preferential attachment. According to this mechanism, a new node preferentially attaches to those that are already well connected. In other words, the likelihood of a new link being created is proportional to the nodes' degree (Barabási & Albert, 1999). As a result, units that are well connected become even better connected. This prompts one of the better known concepts in the sociology of science: the Matthew effect. The term—coined by a couple of American sociologists, Harriet Zuckerman and Robert Merton—originally referred to the cumulative advantage of credit allocation in scientific communities (Merton, 1968; Merton, 1988).[4] But the notion of the Matthew effect equally depicts the process of accumulating new collaborative relationships by units—either individuals, organisations, cities, regions, or even countries—that already have extensive collaboration networks.

5.2.6 Disciplinary spatial bias

All the above described mechanisms shaping spatial patterns of scientific collaborations can be found in every scientific discipline. However, the level of their expression—the genetic analogy comes in handy—varies in accordance with the field and the type of scientific endeavour. This effect goes far beyond the frequently discussed discipline differences in the mean number of authors per paper or the typical project team size. Consider the structure of collaboration networks in particle physics, where large teams of researchers depend on a unique infrastructure, as opposed to the collaborative patterns in mathematics, where specialised equipment is rarely required, and where solo or small team projects prevail (mavericks of the Erdős type being notable exceptions). Undoubtedly, collaboration in experimental particle physics is far more spatially bound than collaboration in the field of theoretical mathematics.

Caroline Wagner (2008) proposed a systematic approach that makes sense of these differences. She distinguished two dimensions that frame collaborative undertakings in contemporary science: spatial and organisational. The spatial axis ranges from geographically centralised to spatially distributed research. The first end of the continuum is exemplified by projects that either need a unique infrastructure (say a large cyclotron) or have to be conducted in a unique environment (e.g., a distinctive Himalayan ecosystem). The other limit of the range encompasses research that can be performed in any—in principle at least—location (such as the previously mentioned theoretical mathematics). The organisational axis refers to the way the research is initiated and managed, from the top-down, hierarchical, precisely planned organisation (typical in drug research), to the bottom-up, networked, ad-hoc organisation (frequently encountered in cross-country comparative studies in social sciences). The juxtaposition of the two axes results in four types of collaborative research: megascience (centralised and top-down), geotic (centralised and bottom-up), participatory (distributed and top-down), and coordinated (distributed and bottom-up).

Each of Wagner's four types is associated with specific spatial patterns of research collaboration. Megascience is defined by a distinctive large-scale research infrastructure, such as Fermilab near Chicago or CERN in Switzerland—the landmarks of big science. This category of research typically involves many individuals, numbering hundreds or thousands. Noticeably, not all of the researchers involved have to conglomerate in the spot where the key equipment is located. On the contrary, megascience teams are frequently spread all over the world (particularly when it comes to the analysis of large amounts of data produced by megascience projects, which can be performed in spatially distant locations).

Geotic research is spatially anchored by unique research conditions. In many disciplines, some places simply need to be visited in order to investigate them or run experiments in specific, unreproducible environments (e.g., the South Pole, a rainforest, or an archaeological site). Researchers from all over the world travel to these unique locations, spend some time there, and return to their home institutions. This temporary collocation, in turn, creates a favourable environment for establishing new spontaneous collaborative relations.

For participatory and coordinated collaborative projects, the exact location of conducted research is largely irrelevant. The difference between the two is in the organisation of the collaborative work. Participatory research projects are initiated in a top-down process and are centrally managed. For example, the Human Genome Project was executed in dozens of laboratories all over the world, each of which had precisely defined responsibilities in order to avoid unnecessary duplication. In contrast, coordinated projects are organised in a bottom-up manner. An example might be the Global Biodiversity Information Facility—an international collaboration focused on collecting and sharing scientific data on biodiversity. Participatory and coordinated research projects often take the form of inter-organisational networks that are characterised—inter alia—by voluntary membership and collaborative governance (Alter & Hage, 1993; Chisholm, 1998; Kilduff & Tsai, 2007). However, a participatory, top-down organisation of research incorporates hierarchical network structures, while coordinated projects involve more horizontal coordination within flat organisational structures.

Participatory and coordinated projects typically make extensive use of information and communication technologies. In this instance, the site that draws collaborators together is not a physical place, but a virtual space, such as a website, common database, or another virtual room created by collaborative software. Undoubtedly, an information and communication infrastructure is important in all four types of research. But with regard to coordinated and participatory research, virtual spaces are much more important, as they typically have no specific place where collaborators need to assemble. Does this mean that these two modes of collaborative projects have no spatial dimension? Certainly not. The conclusion is slightly more moderate: spatial patterns of participatory and coordinated research are subject to the general forces that shape spatial patterns of scientific collaboration: spatial and non-spatial distance, gravity and fitness of nodes, and the preferential attachment principle. In contrast, megascience and geotic research can modify the way in which these forces operate—for instance, the establishment of a unique infrastructure generates new proximities and new forces of attraction.

5.3 Explaining the impacts of scientific collaboration

The preceding subchapter considered selected concepts, explaining how territorial features influence scientific collaboration. The current part focuses on the other side of the relationship: the impact of scientific collaboration on the territory. In this context the most vital question is how scientific collaboration boosts progress in science and—at the end of the day—the economic development of cities, communities, and regions. The first part of the question lies in the main current of scholarly debate, however, the answers are often limited to the immediate effects rather than long-term impacts. The second part of the question is rarely, if ever, asked explicitly. A rich variety of regional and local development theories discuss the role of research capacities and processes. The debate focuses, in particular, on mechanisms of innovativeness and on intersectoral links—namely, knowledge flows between science and industry—while purely scientific collaboration remains in the background. However, understanding the processes of socioeconomic development through the lenses of scientific collaboration is not feasible without accounting for the mechanisms of scientific collaboration impact on the science sector itself.

This part of the book brings to light factors and processes that determine the impacts of scientific collaboration on science and on regional development. The review covers sources from theories developed within various disciplines, such as sociology of science, economic geography, innovation studies, and organisation management. As regards perspective, the theories span from micro-level approaches oriented on organisational units, such as the industrial district, clusters concepts, and the strength of weak ties, towards macro-level approaches that are regionally oriented, such as the regional innovation systems, the triple helix, and the learning region. The concepts in question differ in many dimensions, but in terms of the impacts of scientific collaboration, their common interests are important. First, the intersectorality of research collaboration, which is accountable for the processes of collective learning that relate to the production and application of knowledge, as well as to enhancing the institutional component of regional development. Second, the concomitance of competition and collaboration, which facilitates gaining an advantage in both science and regional development. Third, the spatial aspect of collaboration, upon which the final rewards from collaboration substantially depend. In this spirit the remaining part of the subchapter will be constructed, heralded by a general reflection on the mechanisms behind the direct and indirect impacts of scientific collaboration.

5.3.1 Direct and indirect effects

Scientific collaboration provides direct and indirect stimuli for the development of science. The direct impact applies to a given collaboration case, while the indirect impact spills over spatially and temporally. The allegedly superior significance and influence of joint work in comparison to individual research has induced scholars to reflect on possible explanations (Beaver, 2004). A remarkable answer to this problem was formulated by philosopher K. Brad Wray as the concept of the epistemic significance of collaborative research. Wray argues that the power of collaborative research lies in its ability to justify scientific discoveries by the scholarly community. The results achieved by a group of collaborating researchers with different backgrounds, knowledge, and methodological approaches are supposed to have a more objective overtone. Collaboration allows for not only the cross-fertilisation of ideas, but also for a cross-validation of assumptions, processes, and outcomes. In turn, the results of collaborative work are more likely to be acknowledged by the academic community. In other words, collaborative work enhances the epistemic validity of research outputs (Wray, 2002).

The indirect impact of collaboration on the development of science relies on the intensification of knowledge spillovers across members of the research community. This mechanism works as a side effect. Cross-fertilisation among collaborators can go beyond the specific subject of the current collaboration. Such knowledge spillovers reinforce the effect of their current and future collaborative research endeavours, undertaken individually or in a different configuration of partners. The way to depict the presence of knowledge spillovers is to look for the consequences of collaborative relationship dissolution. The premature death of a scholar provides a quasi-experimental situation in which collaboration is ended by an exogenous factor. The study of the collaborative networks of 112 eminent life scientists who unexpectedly passed away confirmed lasting detrimental effects on the research performance of their collaborators. The long-term decline in their quality-adjusted publication rate was shown to be as high as 5–8 percent (Azoulay, Graff Zivin, & Wang, 2010). Congruent conclusions stem from another quasi-experimental situation. During World War I, the world split into two: the Allied camp (the United Kingdom, France, the United States, and a number of smaller countries) and the Central camp (Germany, Austria-Hungary, the Ottoman Empire, Bulgaria). This resulted in the disruption of knowledge flows between scholars belonging to the two detached groups. This was visible in the decrease in citations between them and the dissimilarity of the titles of scientific papers produced by the separated groups of scholars. The lower accessibility of recent knowledge negatively affected the quality of scientific outcomes: scholars who based their work on frontier, cutting-edge science published fewer papers in top scientific journals, took part in fewer Nobel Prize–nominated research projects, and introduced fewer novel scientific words in both papers and patent applications (Iaria, Schwarz, & Waldinger, 2018).

The indirect impacts of scientific collaboration are even more evident in non-science sectors, where knowledge spills over into activities undertaken by other regional actors. The reason for this is twofold. First, scientific endeavours take place in various kinds of organisations, not only universities and research institutes, but also companies, corporations, and non-profit private laboratories. Second, the outputs of research carried out in the R&D sector are translated into socioeconomic practice. In other words, applied knowledge very often results from collaborative work. Hence, scientific collaboration indirectly influences regional development. Nevertheless, there is also a reverse causation flow from the regional environment to scientific practice. The external environment elicits new ideas and provides opportunities (and funding) to develop, test, and modify scientific theories (see for instance Goddard & Vallance, 2013; Sánchez-Barrioluengo, 2014). However, the so-called environmental effect depends on the region's level of development and technological advancement. On one end of the continuum there are economically lagging regions with low levels of innovativeness, on the other—highly developed locations and strong innovators. Developed regions have the advantage of a vibrant business sector. In such regions, companies are characterised by greater accumulated expertise, higher capacities to absorb new knowledge, more employment opportunities for university graduates, and greater willingness to collaborate with the R&D sector, contrary to their counterparts from peripheral regions (Bonaccorsi & Secondi, 2017). This logic also applies to the inverted science-region relationship. On the one hand, a weak science sector is able to produce knowledge flows of imitative character, which can only be of mediocre use to regional development. On the other, high-value knowledge can lead to more spectacular development and may also be applied more broadly, beyond the regional boundaries.

5.3.2 Intersectoral knowledge flows

The indirect impacts of scientific collaboration on science advancement and knowledge-based regional development are facilitated by intersectorality. This works on different levels and dimensions, as intersectorality greases the wheels of knowledge production, circulation, and application that require links among various sectors. The application stage is essential for processes of regional development because the balance between the demand and the supply of knowledge can be achieved in the process of intersectoral collaboration. Strongly connected producers, transmitters, and users of knowledge of different sectoral provenances ensure that knowledge is attuned to the regional needs. This can increase innovativeness and, in the long run, positively affect regional performance.

Regional development theories see scientific collaboration predominantly as an intersectoral phenomenon which takes place in diverse environments among manifold interrelated actors involved in multilevel knowledge production, transfer, and utilisation. The names of some theories directly allude to the meaningful contribution of intersectoral processes to regional growth. For instance, the name of the triple helix theory, formulated by the duo of eminent innovation scholars, Henry Etzkowitz and Loet Leydesdorff (1995), uses a metaphor borrowed from the natural sciences. It suggests the presence of interactions among three systems, referred to here as helices: science, business, and public administration. The above-mentioned theoretical concepts derive intersectorality from different premises. The regional system of innovation perceives collaboration as a consequence of the systemic nature of innovation, which requires interactions among sectors. The triple helix concept derives intersectorality from the growing role in regional development played by science and its interactions with other sectors. Meanwhile, the cluster theory explains intersectorality as the requirements of businesses in the knowledge-based economy.

Two complementary mechanisms are triggered by intersectorality: collective learning and the regulatory role of institutions. Regional collective learning is a dynamic, interactive, and cumulative process which brings about the enlargement and improvement of knowledge. Intersectorality allows each sector to capitalise on the resources and skills of other sectors, thus triggering synergies in the region through the common use of available knowledge, mutual evaluation of ideas, and monitoring of each sector's outputs. To put it simply, regional collective learning is a "territorial counterpart of the learning that takes place within the firm" (Capello, 2007, pp. 198–199). This supposition creates foundations for the *milieu innovateur* concept, developed in the 1980s by the Groupe de Recherche Européen (GREMI) (Aydalot, 1986). Knowledge spillovers within the milieu are facilitated by high mobility of the labour force, cooperation for innovation among knowledge suppliers and users, and local spin-offs (Camagni, 1991b). Based on the assumption that the region acts as a focal point for knowledge creation and learning, Richard Florida coined the notion of the learning region (1995). This has been further autonomously developed in the groundbreaking works of Bengt-Åke Lundvall (1996), Bjørn Asheim (1996), Kevin Morgan (1997), and many others (see: Rutten & Boekema, 2007). While the learning region concentrates on the processes of learning based on interactions among sectors in the region, the triple helix underlines the role of functional substitution in these sectors: universities are increasingly involved in the commercialisation of knowledge, enterprises are developing academic functions, and administration is becoming entrepreneurial (Etzkowitz & Leydesdorff, 1995).

At the same time, all the above-mentioned concepts highlight the key role of regional institutions in the process of multisectoral collective learning. Institutions are represented by the set of norms, codes, and rules in which regional actors operate. Moreover, these rules of the game are embodied in concrete institutions, i.e., organisations. The relative richness or scarcity of institutional structures—so-called institutional thickness—allegedly determines the economic development of regions (Beer & Lester, 2015; Henry & Pinch, 2001). Synergies of interacting institutions facilitate interactive learning (Amin & Thrift, 1994). A unique institutional infrastructure supports innovation within the production structure of the region (Asheim & Gertler, 2005). The role of institutions in the cluster concept is to ensure its smooth and effective operation (Porter, 1998). Interacting institutions in regions are hypothesised to form distinct regional innovation systems—a concept framed by Philip Cooke (1992). The regional innovation system sustains intensive knowledge interactions that take place within and between two institutional subsystems: (1) knowledge generation and diffusion, and (2) knowledge application and exploitation. Both subsystems are embedded in a common regional socioeconomic and cultural setting, influenced by regional policy and linked to national and international innovation systems (Autio, 1998; Cooke, 1998a; Tödtling & Trippl, 2005). The institutional layer is also an important element of the triple helix concept, although here the emphasis is placed on the establishment of new institutions triggered by the interrelation of regional subsectors. Intermediate institutions such as spin-offs, academic incubators, technology transfer centres, technological parks, patent offices, and local production agreements integrate the functions of the three helices and ease interactions within the whole regional system. This, in turn, stimulates knowledge production (as in Mode 2 described in section 5.1) and facilitates knowledge transfer and consumption (Etzkowitz & Leydesdorff, 2000).

Recent progress in the presented concepts gives even more weight to the growing role of intersectorality. This is evident in the case of the triple helix, the evolution of which led to two more sectors being added to the initial concept (Carayannis, Campbell, & Rehman, 2016). The quadruple helix adds a social dimension—the civil society helix. This helix defines the demand for innovation. The quintuple helix incorporates the helix of the natural environment. These developments place the system of collaborative knowledge creation and use in an up-to-date context, acknowledging the role of social innovation and sustainable development.

5.3.3 Coopetition

Relationships among individuals and organisations are not necessarily collaborative. Collaboration is frequently—perhaps always and necessarily—accompanied by competition. The effects of collaboration can be more spectacular if achieved in a competitive environment. At the same time, competition is stimulated by collaboration, which is crucial to gaining advantage both in science and in regional development. The relationship between collaboration and competition is thus interdependent: "Collaboration and competition are not mutually exclusive, they are two aspects of the same more general process" (Atkinson et al., 1998, p. 230). Moreover, as David Smith aptly noticed, "Collaboration and competition co-exist along a continuum; the boundary between the two is rarely neat or tidy" (2001, p. 142). The co-occurrence and dynamic equilibrium between competition and collaboration is referred as coopetition, a term coined within the framework of business management (Brandenburger & Nalebuff, 1996).

The processes of collaboration and competition might seem contradictory, as they are based on opposing logics of interaction. However, the coexistence of collaboration and competition is common. Numerous examples from the business sector, mostly involving large companies, confirm that cooperation with competitors is seen as the most advantageous strategy for improving business performance, in particular in the field of innovation (Bengtsson & Kock, 2000; Gnyawali & Park, 2011). But make no mistake: coopetition also contributes to the development of small and medium-size enterprises, as already acknowledged by Italian scholars, the fathers of industrial district theory (Ottati, 1994). Moreover, the positive influence of coopetition can also be extended beyond the business sector. It can be applied equally well to the science sector.

The naïve picture of scholars who avoid competitive behaviour and prefer to collaborate is out of touch with the complex realm of scientific work. Robert Merton, in his pioneering work on the sociology of science (1973), described science as a process of competitive cooperation. He described scientists as competitive peers (compeers) to underline that science is as much competitive as collaborative. It is undeniable that the scientific rewards go to those scholars who win the race to a new discovery, are first to observe a new phenomenon, or present brand new results. Simultaneously, one can hardly win a competition without being part of cooperative structures. Thus, while scholars and research organisations rival each other, to gain success they readily strive to join their efforts, resources, and knowledge. Researchers compete to achieve breakthrough results and, correspondingly, gain access to funds awarded by a grant formula. Scholarly organisations compete for talented staff and students, as well as for a high-profile reputation as shown in various rankings. Yet, simultaneously, collaboration occurs and is necessary in the same fields as competition: Teams of excellent scholars are better prepared to win research grants. A pool of talented staff can be created through collaboration. The organisation of larger scientific endeavours or events, such as international congresses, is easier in larger teams, while joint promotional actions abroad facilitate student enrolment. Collaboration enhances competition, but the reverse causation also applies here: a competitive environment is a prerequisite for better results of scholarly collaboration. Joint research performed under pressure of rivalry limits negative outcomes, such as duplication of efforts or experiments, delays in preparing probes or data, lack of peer feedback, or publishing only partial results (Atkinson et al., 1998; Nickelsen & Krämer, 2016).

Coopetition strategies adopted by scientific institutions, likewise enterprises, depend on various variables, e.g., the overlap of their fields of specialisation, the number of interacting partners, the temporal dimension, and spatial collocation (Gnyawali, He, & Madhavan, 2008). Collaboration among competitors might be impeded by geographical overlapping. In this case, the relevance of both collaboration (for example joint purchases) and competition (for instance for students) becomes very high (Dal-Soto & Monticelli, 2017). The temporal dimension of coopetition depends on the dynamics of the relationships between research institutions, which can cooperate and compete simultaneously, at different points in time or sequentially (Chien & Peng, 2005).

Natalie Angier, a science writer, observed that "To thrive in science, you must be both a consummate collaborator and a relentless competitor. You must balance, with an almost gymnastic precision, the need to cooperate against the call to battle" (1988, p. 14). The trick is to understand the mechanisms behind coopetition in order to adopt an appropriate strategy in which rivalry does not prevail, but is stimulating enough to gain the most from collaboration. A telling example is the analysis of the micropolitics of an informal research coalition which led to the breakthrough discovery of the gene responsible for myotonic dystrophy, followed by the simultaneous publication of three collaborative papers in *Nature*. The dynamics of collaboration and competition among these research groups depended on the phase of the research. Open flows of information and probes—however carefully managed—as well as personal ties among researchers belonging to different groups gradually decreased as the study progressed. The fiercest rivalry, combined with harsh relations among scholars, occurred when the discovery was about to be published. The individual race for publication and the related rewards in the form of recognition, access to funding, and career enhancement replaced collective work. The pendulum swung again in favour of collaboration after the disclosure of the discovery. It set up the research scene anew: once more, each group of scholars possessed the same knowledge and had no marginal advantage related to timing, research material, or methodology. It was also a period of playing straight because new lines of scientific inquiry needed to be mapped out and new coalitions had to be formed (Atkinson et al., 1998).

Besides relations within the science sector, ties existing among scientific institutions, enterprises, and public administration also bear the hallmarks of coopetition. Such ties are forged within "a coalition which brings together actively involved people who belong to different sectors, but share the same interests, values and common goals" (Daidj & Jung, 2011, p. 40). Coopetition increases the dynamic of relations, spurs the process of mutual learning, and, as a result, can improve the efficiency of the whole regional economy. In other words, coopetition works as a catalyst of relations among various regional players and as an accelerator of positive synergies leading to regional growth. The coopetitive approach provides the essence of cluster theory (Porter, 1990) and theories of regional growth in general, although intersectoral relations are investigated less commonly than those among enterprises (Bengtsson & Raza-Ullah, 2016). The triple helix concept, due to the overlapping roles of different sectors, is naturally based on the competition of collaborating partners (Mongkhonvanit, 2014). This interplay among the roles of helices may cause positive outcomes, likewise the concurrence of three types of interaction within systems of innovation (Edquist, 2005): competition, networking, and transaction. Together they constitute a growth-friendly environment and increase the performance of the given system of innovation (OECD, 2002; Stamboulis, 2007).

However, apart from positive results, coopetition may challenge regional development by demanding greater coordination and dynamic adjustment of each actor's strategy. For instance, the level of coopetitive tension influences enterprises' inclination to adopt an open model of innovation (Mention, 2011). Corporate strategy choices may further impact the behaviour of other regional actors (including those from the science sector), limit the innovativeness of the whole system, and detrimentally influence regional performance (Ritala, Huizingh, Almpanopoulou, & Wijbenga, 2017).

5.3.4 Local and global networks

The impacts of scientific collaboration, both direct and indirect, are spatially dependent. The space dividing collaborators modulates the results of research collaboration. However, it is not clear whether close or distant partnerships are of greater value. Concurrent concepts and approaches provide seemingly contradictory evidence: some underline the role of proximity; others favour distance. Theories that favour proximity rely on the assumption that the regional environment provides an optimum mix of factors for knowledge-based development. The favourable conditions for the innovative interplay among various regional actors enhance dissemination of tacit knowledge that is believed to be socially and economically sticky (Cowan, David, & Foray, 2000). The positive influence of actors' proximity on collaboration impact is rooted in the concept of industrial districts, initialised in the late 19th century by Alfred Marshal. He noticed that the spatial concentration of business entities gives a number of advantages for the entire network of firms in the given location (Lazerson & Lorenzoni, 1999). The importance of regional settings was afterwards tested through investigating the miracle of the so-called Third Italy observed during the economic crisis of the 1970s (Becattini, 2002; Capello, 2007). Michael Porter explained these regularities within the framework of the diamond of competitiveness, in which geographic proximity is the fundamental factor for cluster development.[5] The fact that geographical proximity of partners releases positive outcomes of collaboration is also underlined in other concepts, such as the regional innovation system, the innovative milieu, and the learning region (Lorentzen, 2008).

Concurrently, regional scientists have long suggested that being reliant mostly, or even exclusively, on proximate, intraregional links limits the positive outcomes that could be achieved by the local economy. The proximity approach gradually became out of tune with globalisation trends. In the globalised economy, the main players build their competitive advantage on multi-locality, not restricting themselves to the immediate environment in obtaining resources, knowledge in particular. The same applies to regions which are less (or perceived as less) self-contained, autarkic systems, but rather entities operating in the global context. As Roberto Camagni argues, local milieu need to be linked to the global network to avoid an "entropic death" (1991a). Amin and Thrift (1992) follow his argument and perceive clusters of locally embedded firms as neo-Marshallian nodes in global networks, while Tödtling (1994) underlines that place cannot be seen as an exclusive driving force for innovative firms to develop, as they are becoming increasingly integrated into the global economy.

Acknowledging that both proximity and distance might influence the impact of collaborative endeavours brings more complexity into regional development theories, but also makes them better able to reflect the economic reality. The contradicting perspectives setting local and global relations in opposition have been replaced by the thesis that collaboration limited to specific geographical boundaries is insufficient in most cases, in particular in the context of the knowledge-based economy (McCann, 2007). As Bathelt aptly noticed, "local cannot be seen in isolation from other spatial levels" (2011, p. 150). The exposure to new perspectives boosts the creativity of the whole system and prevents a cognitive lock-in effect (Fleming et al., 2007). The role of different external links of national, inter-regional, and global character for the purpose of maximising collaboration impact became the key point in the evolution of the industrial district concept (Rabellotti, Carabelli, & Hirsch, 2009). Processes of knowledge creation and application typically involve collaboration on various spatial levels, as underlined in the complex interrelations among theories of sectoral, regional, national, and global innovation systems (Asheim & Gertler, 2005; Binz & Truffer, 2017; Lundvall, 2007). Remarkably, this open approach is not recent—it was already present in Phillip Cooke's classic typology of regional innovation systems (Cooke, 1998b).

In the context of scientific collaboration, the empirical evidence for the superior importance of distant relations prevails. Papers co-authored with remote collaborators have a greater chance of accumulating citations than papers co-authored by spatially proximate groups. Long distance usually equates to international collaboration—thus, a higher level of internationalisation is associated with greater impact, at least when measured by citations (for a detailed discussion of the evidence, see section 4.3). However, this does not mean that local cooperation is irrelevant. The key distinction is not between local and long-distance collaboration, but between collaboration and its absence. As Katz and Hicks stated in their classic work on collaboration and citations, the impact of papers is higher "if there is collaboration of some kind" (1997, p. 554). Considering the quality, visibility, and impact of research outputs, local collaboration is definitely better than solitary work. Furthermore, a wider, more distant network of collaboration is more advantageous than exclusively local links.

The discussion has so far focused on demonstrating the complexity of the relationship between the extent of cooperation and its impact, both within the realms of science and in the wider context of regional and local development. However, the key question is, how can one explain the positive impacts of both proximity and distance on collaboration effects? One possible answer is given by the theory of the strength of weak ties, coined by Mark Granovetter in the 1970s. The American sociologist showed that not only strong ties—i.e., those among family members, friends, or close collaborators—have practical value. Weak ties—those with distant acquaintances—in some circumstances might be even more valuable, as they provide access to information and opportunities not accessible via strong ties (Granovetter, 1973). Similar conclusions can be drawn from the later theory of structural holes proposed by American sociologist Ronald Stuart Burt. A structural hole is an existing or possible relation between two nodes in a network, connecting groups of nodes that are otherwise isolated. Being in the position of a structural gap in the network is particularly beneficial because it gives access to complementary sources of information and can even allow you to control the flows of information in the network (Burt, 1992). We can assume—somewhat simplistically—that Burt's structural holes are equivalent to Granovetter's weak ties (Borgatti & Lopez-Kidwell, 2011). Moreover, in the context of geography, we can expect that as the distance between nodes grows, the relationships between them are increasingly likely to be weaker and to be characterised as structural holes.

Further application of this approach to innovative studies has led to the conclusion that strong and weak relations have different impacts on the collaboration result. Strong ties, understood as intensive and close links among various units (peoples, organisations, territories) facilitate flows of tacit and highly complex knowledge because closely related units tend to have a common knowledge base. On the contrary, weak ties that loosely link distant entities featuring limited knowledge redundancy are characteristic of the transmission of codified and less compound knowledge (Fleming, King, & Juda, 2007). In the innovative process, weak ties provide opportunities to access new sources of knowledge and can lead to groundbreaking inventions. That is hardly possible in the case of strong ties, which lead rather to incremental innovations (Hauser, Tappeiner, & Walde, 2007). Additionally, weak ties can compensate for a peripheral position in the network by providing access to the most influential nodes and offering the chance to gain a fine share of the knowledge pie. This is due to the fact that the position in the network matters more than the strength of relations.

The model of local buzz versus global pipelines adapts the strength of the weak ties concept to the spatial context. The point of departure for the idea of global pipelines was a refutation of the thesis that sustained, direct, and strong interactions related to knowledge flows in the local environment are sufficient for innovative development (Storper & Venables, 2004). Local buzz—which results from physical as well as cognitive, organisational, and technological proximity—usually does not provide enough input for knowledge-based development. Insufficient openness to impulses from outside the region hinders regional performance (Bathelt, Malmberg, & Maskell, 2004). Effective knowledge creation and learning processes therefore require the co-occurrence of both local and non-local research relations (Amin & Robins, 1991; Asheim & Isaksen, 2002; De Noni, Ganzaroli, & Orsi, 2017; Torre & Rallet, 2005). Collaboration with distant partners can secure advantages of a totally different kind than collaboration with close neighbours (Oinas & Lagendijk, 2005).

An analogous approach can be directly applied to collaborative relations in science. Among US information management scholars, a higher g-index[6] is obtained by those that established numerous connections with top peers, engage in long-lasting collaboration, and avoid co-authoring with researchers within the same cluster of partners (Abassi, Altman, & Hossain, 2011). According to Ortega (2014), scholars with dense, overlapping collaboration networks achieve poorer scientific performance than those with sparser networks. Both studies are clearly in line with the assumptions of the structural holes theory: a position in a network that provides good access to complementary resources, expertise, and knowledge is a good predictor of a superior research performance.

The structural holes theory also gives an interesting perspective to academic mobility in enhancing collaboration impact. The moderating role of returning scholars has been observed in Chinese nanotechnology: articles prepared by Chinese scholars together with returnees were published in journals with a higher impact factor than those written with no such support (Tang & Shapira, 2012). Similarly, the foreign work experience of Argentinian returnees increased the propensity to publish collaborative papers in high impact factor journals (Jonkers & Cruz-Castro, 2013). In this case co-authorship with returnees served as a substitute for international collaboration: a large share of collaborative papers with returnees was published without international co-authorship. In other words, valuable knowledge improvements may be achieved by filling the structural hole with international ties either directly, through international collaboration, or indirectly, by the linkages—and foreign experience—of returning scholars. The returnees constitute an important asset for a national, regional, or local R&D sector since their strong embeddedness in exterior networks facilitates knowledge flows to the internal network (Jonkers & Tijssen, 2008).

Establishing and maintaining global pipelines can be particularly beneficial for lagging regions.[7] Due to the feeble science sector and low absorptive capacity of resident businesses, these regions are not able to benefit from local buzz. To gain access to new sources of knowledge and to stimulate weak endogenous potential for innovative growth, regional actors must refer to global pipelines (Fitjar & Rodriguez-Pose, 2011; Lorentzen, 2007; Wanzenböck, Scherngell, & Brenner, 2014; Žížalová, 2010). However, since small and weak organisations, typical of less developed regions, usually have limited absorptive capacity, it is often beyond their capabilities to engage in both regional and extra-regional interactions simultaneously. In this case, maintaining only one of the two types of relations is not only necessary, but indeed can provide optimal effects (Aarstad, Kvitastein, & Jakobsen, 2016). Similarly, the performance argument explained above is also used in the case of impacts in the science sector. The level of advancement of a given discipline in a country may influence the strength of the relation between collaboration and citation levels. More developed scientific fields are less dependent on international co-authorship. The Slovenian case provides evidence for this hypothesis through contrasting patterns observed in traditionally strong fields (physics and chemistry) and less developed ones (biomedicine) (Pedin, Južnic, Blagus, Sajko, & Stare, 2012). This example fits well into the local buzz and global pipelines theory. In the case of strong national environments, dense relations among highly performing scientific entities—local buzz—are the most beneficial, while in case of weak environments, global pipelines act as a vital fuel for scientific excellence.

* * *

Although there is no specific theory of scientific collaboration in the territorial perspective, this chapter provides a framework for such a theory. It should address three key aspects of the geography of scientific collaboration, namely: (1) the growth of collaboration, (2) the formation and evolution of its spatial patterns, and (3) the impacts of research collaboration on science and regional development. Furthermore, the theory should not be built from scratch, but it can be based on the numerous concepts, approaches, and traditions analysed throughout the chapter. Some of them are complementary; others lead to ambiguous and sometimes even contradictory conclusions. One of the most attention-grabbing tensions is related to the role of spatial proximity. While spatial proximity is conducive to establishing cooperation, the impact of collective work—on the contrary—positively correlates with greater distance, or at least with an adequate proportion between distant and close links. The contradiction between circumstances in favour of establishing collaboration and those assuring advantages from joint research may have far-reaching consequences, not only for spatial scientometrics, but also for scientific collaboration policy.

Notes

1 Later polemics have revealed, by using examples from the history of science, that Mode 2 was already in effect as far back as the 17th century, before the professionalisation of science (Etzkowitz & Leydesdorff, 2000). The long prevalence of Mode 1

stemmed from the need to assure the independence of scientific endeavours rather than weak links between science and its socioeconomic environment (Hessels & van Lente, 2008).
2 Trott and Hartmann claimed that Chesbrough created a false dichotomy, and that the need for external linkages of firms was already underlined in the 1960s, thus, open innovation is an "old wine in a new bottle" case (Trott & Hartmann, 2009). Similar criticisms can be applied to the dichotomous concepts of Mode 2 vs. Mode 1.
3 Technically, scientific collaboration networks cannot be named as scale free—as physicist Mark Newman from the University of Michigan argues. The node degree distribution is not a proper power law, but power law with an exponential cutoff (Newman, 2004; see also Clauset, Shalizi, & Newman, 2009).
4 The Matthew effect was originally used to describe the phenomenon that eminent, famous scholars tend to gain more credit than less known researchers, even if their work is equally solid and significant.
5 According to Porter's definition a cluster is "a geographic proximate group of interconnected companies and associated institutions in a particular field, linked by commonalities and complementarities" (2000, p. 16).
6 An alternative to the h-index measure of scientific productivity on the individual level developed by Egghe (2006).
7 Nevertheless, even in highly innovative locations, the assumption of the prevalence of internal technological knowledge spillovers, thus relying on the local buzz, can be questioned (Huber, 2012).

6 Scientific collaboration policy

Scientific collaboration policy is a set of ideas and measures intended to manage scientific collaboration. Often it is understood as actions aimed at increasing scientific collaboration (Achachi et al., 2016; Amanatidou, 2002; Melin & Persson, 1996). However, its scope is much wider. From the perspective of policy objectives, it can be targeted not only at increasing collaboration, but also its effectiveness and efficiency, which might include termination of needless or underperforming partnerships. Moreover, scientific collaboration policy can be seen as (1) a subset of science policy and (2) a feature of science policy. In the first approach, measures directly aimed at collaboration—e.g., funding schemes supporting international research projects—are used to complement the science policy toolbox. In the second approach, science policy addresses scientific collaboration in a horizontal manner. The present-day ubiquity of scientific collaboration makes the second approach progressively more valid and useful for science policy analysis, development, and evaluation. Contemporary science policy simply cannot ignore multilevel networks that link scholars, research units, institutions, and countries.

The collaborative thread has to be carefully unwoven from the complex fabric of science policy. To this aim, we have based the present chapter on three case studies. We review scientific collaboration policies and their determinants and circumstances in three contexts: the United States, Europe (with the focus on the European Union level), and China. Our analysis focuses on central government policies, although subnational or institutional levels are also mentioned if needed for a proper understanding of a given setting. The chapter concludes with the mapping of the main scientific collaboration policy tools and some evidence shedding light on the evaluation of their effectiveness and efficiency. Before reaching this point, we have to begin our inquiry by placing scientific collaboration policy in the wider context of science policy—its origins, varieties, and developments.

6.1 Policy through science and for science

Initially, state incentives for research and innovation focused primarily on practical aims. They sought to exploit scientific discoveries for the benefit of areas of governmental concern. Jean-Jacques Salomon (1929–2008), a prominent French science scholar, called it a *policy through science* (Salomon, 1977). The pioneering example of such an initiative is the Longitude Act—passed by the British Parliament in 1714—which provided a lucrative reward amounting to circa $3 million (in 2016 dollars) for the precise determination of a ship's longitude at sea. The British government desperately sought to solve the so-called longitude problem since they managed the largest navy and merchant fleet in the world (Woolfson, 2015). The British Scientific Society, despite years of effort and with the brightest naturalists on board—it suffices to mention one of them: Isaac Newton—failed to solve the puzzle. At that point, the brain teaser was presented to the general public in the form of—using contemporary terms—a call for proposals. Fifty years later, self-taught clockmaker and carpenter John Harrison (1693–1776) found the answer: the marine chronometer, H4, or simply sea watch (Sobel, 1996). This invention, the result of a targeted science policy intervention, gave additional power to British global expansion, and in turn built its colonial empire.

The Longitude Act, although 300 years old, could still serve as an example of good practice for designing incentives of the policy through science type (Spencer, 2012). It outlined a specific goal and showed its strategic significance. It clearly described the desired outcome, but it did not suggest or exclude particular solutions. It defined the way in which the achievement of this outcome would be identified and evaluated. For this task, a distinct review body—the Board of Longitude—was established, and its tasks and competences were specified. Another significant feature of the Longitude Act was the set of conditions for granting rewards. It was assumed that the solution to the problem could be more or less accurate—and even less successful attempts should be somehow valued, because they could consequently lead to better ones. In this vein, the Act offered the full prize for the best solution, but also lesser prizes for less accurate tries. Last but not least, the call was wide open. There were no restrictions to participating—and this approach proved wise, as the best solution was invented by a self-educated commoner.

In the first half of the 20th century, science policy progressively attracted the strategic attention of policymakers, and it became more organised and institutionalised. It was the time when policy through science was combined with and complemented by *policy for science* (Salomon, 1977). The latter means the provision of favourable conditions for science and technology development but without specific expectations of direct and prompt profits from scientific research. This shift was perhaps most clearly visible in the US. Until the 1930s, American scholars depended almost entirely on funds provided by industry or philanthropists (Dupree, 1957). In the early 1940s, the first noteworthy federal funding was assigned for improving research and development in agriculture and public health (Bok, 2015). But the real change came with World War II and its aftermath. On the one hand, the atomic bomb made within the framework of the Manhattan Project—a clear example of policy through science—made the ultimate argument for the importance of science. On the other hand, generous federal funding for military-oriented research enhanced US scientific capacity. After the war, federal engagement in science was continued, and it largely took the form of policy for science. An authoritative figure behind this policy development was Vannevar Bush (1890–1974) with his influential 1945 report to the president of the United States entitled *Science, The Endless Frontier*. Bush emphasised the critical importance of basic research:

> Basic research leads to new knowledge. It provides scientific capital. It creates the fund from which the practical applications of knowledge must be drawn. New products and new processes do not appear full-grown. They are founded on new principles and new conceptions, which in turn are painstakingly developed by research in the purest realms of science. Today, it is truer than ever that basic research is the pacemaker of technological progress. [...] A nation which depends upon others for its new basic scientific knowledge will be slow in its industrial progress and weak in its competitive position in world trade, regardless of its mechanical skill
>
> (1945, p. 13–14).

In this vein, the American taxpayers' money was channelled into supporting basic research—which has become the main task of the National Science Foundation established in 1950. However, as the above quote from Vannevar Bush shows, from a policy perspective, even basic research is expected to induce profits for society and the economy. The main difference between policy through science and policy for science is that the first expects direct economic and social profits, while the other accepts long-term, indirect, and unanticipated impacts.

6.2 Policy shift towards collaboration

In the second half of the 20th century and at the dawn of the third millennium, science policy changed substantially in response to contemporary challenges and the logic of a collaborative turn in science. As early as 1996, an article in *Scientometrics* observed that "From a science policy perspective research collaboration has become a central issue" (Melin & Persson, 1996, p. 363–364). Two decades later, Ben Martin (2016) emphasised the gradual shift from science policy focused on an individual researcher, single laboratory, or an enterprise, to policy aimed at collaborations and networks. He points out that this policy change is intertwined with other shifts: from linear to systemic thinking about R&D and innovation, from national to multilevel governance, and from individual policies to policy mixes. That runs in line with the argument of Caroline Wagner who noticed the "shift from a nationally centred scientific system to a global one in which researchers, not national authorities, set the rules" (2008, p. 10). She claims that contemporary global science can be understood as a "new invisible college"—the term Wagner used as the title of her 2009 book. There she argues that the emergence of the new invisible college challenged traditional governmental science policies that have had to be reoriented to include new collaborative and open circumstances in designing incentives for science.

Many national and regional governments, as well as non-governmental institutions, have already reacted to the new collaborative logic of scientific activity and have implemented various instruments aimed at strengthening links among scholars (see: Caloghirou, Vonortas, & Ioannides, 2002; Cooke & Hilton, 2015; Cunningham & Gök, 2012; Hicks & Katz, 1996; Sakakibara & Cho, 2002; Stephan, 2012; Turpin, Garrett-Jones, & Woolley, 2011). For instance, in Germany the annual number of publicly subsidised collaborative R&D projects exceeded the number of single projects as early as 1999 (Czarnitzki & Fier, 2003). Since then, joint research ventures have significantly outnumbered single-institution grants funded by the German Federal Government. All in all, an impressive number of circa 60,000 collaborative projects were carried out in Germany in the period 1969–2012, more than one-third of the overall number of federally funded research studies. Cross-sectoral, science-industry joint research ventures largely contributed to this figure (Umlauf, 2016).

For the most scientifically advanced and wealthy nations, research collaboration—often international—is a way to amass resources and target the endless frontier of science with a force unfeasible for a single country. This tactic led to the rise of big science, exemplified by the European Organization for Nuclear Research widely known as CERN (an abbreviation derived from its historic French name, *Conseil Européen pour la Recherche Nucléaire*). CERN, the brainchild of atomic physicists, was established in 1954 by 12 European countries with the general mission to "provide for collaboration among European States in nuclear research of a pure scientific and fundamental character", as stated in the CERN Convention ("Convention for the Establishment of a European Organization for Nuclear Research", 1953, Article II). The idea behind CERN was to rebuild Europe's research capability and effectively face the intense competition with the US in the field of nuclear physics. Today, CERN includes 22 member states and involves a further 60 countries outside Europe. The laboratory employs about 15,000 scientists from around the world. Several revolutionary discoveries encapsulate the tremendous results of the CERN operation till today. Two of them were honoured with Nobel Prizes: the discoveries of the W and Z bosons by Simon van der Meer (1925–2011) and Carlo Rubbia (born in 1934), and the invention and development of particle detectors by Georges Charpak (1924–2010).

The promise of scientific excellence, improved by linking scientists in collaborative networks, turns out to be particularly attractive in resource-constrained conditions. The expectation arises that collaboration can substitute—at least to some degree—for R&D spending and lack of local skills and knowledge resources. This approach is essentially valid for less scientifically advanced and less well-off institutions and countries. In their case, science policy focused solely on the development of endogenous capacities is very unlikely to be successful. They need to look for exogenous resources and find ways to plug themselves into the global scientific networks. In practice, however, both endogenous and exogenous approaches have to be combined in a policy mix appropriate for the given institution or country; the reason for this is that a certain level of internal assets—or absorptive capacity (see: Cohen & Levinthal, 1990; Criscuolo & Narula, 2008)—is a prerequisite for effective use of external feeds. Caroline Wagner labels it a dual strategy, where "sinking" of investments on local territory is combined with "linking" to the global network (Wagner, 2008). The call for a dual strategy is—not surprisingly—equally applicable to scientifically lagging and developing as well as advanced countries. The three case studies described in the coming pages illustrate the rich variety of possible policy mixes in terms of scientific collaboration policy and its place in the overall science policy in a given national or institutional milieu.

6.3 Europe: towards the European Research Area

After World War II, the unprecedented integration process in Europe created a unique political framework—the European Union—for a variety of collaborative activities, including science. The main feature of the scientific collaboration policy in Europe is multilevel governance. It consists of, and emerges from, national policies and activities, intergovernmental agreements between sovereign countries, and supranational regulations and programmes at the EU level. Yet the European level of science policy is quite modest in comparison to policies at other levels. The average annual budget of Horizon 2020—the largest EU science policy instrument—accounts for only about 3.5 percent of the total annual gross domestic expenditure on research and development of the 28 UE Member States as of 2014 ("Breakdown of Horizon 2020 budget", 2011). Nevertheless, the EU science policy realises the central goal of stimulating transnational collaboration (Calvert & Martin, 2001; Hoekman et al., 2013), which has always been the apple of the EU policy makers' eye. As Luke Georghiou describes it, "The basic tenet of EU RTD [research and technological development] policy is the promotion of co-operation" (2001, p. 893). It is seen as essential to overcome fragmentation—Europe's main disadvantage, blamed for the continent's lagging in the worldwide R&D race (Georghiou, 2001). This chapter presents the reasoning, evolution, and architecture of the European scientific collaboration policy, within the EU and with non-EU countries. The main focus is on the EU-level initiatives. However, several examples from the country level are also presented.

6.3.1 Integrating Europe

The rationale behind supporting scientific collaboration on the EU level is twofold: (1) to enhance Europe's scientific excellence, and (2) to spur European integration. The scientific motivation is derived from the advantages of joint research in comparison to non-collaborative undertakings. Collaboration boosts scientific performance and impact, which may, in the long term, increase innovativeness and competitiveness, crucial drivers of the contemporary knowledge-based economy as it is understood and underlined in various European Union policy papers and strategies (e.g., the Lisbon Strategy from 2000 and the Europe 2020 strategy proposed in 2010). The integrative reasoning originates from the assumption that any form of collaboration strengthens EU integration (Gorzelak & Zawalińska, 2013). Fostering international collaboration is thus justified even if the only positive outcome is bringing European countries together. The strong support that scientific collaboration receives from the EU is manifested in numerous programmes, projects, actions, and regulations, as well as specific institutions.

This rich instrumentation did not appear out of the blue. The initial wave of pro-collaborative initiatives appeared in Europe during the first post-war decades, when several organisations supporting joint research were established, such as the aforementioned CERN established in 1954, the European Organization for Astronomical Research in the Southern Hemisphere launched in 1962, and the European Molecular Biology Organization established in 1964. The idea of a common policy supporting European science regardless of the discipline materialised in 1971 in the form of the European Cooperation in Science and Technology (COST). COST is the longest-running European intergovernmental framework aimed directly at supporting scientific collaboration through providing researchers with the opportunity to participate in science and technology networks. Three years later the EU policymakers set up two more institutions to foster and facilitate collaboration: Scientific and Technical Research Committee (CREST) and European Science Foundation (Commission of the European Communities, 1975).

The next wave of pro-collaborative impetus came to the surface in the first half of the 1980s. In 1983 the first European Strategic Programme for Research in Information Technologies (ESPRIT) was launched. Four editions of ESPRIT provided cross-sectoral financial support for information technology research and industrial technology transfer to industry. Two years after ESPRIT, EUREKA was founded as an intergovernmental organisation for funding and coordinating pan-European research and development, involving both EU and non-EU countries. It represents a bottom-up approach in which private companies decide themselves which research projects should be developed. The Framework Programme for Research and Technological Development (FP), the flagship initiative of EU scientific collaboration policy, was also initiated in the 1980s. The programme was intended to address the problem of insufficient coordination of individual R&D activities at the EU level, all of them requiring a large number of the European Council's decisions (Georghiou, 2001).

At the beginning of the 21st century, EU science policy goals started to move from coordination of national policies towards genuine integration of European research. The emphasis was no longer on collaboration *per se*, but more on global competition and research excellence (Luukkonen & Nedeva, 2010). Stronger focus on competition actually fosters research collaboration since staying at the frontier of worldwide science requires joint effort and resources

(Cruz-Castro, Jonkers, & Sanz-Menéndez, 2015). This shift was compliant with increased interest at EU political forums in research and knowledge production, as manifested in the Lisbon Strategy. The document called for making the EU "the most competitive and dynamic knowledge-based economy in the world" (Lisbon European Council, 2000, para. 5).

The idea to deepen European scientific integration was promoted as early as the 1970s by EU Commissioner for Research, Science, and Education, Ralf Dahrendorf (1929–2009). But it was only in 2000 when the concept materialised in the form of the European Research Area (ERA). The aim of ERA is to create

> a unified research area open to the world based on the Internal Market, in which researchers, scientific knowledge and technology circulate freely and through which the Union and its Member States strengthen their scientific and technological bases, their competitiveness and their capacity to collectively address grand challenges
>
> (European Commission, 2012).

ERA is not a single programme, but rather a European-level policy that is implemented through various initiatives, in many cases already pre-existing, such as the Framework Programmes. ERA's aim to foster free circulation of researchers, knowledge, and technology—the so-called "fifth freedom"—supplements four fundamental EU freedoms of movement: of capital, goods, services, and people (Andrée, 2009; Madesn, 2010; Nedeva & Stampfer, 2012).

Apart from the Framework Programmes, ERA is implemented through other collaborative instruments, although their budgets are smaller. An example could be the Joint Programming Initiatives, commenced at the end of 2008 and aimed at major societal challenges, such as Alzheimer's disease, water challenges, and demographic changes (Commission of the European Communities, 2008). Up until 2016, ten initiatives were launched, gathering partners from 29 countries (including eight non-EU countries), with a total budget of around €500 million (European Commission, 2016a). 2008 also witnessed the birth of another collaboration initiative—the European Institute of Innovation and Technology (EIIT). The idea of a network organisation combining world-class education and research with innovation and application was inspired by the Massachusetts Institute of Technology (Gilbert, 2011). The EIIT, supported with almost €3 billion, was intended to fuel the EU's innovativeness by transferring knowledge from academia to business. A recent audit revealed that this ambitious goal has been held back by oversized bureaucracy, management deficiencies, and defective design. This has been reflected in geographical dispersion as a result of arguments between EU member states about who will host the EIIT's headquarters (Schiermeier, 2016). This perfectly exemplifies the challenges that EU scientific collaboration policy has been facing since its very beginning: the tensions between EU-level priorities and national interests, as well as the nature of scientific collaboration, which is difficult to impose in a top-down manner.

6.3.2 The world's largest collaborative programme

The Framework Programmes for Research and Technological Development became the flagship of the EU science policy: "the behemoth of the Community's science engagement" (Madsen, 2010, p. 196). They enabled breakthrough discoveries, such as contributing to the development of the global standard for 2G and 3G mobile phone communications or a wearable artificial kidney to replace dialysis (Migliaccio & Philipsen, 2006). In the mid-1980s, when the programme was launched, the main operational aim of its initiator, Étienne Davignon (the European Commissioner for Industrial Affairs and Energy), was to coordinate numerous R&D activities taken at the EU level that linked researchers with big industrial players, in order to identify and implement solutions needed to compete with the US and Japan (Georghiou, 2001; Nedeva, 2013). The approach applied in the programme design was based on the model of successful Japanese R&D collaborative networks of the Ministry of International Trade and Industry, adapted to the European context (Andrée, 2009; Fraunhofer ISI, Idea Consult, & SPRU, 2009). FPs have evolved in terms of scale and design, as well as thematic focus, yet their strategic objective of fostering scientific collaboration has remained unchanged.

The FPs' budget has grown systematically, from €0.8 billion per year in the first four-year edition (1984–1987) to €11.3 billion per year in the last seven-year edition (2014–2020). In effect, over eight editions of the FPs, European science has received almost €200 billion (European Parliamentary Research Service, 2015). Most of the FP funds are dedicated to consortia that include partners from different countries, preferably geographically dispersed. During the programme's lifespan the requirement for international collaboration has systematically evolved. Initially, project consortia had to be composed of institutions from at least two EU countries. Since the sixth FP (2002–2006), the requirement has been strengthened to include participants based in at least three different EU member states. In an increasingly competitive scientific environment this precondition may lead to honorary project partnership (similar to the honorary authorship described in Chapter 2), where an institution is added to the consortium only—or mostly—in order to meet the formal criteria, although the project would also be feasible without its involvement.

Apart from supporting collaboration through grants dedicated to transnational consortia, all editions of the FPs have provided funds for researchers' international mobility through special initiatives: Stimulation in FP1, Science in FP2, and since FP3 as one of the programme's thematic axes. All these initiatives have paved the way for the largest EU mobility programme: Marie Skłodowska-Curie Actions (MSCA), launched in 1996. Up until 2013, the MSCA supported the international mobility of more than 65,000 researchers from over 130 countries, with 30 percent of them coming from outside Europe (European Commission, 2013). Each year about 9,000 scientists receive support under MSCA to move within the EU, to the EU, or from the EU to third countries.

Increases in the budget and changes in the programme's design were made in line with its evolving priorities: from those of an almost purely applied, industry-led instrument focused on several thematic areas, to those of a comprehensive multi-theme initiative providing funds for both basic and applied research (European Commission, 2011). The first edition of the Framework Programme was largely industry oriented. Half of its budget was dedicated to energy research, especially nuclear energy and thermonuclear fusion, while one-fifth went to new technologies, such as IT, biotechnology, and telecommunications (Boekholt, 1994). The second FP edition (1987–91) was marked by a shift towards IT, in accordance with the OECD recommendation to follow the spectacular Japanese achievements in consumer electronics of the late 1970s. In this edition, to provide access to the unique scientific infrastructure, especially for scientists from smaller countries, a special programme was launched: Access to Research Infrastructure. The third FP round (1990–94) was characterised by a diminishing role of nuclear energy in favour of, among others, environmental research. In 1993, the Maastricht Treaty came into force, adding new FP criteria. The addendum made it possible to include almost any research topic as an FP theme. From the time of FP4 (1994–98), the set of themes supported by the programme was broadened by a few new topics, such as socioeconomic research. Apart from thematic axes, horizontal programmes were also introduced, including those facilitating collaboration: the promotion of cooperation with third countries and international organisations (INCO), as well as the training and mobility of researchers. The horizontal themes were even more emphasised in the FP's fifth edition (1998–2002) as one more collaborative theme was added: promotion of innovation and encouraging the participation of small and medium-sized enterprises (SME). The SME component was strengthened in FP6 (2002–06) through the CRAFT programme (Co-operative Research), dedicated to SMEs in cross-border innovative research partnerships. In 2002, new instruments related to the European Research Area were introduced: ERA-NET (a bottom-up scheme supporting coordination of national and regional programmes), Integrated Projects (large research projects), and Network of Excellence (supporting coordination between research organisations) (ERA-NET Review 2006, 2006). The themes supported in the last two editions of the Programme (FP7 and Horizon 2020) have been very diverse and wide-ranging, covering almost all scientific disciplines. However, as for the whole FP lifespan, the topics of the specific calls for proposals have always been defined by the European Commission.

The last completed edition of the Framework Programmes, FP7, financed about 26,000 joint projects[1] and generated over 500,000 pairs of collaborative links between scientific institutions (Abbott, Butler, Gibney, Schiermeier, & Van Noorden, 2016). The number of organisations per average FP7 collaborative project[2] reached 10.5, while the number of countries represented by collaborating institutions amounted to 6.2. Joint research within FP7 resulted in many multi-institutional publications. The average share of international co-publications from programme participants increased by 10 percentage points (from 49 to 59 percent) in comparison to their achievements before joining the programme. For

142 *Scientific collaboration policy*

sub-programmes dedicated exclusively to research teams (not individual scientists) the difference amounted to almost 12 percentage points (Science-Metrix, Fraunhofer ISI, & Oxford Research, 2015). Moreover, qualitative studies reveal that 90 percent of evaluated researchers confirm that participation in FPs has had a marked effect on their international networks of collaborators (Idea Consult, iFQ, & PPMI, 2014).

6.3.3 Connecting Europe with third countries

The idea of the European Research Area—creating a common research space—is unquestionably alluring, although it can be criticised on the grounds that it might lead to the continent's lock-in by hampering collaboration with non-EU partners. One way to address the risk of lock-in is to improve institutionalised scientific cooperation of the European Union with so-called third countries. This dates back to 1983 when the Science and Technology for Development programme was launched. Twenty-five years later, the Strategic Forum for International Science and Technology Cooperation (SFIC) was set up—a platform for establishing the common strategy of EU member states for scientific collaboration with selected non-EU partners. Targeted strategies of research collaboration with third countries take the form of multiannual roadmaps. Up until 2015, the EU had signed bilateral agreements with 20 countries. The partners are chosen based on specific scientific, economic, and political criteria and include both emerging scientific powers (China, India, Brazil) and established global science players (US, Canada, Japan, South Korea) (European Parliament, 2015). Scientific collaboration with non-EU countries was also treated as a way to integrate future EU member states. An example could be the scheme for Central and Eastern European countries launched in 1992. As potential future members of the union, they gained access to €55 million for collaboration with EU countries through joint projects, researcher mobility, and networking (CESAER, 2016). Furthermore, the participation of new member states in research consortia has always been positively assessed during proposal evaluations (Arnold et al., 2008).

Let us take the Framework Programmes as an example of third countries' involvement in scientific collaboration with European countries. One in five of the FP7 projects included partners from neither the EU nor associated countries, accounting for about five percent of the total number of FP7 participants. In the current Framework Programme edition—Horizon 2020—partners from non-EU countries can participate in all programmes and projects, even if the call for proposals does not have an explicit condition of such participation. Additionally, several thematic areas strongly encourage, or sometimes require, cooperation with third countries, e.g., climate change, food production, and migration. Such projects accounted for about 20 percent of the Horizon 2020 calls for proposals in 2014–2015. Although today participation in the FP is very open, non-EU countries vary in terms of their level of eligibility for EU FP funds. Partners from enlargement and neighbourhood countries associated with the Horizon 2020 contribute to the FP budget and share both the rights and obligations of their EU counterparts.[3] More than 120 developing countries form a group of International Cooperation Partner Countries (ICPC) and are able to participate in the FP without the status of an associated country (European Parliament, 2015). The rest of the world has the status of non-EU countries not automatically eligible for funding, which means that they can participate in the projects but have to fund the participation of their institutions themselves, with the exception of cases when their participation is recognised as essential for the project (European Commission, 2016b).

Collaboration with non-EU partners is also driven by the unique scientific infrastructure marking the European scientific landscape, like the emblematic Large Hadron Collider (Hallonsten, 2016; Nedeva & Stampfer, 2012). For the last 60 years, the most expensive and advanced facilities and installations have been built in Europe based on intergovernmental agreements and multinational funds. Since 2002 these kinds of research investments have been coordinated and examined by the European Strategy Forum on Research Infrastructures through special biannual roadmaps of new research infrastructure of pan-European interest. The forum gathers representatives of the EU member states and the European Commission, as well as associated countries.

6.3.4 From national interests to European added value

Scientific collaboration in Europe also receives support through numerous policy initiatives implemented at the national level, where the majority of R&D funds are managed (Delanghe, Muldur, & Soete, 2009). The most common are grants for projects carried out by international or national research teams, such as the Collaborative Research Grants of the Carnegie Trust for the Universities of Scotland, the Scientific Networks within the Individual Grants Programme of the German Research Foundation, the Research Network grant scheme of the Danish Council for Independent Research, the Harmonia programme of the Polish National Science Centre, the Academy Project funding scheme in Finland, International Collaborative Research Projects of the French National Research Agency, the TOP grants for research groups of the Netherlands Organisation for Scientific Research, and the NordForsk programmes in the Nordic region. The pro-collaborative dimension is also present in measures supporting researcher mobility, such as the DFF-MOBILEX mobility grants of the Danish Council for Independent Research, the Arts & Humanities Research Council International Placement Scheme in the UK, and the International Short Visits scheme of the Swiss National Science Foundation. Some countries dedicate special programmes to foreign researchers visiting national institutions, e.g., the POLONEZ programme of the Polish National Science Centre, the Visiting Scientist Programme of the Hungarian Academy of Sciences, the Visitor's Travel Grants of the Netherlands Organisation for Scientific Research, or the grants for recruitment of leading researchers of the Swedish Research Council. European governments also offer a range of instruments aimed directly at fostering and facilitating the establishment of collaboration, partly through building mutual trust. The British

Arts & Humanities Research Council established the Research Networking Scheme, which supports multi-institutional applicants in the process of exchange of ideas on a specific issue. Within the scheme, custom-made networking activities can be financed, especially those enabling the crossing of boundaries—disciplinary, theoretical, methodological, and international.

National support for scientific collaboration, as with the EU-level interventions, also has an integrative dimension. A telling example is Belgium which, in order to deal with its Flemish-Walloon internal divisions, launched, through the Belgian Federal Science Policy Office, the Interuniversity Attraction Poles (IAP) programme. During the seventh five-year phase of the IAP programme, a total budget of about €671 million was allocated to stimulate the development of the excellent interuniversity networks in basic research representing various disciplines. In the most recent phase, which started in 2012, it is envisaged that €156 million will be allocated to support 47 networks with circa 370 partners, from which more than 110 are from abroad. Each network comprises at least four partners representing universities from the two Belgian regions, Flanders and Wallonia. This will make it possible to achieve both aims: to create a sufficient critical mass of human and material resources and help Belgian researchers find a place in the international scientific landscape, as well as to build long-term, structured cooperation links between scientific institutions from the different linguistic communities. Spatial balance is one of the programme's concerns—the last completed programme reveals that 56 percent of the IAP's budget was allocated to universities of the Flemish Community and 44 percent to institutions in the French part of Belgium (Idea Consult & ADE, 2011).

National scientific budgets also support collaboration with third countries. According to the 2014 ERA survey,[4] funders in two-thirds of the EU member states allocate on average 0.7 percent[5] of their budgets to this type of scientific collaboration. The highest shares (above 2.5 percent) are granted by Germany (a European leader in collaboration with the US and Russia), France (focusing on cooperation with BRIC[6] countries, Japan, and South Korea), and Portugal (distinguished by collaboration with Portuguese-speaking countries) (European Commission, 2014).

Initiatives supporting scientific collaboration at the European Union level work in parallel with national science policies, which also address joint research in various ways. In the last few decades, along with the rising number and budgets of transnational programmes and initiatives, the role of EU-level interventions has been increasing. However, the national dimension is still strong. The compatible coexistence of the two levels is a result of political negotiations, bargains, and tensions that create and maintain the balance between supporting collaboration at the EU level, aimed at the common good, and national self-interests. European collaboration "is not undertaken at the expense of self-interest; it is rather the pursuit of one's interests by other means" (Krige, 2003, p. 900).

The rationale for many EU policies, balanced between national interests and a common goal, is derived from the subsidiarity rule, which states that actions at the EU level are undertaken only if and in so far as the objectives cannot be achieved by the member states and can be better achieved at the EU level. This applies especially to issues with a strong international aspect, thus, those involving or even requiring collaboration. In these cases, EU-level policy brings additional benefits called European added value (Georghiou, 1998). It is understood as "the value resulting from an EU intervention which is additional to the value that would have been otherwise created by Member State action alone" (European Commission, 2011, p. 2). Scientific cooperation and networking is the very sphere in which European added value can be created.

6.4 The United States: collaborative culture

There is no distinct scientific collaboration policy in the US. Despite this fact—which runs in line with the American tradition of limited government—collaboration among American scientists flourishes, including inter-organisational and inter-state collaboration. The well-developed and amply financed US science sector operates in an environment that enables collaborative behaviour. The high spatial mobility of the population, inclusive organisational culture, and common language are all factors that make scientific collaboration far easier than, say, between countries in Europe. Even so, when it comes to international collaboration, the US to some extent lags behind the most scientifically collaborative nations (compare Chapter 4). On these grounds, there have been new calls for greater appreciation of the considerable benefits of international scientific collaboration to American prosperity (see: Lyons et al., 2016). This does not mean that there is no scientific collaboration policy in the US. On the contrary, it is easy to find numerous initiatives of different scale, origin, and significance. The point is that central (federal) and strategic coordination of these undertakings is limited (Hane, 2008). Hence, the overall scientific collaboration policy in the US can be seen as a largely bottom-up, emerging phenomenon. Of course, large-scale research is powered by federal agencies, but the bread and butter of everyday scientific collaboration has a predominantly grassroots flavour.

This section focuses on selected features of the American scientific collaboration policy and its particular underpinnings, from the diversity of sources of science policy, through its collaborative culture, to the importance of science-industry cooperation and academic mobility, and finally to its multilevel international collaboration efforts.

6.4.1 Multitudes of science policies in the US

In the second half of the 20th century, the United States became an unquestionable leader in science. The US formed a highly competitive national innovation system, characterised by a vast scale and institutional complexity (Nelson, 1993). The large number of players on the American R&D scene produce almost unlimited opportunities to collaborate. On the other hand, institutional complexity relates to the diversity of actors involved in the framing of science policy, including scientific collaboration policy. This diversity has three facets. First, on the federal level, the task of making and implementing science policy is distributed among various organisations. High-level policy decisions involve the president and the congress. On the implementation side, many federal departments and agencies manage their own R&D budgets. The Department of Defense controls by far the bulkiest science funds ($66.1 billion in 2014).[7] The Department of Health and Human Services has the second largest R&D budget ($30.8 billion). Then comes NASA—the National Aeronautics and Space Administration ($11.5 billion) and the Department of Energy ($11.4 billion). The National Science Foundation—the only federal agency with the principal objective of funding science—has a considerably smaller budget ($5.5 billion). The combined R&D budgets of the other departments amount to about $10 billion. In such circumstances, the resultant federal science policy does not only originate from the largely independent decisions of a good dozen organisations, but it is also well-aligned with other policies (security, health, energy, etc.), and this—in turn—strengthens the applicatory flavour of US science.

Second, science policy in the US is characterised by multilevel governance. In the American intergovernmental system (Stephens & Wikstrom, 2007) the making of science policy is not limited to the central government—as it is in the case of many countries—but the process engages states and even local governments. However, science policy at the state level is usually seen not as an independent political field, but rather as an instrument in the service of economic development. This makes state-level science policies largely oriented on research, technology transfer, and university-industry relations (Rees & Bradley, 1988). A well-known example of such state-level policies, operating since 1982, is Pennsylvania's Ben Franklin Technology Partners, previously branded as the Ben Franklin Partnership Program (Rahm & Luce, 1992). However, some state initiatives also target basic research. This is the case of the California Institute for Regenerative Medicine, established in 2004 after approval in a state-wide referendum, which focuses its funding on basic stem cell research (Adelson & Weinberg, 2010).

Third, the profile of US science is shaped by both governmental and nongovernmental institutions. The nongovernmental actors—companies and nonprofits—do not only influence government decisions but also proactively shape science policy. They control significant R&D budgets that can be allocated to pursuing research themes independent of the current administration's science priorities. Certainly, in almost every industrialised country, a substantial part of R&D budgets comes from nongovernmental sources (primarily business). But again, the US seems outstanding in this respect because of the abundance of wealthy corporations, private foundations (e.g., the Kavli Foundation, Alfred P. Sloan Foundation, and the Research Corporation for Science Advancement, to name only a few landmark ones),[8] and, last but not least, private universities, many of which enjoy multi-billion-dollar endowments (the world's largest is Harvard University's endowment, amounting to $36.5 billion in 2015). The interest from endowments, royalties from patents and copyrights, and tuition fees provide US universities (mainly private ones) with resources that make them autonomous and significant players in framing their own science policies and the resultant national policy.

All in all, science policy in the US can be seen as the sum of various initiatives pursued by a diverse group of (semi)independent actors. In such an institutional ecosystem, keeping track of scientific collaboration policies and measures is not a straightforward task. Take, for instance, one of the latest comprehensive overviews of US science policy, *Beyond Sputnik: US Science Policy in the Twenty-First Century* (Neal, Smith, & McCormick, 2008). This almost-400-page volume does not include a specific section dedicated to scientific collaboration policies, but make no mistake—the topic is present, though scattered across various chapters and sections.

6.4.2 Scientific collaboration in collaborative culture

Scientific collaboration in the US largely relies on the policies of individual institutions, which voluntarily form various—often overlapping—networks. It can be seen as a form of "low-level" policy—in contrast to "high-level" policies made by federal and state governments. The wide variety of academic associations are a case in point, from the inclusive Association of American Colleges & Universities, comprising nearly 1,400 member institutions, through the field-specific Association of Independent Technological Universities, to the elite Association of American Universities, which has 60 members in the US and two in Canada. Many initiatives bring together institutions from numerous states, but there are also single-state forms of cooperation, for instance, the University Research Corridor in Michigan: an alliance of Michigan State University, the University of Michigan, and Wayne State University.

Interestingly and specifically, many territorial groupings of US universities are linked to the inter-college sports competitions which are organised into regional associations (conferences). The prestigious Ivy League—a grouping of eight world-class, excellent, and selective northeastern universities[9]—originated as a collegiate athletic conference. Collaboration among Ivy League institutions extends far beyond sporting rivalries. The partnership is coordinated by the Council of Ivy Group Presidents and by the student-led Ivy Council. Another example might be the Big Ten Academic Alliance (from its founding in 1958 until June 2016 known as the Committee on Institutional Cooperation). This grouping of 14 large, mainly public universities[10] located in the northeastern and midwestern states has evolved as an academic counterpart of the inter-college sports Big Ten Conference. The alliance initiatives cover a broad range of activities, from somewhat traditional reciprocal library borrowing, through shared courses, organisational know-how exchanges, capacity-building initiatives, and common purchasing, to IT support for collaborative research (a cutting-edge fibre optic network between participating universities) and joint research projects. The coalition does not limit its activities to enhancing internal collaboration. The participating institutions build on their outstanding joint capacity to improve their external collaboration and outreach. They share study abroad programmes and work together to increase national and international research collaboration. A case in point is the Traumatic Brain Injury Research Collaboration. The initiative brings together the Big Ten and aforementioned Ivy League institutions to study the causes and long-term effects of sport-related concussion and head injuries. The feasibility and success of the project rely on the unique resources of the 23 participating universities, namely, circa 17,500 student athletes.

A variety of collaborative frameworks in the US can be attributed to the unique American culture of collaboration. Formal, as well as informal, un-codified partnerships play a critical role in the US science and innovation system (Atkinson, 2014; Committee on Science and Technology, 1998). This collaborative culture is deeply rooted in the American national character and is famously portrayed by 19th-century French intellectual Alexis de Tocqueville (1805–1859). In his epic *Democracy in America*, Tocqueville declared:

> In America I encountered sorts of associations of which, I confess, I had no idea, and I often admired the infinite art with which the inhabitants of the United States managed to fix a common goal to the efforts of many men and to get them to advance to it freely
>
> (2000, p. 489).

In the context of the contemporary American R&D sector, collaborative culture is displayed—inter alia—in the rise of open innovation (Chesbrough, 2003). At the beginning of the third millennium about two-thirds of award-winning US innovations (as recognised by *R&D Magazine*) involved inter-organisational collaboration between business and government, including federal laboratories and research universities (Block & Keller, 2009).

6.4.3 Scientific collaboration and industrial R&D policies

A solid chunk of science policy in the US focuses on science-industry collaboration. Make no mistake, policies supporting collaboration between science and industry are not limited to the US; quite the contrary—they can be found in all developed countries. Nonetheless, it is in the US that the application of research outcomes is particularly emphasised and extensively supported, e.g., through intellectual property law (Bayh-Dole Act), which permits universities and other non-profit research institutions to benefit from inventions made with federal funding. Technology transfer—or in broader terms, knowledge transfer—from the R&D sector to business and social practice extends beyond the scope and aims of this book. Moreover, a vast body of literature already covers this topic (see: Link, Siegel, & Wright, 2015). Nevertheless, it is indispensable to highlight that some science-industry collaboration measures directly influence science-science collaboration. This is the case, firstly, when science-sector-based scholars collaborate with researchers in company-run R&D labs, for instance in the framework of Cooperative

Research and Development Agreements—CRADAs (Kraemer, 2006; Neal et al., 2008). Secondly, measures aimed at creating links between science and industry can—directly or indirectly—encourage collaboration between scientific institutions which, working together, can increase their critical mass and offer more comprehensive solutions for their business partners. A good example of a policy instrument targeted at the industrial application of research, which at the same time directly reinforces science-science collaboration, is the Industry-University Cooperative Research Centers (IUCRC) programme.

The IUCRC is a programme led by the National Science Foundation (NSF) since 1973. The programme's main objective is to transfer new knowledge and technology from science to industry. However, it also has supplementary goals, such as enhancing the engineering and science workforce, developing the research infrastructure base, and stimulating additional funding for pre-competitive research from the industrial sector. Each centre has to be dedicated to a specific research or technology area (IUCRCs should not overlap in their research foci). Centres are run by higher education institutions and have to involve members from business, government, and non-profit sectors (in the spirit of the triple-helix approach—see Chapter 5). Such an approach, where universities mediate industry-government relations, enables the government to reduce the risk of being blamed for "picking winners and losers in the private sector" (Neal et al., 2008, p. 144).

Formally, an IUCRC can be run by a single university, but the NSF explicitly favours institutional partnerships: "multi-university IUCRCs are preferred to single-university IUCRCs because multi-university Centers contribute to an increased research base as well as to increased interaction among Center participants" ("About the IUCRC Program", n.d., para. 4). In this way, the policy measure focused on technology transfer supports—somewhat incidentally—collaboration between universities. However, the multi-university preference is relatively new. Initially, a vast majority of IUCRCs were established at a single university. Only in 2002 did the number of multi-site centres exceed the sum of single-site centres (respectively 26 to 19). In 2016, almost all of the centres were multi-site (63) and only five were run by a single university. Altogether, 68 IUCRCs involved 182 universities from virtually all states, i.e., circa 2.6 universities per single collaborative centre (Leonchuk, McGowen, & Gray, 2016). Additionally, five centres formally partnered up with foreign universities (KU Leuven, Belgium; Dubna International University, Russia; Dharmsinh Desai University, India; Tampere University of Technology, Finland; Leibniz University, Germany). The programme—along with another similar initiative of the NSF: the Engineering Research Center program (for more details see Section 6.6.3)—proved to be successful and also contributed to the popularisation of the cooperative research centre (CRC) model of supporting knowledge and technology transfer and cross-sector collaboration. Rivers and Gray (2013) estimate that between 15 and 25 percent of the 24,000 government or university-based and other non-profit research centres in the US and Canada meet the characteristics of the cooperative research centre.

Similarly, science policies on the state level also lean toward science-industry collaboration. This is the case with the above-mentioned Ben Franklin Partnership Program in Pennsylvania, but parallel initiatives have been adopted by many other states, for example, Ohio's Thomas Edison Program launched in 1983 (Wessner, 2013), the Georgia Research Alliance established in 1990 (Lambright, 2000), and Michigan's Life Sciences Corridor initiated in 1999 and slowed down just a few years later due to state budget limitations (Geiger & Sá, 2005).

6.4.4 Academic mobility in a mobile society

US internal scientific collaboration is facilitated by the significant spatial mobility of researchers. According to a study based on affiliations of publications published in the period of 1996–2011 and indexed in Scopus, almost one in four US researchers reported affiliations to institutions located in two or more US states. This can be roughly interpreted as inter-state mobility. If we assume that the US inter-state mobility is analogous to the inter-country mobility in Europe, an intriguing picture arises: European researchers move within Europe more than three times less frequently than Americans move inter-state (6.8 versus 22.2 percent). Moreover, fewer European scientists experience mobility outside the continent than Americans do outside the US (5.5 versus 8.4 percent) (Kamalski & Plume, 2013).

Academic mobility in the United States fits squarely into the American culture of geographic mobility. Americans are one of the most spatially mobile nations. A Gallup survey conducted in 2011 and 2012 showed that in a five-year timeframe, 24 percent of US adults reported moving house within the country, while the world average was only eight percent (Esipova, Pugliese, & Ray, 2013). An average American changes residence much more frequently than Europeans do. The Federal Census Bureau estimated that, as of 2007, a typical American moves 11.7 times in his or her lifetime (Chalabi, 2015). Estimates from 2016 showed that an average European moves about four times (Chandler, 2016)—with some nations significantly less prone to mobility (in Poland, Slovakia, and Spain the average is around two moves) and others visibly more mobile (in Finland, Sweden, and Switzerland people typically move six times, in the UK five times) (RE/MAX, 2015).

This mobility of researchers within the US results in them forming a network of former colleagues, which facilitates inter-institutional and inter-state collaboration—with social closeness being the major enabling factor. This process, in turn, is amplified by the fact that a vast majority of America's professors earned PhDs from a very narrow group of universities. A 2015 careful study of nearly 19,000 faculty in three disciplines—computer science, business, and history—showed that 71 to 86 percent of all tenure-track faculty (depending on the discipline) originated from only 25 percent of institutions (Clauset, Arbesman, & Larremore, 2015). Acquaintances and friends made in graduate schools or during postdocs often prove handy collaborators at further steps of an academic career.

Furthermore, the international dimension of academic mobility also shapes the American R&D sector. The US is exceptionally efficacious in attracting external talent. Foreign-born and foreign-educated scholars make an exceptional contribution to American science. This is evidenced by higher-than-expected representation of foreign-born individuals (1) elected to the National Academy of Sciences and National Academy of Engineering, (2) being most cited authors, being authors of (3) "citation classics", and (4) highly-cited patents, and (5) playing a crucial role in launching biotechnology enterprises (Stephan & Levin, 2001). This extraordinary gravitational pull gives rise to accusations of a brain drain that profits the US at the expense of other countries, mostly less developed. As *The Economist* forcefully summarised:

> Depending on your point of view, America is either a land of opportunity in which genius blossoms in ways that are impossible at home; or a talent-sucking vampire that bleeds other countries of their human capital by wickedly paying more and offering better laboratory facilities
> ("Proteins and particles", 1999, p. 85).

Real life, though, eludes this simple binomial model. The brain drain and gain approach is gradually being replaced by the notion of brain circulation (Saxenian, 2002), which emphasises that both receiving and sending countries can profit from accelerated mobility. Even if migrating scholars do not return, they often collaborate with colleagues in their former country (Scellato, Franzoni, & Stephan, 2015).

Various policies influence international academic mobility. By and large, American efforts are focused on attracting foreign students and exceptionally skilled scientists. Many universities make significant efforts to take their piece of the global higher education market. These efforts range from intensive advertising to offering free online courses and educational material, funding short and long-term incoming and outgoing scholarships, and launching overseas offices. In 2016, eight out of fourteen members of the above-mentioned Big Ten Academic Alliance operated permanently staffed foreign offices—some of them in up to four different locations—mostly in China, but also in Brazil, Colombia, Germany, India, Qatar, Turkey, and the United Arab Emirates. Overseas offices focus on recruiting students, but their mission often includes support for faculty research collaboration (Big Ten Academic Alliance, 2016). The initiatives of numerous individual institutions contribute to the critical mass that draws foreign talent to American higher education and R&D sector. Nevertheless, the landmark academic mobility policy lies at the federal level: this is the Fulbright Program, named after Senator James William Fulbright (1905–1995), who envisioned the international exchange program. Founded in 1946, the Fulbright Program provides grants for foreigners to pursue study, teaching, or research in the US, as well as for American students and researchers to go abroad (in recent years the programme has provided grants to circa 8,000 individuals annually). There is tangible evidence that the brain circulation stimulated by the Fulbright Program has increased international collaboration. Foreign Fulbright scholars, after returning to their countries of origin, are highly likely to continue collaboration with their US colleagues, as shown by the co-authorship of scientific papers (Kahn & MacGarvie, 2011; Røsdal, Lekve, Scordato, Aanstad, & Piro, 2014).

6.4.5 International focus

The Fulbright Program and other efforts to stimulate academic mobility are only a part of US international scientific collaboration policy. In fact, it occurs through multiple channels and on multiple levels. First, the US takes part in large-scale international projects—for example, the Human Genome Project, the International Thermonuclear Experimental Reactor, and the International Space Station. The US frequently plays a leading role in such projects, not necessarily as an official leader, but de facto as a major contributor. Second, large-scale, often multilateral initiatives are accompanied by bilateral cooperation frameworks, which the US has established with almost all countries. This can take the form of high-level government-to-government agreements and resulting coordination bodies such as the US-China Joint Commission on Science and Technology Cooperation and the US-France Science and Technology Cooperation. High-level official arrangements are essential tools of science diplomacy, but they do not necessarily directly translate into specific cooperation programmes and actual funding. Typically, the US government—through its various agencies—backs the US side of collaborative projects, expecting the foreign part to be financed by cooperating country sources. Nonetheless, the US fully funds or co-funds collaborative research programmes with many countries. These programmes frequently focus on a particular topic or challenge, as for instance, the US-India Collaborative Vision Research program, the US-China Clean Energy Cooperation, or the US-Israel Collaboration in Computer Science.

Federal-level science funding organisations pursue numerous international collaboration actions. For instance, the National Institute of Health (NIH)—an agency of the Department of Health and Human Services—through its Extramural Research Program supports international collaboration by awarding research grants, as well as exchange and educational projects. Many of the NIH's 27 institutes and centres conduct or promote international collaboration in specific disciplines of biomedical science. One of the NIH centres is specifically devoted to international collaboration. This is Fogarty International Center (FIC), named after Congressman John Edward Fogarty (1913–1967), an avid advocate of international health research. Initially named Health for Peace, FIC was opened in 1968. Today FIC runs projects that connect US scientists with colleagues from over 100 countries.

The organisational variety of US international scientific collaboration frameworks can be illustrated by the Global Innovation Initiative launched in 2013. This is a competitive grant program, financed jointly by the US and the UK, directed to university consortia in science, technology, engineering, and mathematics, focusing on issues of global significance (e.g., access to safe drinking water and the relation between land use changes and infectious vector-borne diseases). The programme funds multilateral projects between UK and US institutions and one—or more—from designated emerging economies (Brazil, China, India, and Indonesia). For the sake of streamlining the management of the programme, grants are administered either by the US (Institute of International Education—operating on behalf of the Department of State) or the UK side (British Council). Without a doubt, the Global Innovation Initiative creates opportunities to foster international collaboration, but the scale of the programme is fairly small. In the first round, 23 projects were awarded a total of $5.1 million. The second cycle resulted in only 14 awarded grants.[11]

Apart from governmental programmes, which are vulnerable to domestic and international political and economic turbulences and, as such, are temporary by nature, international collaboration frameworks in some cases take a more persistent institutional form. This is the case of the US-Israel Binational Science Foundation (BSF) endowed in equal parts by the two countries in 1972. Through the decades, BSF has awarded over 4,000 collaborative research projects, with a combined budget amounting to almost $0.5 billion. In 2012, facing the growing costs of research undertakings and stagnating returns on endowments, the BSF began a joint funding program with the National Science Foundation (in 2016 the joint NSF-BSF programme awarded 53 grants). Bilateral scientific collaboration frameworks occasionally take the form of public-private partnerships and involve non-profit, non-governmental organisations. This approach is exemplified by the Partner University Fund (PUF), which supports research collaboration between French and American institutions. The PUF was established in 2007 by the French government and the US-based French American Cultural Exchange Foundation, along with American private donors.

Individual scientific institutions also often have their own collaboration policies focused on the international dimension. This is particularly seen in the case of the most affluent and prestigious universities, which largely operate on the global scale. Take for example Massachusetts Institute of Technology (MIT). Its Global Seed Funds support new collaborations between MIT scholars and their foreign colleagues. Besides this general fund, MIT provides distinct funding for developing collaboration with institutions from 16 selected countries. Certain institutions go even further and establish overseas satellite campuses or partner with foreign counterparts in developing new joint study programmes or institutes. In 2011, MIT joined up with the Russian government to launch Skolkovo Institute of Science and Technology (Skoltech), which is intended to become one of the R&D engines of the Skolkovo Innovation Center—a high-tech park on Moscow's outskirts (Stone, 2016). Four American universities—the University of Wisconsin-Madison, the University of Pittsburgh, Duke University, and the University of Pennsylvania—have partnered with Kazakhstan's newly established (in 2010) Nazarbayev University in its aim to quickly secure an above-average position in international university league tables (Mahon & Niklas, 2016). After

2000, several American universities opened branches or programmes in the Persian Gulf states, which were quickly developing and eager to wisely invest their petrodollars. These initiatives include, among others, Weill Cornell Medical College of Cornell University in Doha, Qatar, and New York University Abu Dhabi and Heriot-Watt University Dubai in the United Arab Emirates (Miller-Idriss & Hanauer, 2011). These ventures focus largely on education, but in the long run, they can evolve into more research-oriented partnerships. However, the proliferation of branch campuses around the world is accompanied by rising doubts as to their long-term sustainability (Altbach, 2010), especially since many satellite campuses operate in countries vulnerable to political tensions and turnarounds.

International scientific collaboration is also susceptible to domestic political burdens. In the US context, these are chiefly related to national security. Technologies considered to have military relevance are principally off-limits to collaborative efforts with scholars from other countries (Vest, 2007). National security should be treated very seriously, but it sometimes leads to constrictions in scientific collaboration that is only at first glance connected to top-secret technologies. Consider the case of the physicist Xiaoxing Xi from Temple University. In 2015, the FBI arrested him for leaking classified semiconductor technology to China. At last—after several expert opinions—it turned out that the FBI agents had confounded different technologies and Xi's research had nothing to do with classified technologies (Otto, 2016).

6.5 China: (r)evolution in science policy

There is nothing small about China, nor about Chinese science. The Chinese scientific sector has experienced incredible growth and one cannot deny that in the last 40 years government policy—with the visible hand of the Chinese state—has played a crucial role in these developments (Liu, Simon, Sun, & Cao, 2011). Although state support for science and innovation has a very long tradition in the Middle Kingdom (Gelber, 2001; Needham, 1954; Wilson, 1999), the Chinese government recognised the vital role of collaboration in this process quite late, i.e., in 1980s. Scientific collaboration policy in China is characterised by high selectivity in three dimensions: thematic, institutional, and geographical (Jakobson, 2007). Firstly, R&D resources have been channelled to the most promising disciplines, to a large extent those giving international recognition to the country. This prioritisation trend has been visible since 1978, when the open-up policy was launched. In 2006, priority was given to, inter alia, information technology, nanotechnology, and biotechnology (State Council of the People's Republic of China, 2006; Cao, Suttmeier, & Simon, 2006; Zhou, 2015). Secondly, institutional selectivity is visible in the state's support of selected universities. The mid-1990s State Plan structured the higher education sector in a very hierarchical way, distinguishing elite research-intensive universities from the vast pool of higher education institutions. Specifically, special central government funding packages were provided to build world-class universities, which are also supported by subsidies from municipal funds (Zha, 2009). This policy has led to spatial variations in the quality of the Chinese science sector. Only a small proportion of the Chinese higher education institutions, predominantly located in the eastern and coastal regions, constitutes the "national team", homed in on the highest quality scientific research (Kafouros, Wang, Piperopoulos, & Zhang, 2015). The third focus area of Chinese scientific collaboration policy is international outreach. At the same time, internal collaboration has been somewhat overlooked and has faced numerous obstacles deeply rooted in the Chinese culture and society.

6.5.1 Collaboration in uncollaborative settings

From the science policy point of view, scientific collaboration among Chinese institutions remains at an unsatisfactory level. Papers co-authored by researchers affiliated in two or more Chinese provinces comprise a meagre 14 percent of papers indexed in the Chinese Science Citation Database. In-province collaboration is slightly more frequent, with 20 percent of papers co-authored by scientists from different institutions but located in the same Chinese province (Libo, 2015). The Chinese Patent Office (SIPO) data demonstrates even lower levels of inter-organisational collaboration in China. Only 1.3 percent of nearly 767,000 patent applications received by SIPO in the years 1985–2008 were the outcomes of intra-regional collaboration, and just one percent resulted from interregional collaborative research. Moreover, the numbers hardly changed during the period in question (Sun & Cao, 2015). These scientometric data show two noteworthy concerns. Firstly, collaborative inter-organisational behaviour in China is much more frequent in the case of research with less direct market value—note the different order of magnitude between co-authorship (14–20) and co-patenting (1–1.3) collaboration rates. Secondly, spatial proximity matters: in-province collaboration is clearly more frequent than collaboration that crosses provincial borders, both for co-publications (20 vs. 14 percent) and joint patent applications (1.3 vs. 1 percent).

Research collaboration in China develops in an environment that can be dubbed uncollaborative. A number of factors contribute to this condition. The roots of the uncollaborative environment are deeply embedded in Chinese culture and history. The grim legacy of the Cultural Revolution (1966–76) led by Mao Zedong (1893–1976) still casts a shadow on Chinese scholarship. During this difficult period Chinese universities were shut down, scientific institutes were dismantled, scholarly journals ceased publication, intellectuals were punished, and millions of students and researchers were sent to the countryside to learn political virtue from poor and uneducated peasants (Wilsdon, 2007). The most significant and long-lasting consequence of this period was the loss of a whole generation of scholars (Jakobson, 2007).

The Confucian tradition does not support collaborative behaviour. It attaches great importance to the social hierarchy, loyalty, and subordination to authority. Chinese education traditionally does not encourage critical thinking and expression of personal opinions (Qiu, 2014). Further, interpersonal relations in Chinese society are determined by *guanxi*—a concept closely related to the philosophy of Confucianism. Guanxi describes a complex system of interpersonal relationships which facilitate private and professional dealings. Development and maintenance of one's guanxi network is based on the exchange of reciprocal favours. Those informal relationships do not only shape collaboration networks in science, but they also regulate access to resources and funding for research projects. This is a big issue in China in the context of the thousands of returnees, who appreciate transparency in the financial system and grant policy (Cao, Li, Li, & Liu, 2013). Moreover, Chinese returnees, after many years spent abroad, may be met with mistrust and reluctance to collaborate, partially derived from their lack of appropriate guanxi (Wang & Bao, 2015). In effect, collaboration among Chinese scholars seems to be more difficult than in more open and less hierarchical organisational cultures (as in the US, for example).

Despite various modernisation reforms and political efforts, the state's organisation and the rules of its operation hamper scientific collaboration in the Middle Kingdom. An example could be the complex system of rights among different organisations and individuals. It was not until 1999, when the Chinese government issued the Decision on Strengthening Technological Innovation, Developing High Technology and Realizing Industrialization, that any organisation could freely decide whether and with whom to collaborate, based on its own interests and the market rules. Before this date, in the early stages of the science and technology sector development and transition towards a market-oriented economy, Chinese organisations were constricted by *tiao* (ministerial/departmental) and *kuai* (regional) relationships (Sun & Cao, 2015). Moreover, unclear rules regarding profit distribution, risk sharing, and ownership of intellectual property rights intensify the reluctance to collaborate. Last but not least, the lack of democracy and freedom in the field of policy and social life also affects scientific collaboration in China. Laura Jakobson aptly concludes in her book that "The S&T [science and technology] landscape faces the same problems as society at large" (2007, p. 28). The political system in China hampers the freedom of choice of scientific topics and partners for collaboration, and the freedom of speech. As such, it is in conflict with the notion of innovativeness and creativity.

The unsatisfactory level of collaboration within the Chinese science sector also results from the all-pervasive bureaucracy and central planning. The number of agencies responsible for science and technology development is enormous, and the institutional system complicated, with insufficient coordination and lack of transparency of financial flows. Several dozen independent research budget holders operate under China's State Council, and only recently (in 2011) has the Chinese government obliged its agencies to disclose information on their R&D expenditures to the wider public. The Ministry of Science and Technology, the Chinese Academy of Sciences, and the Natural Science Foundation of China control more than 70 percent of the central R&D spending through 71 agencies that disclosed their budgets in 2011 (Sun & Cao, 2014). Other important players are the Ministry of Industry and Information Technology, the Ministry of Education, the Ministry of Agriculture, the Ministry of Health, and the National Development and Reform Commission. At the same time, the top governing body of the science and technology system—the Leading Group of Science, Technology and Education, which operates within the Chinese Communist Party Central Committee—is blamed for inefficient coordination of activities among numerous agencies. For instance, although the Leading Group comprises heads of ministries involved in science and other related areas, it failed to efficiently coordinate scientific activities and resources in the face of the SARS syndrome in 2003 (Cao, 2014).

Insufficient exchange of information within and among founding bodies and a lack of national quality standards lead to misuse of funds. Different governmental agencies announce calls for the same undertakings without any coordination (IDRC & State Science and Technology Commission People's Republic of China, 1998; Sun & Liu, 2014), while scholars submit identical research proposals simultaneously to many funding bodies. Moreover, budgets for single grants are usually insufficient, forcing researchers to apply for several projects at the same time. Interviews with members of the Chinese Academy of Sciences revealed that more than half are under acute pressure to compete for funds because they can barely cover their basic living expenses (Luo, Ordonez-Matamoros, & Kuhlmann, 2015). Fierce competition for resources hampers collaboration and makes the research projects fragmented (Poo & Wang, 2014).

Another issue influencing Chinese scholars' attitudes to teamwork is the system of research evaluation. This is based almost entirely on publication output and therefore strongly encourages the publish or perish strategy. Domestic institutions judge scholars' status by the number of papers published each year. The story of Tu Youyou, the 2015 Nobel Prize winner in Physiology or Medicine, revealed how inadequate the system is in recognising talent. Although Youyou's discovery of a new cure for malaria became globally recognised and has saved millions of lives, she has never been elected to be an academician—the top domestic title for a Chinese researcher ("Reform of scientific research still needed despite Tu's Nobel", 2015). Furthermore, the evaluation system undervalues the contributions from researchers who are neither the first nor the corresponding author. This rule hampers young scientists in particular, who at the same time experience high pressure to publish in high-impact journals (Qiu, 2015). The system reduces willingness to collaborate because collaborative papers are less valuable than independent works. This means that in many situations, Chinese researchers do not work together, even if it would be more beneficial for national scientific capability (Qiu, 2014). The evaluation system also boosts plagiarism tendencies among researchers (Cao, 2014), and thereby increases mistrust within the scientific community. Ze Zhong, the former vice president of Beijing University of Technology, bitterly summarises, "Collaboration becomes very difficult. You can't trust people not to steal your work. Everyone works with the door closed, in secret" (Wilsdon, 2007).

158 *Scientific collaboration policy*

6.5.2 Reshaping institutions for collaboration

The Chinese science sector has been through significant changes over the last few decades. Deep organisational reforms have affected scientific collaboration An example of a policy aimed at spurring internal collaboration among Chinese scholars is the institutional reform of the Chinese Academy of Sciences (CAS). The CAS was established in the first month of the People's Republic of China in 1949 and still dominates the scientific landscape, serving over 70 percent of national science infrastructure and facilities. Zhou Enlai (1898–1976), the then premier of the State Council of the People's Republic of China, was determined to pool the resources of the whole nation in order to set up the CAS. He commented, "Give them people if they need people, land if they need land, buildings if they need buildings" (Poo & Wang, 2014, p. 3). Outstanding scientists, among them returnees from abroad, were concentrated in the new institution. Moreover, financial resources guaranteed the CAS an unquestionable position not only in science itself, but also in science policy. The institution adopted a very broad and complex mission. Until today it has undertaken basic and technological research, knowledge transfer, and commercialisation activities, conducted nationally strategic research for long-term development, developed higher education, run big-science facilities, and supplied advice on science policy decision-making. To fulfil its various functions, CAS employs 48,500 researchers and more than 12,000 other staff in 1,000 sites and stations across the country. It consists of 104 research institutes, 12 branch academies and three universities.[12]

Due to its multiple tasks, mammoth size, and complex structure, governance of the CAS became very challenging and caused tensions among various actors and institutions. On this account, in the last two decades several reforms have been undertaken to simplify the CAS structures and increase its strategic and financial efficiency: the Knowledge Innovation Programme (KIP) in the years 1997–2010, CAS Innovation 2020 in 2006, Innovation 2050 in 2009, and, most recently, the Pioneer Action Plan initiated in 2014 (Luo et al., 2015). In the framework of the KIP, research institutes were restructured and categorised under 10 prioritised funding fields. As a result, the number of independent institutes was reduced by one-fifth. Moreover, to decrease maintenance costs, about 25,000 researchers in CAS lost tenured positions. Nevertheless, the KIP reform brought positive results to the academy's productivity, which improved by 12.5 percent.

Another turning point was the CAS conference held in 2012. During the event, Bai Chunli, president of the academy, drew attention to the lack of collaboration among researchers running interrelated, but not linked, research programmes on LED employed in 20 different CAS institutes. The same was true for nearly 20 biological institutes. The scientists were not aware of their colleagues' work and were reluctant to discuss research results and share knowledge with the industry (Poo & Wang, 2014). To boost teamwork within the academy, consolidate research efforts, and limit the fragmentation of research programmes, the CAS institutes have been grouped into four broad categories: (1) innovation academies dealing with applied research in the fields of microsatellites, space science, marine information science, information technology, drug development, and nuclear energy, (2) centres of excellence performing basic science research, (3) big science facilities, such as the Particle Collider in Beijing or the Heavy Ion Source Facility in Guangzhou, and (4) specialised institutes responsible for relevant regional research, such as the environmental and social effects of natural disasters. Promising scientists were invited to work in these organisations, with assurance of better working conditions and higher salaries (which were previously lower than the Chinese average and therefore made scientists dependent on short-term grants). By this, the CAS encouraged scientists to collaborate on fewer, larger problems, rather than diverting their efforts to marginal advances in disparate projects (Cyranoski, 2014; Poo & Wang, 2014).

Similar deep reforms were applied to Chinese higher education. Until 1995, the institutional structure of higher education in China did not support collaboration. Different scientific disciplines were strictly separated within dedicated higher education institutions governed either by one of the ministries within central government, or by provincial and even local authorities. The reform merged universities and colleges into comprehensive institutions. By 2000, 556 universities had been merged and an additional 232 dissolved (Huang & Zhang, 2000; Mok, 2005). The reform assumed that merging mono-disciplinary institutions into comprehensive universities would improve managerial efficiency and international recognition, and increase opportunities to interdisciplinary collaboration.

6.5.3 China goes global

In recent decades, fostering international collaboration in science, technology, and innovation has been a strategic aim of the Chinese approach towards development. Each of the government's three major agencies for science and technology—the Ministry of Science and Technology, the National Natural Science Foundation of China, and the Chinese Academy of Sciences—has its own international departments to promote collaboration (Tian, 2015). Due to intensive science diplomacy, the Chinese science system is today closely intertwined with the worldwide network of connections (Bound, Saunders, Wildson, & Adams, 2013). According to figures from 2014, China has established scientific cooperation relations with over 150 countries and regions, signed over 100 intergovernmental collaboration agreements, and joined more than 200 international science and technology cooperation organisations (Simon, 2014).

The priority given by the Chinese government to international scientific collaboration is manifested in the Chinese presence in numerous international research projects, including the largest and the most cutting-edge. Examples could be the International Thermonuclear Experimental Reactor, Galileo, the Integrated Ocean Drilling Program, fourth gen nuclear energy, the Global Earth Observation System, CERN Large Hadron Collider, the Human Genome Project, the Alpha Magnetic Spectrometer, and the World Climate Research Programme. The Middle Kingdom actively participated in the latest discoveries and changes in the international scientific landscape. In response to the detection of gravitational waves by the LIGO project in February 2016, the Chinese government has initiated a 15-billion-yuan (circa $2.3 billion in 2016 dollars) research project led by Sun Yat-Sen University. The TianQuin project will study space-borne gravitational waves with the use of three spacecrafts in Earth's orbit and other exceptional equipment such as an ultra-quiet cave laboratory. To foster interest in the project and attract international talent, a new funding scheme for overseas scholars was launched, with competitive annual salaries of up to $153,000 (Chi, 2016; Luo et al., 2016; Xinhua, 2016a, 2016b; Yingqi, 2016).

Apart from individual projects, China is also involved in many large scientific programmes established by international organisations or based on bilateral agreements. For instance, the research collaboration agreement between China and the European Union was signed initially in 1998 and renewed in 2009. The volume of joint research has gradually increased under the European Union's Framework Programmes, placing China third, after the US and Russia, in terms of the total number of non-European participants (Bound et al., 2013). 383 Chinese organisations participated in 274 collaborative research projects between 2007 and 2013, with a total EU contribution of €35 million. In relation to the Horizon 2020 programme, the EU and China have launched a new Co-Funding Mechanism to support joint research and innovation activities. Each year, more than €100 million from the EU will be matched by at least 200 million yuan (almost €30 million) from Chinese programmes of the Ministry of Science and Technology for projects involving partners from Europe (Tian, 2015).

China consistently links its science sector to the international corporate R&D scene through the inflow and outflow of foreign direct investments. Many large Chinese companies are now firmly established overseas. The flagship telecommunication company Huawei operates several of its many R&D centres all over the world, e.g., in France, Germany, India, Italy, Sweden, Russia, the US, and the UK. The same stands for another renowned telecommunication equipment manufacturer, ZTE Corporation, which established its first R&D site in the United States, and later on also in Sweden, France, and Canada. The 2007 OECD review of the innovation policy in China reported that Chinese companies increasingly place their R&D centres in prestigious locations. Haier (consumer electronics and home appliances), Konka (electronics and telecommunications), Suning Commerce Group (retail), BAIC Group (automobiles and machinery), and DJI (a leading company in the civilian-drone industry) all set up their R&D sites in Silicon Valley (Sedgwick, 2015; Somerville, 2013; Terdiman, 2015).

Despite the increasing scale of international collaboration, the big issue is the character of the involvement of Chinese participants in international scientific projects. The role of Chinese scholars is gradually changing, from being passive workers to proactive collaborators, based on a win-win basis and with more equal responsibilities and tasks (Zhou, 2015). "International cooperation is both an effective means to bring in, absorb, and utilize worldwide scientific progress, resources, and talent for innovation, and a way for CAS to contribute to the global science progress and the tackling of various global challenges," says Bai Chunli, president of the Chinese Academy of Sciences, underlining the mutual benefits of international collaboration for Chinese and non-Chinese individuals and organisations (Jing, 2011).

The nature of involvement in a research project depends heavily on the maturity of the given scientific discipline or specialisation in China. As Jian Lin, marine geophysicist at the Woods Hole Oceanographic Institution in Massachusetts, said, "In many areas of research, Chinese scientists have changed from being a raw-data exporter to the source of creative ideas" (Qiu, 2015, p. 243). A major example of this shift in scientific partnerships is the Human Liver Proteome Project, the large-scale international collaborative initiative proposed in 2002 aimed at generating a comprehensive protein atlas of the human liver. Fuchu He, the chief scientist of CAS, initially co-chaired the project and developed its scientific strategy (Zhou, 2015). Another factor facilitating the change in the role of Chinese scientists in international research initiatives is the increased funding coming from Chinese institutes. Nevertheless, the key factor behind these processes is the growing international experience of Chinese scholars gained through studying and working abroad.

6.5.4 From brain drain to brain circulation

Since the 1890s, China has been sending its students abroad to rejuvenate the ancient civilisation (Gelber, 2001). The returnees from the early days have played important roles in the modernisation of Chinese society, bringing back experience, knowledge and international contacts. Statistics reveal that:

> 81% of members of the Chinese Academy of Sciences, 54% of engineering schools research fellows, and 72% of researchers in charge of the large 863 state-financed research projects have studied abroad [...] 77% of the university rectors of MoE[Chinese Ministry of Education]-administered universities are returnees, as are 94% of recipients of the prestigious Yangtze Scholars scheme
>
> (Welch, 2015, p. 99).

Sending students and scientists abroad is beneficial for the individuals, but at the state level it can lead to a brain drain—a loss of the most valuable part of the country's human capital. Of the 2.24 million students and scholars that went overseas in the years 1978–2012, only one-third have returned to China (Tai & Truex, 2015). This loss of human capital has been a major concern for the Chinese government. Thus, it is not surprising that China has implemented many programmes focused on its highly skilled overseas diaspora. The most prestigious Chinese schemes to attract academics from abroad are the Distinguished Young Scholars programme introduced by the National Natural Science Foundation of China in 1994 and the Chang Jiang Scholars Program co-founded by the Li Ka Shing Foundation and the Ministry of Education in 1998. Another recent scheme is the Recruitment

Program of Global Experts, known as 1,000 Talents, designed to attract Chinese-born scientists to return from overseas. Over a period of 5–10 years, the program has sought to attract about 2,000 leading scholars aged below 55, holding professorships or equivalent positions in renowned research institutions or universities (Welch & Hao, 2014). From its initiation in 2008 to mid-2014, the program helped to attract more than 4,000 (two times more than initially expected) top-level scientists from abroad. The overall number of returnees is even more impressive. In 2014, the cumulative number of returned PhD holders reached 110,000 (Zhou, 2015). However, the search for top-notch human capital is not only restricted to Chinese nationals. Several talent schemes are directed towards highly skilled overseas scholars, regardless of their nationality, such as the 100 Talent Program of the Chinese Academy of Sciences or the Chang Jiang Scholars Program (Welch & Hao, 2014). In 2007, the CAS also launched the Award for International Cooperation in Science and Technology, and in 2011, the International Cooperation Award for Overseas Young Scientists to further encourage cross-cultural exchanges and scientific cooperation (Jing, 2011).

Apart from central government action, provincial and municipal programs also try to attract talented people to specific places. Usually, these projects aim to raise the number of innovative start-ups funded by highly skilled specialists from abroad, promote returnee entrepreneurship, and attract quality scholars. For instance, Beijing Overseas Talents Center (BOTC) established in 2008, the first provincial-level service unit for overseas talents established in China, undertakes multifaceted activities on behalf of the Beijing municipal government. BOTC, under the so-called Haiju Program, head-hunts scholars worldwide and offers them comprehensive assistance when they return to their homeland: it awards grants of up to 1 million yuan, provides medical insurance and education stipends for dependents, and resolves visa and other formal issues. BOTC arranges visits to Australia, the US, and the UK to look for overseas Chinese high-level talents and present Beijing's preferential policies to returnees. The Beijing Forum for Overseas Talents, organised by BOTC, integrates the returnee community in Beijing and provides assistance with everyday difficulties in order to facilitate adaptation to current Chinese circumstances. By 2015, BOTC had recruited 627 high-level experts and entrepreneurs (Huang, 2015).

The diaspora policy is also reflected in the preference for returnees in the Chinese residential regulations. A powerful policy in favour of returnees is the conferment of local *hukou*, a Chinese household registration system that segregates the workforce according to regions. The situation regarding hukou is different for graduates of domestic and foreign higher education institutions. For the former group it remains extremely difficult to transfer their hukou to another location. Even if they work in a given city for a long period of time, they lack the formal status of a local resident, and consequently cannot enjoy the welfare entitlements provided by the city government. This means that they are not eligible for local government services, education, and health care. In contrast, the overseas Chinese graduates are allowed to select their preferred city of employment and transfer their hukou accordingly (Welch & Hao, 2014).

An important policy development occurred in 2001, when China shifted its diaspora policy from the notion of "return and serve the homeland" (*huiguo fuwu*) to a more flexible "serve the homeland" (*weiguo fuwu*), which means keeping contacts with the homeland, collaborating from a distance, and supporting the development of Chinese science, but not necessarily returning to China (Cai, 2012). This new approach was clearly expressed in the speech given by Chinese President Xi Jinping in 2013 at the 100th anniversary celebration of the establishment of the Western Returned Scholars Association in Beijing: "We welcome overseas-educated talent, whether at home or abroad, to contribute to China's development" (Jun, 2016). This is in line with recent observations that the concepts of brain drain and brain gain are no longer appropriate in the globalised world and should be replaced by the more comprehensive idea of brain circulation. A country profits not only when emigrants eventually return to the homeland, but also when they act as foreign liaisons that facilitate international collaboration, and connect local institutions to the global scientific network.

6.6 Tools for scientific collaboration policy

With the growth of collaborative practices in today's world of research, scientific collaboration policy becomes a must-have for every scientifically active nation. The case studies of China, Europe, and the United States revealed the wealth of initiatives and environments stimulating scientific collaboration. Governmental scientific collaboration policy is usually accompanied by policies formulated and implemented by various individual organisations: funding agencies, universities, R&D institutions, NGOs, enterprises, and international organisations. To accurately make sense of this abundant variety of scientific collaboration tools, a systematic classification would be beneficial.

Tools for scientific collaboration policy can be thought of as direct or indirect. Direct tools explicitly aim at the development of scientific collaboration. Indirect tools embrace the collaborative component implicitly. The first type actively promotes scientific joint ventures, while the second merely enables collaboration and reduces barriers to its development. Thus, the two approaches differ primarily in perspective. Ultimately, both recognise scientific collaboration as a measure that supports the attainment of other science policy goals, namely enhancement of research quantity and quality. Therefore, scientific collaboration is a tool of science policy, not its target.

Direct and indirect scientific collaboration tools relate to Jean-Jacques Salomon's distinction between policy for science and policy through science (Salomon, 1977). They can be named, respectively: science policy for scientific collaboration and science policy through scientific collaboration. Remarkably, the difference between the two approaches is, to some extent, country specific. EU science policy resembles the first type, while in the US the second category prevails. Risking overgeneralisation, it is arguable that in Europe—at the EU level and in individual countries—policies towards scientific collaboration are mostly top-down, actively promoting collaboration and employing funding mechanisms. In contrast, the US policy towards scientific collaboration is rather bottom-up, enabling and employing regulatory mechanisms (Caloghirou et al., 2002). This diversity is expected, since scientific collaboration policy mixes vary considerably among countries. National innovation systems are country specific, thus, "To govern these systems, policymakers must understand their dynamics and then devise incentives that will lead individual scientists to make the decisions they want" (Wagner, 2008, p. 106).

The following paragraphs summarise broad categories of scientific collaboration tools, their objectives, underlying mechanisms, and—if applicable—unexpected by-products. The review covers science diplomacy, infrastructure for collaboration, collaborative projects and programmes, R&D network management, mobility programmes, the collaborative regulatory environment, and research evaluation criteria. Naturally, the proposed categories overlap, due to the fact that they concern various policy levels. For instance, science diplomacy prepares the ground for other measures to be implemented in the international setting. Research evaluation criteria constitute a part of a wider collaborative regulatory environment. And good practices in R&D network management apply to all of the categories.

6.6.1 Science diplomacy

Science diplomacy creates the overall framework for the international research collaboration of a given nation. It can take the form of bilateral agreements that acknowledge the common will to collaborate in the area of science. More precisely, science diplomacy is "the process by which states represent themselves and their interests in the international arena when it comes to areas of knowledge" (Turekian et al., 2014, p. 4). Science diplomacy consists of three types of activity: (1) diplomacy for science, (2) science for diplomacy, and (3) science in diplomacy. The latter refers to providing policy makers with adequate knowledge of the globalised world and its current challenges together with policy recommendations. The Intergovernmental Panel on Climate Change, established in 1988 by the World Meteorological Organization and the United Nations Environment Programme, can serve as an illustration. Hence, science in diplomacy does not concentrate on science or scientific collaboration, but rather on a state's foreign policy goals (The Royal Society, 2010). Meanwhile, the first two types largely rely on international scientific collaboration.

Diplomacy for science facilitates international scientific collaboration through international agreements, bi- and multilateral collaborative programmes, mobility actions, and joint institutions (both big-science initiatives—such as CERN, the Square Kilometre Array, or the International Thermonuclear Experimental Reactor—and small-scale institutes). High-level government talks often precede working relations and the launch of concrete scientific collaboration policy measures. Diplomacy for science also includes international research marketing—a broad spectrum of measures homed in on the promotion of a given country as a leading location for conducting science, a destination for academic mobility, or a valuable scientific collaborator. Germany has adopted a comprehensive approach to international research marketing. Since 2006, the Federal Ministry of Education and Research has carried out an initiative called "Promoting Innovation and Research in Germany". It aims to attract to Germany foreign R&D investments and highly skilled researchers, as well as fostering international scientific collaboration (Fähnrich, 2015). The initiative is implemented, inter alia, by the network of science representatives based in German embassies, foreign representative offices of German research and intermediary organisations, the alliance for international research marketing,[13] several dozens of temporary R&D networks, international events, and two comprehensive portals: Research in Germany—Land of Ideas (www.research-in-germany.de) and Kooperation international (www.kooperation-international.de). The former targets foreigners interested in R&D collaboration with German partners or willing to pursue study or research in Germany. The latter provides information on international cooperation opportunities for German scientists and companies (Federal Ministry of Education and Research, 2014).

Science for diplomacy means using science cooperation to improve international relations between countries, particularly in a situation where the political environment is tense and official political relations are limited. Examples include the US-Japan Committee on Science Cooperation inaugurated in 1961, the scientific collaboration between Israel's Weizmann Institute and Germany's Max Planck Society initiated in the late 1950s, and the Middle East Research Cooperation programme run by the US Agency for International Development, which since 1981 has established scientific collaboration with Arab and Israeli partners. These initiatives illustrate that scientific interactions can lay the foundation for bringing back diplomatic relations between countries. Science for diplomacy takes the form of mobility programmes, educational scholarships, or science festivals and exhibitions—activities that can be undertaken even if diplomatic relations between countries are frozen (see: Bound et al., 2013).

6.6.2 Infrastructure for collaboration

Collaboration patterns in science are shaped, to some extent, by the availability of specific infrastructure. Two types of infrastructure for scientific collaboration can be distinguished: (1) unique facilities, often—but not necessarily—related to big science, and (2) communication and virtual collaboration tools. The unique infrastructure attracts researchers and, consequently, the places where it is located become collaboration hubs. Here, three cases in point are CERN near Geneva in Switzerland, Fermilab near Chicago in the US, and the Very Large Telescope observatory in the Atacama Desert of northern Chile. Megascience infrastructure does not only play a role in organising scientific collaboration. The uniqueness of facilities and equipment operates on various scales, from globally unique structures (such as the International Space Station), through one-and-only facilities in a country or a region, to single apparatuses within a given organisation. The context-specific uniqueness of infrastructure constitutes its collaborative capability. For this reason, collaboration based solely on shared infrastructure can be easily cut off when collaborators acquire their own facilities. Such a process was observed in Poland after its accession to the European Union in 2004, when many universities and research institutes obtained scientific instruments sponsored by European Union Funds. Consequently, some of the infrastructure-based collaborations became irrelevant and were terminated (Celińska-Janowicz, Wojnar, Olechnicka, & Ploszaj, 2017).

The second type of collaborative infrastructure—communication technologies and virtual collaboration tools—derives its collaborative capability not from uniqueness, but from ubiquity. According to the logic of network externalities, the utility of a given communication tool rises with the number of connected people—the more individuals use telephone, fax, email, or a social networking service, the more useful it is for everyone (Katz & Shapiro, 1985; Rogers, 2003). The enabling and facilitating role of information and communication technologies in scientific collaboration is undeniable. It is no accident that international scientific collaboration gradually increased with the worldwide proliferation of the internet, initiated in the early 1990s and quickly transforming global society and economy (Castells, 1996). Contemporary science is unimaginable without information and communication technologies, which have become omnipresent and almost translucent to the point where it is hard to differentiate between scholars' collaborative behaviour and productivity. A 2009 paper published in *Research Policy* concluded that:

> At earlier stages of the introduction of the internet, its use might have given researchers who were early adopters an added advantage in information exchange and coordination from a distance. However, in a context where use of email has become an everyday routine, email communication proved not as important for research productivity
> (Vasileiadou & Vliegenthart, 2009, p. 1266).

But make no mistake, the diminishing impact of ICT on scientific collaboration concerns primarily the most basic tools (e.g., email), which have become almost universally available, even for scholars in developing countries (Shrum et al., 2014). It is the quality of the ICT infrastructure that makes a difference—for instance, the availability of higher internet bandwidths correlates with academic productivity (da Fonseca Pachi, Yamamoto, da Costa, & Lopez, 2012). Furthermore, the vast diversity of advanced virtual collaboration tool types—collaboratories, e-Science, cyber-infrastructure, virtual research environments, collaborative software, groupware, remote conferencing services, scholarly social networking sites, and workflow systems, to point out only a few of many categories and competing concepts—is progressively transforming the practices of scientific collaboration (for details and examples, see: Carusi & Reimer, 2010; Jirotka, Lee, & Olson, 2013; Olson & Olson, 2013; Olson, Zimmerman, & Bos, 2008).

6.6.3 Collaborative projects and programmes

The most apparent collaboration policy tool is a collaborative project. The idea is straightforward: funding agencies can specify collaboration as a prerequisite for approving a project, or include collaboration incentives in the evaluation criteria for project selection, which in turn makes joint proposals more likely to be funded. Many grant competitions use one of these approaches. This is the case with cross-sectoral programmes, mainly those focused on cooperation between science and business, or programmes for inter-firm research joint ventures (see: Vonortas, 1997). Support schemes available primarily for R&D institutions also apply this approach. For instance, participation in the Framework Programmes—the main measure used to stimulate international scientific collaboration in the European Union—initially required at least two partner institutions from different countries. Following the EU enlargements, the bar was raised to include three or more organisations based in the various countries.

Programmes for collaborative projects are often focused on international collaboration. However, there are a number of worthy examples of measures aimed at domestic networks. Taking the US as an example, we can mention the well-known Engineering Research Centers programme (and its older sister, the Industry-University Cooperative Research Centers programme depicted in Section 6.4.3 above). The Engineering Research Centers initiative was authorised by the US Congress in 1985 to bridge university research, education, and industrial innovation. The programme funded consortia composed primarily of research universities that were expected to form partnerships with industry (Bozeman & Boardman, 2004). The first (1985–1990) and second (1994–2006) generations of the programme financed 40 centres. The third generation started in 2008 and, by 2016, had awarded ten centres. The collaboration requirement varied over time. In the current iteration of the programme, partnerships are expected to include not only domestic partners—a lead university plus one to four partner universities—but also one to three foreign higher education institutions. One of the large-scale and long-operating Engineering Research Centers was the Mid-America Earthquake (MAE) Center. MAE was led by the University of Illinois at Urbana-Champaign in collaboration with Georgia Institute of Technology, the University of Memphis, Massachusetts Institute of Technology, St. Louis University, Texas A&M University, and Washington University. A well-grounded evaluation of the MAE Center proved that it increased collaborative behaviour. Its members collaborated more often than non-affiliates, in particular with industry and in cross-disciplinary teams. The various opportunities to interact across organisational, sectoral, and disciplinary boundaries provided by collaborative research centres was shown to increase not only collaboration, but also research productivity (Ponomariov & Boardman 2010).

Another example of measures directly aimed at intensifying domestic scientific collaboration is the German Excellence Programme. This joint initiative of German federal and state government started in 2006 and is implemented by the German Research Foundation and the German Council of Science and Humanities. The programme has amassed a weighty budget of up to 3.2 percent of the R&D expenditure of the German higher education system. It aims to enhance scientific excellence through intensifying domestic collaboration among universities and major non-university institutions, namely, the Helmholtz Association, the Max Planck Society, the Leibniz Association and the Fraunhofer Society. The underlying premise of the programme—and an essential feature of the German science system—is that non-university research organisations accumulate a great deal of top-level scientific activities. Thus, universities were expected to significantly profit from intensified collaboration with these research organisations, not only increasing their scientific performance but also climbing in global university rankings. The programme resulted in the growth of highly cited joint publications of universities and non-university institutions. However, the positive effect was greater for the latter (Möller, Schmidt, & Hornbostel, 2016), providing a conspicuous example of the Matthew effect generated by science policy.

A distinct category of collaborative schemes is formed by big science projects. Firstly, they are very uncommon for the simple reason that they generate extremely high costs. Secondly, scientific collaboration plays a major role in big science—large, often international partnerships are needed to amass the necessary resources and skills. In this case, collaboration can be seen as a *sine qua non* condition for a project execution. As such, big science projects are responsible for increased scientific collaboration, and consequently for the collaborative turn in science. However, they can hardly be seen as a policy tool aimed directly at scientific collaboration. Policy makers do not fund cutting-edge, large-scale, expensive research to merely influence scientific collaboration, but to enable discoveries and inventions, solve pressing social problems, boost the economy, or achieve military supremacy. Big science clearly shows that scientific collaboration is—ultimately—a measure of science policy, not its objective.

6.6.4 R&D network management

This broad category of scientific collaboration tools focuses on (1) initiating new links between researchers, and (2) developing and enhancing the efficiency of existing R&D networks. Scientific network management initiatives usually take the form of small-scale soft measures which directly address research collaboration. In essence, they supplement initiatives oriented towards research outcomes. A typical example is a small grant scheme aimed at establishing new partnerships, which subsequently can apply for a collaborative project or funding for shared infrastructure. This kind of "glue money", or "seed grant", supports meetings, covers travel costs, brings scientists together, and facilitates communication. Such simple activities can be highly beneficial, specifically with regard to international and interdisciplinary partnerships—typically harder to establish compared to domestic and same-discipline collaborations (Cooke & Hilton, 2015).

On a micro scale, the management of interactions among researchers can be based on the pro-collaborative design of campuses, laboratories, and office spaces. Scientific collaboration is "a body-contact sport—people have to be running into each other to make it work" (National Academies et al., 2005, p. 94). Many organisations deliberately arrange various shared spaces, cafeterias, common rooms, and corridors in a way that increases the number of occasions for people to mingle together. There is growing empirical evidence—on top of common-sense intuition—that the physical features of a workplace environment can impact collaborative behaviour (Doorley & Witthoft, 2012; Owen-Smith, 2013; Sailer & McColloh, 2012; Toker & Gray, 2008). Here, the key role is played by co-location, either long-term or temporary (Boudreau et al., 2017; Catalini, 2017; Kabo et al., 2014).

Efficient research collaboration requires specific personal skills, organisational arrangements, and managerial practices. Collaboration can be risky and inefficient, and it can fail if not managed properly. The need for insight into the mechanisms governing research collaboration and practical advice to manage it well has motivated the rise of a new area of inquiry: the science of team science. This examines "the processes by which scientific teams organize, communicate and conduct research" (Börner et al., 2010). Simultaneously, a number of manuals, handbooks, and best-practices compendia for effective and efficient research collaboration have been proposed. The US National Academy of Sciences has prepared two particularly remarkable practice-oriented publications: *Facilitating Interdisciplinary Research* in 2005 (National Academies et al., 2005) and *Enhancing the Effectiveness of Team Science* in 2015 (Cooke & Hilton, 2015).

6.6.5 Mobility programmes

Mobility programmes create possibilities for students and researchers to spend a period of time in another institution, usually abroad. This is a very common measure implemented on a governmental level by almost all scientifically advanced countries. The most representative example is the US Fulbright Program, while the largest—regarding the number of participants—is the student-oriented EU Erasmus Programme. Many research organisations have also adopted mobility programmes, for example, in the form of bilateral exchange arrangements or subsidised overseas sabbaticals. The temporary relocation of students and researchers is believed to have a positive influence on their knowledge and skills; hence, the main aim of academic mobility is to improve human capital. However, it turns out that the mobility of students and researchers also often results in increased scientific collaboration (Scellato et al., 2015).

There are two mechanisms for gaining collaborative benefits from mobility programmes: return and circulation. The return mechanism relies on the assumption that home-coming scientists bring back and make available their foreign contacts, along with their knowledge and expertise gained abroad. Less-performing countries, like China, India, Argentina, or many African states, build their merit in science by relying on the international exchange of students and scholars. As Jacob and Meek stated, "Mobility and internationalization are increasingly becoming entry costs for engaging in scientific research in some fields of endeavour" (2013, p. 333). The example of China, which since the late 1990s has introduced numerous schemes for returnees, such as the Yangtze River Scholar Plan, the 100 Talents Program and the 1,000 Talents Program, shows that the policy towards returnees was able to bring back its citizens, and they have had an impact on Chinese international scientific collaboration (Hao, Yan, Guo, & Wang, 2017; Xian, 2015). However, the bottom line is that the most talented scholars—meaning also those most engaged in collaboration—rarely returned to China (Zweig & Wang, 2013).

The circulation mechanism can be seen from two opposite perspectives. From the standpoint of the outflow country, it relies on building strong links between the diasporas and the domestic scholar community. Chinese evidence shows that scientists working in China benefited in particular from collaboration with overseas Chinese, thus, encouraging greater collaboration with the scientific diaspora can contribute significantly to scientific progress (Fangmeng, 2016). On the other hand, from the perspective of the inflow country, the circulation mechanism relies on the establishment of long-lasting collaboration with visiting scholars who eventually go back to their homelands. A meticulous study of 1,800 academics from 93 countries who visited Germany under the Humboldt Research Fellowship programme during the second half of the 20th century reveals the positive outcomes of international collaboration. After their return, Humboldt research fellows collaborated with German peers more intensively than other researchers. The study concludes that the Humboldt mobility programme contributed significantly to Germany's strong position in the global scientific collaboration network (Jöns, 2009).

6.6.6 The collaborative regulatory environment

The regulatory environment constitutes a framework in which legal incentives and deterrents shape collaborative behaviour. The impact of legislation on scientific collaboration can be powerful. This is exemplified by the American Bayh-Dole Act adopted in 1980. The legislation, officially named as the Patent and Trademark Law Amendments Act, permitted universities, small businesses, and non-profit institutions to benefit from inventions made with federal funding. This new regulatory environment contributed to the amplification of university-industry R&D collaboration in the US in the 1980s and 1990s (National Academies et al., 2005). On the other hand, the intellectual property monetary value of university research, strengthened by the Bayh-Dole Act, is occasionally blamed for deterring international scientific collaboration, especially between developing and developed nations. Clemente Forero-Pineda, from the University of los Andes in Bogotá, Colombia, mentioned the case of a failed attempt at collaboration between a South American institution and a US research university. The cooperative research agreement was not signed because the US university insisted on keeping all the patent rights resulting from the collaboration (Forero-Pineda, 2006).

Another example of legislation relevant to R&D collaboration is immigration law. Easy movement of scholars across borders is of growing importance in the increasingly internationalised science sector. The idea of the free circulation of researchers is central to the policy framework of the European Research Area. Besides, many developed countries have implemented specific immigration regulations streamlining the entry of foreign scientists. For instance, the US has adopted a visa category for "aliens of extraordinary ability". Under the law, outstanding scholars are granted temporary or permanent residency visas.

Intellectual property rights and immigration law are examples of national-level regulations that can influence scientific collaboration. However, other science policy levels are also relevant here. Above all, research funding agencies have at their disposal a number of regulatory tools that can facilitate or boost collaboration. Simple recognition that a project can be led by multiple principal investigators can facilitate research joint ventures—this approach is implemented, for example, by the US National Institute of Health (McGovern, 2009). However, the largest possible impact of pro-collaborative rules relates to international collaboration. Typically, funding agencies operate within national borders. Crossing country borders in the framework of a funded project is usually impossible or requires significant additional administrative effort. Funding agencies reduce this burden by the application of specific regulations. A guide prepared in 2014 by Science Europe—an association of major European research funding and research performing organisations—recommends three models to facilitate cross-border collaboration: (1) money follows researcher, (2) money follows cooperation line, and (3) the lead agency procedure.

The first scheme allows for cross-border transferability of grants. A researcher relocating to another country can take his or her current grant and continue to work on it in a new research organisation abroad. The model targets international collaboration, somewhat indirectly, by easing international academic mobility. It is argued that "the start at a new host institution and in a new country is easier for the scientists if they are able to bring along their own research funds in a simple and non-bureaucratic way" (Science Europe, 2014, p. 8). Such an approach was initiated in 2003 by the German Research Foundation, the Austrian Science Fund, and the Swiss National Science Foundation. The agreement allows the cross-border transfer of national grants between Austria, Germany, and Switzerland.

The second scheme (money follows co-operation line) allows for the funding of foreign investigators directly, in a national grant. The method enables international collaboration in a simple manner: there is no need for the involvement of foreign funding organisations or any additional international decision-making process. This was implemented in 2007 by the UK's Economic and Social Research Council under the name "International Co-investigators Policy". After several rounds of funding, the council declared that the proposals which included international co-investigators achieved significantly higher success rates in comparison to the purely UK-based proposals (Science Europe, 2014).

The idea of the third scheme, the lead agency procedure, is straightforward: international research projects are funded by national agencies in parallel—i.e., each agency funds its own part of the project and no money is transferred across borders—while one of the cooperating agencies takes the responsibility of reviewing and recommending project applications. However, this is also a more complex model than the two discussed above. The lead agency procedure requires not only a substantial agreement between research funding organisations, but also a high degree of mutual trust. Cooperating organisations have to agree on procedures (which can significantly differ from those to which they are accustomed) and rely on the leading agency's work quality. This additional effort is outweighed by the benefits of simplifying the application process for international partnerships, which need to prepare only one proposal instead of multiple applications submitted separately in each country. Likewise, research funding organisations also benefit from the reduction in processing the same proposals concurrently. The scheme has been adopted by the American National Science Foundation, which partners with the Netherlands Organisation for Scientific Research, and by the French National Research Agency and the Austrian Science Fund, as well as by the Luxembourg National Research Fund and the Swiss National Science Foundation—to name only a few examples (for more details see: Science Europe, 2014).

6.6.7 Research evaluation criteria

Scientific performance evaluation can be a powerful framework for influencing the collaborative behaviour of individuals, as well as institutional policies towards collaboration. The influence can be particularly strong when the result of an evaluation translates into individual or institutional profits, such as career development or access to finance. The latter case relates particularly to performance-based research funding systems implemented in many countries, such as those initiated by the UK in 1986, then followed by Australia and New Zealand, Hong Kong, and a number of European Countries, in particular the Nordic states, but also Belgium (the Flemish Community), Italy, Poland, Portugal, the Slovak Republic, and Spain (Hicks, 2012). Research evaluation frameworks address collaboration in two ways: (1) explicitly, when collaboration is one of the assessment criteria, and (2) implicitly, when other criteria affect collaborative behaviour (e.g., fractional or whole counting of publications). Furthermore, collaborative performance assessment targets individuals or organisations. Expected behavioural change mechanisms vary across these two levels. However, personal and organisational levels of evaluation are to some degree intertwined, due to the fact that institutional evaluation criteria are often seen as a point of reference for individual assessments. In this way, incentives of national performance-based research funding systems trickle down to the level of a single scholar (Aagaard, 2015).

On the individual level, the most obvious and explicit evaluation-induced incentives for collaboration are related to career development. The ability to develop collaborative networks, evidenced by a vast, heterogeneous constellation of collaborators, is a significant plus on the academic job market. Many institutions, in advertising job posts, include experience in scientific collaboration (often international or with industry) as a prerequisite or an appreciated advantage.

Likewise, engagement in collaboration can be checked during periodic performance assessments and tenure or promotion reviews. This can provide a clear message for scholars that might easily translate into more collaborative undertakings. The issue is more complicated than one might expect. Collaboration is often seen as the tricky part of promotion and tenure reviews. Even though science is increasingly collaborative, the key to getting tenure is individual performance (McGovern, 2009; Misra, Smith-Doerr, Dasgupta, Weaver, & Normanly, 2017; Zucker, 2012). Not surprisingly, "A common piece of advice that is given to job candidates and newly hired assistant professors is that it is important to work independently of other faculty so that one's accomplishments can be measured easily" (Jorgensen, 2007, p. 2967). However, the main point is not to discourage collaboration, but to adjust performance assessment rule books to the contemporary collaborative era in science. Some comprehensive frameworks to evaluate individual performance in highly collaborative contexts have already been proposed (see: Mazumdar et al., 2015). A significant related development that facilitates individual performance assessment is the proliferation of scientific journal policies requiring a detailed description of each author's contribution to the given paper (Marušić, Bošnjak, & Jerončić, 2011; Rennie, Yank, & Emanuel, 1997; Tscharntke, Hochberg, Rand, Resh, & Krauss, 2007).

Collaboration as a criterion for evaluation of individual scientists may be closely connected to academic mobility. Experience gained in various institutions (often abroad) is seen not only as an enhancement of one's knowledge and skills but also as a sign of relational capital: the capital of relationships with former colleagues that can be turned into new inter-organisational collaborations. In North America, a typical—and expected by tenure-track search committees—education and career path includes at least two or three major stops at different institutions (undergraduate program, graduate school, and postdoctoral fellowship, for example). Remarkably, this mobility requirement operates largely as an unwritten rule, deeply embedded in the American academic culture. This contrasts with Europe, where academic mobility is decidedly lower, and policymakers try to stimulate or even—occasionally—force institutional mobility. A case in point is Germany, where a rigid mobility requirement has been introduced. PhD graduates are not allowed to work at their alma mater for a period of six years after graduation (Enders, 2001). However, the mobility requirement is usually less strict. For example, in the Czech Republic, some experience abroad is one of the prerequisites for a PhD defence—and in this case, the requirement can be satisfied by participation in summer schools or even academic conferences.

Research performance assessments on the institutional level can approach collaboration criteria qualitatively or quantitatively. Qualitative approaches, based on peer review (such as the Research Excellence Framework in the UK), rarely directly focus on scientific collaboration, due to the fact that evaluators can directly assess the quality and impact of the examined institution. In this instance, scientific collaboration is properly handled as a means, not an end. In quantitative approaches, based on metrics (applied in, inter alia, Australia, China, Denmark, Italy, Norway, and Poland), the criterion of collaboration plays a much more important role and is applied in many ways, from counting episodes of collaboration and mobility, through taking into account the monetary value of collaborative projects, up to measuring the outcomes of collaboration, namely co-authored publications or patent applications. In relation to collaborative projects, different weights can be assigned to various types of projects (e.g., domestic or international) and the roles of an assessed institution (e.g., overall coordination, coordination of a working package, or just participation in a consortium).

Quantitative performance assessment frameworks raise concerns over their indirect—either intentional or unintentional—impact on collaborative behaviour. This is particularly the case with bibliometric indicators. It has been speculated that fractional counting may discourage co-authorships for the reason that co-authored works give fewer credits than those that are single authored; this applies primarily to fields in which publications typically involve dozens or even hundreds of authors or institutions (Bloch & Schneider, 2016). On the contrary, whole counting is seen as a favourable approach to co-authorship because it allocates full credit to all collaborating parties. Some even argue that it can induce "an artificial collaboration initiated only for the purpose of dealing with the evaluation system" (Kulczycki, 2017). However, to date, there is no solid evidence of either effect. Analyses of evaluation models applied in Australia (whole counting), Norway (fractional counting), and Denmark (fractional counting with a bonus for collaborative publications—institutional fractions are multiplied by 1.25) find no relationship between the method of counting publications in performance assessments and collaborative behaviour (Aagaard, Bloch, & Schneider, 2015; Schneider, Aagaard, & Bloch, 2016; Schneider, 2009; Ingwersen & Larsen, 2014; Sivertsen, 2016).

* * *

Due to the omnipresence of collaboration in contemporary science, there is almost no area of science policy that does not affect research collaboration. Besides the plethora of specific tools for scientific collaboration, network-oriented science policy encompasses measures that influence collaboration indirectly. In consequence, scientific collaboration policy has to be seen as an increasingly horizontal and inherent feature of science policy, not merely a subset of its objectives and tools. This fusion of scientific collaboration policies and overall science policy certainly makes decision-making and policy-making processes more challenging. Nonetheless, it also opens up possibilities for more comprehensive and effective science policy that is collaboration-aware.

Notes

1 Not all FP7 projects were collaborative. Two programme axes—Ideas and People—were not specifically designed to support cooperation (i.e., collaboration was not a prerequisite requirement).
2 Excluding the two non-collaborative programme axes: People and Ideas.

3 As of 1 January 2017, the countries associated with Horizon 2020 are Iceland, Norway, Albania, Bosnia and Herzegovina, the Former Yugoslav Republic of Macedonia, Montenegro, Serbia, Turkey, Israel, Moldova, Switzerland, Faroe Islands, Ukraine, Tunisia, Georgia, and Armenia.
4 The survey was addressed to around 600 European public funders and 8,500 research-performing organisations, of which 1,265 responded (representing one-third of the total government budget appropriations or outlays for research and development in the EU).
5 For comparison, 0.35 percent of the FP7 budget was allocated for international cooperation with non-EU countries.
6 Brazil, Russia, India, and China.
7 The data are sourced from UNESCO, 2015.
8 According to the Science Philanthropy Alliance, private funding for basic research in life sciences reached more than $1 billion in 2015 ("Private funding for science", 2016).
9 The eight institutions are Brown University, Columbia University, Cornell University, Dartmouth College, Harvard University, the University of Pennsylvania, Princeton University, and Yale University.
10 Indiana University, Michigan State University, Northwestern University, Ohio State University, Penn State University, Purdue University, Rutgers University, University of Illinois, University of Iowa, University of Maryland, University of Michigan, University of Minnesota, University of Nebraska-Lincoln, University of Wisconsin-Madison.
11 As of the beginning of 2017, the continuation of the initiative is neither confirmed nor foredoomed. http://global-innovation-initiative.org/
12 Data from http://english.cas.cn, visited 17.02.16.
13 The alliance joins four key players of the German innovation system: Alexander von Humboldt Foundation (AvH), German Academic Exchange Service (DAAD), German Research Foundation (DFG), and the Fraunhofer Gesellschaft (FhG).

7 Conclusions

The accelerating accumulation of scientific knowledge, increasing specialisation, and competition for resources and recognition make the way to the knowledge frontier increasingly difficult for a sole scientist, an individual organisation, or a single country. Consequently, policymakers, research organisation managers, and individual scholars recognise collaboration as a valuable tool to allocate resources efficiently and to increase the quantity and quality of scholarly outputs. Everyone jumps on the collaborative bandwagon, as it brings the promise of increased capacities to push forward the knowledge frontier. The unprecedented contemporary growth of research collaboration—the collaborative turn—is transforming scientific endeavour. The organisation of research and scholarly work is progressively defined by multidimensional networks, which connect researchers, organisations, policymakers, infrastructures, professional and general media, and the lay public. However, at the same time, the global geography of science has not changed substantially. Similarly, the highly hierarchical structure of scholarship remains fundamentally constant. The collaborative turn has not flattened the world of science, as globalisation has not levelled global socioeconomic disparities. The overall global landscape of science remains spiky.

On the one hand, the collaborative turn disrupts the processes and practices of doing science. On the other, spatial structures of scientific endeavour can be seen to persist rather than considerably transform. The closing section of the book reflects on this tension. We summarise the mutual relations between scientific collaboration and the geography of science. Then, we look to the future of scientific collaboration and its possible impact on the spatial features of research and scholarship. The chapter concludes with thoughts on science policy challenges in the collaborative turn era.

7.1 Research collaboration and the geography of science

Geography matters in scientific collaboration. The spatial location of research infrastructure, higher education institutions, and individual scholars defines possible nodes of scientific collaboration networks. The geographic distribution of research activities provides a scaffold over which the web of collaboration is stretched. This scaffolding was set up long before the collaborative turn in science materialised. The increasing research collaboration has filled existing structures, rather reinforcing than reshaping the geography of science.

Furthermore, the spatial distance between the nodes in scientific networks modulates the likelihood of collaborative links emerging, as well as the development and intensity of collaboration. Despite significant improvements in transportation, along with advances in information and communication technologies—which have reduced the costs and smoothed the flows of goods, people, and ideas on a global scale—spatially separated organisations and scholars are less likely to collaborate than those located in proximity to each other. However, the role of the proximity-distance variable is different when it comes to the impact of collaborative research. Spatially distant collaboration tends to provide more sound results than short-haul relations. The latter are likely to have overlapping capacities, while spatially separated collaborations create opportunities to combine complementary skills and resources. Thus, overcoming the hardships of distant collaboration can be a smart strategy in order to invade the cutting edge of science. On this account, we can understand why distant collaboration in science is constantly on the rise despite the persistent significance of spatial proximity.

On the other hand, scientific collaboration matters for the geography of science. Research collaboration cements the long-term, hierarchical, core-periphery structure of the global distribution of research excellence. Top-notch research organisations tend to collaborate with each other. In effect, they gain additional advantage over scientifically less developed entities. Collaboration between more and less scientifically advanced organisations, places, or countries happens very often. However, the effects of such cooperation are not necessarily evenly distributed among partners. Although less scientifically advanced partners benefit—through the diffusion of knowledge—from relations with more developed collaborators, the latter profit even more because they are able to impose their own paradigms, research agendas, and long-term objectives.

Simultaneously, less advanced players, positioned on the outskirts of the global scientific collaboration network, have no other option to increase their performance but to collaborate with the scientific core. Yet collaboration is not a sufficient factor to turn scientific latecomers into state-of-the-art performers. The recent rise of China as a new scientific superpower—a rare breakthrough in the petrified structure of the contemporary global science system—provides a prime example here. The outstanding development of the research sector in China has resulted predominantly from massive investments from the Chinese government and has less to do with networks and collaboration. Moreover, this amazing rise has taken place despite the cultural and organisational obstacles to scientific collaboration in China. On the one hand, it implies that even if contemporary science is highly saturated by the logic of collaboration, tangible resources remain the most important stimuli for the development of the research sector. On the other hand, one can hypothesise that cultural and institutional impediments to collaboration may hinder further expansion of the research sector in specific national or organisational environments.

The tension between the collaborative turn that disrupts scientific endeavour and the persistency of the global geography of science can be further understood in light of spatial transaction and transmission costs. Interacting across geographical space involves specific spatial transaction costs. Among them, a subgroup of spatial transmission costs related to moving information, goods, and people can be distinguished. Due to the development of transportation, information, and communication technologies, spatial transmission costs have been significantly reduced in recent decades (Gaspar & Glaeser, 1998; Glaeser & Kohlhase, 2004). This fall in spatial transmission costs has contributed to the rise of scientific collaboration. However, once basic information can be transmitted virtually for free, access to complex knowledge, typically of tacit nature, gains significance in building a competitive advantage. The cost of handling complex knowledge across space remains relatively high because it requires face-to-face interaction and long-term, trusted relationships. In consequence, the overall spatial transaction costs have risen, even if spatial transmission costs have fallen (McCann, 2013). The fact that there are more collaborative flows in the global research network does not necessarily change its structure. The tide of collaboration has raised all boats, but those that were already in the centre are still there, and those that were far away still drift on the periphery.

Moreover, the relations between space and scientific collaboration take place on many levels, from the location and movements of individual scholars, through the internal organisation of research facilities, offices, and campuses, as well as inter-organisational relations, to interurban, inter-regional, and international mega-spaces of knowledge flows. Notably, the multidimensional nature of scientific collaboration in space goes beyond the simple observation that flows occur on different scales. Some regularities vary across spatial levels. This phenomenon is well illustrated by three facets of research internationalisation. First, despite the exceptional growth of international collaboration, domestic—interurban—collaboration not only remains significant but tends to grow faster than international collaboration. Second, due to the aggregation bias, the internationalisation degree tends to be higher at the subnational level than at the national or global scale. Third, at the global level, the relationship between the volume of scientific production and its internationalisation is negative, while at the subnational level, areas with higher scientific output tend to be more involved in international research collaboration. As a result, the comprehensive theoretical approaches to the geography of scientific collaboration should embrace micro and macro perspectives. The two approaches can be simultaneously complementary and contradictory—as in the case of classical and quantum physics or micro and macroeconomics—but both are indispensable to understanding scientific collaboration in space.

7.2 Future geographies of scientific collaboration

The collaborative turn in science is not over—it constantly develops. Most likely, it will continue to change the scholarship in the years to come. We can expect that the future geographies of science will be increasingly conditioned by collaboration, in accordance with the logic of networks. As Manuel Castells observed:

> dominant functions and processes in the Information Age are increasingly organized around networks. Networks constitute the new social morphology of our societies, and the diffusion of networking logic substantially modifies the operation and outcomes in processes of production, experience, power, and culture
>
> (1996, p. 467).

It is indeed difficult to predict what the future will look like. Still, we can reflect on key contemporary trends in scientific cooperation and try to imagine how they might impact the future geographies of science. Four issues are particularly important: (1) the further growth of mass collaboration, (2) the rise of citizen science, (3) the limits of collaboration, and (4) threats to global research networks.

Mass collaboration refers to situations in which collaboration exceeds a typical scale. This is epitomised by scientific hyper-authorship. In 1993, the Ig Nobel Prize went to a group of 972 scholars recognised for co-authoring an article that had 100 times as many authors as pages (Cho & McKee, 2002). As of March 2018, the highest number of co-authors—precisely 5,154—was achieved by a paper estimating the size of the Higgs boson published in *Physical Review Letters* in 2015. The achievement was accurately depicted in *Nature*: "Only the first nine pages in the 33-page article [...] describe the research itself—including references. The other 24 pages list the authors and their institutions" (Castelvecchi, 2015, para. 2). New co-authorship records can only be a matter of time. Large-scale, multi-organisational, and multi-national collaborations proliferate. The sizes of research teams that were incredible yesterday are today typical, and tomorrow will be seen as modest. So what could be the spatial impact of these increasingly common, enormous research teams? Recent years have shown that more flows and denser networks do not necessarily mean that the spatial distribution of network nodes evolves. On the contrary, the network logic seems to replicate pre-existing spatial structures. On this basis, we can hypothesise that larger research teams will create even greater benefits for current cores and increase their advantage over the scientific periphery. Larger teams need more coordination, and if coordinating a team gives power, coordinating a larger team gives even more power. The new logic of networks goes hand in hand here with the old logic of the Matthew effect.

If teams of collaborating scholars can grow to enormous sizes, citizen science—also known as networked science or crowd science—means even larger collaborations. The first iteration of the Galaxy Zoo crowdsourced astronomy project attracted 150,000 citizen scientists who classified 900,000 galaxies (Lintott et al., 2010). Another astronomy project, SETI@home, involved, as of 2016, about 1.5 million volunteers from all over the world who agreed to allocate their personal computers' idle processing resources to analyse radio signals in search of extra-terrestrial intelligence.[1] Although citizen science has limitations—as it is useful only in specific cases—and raises concerns about the quality of results (*The rise of...*, 2015; Thelen & Thiet, 2008), it has already contributed to the development of scientific knowledge. A good example is the online puzzle video game known as Foldit. The aim of the game is to fold structures of proteins—a demanding task that requires strong spatial imagination. The game has attracted hundreds of thousands of players and has contributed to significant discoveries. In 2011, Foldit gamers solved the crystal structure of a monomeric retroviral protease, a long-unsolved problem in HIV/AIDS research (Khatib et al., 2011). A year later, the volunteer crowd reengineered a protein widely used in synthetic chemistry, increasing its activity by more than 18 times (Eiben et al., 2012). The number of citizen science initiatives is impressive: in late 2016, the website named SciStarter—a crowd science directory—listed circa 1,000 active projects. Although at present the number of publications based on citizen science is rather low (e.g., 124 in 2010 and 402 in 2015), it is growing faster than the overall publication output (Kullenberg & Kasperowski, 2016). So, perhaps citizen science can flatten the spiky geography of science? Empty hopes. Involvement in citizen science projects usually requires access to personal computers and a stable internet connection (technology), some basic skills and competencies (human capital), and—last but not least—the luxury of spending time on this type of activity (quality of life). Such capacities are unequally distributed across the globe. Again, better-developed places occupy a privileged position, while underdeveloped locations often cannot even take part in the race.

Throughout the book we have frequently focused on increasing collaboration in science. But we cannot assume that collaboration will grow endlessly. The growth of collaboration has its limits. This is well demonstrated in the case of internationalisation (Ponds, 2009). In many countries the share of papers co-authored with foreign collaborators has been rising linearly in recent decades. As a result, in numerous cases, the percentage of internationally co-authored publications exceeds 50 or 60 percent (see Chapter 4). Common sense suggests that this increase will be less and less dynamic as it approaches 100 percent. At some point, the growth curve will flatten out. The saturation point will be achieved. Similarly, at the individual and organisational level, collaboration cannot increase forever. Indeed, "no one can collaborate with an infinite number of people in a finite period of time" (Newman, 2001a, p. 9). We can expect that further increases in scientific collaboration will fall under the law of diminishing marginal returns. At some point, an additional collaborator brings fewer and fewer benefits. Moreover, when collaboration becomes a new norm, its beneficial impact may cease to matter or will at least be significantly reduced. In the context of geography, this means that collaborative flows may have increasingly less capacity to redefine the fundamental spatial structures of science.

Last but not least, we cannot dismiss the scenario in which research collaboration declines. In recent years, we have become accustomed to the successive increase of collaboration, especially in its international dimension. But what if national isolationism once more gains an advantage over international cooperation and integration? The UK's withdrawal from the EU, a process that began after the

Brexit referendum in 2016, poses a significant threat to the prospects and capacities of the European Research Area. Isolationist tendencies under the Donald Trump administration—e.g., the travel ban for citizens of selected countries and quarrels with Mexico and China—undermine the international connections of US research and higher education institutions. Threats related to international affairs are strengthened by centrifugal social forces. Anti-science movements, epitomised by climate change denial and anti-vaccine beliefs, are gaining momentum all over the world (Otto, 2016). The collapse of international scientific networks, although unlikely, looms on the horizon. If an unfavourable scenario comes true, the less scientifically advanced countries will be the most exposed to negative consequences due to their dependency on knowledge flows from the scientific core. But, more importantly, the biggest loser will be scientific advancement. In turn, the overall social and economic progress of humanity may slow down. The advantages of the contemporary collaborative turn in science are not given once and for all. Wise policies are necessary to sustain global scientific networks.

7.3 Towards smart policies for scientific collaboration

The journey that has taken us from historical, through present, to upcoming places and spaces of scientific collaboration concludes with takeaways for science policy. Ready-to-use recommendations often fail to fulfil their promises, particularly in the long run. Thus, to avoid the trap of one-size-fits-all advice, we have formulated several policy challenges to be addressed in order to craft smart policies in given circumstances. The smart approach towards scientific collaboration policy is necessary for at least two reasons: the horizontal nature of scientific collaboration policies, and the variety of levels at which science policies can be designed and implemented.

The horizontality of scientific collaboration policy calls for integrated approaches. Because contemporary science is increasingly collaborative, the overall science policy should be collaboration-aware, even in areas where connections to collaboration are indirect, such as the architectural design of research facilities or academic promotion criteria. On the other hand, scientific collaboration policy should be coherent with the broader context of science policy. If research collaboration is treated as a distinct policy focus, the risk of inefficiency arises. This comes from two sources. The first source is found within scientific collaboration policy. Once this policy area is delineated, a goal of increasing collaboration tends to be pursued, irrespective of its overall long-term usefulness and its cost-benefit ratio. The second source relates to the overall science policy. If the policy sees scientific collaboration as overseen by designated, separate programmes, measures, and initiatives, the threat of unintended and undesirable interference arises. In an extreme scenario, the overall science policy might countervail the undertakings of a "department for scientific collaboration". This might be exemplified by research performance assessment criteria that do not properly take into account the collaborative nature of contemporary science, thereby hindering joint research.

Scholarly collaboration relates to multiple policy levels: individual, organisational, local, regional, national, transnational, and even global. These levels vary in relevance and their capacity to impact the prospects of collaboration. By and large, the most significant role is played by nation-state policies, as they provide frameworks for organisational and individual strategies. Subnational (local, urban, regional) and supranational levels are less relevant. A special case is the European Union, in which the transnational level has gained much importance. All in all, the spectrum of possible policy options depends on the level considered. Furthermore, various policy levels are interdependent. Such multilevel relations can release synergies. However, at times, policy objectives formulated at different levels can contradict each other and successively produce suboptimal outcomes. Consequently, the answers to the collaboration-relevant policy questions are determined—to some extent—by the place of the given entity in the global knowledge production system.

The fundamental question relates to the ultimate objective of science policy. Should the policy focus on cutting-edge science that pushes back the global knowledge frontier? Or, alternatively, should the policy strive for the development of those research capacities that will contribute to the reinforcement of a given urban, regional, or national economy? The two approaches converge in the long run, but in the short run, they tend to translate into divergent mid-term aims, measures, and milestones. The difference is particularly vital for less scientifically advanced places. In their case, the cutting-edge research agenda is not only implausible, but is also of little use for local socioeconomic development. In such circumstances, focusing on research goals related to local capacities and challenges might prove more reasonable. All things considered, possible strategies for scientific cooperation are conditioned by two approaches. The approach that favours cutting-edge science most likely translates into policies that concentrate on collaboration between highly performing organisations and places. In consequence, less scientifically developed areas can be overlooked and their peripheral position may become more firmly cemented. The approach that gives priority to the applied value of research as an essential factor of urban and regional development has a slightly different policy-choice spectrum. In this case, the encouragement of collaboration between places with varied levels of scientific capacities is more desirable, as it supports knowledge diffusion from the core—a process that can fuel the development of scientific peripheries.

Though less often than core-core collaborations, core-periphery partnerships can also produce cutting-edge science. This implies that the range of scientific collaboration policy goes beyond the duality delineated in the previous paragraph. The idea of place-based and place-neutral policies helps make sense of this variety. The place-neutral approach—also known as spatially-blind—deliberately ignores geography in order to fulfil the ideal of a policy that treats all its subjects impartially. In contrast, the place-based approach takes into account the specific needs, challenges, and capacities of a given territory (Barca, McCann, & Rodríguez-Pose, 2012). As such, the place-neutral approach fits into the cutting-edge science agenda, while the place-based approach leans towards a research strategy that enhances local or regional development. However, other combinations are also possible. Specifically, the place-neutral science policy can be focused on developmental goals defined at the national level. In this scenario, subnational diversity is not taken into account, and the policy can even increase the pre-existing diversity of scientific capacities across geographical space. Likewise, the place-based approach can be combined with the cutting-edge science agenda. Now and then, the specific features of a given territory make it a particularly convenient place to achieve outstanding scientific results. As a result, the territory attracts collaborators regardless of its scientific capacity. For example, specific conditions for astronomical observations fuel collaboration between Chile and many other nations. On the whole, the place-based policy of international scientific collaboration can aim at cutting-edge science, especially within clearly defined research domains or problems, such as environmental management, neglected diseases, or public health.

Science policy should also take into account the hierarchical structure of scientific collaboration grounded in the uneven distribution of collaborative advantage among collaborators. Should the policy focus on supporting collaboration between the best so that they can become even better? Alternatively, should it stimulate knowledge flows between weaker and stronger partners to enhance the overall knowledge production system? The resulting policy options span from polarisation to cohesion. Supporting collaboration among the most advanced entities certainly increases the chance of groundbreaking discoveries, but it also reinforces tendencies of polarisation that are intrinsic to research collaboration. Supporting collaboration between more and less scientifically advanced areas will undoubtedly benefit the latter, and in turn, it can foster more cohesive distribution of research capacities and impacts—but it might be less effective in advancing scientific progress, at least in the short-term. However, cooperation within a hierarchical structure can also lead to polarisation. Stronger partners have the power to impose research topics, objectives, and paradigms on their collaborators. In an extreme scenario, weaker partners might be exploited rather than advantaged. Thus, the cohesion approach in scientific collaboration policy should not only consider how to encourage stronger partners to collaborate with less advanced ones, but also how to secure a fair—though not necessarily equal—distribution of benefits from collaboration.

The unique scientific collaboration policy challenge relates to the proximity-distance nexus. Proximate collaboration is easier to establish and sustain, while distant collaboration unlocks more unusual possibilities and tends to bring more resounding impact. So, in which circumstances is greater proximity needed and in which is greater distance preferred? Or, what would be the right mix of close and distant collaboration? A lack of collaboration calls for simple solutions: facilitating joint research with geographically closer partners. Successively, experience from initial collaborations and accumulated relational capital can support the establishment of more demanding, often distant, partnerships. When the reservoir of possible partners becomes larger, the tactics of partner selection gain importance, particularly in relation to the expected impact of collaboration. Moreover, the geographical dimension of the proximity-distance dilemma intertwines with other types of proximities: cognitive, cultural, economic, institutional, organisational, social, and technological. Therefore, the actual policy challenge is to find the proper equilibrium on the multilevel proximity-distance continuum.

A responsible policy approach to scientific collaboration should consider not only the benefits from collaboration but also its associated costs. By and large, both benefits and costs increase with an expanding collaboration range, be it geographical distance, the number of scholars, the variety of scientific disciplines, or the cultural and organisational diversification of research teams. But, to what point do the benefits from expanding collaboration offset its rising costs? How extensive or selective should collaboration be in a given case? The choice between extensive and selective collaboration strategies calls for a careful cost-benefit analysis, which is no trivial task, given the complex nature of research collaboration. On the one hand, we have collaboration's direct effects and indirect impacts—often significantly postponed—on the other hand, there are direct material costs and overheads, as well as alternative (opportunity) costs.

The final policy challenge relates to the tension between collaboration and competition in science. Relations that drive the research universe are not limited to scientific collaboration. Competition has always been widespread in academia. In fact, both types of relationships coexist, and this is captured by the concept of coopetition. On that basis, important policy questions arise: What is the right mix of collaboration and competition in science? In which circumstances is collaboration desirable and when does competition provide significant efficiencies? The competition-collaboration dilemma is particularly relevant for policy levels that create overall frameworks for scientific communities. In particular, national science policies must carefully address this issue when crafting research funding schemes, intellectual property rights, and research performance assessment criteria. The adequate balance between competition and cooperation should not only maximise the overall efficiency of a research sector, but also ensure the social value of science.

Note

1 The rise of citizen science is greatly facilitated by the development of information and communication technologies, but the origins of this movement are neither new nor related to ICT. Very early examples of citizen science were of an entirely analogue character. The North American Bird Phenology Program ran from 1881 to 1970. At its peak, the programme involved about 3,000 volunteers who documented observations of birds' arrival dates on about six million Migration Observer Cards (Miller-Rushing, Primack, & Bonney, 2012).

References

Aagaard, K. (2015). How Incentives Trickle Down: Local Use of a National Bibliometric Indicator System. *Science & Public Policy, 42*(5), 725–737.

Aagaard, K., Bloch, C., & Schneider, J. W. (2015). Impacts of Performance-Based Research Funding Systems: The Case of the Norwegian Publication Indicator. *Research Evaluation, 24*(2), 106–117. doi:10.1093/reseval/rvv003

Aarstad, J., Kvitastein, O. A., & Jakobsen, S. E. (2016). Local Buzz, Global Pipelines, or Simply Too Much Buzz? A Critical Study. *Geoforum, 75,* 129–133.

Abbasi, A., Altmann, J., & Hossain, L. (2011). Identifying the Effects of Co-Authorship Networks on the Performance of Scholars: A Correlation and Regression Analysis of Performance Measures and Social Network Analysis Measures. *Journal of Informetrics, 5*(4), 594–607.

Abbasi, A., & Jaafari, A. (2013). Research Impact and Scholars' Geographical Diversity. *Journal of Informetrics, 7*(3), 683–692.

Abbott, A., Butler, D., Gibney, E., Schiermeier, Q., & Van Noorden, R. (2016). Boon or Burden: What Has the EU Ever Done for Science? *Nature, 534,* 307–309.

Abramo, G., D'Angelo, C. A., & Murgia, G. (2014). Variation in Research Collaboration Patterns across Academic Ranks. *Scientometrics, 98*(3), 2275–2294.

Achachi, H., Amor, Z., Dahel-Mekhancha, C. C., Cherraj, M., Bouabid, H., Selmanovic, S., & Larivière, V. (2016). Factors Affecting Researchers' Collaborative Patterns: A Case Study from Maghreb Universities/Les Facteurs Affectant Les Pratiques De Collaboration Des Chercheurs: Une Étude De Cas Des Universités Maghrébines. *Canadian Journal of Information and Library Science, 40*(3), 234–253.

Aczel, A. D. (2006). *The Artist and the Mathematician: The Story of Nicolas Bourbaki, the Genius Mathematician Who Never Existed.* New York, NY: Thunder's Mouth Press.

Adams, J. (2013). The Fourth Age of Research. *Nature, 497,* 557–560.

Idea Conslut & ADE. (2011, January). *Ex-Post Evaluation of the IAP Programme (Phase VI, 2007–2011).* Brussels. Retrieved from http://www.belspo.be/belspo/iap/publ/iap%20evaluation%20-%20main%20report.pdf

Adelson, J. W., & Weinberg, J. K. (2010). The California Stem Cell Initiative: Persuasion, Politics, and Public Science. *American Journal of Public Health, 100*(3), 446–451.

Agar, J. (2012). *Science in the Twentieth Century and Beyond.* Cambridge, UK: Polity Press.

Agrawal, A., Kapur, D., & McHale, J. (2008). How Do Spatial and Social Proximity Influence Knowledge Flows? Evidence from Patent Data. *Journal of Urban Economics, 64*(2), 258–269.

Agrawal, A., McHale, J., & Oettl, A. (2014). Collaboration, Stars, and the Changing Organization of Science: Evidence from Evolutionary Biology. In A. B. Jaffe & B. F. Jones (Eds.), *The Changing Frontier: Rethinking Science and Innovation Policy* (pp. 75–102). Chicago, IL: University of Chicago Press.

References

Ahlgren, P., Persson, O., & Tijssen, R. (2013). Geographical Distance in Bibliometric Relations within Epistemic Communities. *Scientometrics*, *95*(2), 771–784.

Ahn, J., Oh, D. H., & Lee, J. D. (2014). The Scientific Impact and Partner Selection in Collaborative Research at Korean Universities. *Scientometrics*, *100*(1), 173–188.

Ajiferuke, I., Burell, Q., & Tague, J. (1988). Collaborative Coefficient: A Single Measure of the Degree of Collaboration in Research. *Scientometrics*, *14*(5–6), 421–433.

Akera, A. (2007). *Calculating a Natural World: Scientists, Engineers, and Computers during the Rise of U.S. Cold War Research*. Cambridge, MA: MIT Press.

Al, U., & Taşkın, Z. (2015). Relationship between Economic Development and Intellectual Production. *Collnet Journal of Scientometrics and Information Management*, *9*(1), 25–35.

Allen, J. T. (1977). *Managing the Flow of Technology: Technology Transfer and the Dissemination of Technologycal Information within the R&D Organization*. Cambridge, MA: The Massachusetts Institute of Technology.

Allen, J. T., & Henn, G. (2007). *The Organization and Architecture of Innovation: Managing the Flow of Technology*. Amsterdam, Netherlands: Elsevier.

Altbach, P. (2010). Why Branch Campuses may be Unsustainable. *International Higher Education*, *58*, 2–3.

Alter, C., & Hage, J. (1993). *Organizations Working Together*. London, UK: Sage.

Amanatidou, E. (2002). Foreign Policy and International R&D Collaboration Policy in Greece. *Science and Public Policy*, *29*(6), 439–450.

Amin, A., & Robins, K. (1991). These are Not Marshallian Times. In R. Camagni (Ed.), *Innovation Network: Spatial Perspective* (pp. 105–120). London, UK: Belhaven.

Amin, A., & Thrift, N. (1992). Neo-Marshallian Nodes in Global Networks. *International Journal of Urban and Regional Research*, *16*(4), 571–587.

Amin, A., & Thrift, N. (1994). Living in the Global. In A. Amin & N. Thrift (Eds.), *Globalization, Institutions, and Regional Development in Europe* (pp. 1–22). Oxford, UK: Oxford University Press.

Anderson, J. E. (2010). *The Gravity Model*. NBER Working Papers 16576. Cambridge, MA: National Bureau of Economic Research, Inc.

Andersson, Å. E., & Persson, O. (1993). Networking Scientists. *The Annals of Regional Science*, *27*(1), 11–21.

Andersson, M., & Ejermo, O. (2005). How Does Accessibility to Knowledge Sources Affect the Innovativeness of Corporations?—Evidence from Sweden. *The Annals of Regional Science*, *39*(4), 741–765.

Andrée, D. (2009). *Priority-Setting in the European Research Framework Programmes*. VINNOVA-Swedish Governmental Agency for Innovation Systems. Retrieved from https://www.vinnova.se/publikationer/priority-setting-in-the-european-research-framework-programmes/

Angier, N. (1988). Nice Guys Don't Win Nobel Prizes [Review of the Book *Science as a Process: An Evolutionary Account of the Social and Conceptual Development of Science*, by D. L. Hull]. *The New York Times*, pp. 14–16.

Arbo, P., & Benneworth, P. (2007). *Understanding the Regional Contribution of Higher Education Institutions: A Literature Review*. OECD Education Working Papers. 9. Paris, France: OECD Publishing. http://doi.org/10.1787/161208155312

Arnold, E., Åström, T., Boekholt, P., Brown, N., Good, B., Holmberg, R., ... & Van Der Veen, G. (2008). *Impacts of the Framework Programme in Sweden*. VINNOVA-Swedish Governmental Agency for Innovation Systems. Retrieved from https://www.vinnova.se/en/publikationer/impacts-of-the-framework-programme-in-sweden/

Asheim, B. R. T. (1996). Industrial Districts as 'Learning Regions': A Condition for Prosperity. *European Planning Studies*, *4*(4), 379–400.

Asheim, B. R. T., & Gertler, M. S. (2005). The Geography of Innovation: Regional Innovation Systems. In J. Fagerberg, D. C. Mowery & R. R. Nelson (Eds.), *The Oxford Handbook of Innovation* (pp. 292–317). Oxford, UK: Oxford University Press.

References

Asheim, B. R. T., & Isaksen, A. (2002). Regional Innovation Systems: The Integration of Local 'Sticky' and Global 'Ubiquitous' Knowledge. *The Journal of Technology Transfer*, 27(1), 77–86.

Atkinson, P., Batchelor, C., & Parsons, E. (1998). Trajectories of Collaboration and Competition in a Medical Discovery. *Science, Technology, & Human Values*, 23(3), 259–284.

Atkinson, R. D. (2014, June). *Understanding the US National Innovation System*. The Information Technology & Innovation Foundation. Retrieved from https://papers.ssrn.com/sol3/papers.cfm?abstract_id=3079822

ATLAS Authorship Committee. (2013, February 8). *ATLAS Authorship Policy*. Retrieved from https://www.cppm.in2p3.fr/~nagy/ATLAS/qualification/A74_AUTHOR_policy_76.pdf

Autant-Bernard, C., Billand, P., Frachisse, D., & Massard, N. (2007). Social Distance versus Spatial Distance in R&D Cooperation: Empirical Evidence from European Collaboration Choices in Micro and Nanotechnologies. *Papers in Regional Science*, 86(3), 495–519.

Autio, E. (1998). Evaluation of RTD in Regional Systems of Innovation. *European Planning Studies*, 6(2), 131–140.

Autio, E., Hameri, A. P., & Nordberg, M. (1996). A Framework of Motivations for Industry-Big Science Collaboration: A Case Study. *Journal of Engineering and Technology Management*, 13(3), 301–314.

Avkiran, N. (1997). Scientific Collaboration in Finance Does Not Lead to Better Quality Research. *Scientometrics*, 39(2), 173–184.

Aydalot, P. (Ed.). (1986). *Milieux Innovateurs En Europe*. Paris, France: GREMI.

Azoulay, P., Graff Zivin, J. S., & Wang, J. (2010). Superstar Extinction. *The Quarterly Journal of Economics*, 125(2), 549–589.

Bakouros, Y. L., Mardas, D. C., & Varsakelis, N. C. (2002). Science Park, a High Tech Fantasy?: An Analysis of the Science Parks of Greece. *Technovation*, 22(2), 123–128.

Balland, P. A. (2012). Proximity and the Evolution of Collaboration Networks: Evidence from Research and Development Projects within the Global Navigation Satellite System (GNSS) Industry. *Regional Studies*, 46(6), 741–756.

Barabási, A. L. (2002). *Linked: The New Science of Networks*. Cambridge, MA: Perseus Publishing.

Barabási, A. L., & Albert, R. (1999). Emergence of Scaling in Random Networks. *Science*, 286(5439), 509–512.

Barandiaran, J. (2015). Reaching for the Stars? Astronomy and Growth in Chile. *Minerva*, 53(2), 141–164.

Barca, F., McCann, P., & Rodríguez-Pose, A. (2012). The Case for Regional Development Intervention: Place-Based versus Place-Neutral Approaches. *Journal of Regional Science*, 52(1), 134–152.

Bar-Ilan, J. (2008). Informetrics at the Beginning of the 21st century—A Review. *Journal of Informetrics*, 2(1), 1–52.

Barjak, F. (2006). The Role of the Internet in Informal Scholarly Communication. *Journal of the American Society for Information Science and Technology*, 57(10), 1350–1367.

Barnard, H., Cowan, R., & Müller, M. (2012). Global Excellence at the Expense of Local Diffusion, or a Bridge between Two Worlds? Research in Science and Technology in the Developing World. *Research Policy*, 41(4), 756–769.

Bathelt, H. (2011). Innovation, Learning and Knowledge Creation in Co-Localized and Distant Contexts. In A. Pike, A. Rodríguez-Pose, & J. Tomaney (Eds.), *Handbook of Local and Regional Development* (pp. 149–161). London, UK: Routledge.

Bathelt, H., Malmberg, A., & Maskell, P. (2004). Clusters and Knowledge: Local Buzz, Global Pipelines and the Process of Knowledge Creation. *Progress in Human Geography*, 28(1), 31–56.

Beaver, D. D. (2001). Reflections on Scientific Collaboration (And Its Study): Past, Present, and Future. *Scientometrics*, 52(3), 365–377.

Beaver, D. D. (2004). Does Collaborative Research Have Greater Epistemic Authority? *Scientometrics*, 60(3), 399–408.

References

Beaver, D. D., & Rosen, R. (1978). Studies in Scientific Collaboration: Part I. The Professional Origins of Scientific Co-Authorship. *Scientometrics*, 1(1), 65–84.

Becattini, G. (2002). From Marshall's to the Italian "Industrial Districts". A Brief Critical Reconstruction. In A. Quadrio Curzio & M. Fortis (Eds.), *Complexity and Industrial Clusters* (pp. 83–106). New York, NY: Physica-Verlag.

Beer, A., & Lester, L. (2015). Institutional Thickness and Institutional Effectiveness: Developing Regional Indices for Policy and Practice in Australia. *Regional Studies, Regional Science*, 2(1), 205–228.

Belyayev, Ye. A. (1973). Geography of Science—Past and Present. *Priroda (Nature)*, 8, 91–93. March 28. (Joint Publication Research Service, JPRS-58596, Trans.) (Original work published 1972).

Ben-David, J. (1984). *The Scientist's Role in Society: A Comparative Study* (2nd ed.). Chicago, IL: University of Chicago Press.

Bengtsson, M., & Kock, S. (2000). "Coopetition" in Business Networks—To Cooperate and Compete Simultaneously. *Industrial Marketing Management*, 29(5), 411–426.

Bengtsson, M., & Raza-Ullah, T. (2016). A Systematic Review of Research on Coopetition: Toward A Multilevel Understanding. *Industrial Marketing Management*, 57, 23–39.

Benneworth, P., & Hospers, G. J. (2007). Urban Competitiveness in the Knowledge Economy: Universities as New Planning Animateurs. *Progress in Planning*, 67(2), 105–197.

Berners-Lee, T., & Fischetti, M. (1999). *Weaving the Web: The Original Design and Ultimate Destiny of the World Wide Web by Its Inventor*. San Francisco, CA: Harper San Francisco.

Berry, D. M. (2008). *Copy, Rip, Burn: The Politics of Copyleft and Open Source*. London, UK: Pluto Press.

Bianconi, G., & Barabási, A. L. (2001). Competition and Multiscaling in Evolving Networks. *Europhysics Letters*, 54(4), 436.

Big Ten Academic Alliance. (2016). *Executive Brief: Overseas Offices*. Retrieved from http://www.btaa.org/docs/default-source/international/global-brief—overseas-offices—july-2016.pdf?sfvrsn=4

Bikard, M., Murray, F., & Gans, J. S. (2015). Exploring Trade-Offs in the Organization of Scientific Work: Collaboration and Scientific Reward. *Management Science*, 61(7), 1473–1495.

Binz, C., & Truffer, B. (2017). Global Innovation Systems—A Conceptual Framework for Innovation Dynamics in Transnational Contexts. *Research Policy*, 46(7), 1284–1298.

Birnholtz, J. P. (2007). When Do Researchers Collaborate? Toward a Model of Collaboration Propensity. *Journal of the American Society for Information Science and Technology*, 58(14), 2226–2239.

Bloch, C., & Schneider, J. W. (2016). Performance-Based Funding Models and Researcher Behavior: An Analysis of the Influence of the Norwegian Publication Indicator at the Individual Level. *Research Evaluation*, 25(4), 371–382.

Block, F., & Keller, M. R. (2009). Where Do Innovations Come From? Transformations in the US Economy, 1970–2006. *Socio-Economic Review*, 7(3), 459–483.

Boekholt, P. E. B. (1994). *The European Community and Innovation Policy: Reorienting Towards Diffusion* (Doctoral Dissertation). Retrieved from Aston University.

Boeri, T. (Ed.). (2012). *Brain Drain and Brain Gain: The Global Competition to Attract High-Skilled Migrants*. Oxford, UK: Oxford University Press.

Boghossian, P. A. (2006). *Fear of Knowledge: Against Relativism and Constructivism*. Oxford, UK: Oxford University Press.

Bok, D. C. (2015). *Higher Education in America* (Revised ed.). Princeton, NJ: Princeton University Press.

Bolaños-Pizarro, M., Thijs, B., & Glänzel, W. (2010). Cardiovascular Research in Spain. A Comparative Scientometric Study. *Scientometrics*, 85(2), 509–526.

Bonaccorsi, A., & Secondi, L. (2017). The Determinants of Research Performance in European Universities: A Large Scale Multilevel Analysis. *Scientometrics*, 112(3), 1147–1178.

Bordons, M., Gomez, I., Fernández, M., Zulueta, M., & Mendez, A. (1996). Local, Domestic and International Scientific Collaboration in Biomedical Research. *Scientometrics*, 37(2), 279–295.

Borel, A. (1998). Twenty-Five Years with Nicolas Bourbaki, 1949–1973. *Notices of the American Mathematical Society, 45*(3), 373–380.
Borgatti, S. P., & Lopez-Kidwell, V. (2011). Network Theory. In J. Scott & P. J. Carrington (Eds.), *The SAGE Handbook of Social Network Analysis* (pp. 40–54). London, UK: SAGE.
Börner, K. (2010). *Atlas of Science: Visualizing What We Know*. Cambridge, MA: MIT Press.
Börner, K. (2015). *Atlas of Knowledge: Anyone Can Map*. Cambridge, MA: MIT Press.
Börner, K., Contractor, N., Falk-Krzesinski, H. J., Fiore, S. M., Hall, K. L., Keyton, J., ... & Uzzi, B. (2010). A Multi-Level Systems Perspective for the Science of Team Science. *Science Translational Medicine, 2*(49), 49cm24.
Börner, K., & Scharnhorst, A. (2009). Visual Conceptualizations and Models of Science. *Journal of Informetrics, 3*, 161–172.
Bornmann, L., Stefaner, M., De Moya Anegón, F., & Mutz, R. (2014). Ranking and Mapping of Universities and Research-Focused Institutions Worldwide Based on Highly-Cited Papers: A Visualisation of Results from Multi-Level Models. *Online Information Review, 38*(1), 43–58.
Bos, N., Zimmerman, A., Olson, J., Yew, J., Yerkie, J., Dahl, E., & Olson, G. (2007). From Shared Databases to Communities of Practice: A Taxonomy of Collaboratories. *Journal of Computer-Mediated Communication, 12*(2), 652–672.
Boschma, R. (2005). Proximity and Innovation: A Critical Assessment. *Regional Studies, 39*(1), 61–74.
Boschma, R., & Iammarino, S. (2009). Related Variety, Trade Linkages, and Regional Growth in Italy. *Economic Geography, 85*(3), 289–311.
Boudreau, K. J., Brady, T., Ganguli, I., Gaule, P., Guinan, E., Hollenberg, A., & Lakhani, K. R. (2017). A Field Experiment on Search Costs and the Formation of Scientific Collaborations. *Review of Economics and Statistics, 99*(4), 565–576.
Bound, K., Saunders, T., Wilsdon, J., & Adams, J. (2013). *China's Absorptive State: Research, Innovation and the Prospects for China-UK Collaboration*. London, UK: NESTA.
Bourdieu, P. (2004). *Science of Science and Reflexivity* (R. Nice, Trans.). Chicago, IL: University of Chicago Press. Original work published 2001.
Boys, J. (2011). *Towards Creative Learning Spaces: Re-Thinking the Architecture of Post-Compulsory Education*. Abingdon, UK: Routledge.
Bozeman, B., & Boardman, P.C. (2004). The NSF Engineering Research Centers and the University–Industry Research Revolution. *The Journal of Technology Transfer, 29*(3–4), 365–375.
Bozeman, B., & Corley, E. (2004). Scientists' Collaboration Strategies: Implications for Scientific and Technical Human Capital. *Research Policy, 33*(4), 599–616.
Bozeman, B., & Gaughan, M. (2011). How Do Men and Women Differ in Research Collaborations? An Analysis of the Collaborative Motives and Strategies of Academic Researchers. *Research Policy, 40*(10), 1393–1402.
Brand, S. (1987). *The Media Lab: Inventing the Future at MIT*. New York, NY: Viking.
Brandenburger, A. M., & Nalebuff, B. J. (1996). *Co-Opetition*. New York, NY: Doubleday.
Braudel, F. (1958). Histoire Et Sciences Sociales: La Longue Durée. Annales. *Histoire, Sciences Sociales, 13*(4), 725–753.
Breakdown of Horizon 2020 Budget. (2011). Retrieved from http://ec.europa.eu/research/horizon2020/pdf/press/horizon_2020_budget_constant_2011.pdf
Brew, A. (2006). *Research and Teaching: Beyond the Divide*. Houndmills, UK: Palgrave Macmillan.
Breznitz, S. M., & Feldman, M. P. (2012). The Engaged University. *The Journal of Technology Transfer, 37*(2), 139–157.
Bridges, D. (2006). The Role of the University in Regional Economic Development. In D. Bridges, P. Juceviciene, R. Jucevicius, T. H. Mclaughlin, & J. Stankeviciute (Eds.), *Higher Education and National Development: Universities and Societies in Transition* (pp. 103–119). London, UK: Routledge.
Broekel, T. (2015). The Co-Evolution of Proximities–A Network Level Study. *Regional Studies, 49*(6), 921–935.

References

Bruce, A., Lyall, C., Tait, J., & Williams, R. (2004). Interdisciplinary Integration in Europe: The Case of the Fifth Framework Programme. *Futures, 36*(4), 457–470.

Burdick, A., Drucker, J., Lunenfeld, P., Presner, T., & Schnapp, J. (2012). *Digital_Humanities*. Cambridge, MA: MIT Press.

Burt, R. S. (1992). *Structural Holes: The Social Structure of Competition*. Cambridge, MA: Harvard University Press.

Bush, V. (1945). *Science, the Endless Frontier: A Report to the President*. United States Office of Scientific Research and Development. Washington, DC: U.S. Govt. Print. Off.

Button, K., Brown, P., Fischer, M., Maggi, R., Ouwersloot, H., Rammer, C., … Salomon, I. (1993). *Academic Links and Communications (Studies of Science in Europe)*. Aldershot, UK: Avebury.

Bynum, W. (2012). *A Little History of Science*. New Haven, CT: Yale University Press.

Cai, H. (2012). Deploying the Chinese Knowledge Diaspora: A Case Study of Peking University. *Asia Pacific Journal of Education, 32*(3), 367–379.

Cairncross, F. (1997). *The Death of Distance: How the Communications Revolution Will Change Our Lives*. Boston, MA: Harvard Business School Press.

Caloghirou, Y., Vonortas, N. S., & Ioannides, S. (2002). Science and Technology Policies Towards Research Joint Ventures. *Science and Public Policy, 29*(2), 82–94.

Calvert, J., & Martin, B. (2001). Science Funding: Europe. In *International Encyclopedia of the Social and Behavioural Sciences* (Vol. 20, pp. 13676–13680). Amsterdam, Netherlands: Elsevier.

Calvo-Sotelo, C. (2011). *Identidad, Innovación Y Entorno En La Universidad Española. Proyectos De Campus De Excelencia Internacional*. Madrid, Spain: Ministerio Educación, Secretaría General de Universidades.

Camagni, R. (1991a). Local 'Milieu', Uncertainty and Innovation Networks: Towards a New Dynamic Theory of Economic Space. In R. Camagni (Ed.), *Innovation Networks: Spatial Perspectives* (pp. 121–142). London, UK: Belhaven.

Camagni, R. (Ed.). (1991b). *Innovation Networks: Spatial Perspectives*. London, UK: Belhaven.

Campbell, D., Roberge, G., Haustein, S., & Archamba, E. (2013). *Intra-European Cooperation Compared to International Collaboration of the ERA Countries*. Brussels: European Commission.

Cao, C. (2014). The Universal Values of Science and China's Nobel Prize Pursuit. *Minerva, 52*(2), 141–160.

Cao, C., Li, N., Li, X., & Liu, L. (2013). Reforming China's S&T System. *Science, 341*(6145), 460–462.

Cao, C., Suttmeier, R. P., & Simon, D. F. (2006). China's 15-Year Science and Technology Plan. *Physics Today, 59*(12), 38.

Capello, R. (2007). *Regional Economics*. Oxon, UK: Routledge.

Capello, R., & Caragliu, A. (2018). Proximities and the Intensity of Scientific Relations: Synergies and Nonlinearities. *International Regional Science Review, 41*(1), 7–44.

Capshew, J. H. (1992). Psychologists on Site: A Reconnaissance of the Historiography of the Laboratory. *American Psychologist, 47*(2), 132–142. doi:10.1037/0003-066X.47.2.132

Carayannis, E. G., Campbell, D. F., & Rehman, S. S. (2016). Mode 3 Knowledge Production: Systems and Systems Theory, Clusters and Networks. *Journal of Innovation and Entrepreneurship, 5*(1), 1–24.

Cardwell, D. S. L. (1972). *Turning Points in Western Technology: A Study of Technology, Science and History*. New York, NY: Science History Publications.

Carey, H. C. (1867). *Principles of Social Science* (Vol. 3). JB Lippincott & Company.

Carillo, M. R., Papagni, E., & Sapio, A. (2013). Do Collaborations Enhance the High-Quality Output of Scientific Institutions? Evidence from the Italian Research Assessment Exercise. *The Journal of Socio-Economics, 47*, 25–36.

Carusi, A., & Reimer, T. (2010). *Virtual Research Environment Collaborative Landscape Study*. Bristol, UK: JISC.

Casadevall, A., & Fang, F. C. (2013). Is the Nobel Prize Good for Science? *The FASEB Journal, 27*(12), 4682–4690.

Casassus, B. (2014). China Predicted to Outspend the US on Science by 2020. *Nature.* November 12. doi:10.1038/nature.2014.16329
Cassi, L., Corrocher, N., Malerba, F., & Vonortas, N. S. (2009). Evaluating the Links between Research and Deployment Networks of Innovation in Information Society in Europe. In F. Malerba & N. S. Vonortas (Eds.), *Innovation Networks in Industries* (Chapter 10). Cheltenham, UK: Edward Elgar.
Cassi, L., Morrison, A., & Rabellotti, R. (2015). Proximity and Scientific Collaboration: Evidence from the Global Wine Industry. *Tijdschrift Voor Economische En Sociale Geografie, 106*(2), 205–219.
Castells, M. (1996). *The Rise of the Network Society.* Cambridge, MA: Blackwell Publishers.
Castells, M., & Hall, P. (1994). *Technopoles of the World: The Making of Twenty-First-Century Industrial Complexes.* London, UK: Routledge.
Castells, M., & Ince, M. (2003). *Conversations with Manuel Castells.* Cambridge, UK: Polity Press.
Castelvecchi, D. (2015). Physics Paper Sets Record with More than 5,000 Authors. *Nature.* May 15. doi:10.1038/nature.2015.17567
Castro, R., & Grossman, J. W. (1999). Famous Trails to Paul Erdős. *The Mathematical Intelligencer, 3*(21), 51–53.
Catalini, C. (2017). Microgeography and the Direction of Inventive Activity. *Management Science.* doi: http://doi.org/10.1287/mnsc.2017.2798
Catalini, C., Fons-Rosen, C., & Gaulé, P. (2016). *Did Cheaper Flights Change the Geography of Scientific Collaboration?* MIT Sloan Research Paper No. 5172-16.
Cattuto, C., Van Den Broeck, W., Barrat, A., Colizza, V., Pinton, J. F., & Vespignani, A. (2010). Dynamics of Person-To-Person Interactions from Distributed RFID Sensor Networks. *PLoS ONE, 5*(7), e11596.
Celińska-Janowicz, D., Wojnar, K., Olechnicka, A., & Ploszaj, A. (2017). Znaczenie Bliskóci W Nawiązywaniu Współpracy Naukowej Przez Polskich Naukowców. *Zagadnienia Naukoz-nawstwa, 53*(3), 285–308.
CESAER. (2016, October 21). *Statement for the Interim Evaluation Horizon 2020.* Conference of European Schools for Advanced Engineering Education and Research, Leuven.
Chalabi, M. (2015, January 29). How Many Times Does The Average Person Move? *Five Thirty Eight.* Retrieved from http://fivethirtyeight.com/datalab/how-many-times-the-average-person-moves/
Chandler, A. (2016, October 21). Why Do Americans Move So Much More Than Europeans? *The Atlantic.* Retrieved from http://www.theatlantic.com/business/archive/2016/10/us-geo graphic-mobility/504968/
Chang, D., Ge, Y., Song, S., Coleman, N., Christensen, J., & Heer, J. (2009). *Visualizing the Republic of Letters.* Stanford, CA: Stanford University. Retrieved from http://web.stanford.edu/group/toolingup/rplviz/papers/Vis_RofL_2009
Chang, H. W., & Huang, M. H. (2013). Prominent Institutions in International Collaboration Network in Astronomy and Astrophysics. *Scientometrics, 97*(2), 443–460.
Chesbrough, H. W. (2003). *Open Innovation: The New Imperative for Creating and Profiting from Technology.* Boston, MA: Harvard Business School Press.
Chi, M. (2016, February 24). China-Led Gravitational Wave Venture Seeks Global Talent. *China Daily.* Retrieved from http://www.chinadaily.com.cn/china/2016-02/24/content_23626552.htm
Chien, T. H., & Peng, T. J. (2005). Competition and Cooperation Intensity in a Network–A Case Study in Taiwan Simulator Industry. *Journal of American Academy of Business, 7*(2), 150–155.
Chinchilla-Rodríguez, Z., Vargas-Quesada, B., Hassan-Montero, Y., González-Molina, A., & Moya-Anegóna, F. (2010). New Approach to the Visualization of International Scientific Collaboration. *Information Visualization, 9*(4), 277–287.
Chisholm, R. F. (1998). *Developing Network Organizations: Learning from Practice and Theory.* Reading, UK: Addison Wesley Longman.

192   References

Cho, M., & McKee, M. (2002, March 1). *Authorship in Biomedical Research—Realities and Expectations*. Retrieved from http://www.sciencemag.org/careers/2002/03/authorship-biomedical-research-realities-and-expectations

Choi, S. (2011). Core-Periphery, New Clusters, or Rising Stars?: International Scientific Collaboration among 'Advanced' countries in the Era of Globalization. *Scientometrics, 90*(1), 25–41.

Chompalov, I., Genuth, J., & Shrum, W. (2002). The Organization of Scientific Collaborations. *Research Policy, 31*(5), 749–767.

Christensen, C. M. (1997). *The Innovator's Dilemma: When New Technologies Cause Great Firms to Fail*. Boston, MA: Harvard Business School Press.

Clark B. (1998). *Creating Entrepreneurial Universities: Organizational Pathways of Transformation*. Oxford, UK: Pergamon for IEU Press.

Clauset, A., Arbesman, S., & Larremore, D. B. (2015). Systematic Inequality and Hierarchy in Faculty Hiring Networks. *Science Advances, 1*(1), February 12. doi:http://doi.org/10.1126/sciadv.1400005

Clauset, A., Shalizi, C. R., & Newman, M. E. (2009). Power-Law Distributions in Empirical Data. *SIAM Review, 51*(4), 661–703.

Coase, R. (1937). The Nature of the Firm. *Economica, New Series, 4*(16), 386–405.

Cobo, M. J., López-Herrera, A. G., Herrera-Viedma, E., & Herrera, F. (2011). Science Mapping Software Tools: Review, Analysis, and Cooperative Study among Tools. *Journal of the American Society for Information Science and Technology, 62*(7), 1382–1402.

Coenen, L., Moodysson, J., & Asheim, B. T. (2004). Nodes, Networks and Proximities: On the Knowledge Dynamics of the Medicon Valley Biotech Cluster. *European Planning Studies, 12*(7), 1003–1018.

Cohen, W., & Levinthal, D. (1990). Absorptive Capacity: A New Perspective on Learning and Innovation. *Administrative Science Quarterly, 35*(1), 128–152. doi:http://doi.org/10.2307/2393553

Coleman, J. (1988). Social Capital in the Creation of Human Capital. *American Journal of Sociology, 94*, S95–S120.

Collaboration. (n.d.). In *Oxford English Dictionary Online*. Retrieved from http://www.oed.com/

Commission of the European Communities. (1975). *The Scientific and Technical Research Committee (CREST). Its Origin, Role and Function*. Retrieved from https://publications.europa.eu/de/publication-detail/-/publication/ff82cd76-5f90-4deb-b26e-b2d5182e1791

Commission of the European Communities. (2008). *Communication from the Commission to the European Parliament, the Council, the European Economic and Social Committee and the Committee of the Regions. Towards Joint Programming in Research: Working Together to Tackle Common Challenges More Effectively*. Brussels, 15.7.2008, COM(2008) 468 final. Retrieved from https://eur-lex.europa.eu/legal-content/EN/TXT/?uri=celex%3A52008DC0468

Committee on Science and Technology (1998, September 1). *Unlocking Our Future: Toward a New National Science Policy*. 105th Congress, 2nd Session, Congressional Committee Materials. U.S. Government Publishing Office. Retrieved from https://www.gpo.gov/fdsys/pkg/GPO-CPRT-105hprt105-b/content-detail.html

Conner, C. (2005). *A People's History of Science: Miners, Midwives, and Low Mechanicks*. New York, NY: Nation Books.

Convention for the Establishment of a European Organization for Nuclear Research. (1953, July 1). Paris. Retrieved from https://council.web.cern.ch/en/content/convention-establishment-european-organization-nuclear-research

Cooke, N. J., & Hilton, M. L. (Eds.). (2015). *Enhancing the Effectiveness of Team Science*. Washington, DC: The National Academies Press.

Cooke, P. (1992). Regional Innovation Systems: Competitive Regulation in the New Europe. *Geoforum, 23*(3), 365–382.

Cooke, P. (1998a). Global Clustering and Regional Innovation. Systemic Integration in Wales. In H. J. Braczyk, P. Cooke, & M. Heidenreich (Eds.), *Regional Innovation Systems: The Role of Governances in a Globalized World* (pp. 245–262). London, UK: UCL Press.

References

Cooke, P. (1998b). Introduction: The Origin of the Concept. In H. J. Braczyk, P. Cooke, & M. Heidenreich (Eds.), *Regional Innovation Systems: The Role of Governances in a Globalized World* (pp. 2–25). London, UK: UCL Press.

Costa, B. M. G., Da Silva Pedro, E., & De Macedo, G. R. (2013). Scientific Collaboration in Biotechnology: The Case of the Northeast Region in Brazil. *Scientometrics, 95*(2), 571–592.

Coulson, J., Roberts, P., & Taylor, I. (2011). *University Planning and Architecture: The Search for Perfection.* Abingdon, UK: Routledge.

Coulson, J., Roberts, P., & Taylor, I. (2015). *University Trends: Contemporary Campus Design.* London, UK: Routledge.

Cowan, R., David, P. A., & Foray, D. (2000). The Explicit Economics of Knowledge Codification and Tacitness. *Industrial and Corporate Change, 9*(2), 211–253.

Crane, D. (1972). *Invisible Colleges: Diffusion of Knowledge in Scientific Communities.* Chicago, IL: University of Chicago Press.

Creamer, E. G. (2004). Assessing Outcomes of Long-Term Research Collaboration. *The Canadian Journal of Higher Education, 34*(1), 27–46.

Criscuolo, P., & Narula, R. (2008). A Novel Approach to National Technological Accumulation and Absorptive Capacity: Aggregating Cohen and Levinthal. *The European Journal of Development Research, 20*(1), 56–73.

Cronin, B. (2001). Hyperauthorship: A Postmodern Perversion or Evidence of A Structural Shift in Scholarly Communication Practices? *Journal of the American Society for Information Science and Technology, 52*(7), 558–569.

Cronin, B., & Weaver-Wozniak, S. (1993). Online Access to Acknowledgements. In M. E. Williams (Ed.), *Proceedings of the 14th National Online Meeting* (pp. 93–98). Medford, NJ: Learned Information.

Cruz-Castro, L., Jonkers, K., & Sanz-Menéndez, L. (2015). The Internationalisation of Research Institutes. In L. Wedlin & M. Nedeva (Eds.), *Towards European Science: Dynamics and Policy of an Evolving European Research Space* (pp. 175–198). Cheltenham, UK: Edward Elgar Publishing.

Cummings, J. N., & Kiesler, S. (2003). Coordination and Success in Multidisciplinary Scientific Collaborations. *ICIS 2003 Proceedings, 25.* Retrieved from http://aisel.aisnet.org/icis2003/25

Cummings, J. N., & Kiesler, S. (2005). Collaborative Research across Disciplinary and Organizational Boundaries. *Social Studies of Science, 35*(5), 703–722.

Cummings, J. N., & Kiesler, S. (2007). Coordination Costs and Project Outcomes in Multi-University Collaborations. *Research Policy, 36*(10), 1620–1634.

Cunningham, P., & Gök, A. (2012). *The Impact and Effectiveness of Policies to Support Collaboration for R&D and Innovation.* Nesta Working Paper No. 12/06.

Cyranoski, D. (2014). Chinese Science Gets Mass Transformation. *Nature, 513*(7519), 468–469.

Czarnitzki, D., & Fier, A. (2003). Publicly Funded R&D Collaborations and Patent Outcome in Germany. *ZEW Discussion Papers, 03-24.* Center for European Economic Research.

Da Fonseca Pachi, C. G., Yamamoto, J. F., Da Costa, A. P. A., & Lopez, L. F. (2012). Relationship between Connectivity and Academic Productivity. *Scientometrics, 93*(2), 265–278.

Daidj, N., & Jung, J. (2011). Strategies in the Media Industry: Towards the Development of Co-Opetition Practices? *Journal of Media Business Studies, 8*(4), 37–57.

Dal-Soto, F., & Monticelli, J. (2017). Coopetition Strategies in the Brazilian Higher Education. *Revista De Administração De Empresas, 57*(1), 65–78.

Day, R. E. (2001). *The Modern Invention of Information: Discourse, History, and Power.* Carbondale, IL: Southern Illinois University Press.

De Noni, I., Ganzaroli, A., & Orsi, L. (2017). The Impact of Intra-And Inter-Regional Knowledge Collaboration and Technological Variety on the Knowledge Productivity of European Regions. *Technological Forecasting and Social Change, 117,* 108–118.

De Prato, G., & Nepelski, D. (2014). Global Technological Collaboration Network: Network Analysis of International Co-Inventions. *The Journal of Technology Transfer, 39*(3), 358–375.

De Sordi, J. O., Conejero, M. A., & Meireles, M. (2016). Bibliometric Indicators in the Context of Regional Repositories: Proposing the D-Index. *Scientometrics, 107*(1), 235–258.

De Stefano, D., Fuccella, V., Vitale, M. P., & Zaccarin, S. (2013). The Use of Different Data Sources in the Analysis of Co-Authorship Networks and Scientific Performance. *Social Networks, 35*(3), 370–381.

De Stefano, D., Giordano, G., & Vitale, M. P. (2011). Issues in the Analysis of Co-Authorship Networks. *Quality & Quantity, 45*(5), 1091–1107.

Delanghe, H., Muldur, U., & Soete, L. (Eds.). (2009). *European Science and Technology Policy: Towards Integration or Fragmentation?* Cheltenham, UK: Edward Elgar.

Desrochers, N., Paul-Hus, A., & Larivière, V. (2016). The Angle Sum Theory: Exploring the Literature on Acknowledgments in Scholarly Communication. In C. R. Sugimoto (Ed.), *Theories of Informetrics and Scholarly Communication* (pp. 225–247). Berlin, Germany: De Gruyter Mouton.

Desrochers, N., Paul-Hus, A., & Pecoskie, J. (2015). Founding Concepts and Foundational Work: Establishing the Framework for the Use of Acknowledgments as Indicators. *Proceedings of the 15th International Conference on Scientometrics and Informetrics*, 890–894.

Didegah, F., & Thelwall, M. (2013). Which Factors Help Authors Produce the Highest Impact Research? Collaboration, Journal and Document Properties. *Journal of Informetrics, 7*(4), 861–873.

Didegah, F., Thelwall, M., & Gazni, A. (2012). An International Comparison of Journal Publishing and Citing Behaviours. *Journal of Informetrics, 6*(4), 516–531.

Dingemanse, M. (2016, June 27). Some Things You Need to Know about Google Scholar. Retrieved from http://ideophone.org/some-things-you-need-to-know-about-google-scholar/

Doorley, S., & Witthoft, S. (2012). *Make Space: How to Set the Stage for Creative Collaboration.* Hoboken, NJ: John Wiley & Sons.

Doré, J. C., Ojasoo, T., Okubo, Y., Durand, T., Dudognon, G., & Miquel, J. F. (1996). Correspondence Factor Analysis of the Publication Patterns of 48 Countries over the Period 1981–1992. *Journal of the American Society for Information Science, 47*(8), 588–602.

Dorn, H. (1991). *The Geography of Science.* Baltimore, MD: Johns Hopkins University Press.

Drucker, J., & Goldstein, H. (2007). Assessing the Regional Economic Development Impacts of Universities: A Review of Current Approaches. *International Regional Science Review, 30*(1), 20–46.

Ductor, L. (2015). Does Co-Authorship Lead to Higher Academic Productivity? *Oxford Bulletin of Economics and Statistics, 77*(3), 385–407.

Dunn, R., & Higgitt, R. (2014). *Finding Longitude: How Ships, Clocks and Stars Helped Solve the Longitude Problem.* Glasgow, UK: Harper Collins UK.

Dupree, A. H. (1957). *Science in the Federal Government: A History of Policies and Activities to 1940.* Cambridge, MA: Belknap Press of Harvard University Press.

Duque, R. B., Ynalvez, M., Sooryamoorthy, R., Mbatia, P., Dzorgbo, D. B. S., & Shrum, W. (2005). Collaboration Paradox Scientific Productivity, the Internet, and Problems of Research in Developing Areas. *Social Studies of Science, 35*(5), 755–785.

Eagle, N., Pentland, A. S., & Lazer, D. (2009). Inferring Friendship Network Structure by Using Mobile Phone Data. *Proceedings of the National Academy of Sciences, 106*(36), 15274–15278.

Eckert, D., Baron, M., & Jégou, L. (2013). Les Villes Et La Science: Apports De La Spatialisation Des Données Bibliométriques Mondiales. *M@Ppemonde, 110*(2). Retrieved from https://mappemonde-archive.mgm.fr/num38/articles/art13201.html

Edelstein, D., Comsa, M., Conroy, M., Kassabova, B., Willan, C., Edmundson, C., Nyaosi, B. (2010). *Voltaire and the Enlightenment. A Case Study within the "Mapping the Republic of Letters" Project.* Retrieved from http://republicofletters.stanford.edu/casestudies/voltaire.html

Edquist, C. (2005). Systems of Innovation. Perspectives and Challenges. In J. Fagerberg, D. C. Mowery, & R. R. Nelson (Eds.), *The Oxford Handbook of Innovation* (pp. 181–208). Oxford, UK: Oxford University Press.

Edwards, B. (2000). *University Architecture.* London, UK: Spon Press.

References

Egghe, L. (2005). Expansion of the field of Informetrics: Origins and Consequences. *Information Processing and Management, 41*, 1311–1316.

Egghe, L. (2006). Theory and Practise of the G-Index. *Scientometrics, 69*(1), 131–152.

Eiben, C. B., Siegel, J. B., Bale, J. B., Cooper, S., Khatib, F., Shen, B. W., … & Baker, D. (2012). Increased Diels-Alderase Activity through Backbone Remodeling Guided by Foldit Players. Nature. *Biotechnology, 30*(2), 190–192.

Einstein, A. (1983). *Essays in Humanism*. New York, NY: Philosophical Library.

Einstein, A. (1994). *Ideas and Opinions*. New York, NY: The Modern Library.

Ejermo, O., & Karlsson, C. (2006). Interregional Inventor Networks as Studied by Patent Coinventorships. *Research Policy, 35*(3), 412–430.

Endenich, C., & Trapp, R. (2015). Cooperation for Publication? an Analysis of Co-Authorship Patterns in Leading Accounting Journals. *European Accounting Review, 25*(3), 613–633.

Enders, J. (2001). A Chair System in Transition: Appointments, Promotions, and Gate-Keeping in German Higher Education. *Higher Education, 41*(1–2), 3–25.

Engers, M., Gans, J., Grant, S., & King, S. (1999). First Author Conditions. *Journal of Political Economy, 107*(4), 859–883.

ERA-NET Review 2006. (2006, December). Retrieved from https://ec.europa.eu/info/research-and-innovation_en

Esipova, N., Pugliese, A., & Ray, J. (2013). The Demographics of Global Internal Migration. *Migration Policy Practice, 3*(2), 3–5.

Etzkowitz, H., & Leydesdorff, L. (1995). The Triple Helix–University-industry-government Relations: A Laboratory for Knowledge Based Economic Development. *EASST Review, 14*(1), 14–19.

Etzkowitz, H., & Leydesdorff, L. (2000). The Dynamics of Innovation: From National Systems and "Mode 2" to a Triple Helix of University–Industry–Government Relations. *Research Policy, 29*(2), 109–123.

European Commission. (2011). *Commission Staff Working Paper: The Added Value of the EU Budget. Accompanying the Document Commission Communication – A Budget for Europe 2020*. Brussels, 29.6.2011, SEC(2011) 867 final. Retrieved from http://ec.europa.eu/budget/library/biblio/documents/fin_fwk1420/working_paper_added_value_EU_budget_SEC-867_en.pdf

European Commission. (2012). *Communication from the Commission to the European Parliament, the Council, the European Economic and Social Committee and the Committee of the Regions: A Reinforced European Research Area Partnership for Excellence and Growth*. Brussels, 17.7.2012, COM/2012/0392 final. Retrieved from https://eur-lex.europa.eu/legal-content/EN/TXT/?uri=COM:2012:0392:FIN

European Commission. (2013, October 23). *Fact Sheet: International Participation in Horizon 2020*. Retrieved from http://ec.europa.eu/programmes/horizon2020/sites/horizon2020/files/Fact sheet_international_participation.pdf

European Commission. (2014). *European Research Area Progress Report 2014*. Retrieved from http://ec.europa.eu/research/era/eraprogress2014_en.htm

European Commission. (2016a). *Evaluation of Joint Programming to Address Grand Societal Challenges Final Report of the Expert Group*. Retrieved from https://www.era-learn.eu/publications/ec-publications/evaluation-of-joint-programming-to-address-grand-societal-challenges-final-report-of-the-expert-group

European Commission. (2016b). *Horizon 2020 Open to the World! Funding of Applicants from non-EU Countries & International Organisations*. Retrieved from http://transvac.org/assets/img/PDF/h2020-hi-3cpart-en.pdf

European Parliament. (2015, July). *EU Scientific Cooperation with Third Countries*. Briefing. Retrieved from http://www.europarl.europa.eu/thinktank/en/document.html?reference=EPRS_BRI(2015)564393

European Parliamentary Research Service. (2015, November). *Horizon 2020 Budget and Implementation. A Guide to the Structure of the Programme*. Retrieved from http://www.europarl.europa.eu/RegData/etudes/IDAN/2015/571312/EPRS_IDA%282015%29571312_EN.pdf

Fähnrich, B. (2015). Science Diplomacy: Investigating the Perspective of Scholars on Politics–Science Collaboration in International Affairs. *Public Understanding of Science*. First Published 21 Nov 2016. doi:10.1177/0963662515616552

Fanelli, D., & Larivière, V. (2016). Researchers' Individual Publication Rate Has Not Increased in a Century. *PLoS ONE*, *11*(3), e0149504.

Fangmeng, T. (2016). Brain Circulation, Diaspora and Scientific Progress: A Study of the International Migration of Chinese Scientists, 1998–2006. *Asian and Pacific Migration Journal*, *25*(3), 296–319.

Federal Ministry of Eduaction and Research. (2014). *International Cooperation. Action Plan of the Federal Ministry of Education and Research (BMBF)*. Retrieved from. https://www.bmbf.de/pub/Action_Plan_International_Cooperation.pdf

Festinger, L., Schachter, S., & Back, K. (1950). The Spatial Ecology of Group Formation. In L. Festinger, S. Schachter, & K. Back (Eds.), *Social Pressure in Informal Groups* (pp. 141–161). New York, NY: Harper & Bros.

Feynman, R. P. (2010). *"Surely You're Joking, Mr. Feynman!": Adventures of a Curious Character*. New York, NY: W. W. Norton & Company.

Fischer, M. M., Scherngell, T., & Jansenberger, E. (2006). The Geography of Knowledge Spillovers between High-Technology Firms in Europe: Evidence from a Spatial Interaction Modeling Perspective. *Geographical Analysis*, *38*(3), 288–309.

Fitjar, R. D., Huber, F., & Rodríguez-Pose, A. (2016). Not Too Close, Not Too Far: Testing the Goldilocks Principle of 'Optimal' distance in Innovation Networks. *Industry and Innovation*, *23*(6), 465–487.

Fitjar, R. D., & Rodriguez-Pose, A. (2011). When Local Interaction Does Not Suffice: Sources of Firm Innovation in Urban Norway. *Environment and Planning A*, *43*(6), 1248–1267.

Flanagin, A., Carey, L. A., Fontanarosa, P. B., Phillips, S. G., Pace, B. P., Lundberg, G. D., & Rennie, D. (1998). Prevalence of Articles with Honorary Authors and Ghost Authors in Peer-Reviewed Medical Journals. *Jama*, *280*(3), 222–224.

Fleming, L., King, C., & Juda, A. I. (2007). Small Worlds and Regional Innovation. *Organization Science*, *18*(6), 938–954.

Florida, R. (1995). Toward the Learning Region. *Futures*, *27*(5), 527–536.

Florida, R. (2002). *The Rise of the Creative Class: And How It's Transforming Work, Leisure, Community and Everyday Life*. New York, NY: Basic Books.

Florida, R. (2005). The World Is Spiky: Globalization Has Changed the Economic Playing Field, but Hasn't Levelled It. *Atlantic Monthly*, *296*(3), 48.

Forero-Pineda, C. (2006). The Impact of Stronger Intellectual Property Rights on Science and Technology in Developing Countries. *Research Policy*, *35*(6), 808–824.

Forgan, S. (1989). The Architecture of Science and the Idea of a University. *Studies in History and Philosophy of Science Part A*, *20*(4), 405–434.

Frame, J. D., Narin, F., & Carpenter, M. P. (1977). The Distribution of World Science. *Social Studies of Science*, *7*(4), 501–516.

Franceschet, M. (2012). The Large-Scale Structure of Journal Citation Networks. *Journal of the Association for Information Science and Technology*, *63*(4), 837–842.

Franceschet, M., & Costantini, A. (2010). The Effect of Scholar Collaboration on Impact and Quality of Academic Papers. *Journal of Informetrics*, *4*(4), 540–553.

Frenken, K., Hardeman, S., & Hoekman, J. (2009). Spatial Scientometrics: Towards a Cumulative Research Program. *Journal of Informetrics*, *3*(3), 222–232.

Friedman, T. L. (2005). *The World Is Flat: A Brief History of the Twenty-First Century*. New York, NY: Farrar, Straus and Giroux.

Frietsch, R., & Jung, T. (2009). *Transnational Patents: Structures, Trends and Recent Developments*. Studien zum deutschen Innovationssystem, 7. Karlsruhe, Germany: Fraunhofer Institute for Systems and Innovation Research.

Galenson, D. (2012, March 7). Collaboration in Science and Art. *Huffington Post*. Retrieved from http://www.huffingtonpost.com/david-galenson/collaboration-in-science-_b_ 1687024.html

Galison, P. (2003). The Collective Author. In M. Biagioli & P. Galison (Eds.), *Scientific Authorship: Credit and Intellectual Property in Science* (pp. 327–355). New York, NY: Routledge.

Galison, P., & Hevly, B. W. (1992). *Big Science: The Growth of Large-Scale Research*. Stanford, CA: Stanford University Press.

Galison, P., & Thompson, E. (Eds.). (1999). *The Architecture of Science*. Cambridge, MA: MIT Press.

Gama, R., Barros, C., & Fernandes, R. (2018). Science Policy, R&D and Knowledge in Portugal: An Application of Social Network Analysis. *Journal of the Knowledge Economy, 9*(2), 329–358.

Garfield, E. (1996). What Is the Primordial Reference for the Phrase 'Publish or Perish'? [Commentary]. *The Scientist, 10*(12), 11. Retrieved from http://the-scientist.com/17052

Gaspar, J., & Glaeser, E. L. (1998). Information Technology and the Future of Cities. *Journal of Urban Economics, 43*(1), 136–156.

Gauffriau, M., Larsen, P., Maye, I., Roulin-Perriard, A., & von Ins, M. (2007). Publication, Cooperation and Productivity Measures in Scientific Research. *Scientometrics, 73*(2), 175–214.

Gaul, G. M. (2015). *Billion-Dollar Ball: A Journey through the Big-Money Culture of College Football*. New York, NY: Penguin Books.

Gazni, A., Sugimoto, C. R., & Didegah, F. (2012). Mapping World Scientific Collaboration: Authors, Institutions, and Countries. *Journal of the Association for Information Science and Technology, 63*(2), 323–335.

Geiger, R. L., & Sá, C. (2005). Beyond Technology Transfer: US State Policies to Harness University Research for Economic Development. *Minerva, 43*(1), 1–21.

Gelber, H. (2001). *Nations Out of Empires. European Nationalism and the Transformation of Asia*. Hampshire, UK: Palgrave.

Georghiou, L. (1998). Global Cooperation in Research. *Research Policy, 27*(6), 611–626.

Georghiou, L. (2001). Evolving Frameworks for European Collaboration in Research and Technology. *Research Policy, 30*(6), 891–903.

Gertler, M. S., & Vinodrai, T. (2005). Anchors of Creativity: How Do Public Universities Create Competitive and Cohesive Communities. In F. Iacobucci & C. J. Tuohy (Eds.), *Taking Public Universities Seriously* (pp. 293–315). Toronto, Canada: University of Toronto Press.

Gibbons, M., Limoges, C., Nowotny, H., Schwartzman, S., Scott, P., & Trow, M. (1994). *The New Production of Knowledge: The Dynamics of Science and Research in Contemporary Societies*. Los Angeles, CA: Sage.

Gibney, E. (2014, July 31). Five-Year Delay Would Spell End of ITER. *Nature*. Retrieved from http://www.nature.com/news/five-year-delay-would-spell-end-of-iter-1.15621

Gieryn, T. F. (2002). Three Truth-Spots. *Journal of the History of the Behavioral Sciences, 38*(2), 113–132.

Gieryn, T. F. (2018). *Truth-Spots*. Chicago, IL: The University of Chicago Press.

Gilbert, N. (2011). Europe's Innovation Hub Finally KICs Off: Large Networks of Researchers and Companies Aim to Develop and Commercialize Marketable Products. *Nature, 470*(7335), 450–451.

Gliboff, S. (2010). Did Paul Kammerer discover epigenetic inheritance? No and why not. *Journal of Experimental Zoology Part B: Molecular and Developmental Evolution, 314*(8), 616-624.

Glaeser, E. L., & Kohlhase, J. E. (2004). Cities, Regions and the Decline of Transport Costs. In R. J. G. M. Florax & D. Plane (Eds.), *Fifty Years of Regional Science* (pp. 197–228). Berlin, Germany: Springer.

Glänzel, W. (2001). National Characteristics in International Scientific Co-Authorship Relations. *Scientometrics, 51*(1), 69–115.

Glänzel, W., & Schubert, A. (2001). Double Effort= Double Impact? A Critical View at International Co-Authorship in Chemistry. *Scientometrics, 50*(2), 199–214.

Glänzel, W., Schubert, A., & Czerwon, H. J. (1999). A Bibliometric Analysis of International Scientific Cooperation of the European Union (1985–1995). *Scientometrics, 45*(2), 185–202.

References

Gmür, M. (2003). Co-Citation Analysis and the Search for Invisible Colleges: A Methodological Evaluation. *Scientometrics*, 57(1), 27–57.

Gnyawali, D. R., He, J.,& Madhavan, R. (2008). Co-Opetition: Promises and Challenges. In C. Wankel (Ed.), *21st Century Management: A Reference Handbook* (pp. 386–398). Thousand Oaks, CA: Sage.

Gnyawali, D. R., & Park, B. J. R. (2011). Coopetition between Giants: Collaboration with Competitors for Technological Innovation. *Research Policy*, 40(5), 650–663.

Goddard, J. (2013). Keep Universities Anchored. *Research Fortnight*, 422, 20–22.

Goddard, J., Kempton, L., Vallance P. (2013). The Civic University: Connecting the Global and the Local. In R. Cappello, A. Olechnicka, & G. Gorzelak (Eds.), *Universities, Cities and Regions: Loci for Knowledge and Innovation Creation* (pp. 43–63). New York, NY: Routledge.

Goddard, J., & Vallance, P. (2011). Universities and Regional Development. In A. Pike, A. Rodríguez-Pose, & J. Tomaney (Eds.), *Handbook of Local and Regional Development* (pp. 425–437). London, UK: Routledge.

Goddard, J., & Vallance, P. (2013). *The University and the City*. London, UK: Routledge.

Godin, B., & Ippersiel, M. P. (1996). Scientific Collaboration at the Regional Level: The Case of a Small Country. *Scientometrics*, 36(1), 59–68.

Goffman, C. (1969). And What Is Your Erdős Number? *The American Mathematical Monthly*, 76(7), 791–791.

Goldfinch, S., Dale, T., & DeRouen, K. (2003). Science from the Periphery: Publication, Collaboration and 'Periphery Effects' in Article Citation Rates of the New Zealand Crown Research Institutes 1995–2000. *Scientometrics*, 57(3), 321–337.

Goldstain, H. (2010). The 'Entrepreneurial Turn' and Regional Economic Development Mission of Universities. *Annals of Regional Science*, 44(1), 83–109.

Goodyear, D. (2016, February 29). The Stress Test. *The New Yorker*. Retrieved from http://www.newyorker.com/magazine/2016/02/29/the-stem-cell-scandal

Gordin, M. D. (2015). *Scientific Babel: How Science Was Done before and after Global English*. Chicago, IL: University of Chicago Press.

Gordon, M. (1980). A Critical Reassessment of Inferred Relations between Multiple Authorship, Scientific Collaboration, the Production of Papers and Their Acceptance for Publication. *Scientometrics*, 2(3), 193–201.

Gorraiz, J., Reimann, R., & Gumpenberger, C. (2012). Key Factors and Considerations in the Assessment of International Collaboration: A Case Study for Austria and Six Countries. *Scientometrics*, 91(2), 417–433.

Gorzelak, G. (2010). Facts and Myths of Regional Development, *Studia Regionalne I Lokalne*, 5–28. Special Issue.

Gorzelak, G., & Zawalińska, K. (Eds.). (2013). *European Territories: From Cooperation to Integration?* Warsaw, Poland: Scholar.

Granovetter, M. S. (1973). The Strength of Weak Ties. *American Journal of Sociology*, 78(6), 1360–1380.

Grasland, C., & Madelin, M. (Eds.). (2006). *The Modifiable Areas Unit Problem. ESPON 3.4.3 Final Report*. Luxembourg: ESPON.

Griffiths, R. (2004). Knowledge Production and the Research–Teaching Nexus: The Case of the Built Environment Disciplines. *Studies in Higher Education*, 29(6), 709–726.

Grossetti, M., Eckert, D., Gingras, Y., Jégou, L., Larivière, V., & Milard, B. (2014). Cities and the Geographical Deconcentration of Scientific Activity: A Multilevel Analysis of Publications (1987–2007). *Urban Studies*, 51(10), 2219–2234.

Grove, J. (2016, March 31). Can a Young University Be a World-Leading University? *Times Higher Education*. Retrieved from https://www.timeshighereducation.com/features/can-a-young-university-be-a-world-leading-university

Guan, J., & Liu, N. (2014). Measuring Scientific Research in Emerging Nano-Energy Field. *Journal of Nanoparticle Research*, 16(4), 2356.

Guellec, D., & De La Potterie, B. V. P. (2001). The Internationalisation of Technology Analysed with Patent Data. *Research Policy, 30*(8), 1253–1266.
Gumprecht, B. (2008). *The American College Town*. Amherst, MA: University of Massachusetts Press.
Gunasekara, C. (2006a). Reframing the Role of Universities in the Development of Regional Innovation Systems. *The Journal of Technology Transfer, 31*(1), 101–113.
Gunasekara, C. (2006b). The Generative and Developmental Roles of Universities in Regional Innovation Systems. *Science and Public Policy, 33*, 137–150.
Gusmão, R. (2001). Research Networks as a Means of European Integration. *Technology in Society, 23*(3), 383–393.
Haar, S. (2011). *The City as Campus: Urbanism and Higher Education in Chicago*. Minneapolis, MN: Unieversity of Minnesota Press.
Hall, P. (2000). Creative Cities and Economic Development. *Urban Studies, 37*(4), 639–649.
Hallonsten, O. (2016). *Big Science Transformed: Science, Politics and Organization in Europe and the United States*. New York, NY: Macmillan Publishers Limited.
Hane, G. (2008). Science, Technology, and Global Reengagement. *Issues in Science and Technology, 25*(1), 85–90.
Hannaway, O. (1986). Laboratory Design and the Aim of Science: Andreas Libavius versus Tycho Brahe. *Isis, 77*(4), 585–610.
Hansen, T. (2013). Bridging Regional Innovation: Cross-Border Collaboration in the Øresund Region. *Geografisk Tidsskrift-Danish Journal of Geography, 113*(1), 25–38.
Hao, X., Yan, K., Guo, S., & Wang, M. (2017). Chinese Returnees' Motivation, Post-Return Status and Impact of Return: A Systematic Review. *Asian and Pacific Migration Journal, 26*(1), 143–157.
Hara, N., Solomon, P., Kim, S. L., & Sonnenwald, D. H. (2003). An Emerging View of Scientific Collaboration: Scientists' Perspectives on Collaboration and Factors that Impact Collaboration. *Journal of the American Society for Information Science and Technology, 54*(10), 952–965.
Harloe, M., & Perry, B. (2004). Universities, Localities and Regional Development: The Emergence of the 'Mode 2' university? *International Journal of Urban and Regional Research, 28*(1), 212–223.
Harris, S. J. (2006). Networks of Travel, Correspondence, and Exchange. In D. C. Lindberg, R. L. Numbers, & R. Porter (Eds.), *The Cambridge History of Science* (Vol. 3, pp. 341–362). Cambridge, UK: Cambridge University Press.
Hart, R. L. (2007). Collaboration and Article Quality in the Literature of Academic Librarianship. *The Journal of Academic Librarianship, 33*(2), 190–195.
Hassell, M. P., & May, R. M. (1974). Aggregation of Predators and Insect Parasites and Its Effect on Stability. *The Journal of Animal Ecology, 43*(2), 567–594.
Hauser, C., Tappeiner, G., & Walde, J. (2007). The Learning Region: The Impact of Social Capital and Weak Ties on Innovation. *Regional Studies, 41*(1), 75–88.
Haustein, S., Costas, R., & Larivière, V. (2015). Characterizing Social Media Metrics of Scholarly Papers: The Effect of Document Properties and Collaboration Patterns. *PLoS One, 10*(3), e0120495.
He, B., Ding, Y., & Ni, C. (2011). Mining Enriched Contextual Information of Scientific Collaboration: A Meso Perspective. *Journal of the American Society for Information Science and Technology, 62*(5), 831–845.
He, B., Ding, Y., & Yan, E. (2012). Mining Patterns of Author Orders in Scientific Publications. *Journal of Informetrics, 6*(3), 359–367.
He, Z. L. (2009). International Collaboration Does Not Have Greater Epistemic Authority. *Journal of the American Society for Information Science and Technology, 60*(10), 2151–2164.
Hennemann, S., Wang, T., & Liefner, I. (2011). Measuring Regional Science Networks in China: A Comparison of International and Domestic Bibliographic Data Sources. *Scientometrics, 88*(2), 535–554.

Henry, N., & Pinch, S. (2001). Neo-Marshallian Nodes, Institutional Thickness, and Britain's 'Motor Sport Valley': Thick or Thin? *Environment and Planning A, 33*(7), 1169–1183.

Heringa, P. W., Horlings, E., Van Der Zouwen, M., Van Den Besselaar, P., & Van Vierssen, W. (2014). How Do Dimensions of Proximity Relate to the Outcomes of Collaboration? A Survey of Knowledge-Intensive Networks in the Dutch Water Sector. *Economics of Innovation and New Technology, 23*(7), 689–716.

Hessels, L. K., & Van Lente, H. (2008). Re-Thinking New Knowledge Production: A Literature Review and A Research Agenda. *Research Policy, 37*(4), 740–760.

Hicks, D. (2012). Performance-Based University Research Funding Systems. *Research Policy, 41*(2), 251–261.

Hicks, D., & Katz, J. S. (1996). Science Policy for a Highly Collaborative Science System. *Science and Public Policy, 23*(1), 39–44.

Hiltzik, M. A. (2015). *Big Science: Ernest Lawrence and the Invention that Launched the Military-Industrial Complex*. New York, NY: Simon & Schuster.

Hoekman, J., Frenken, K., & Tijssen, R. J. (2010). Research Collaboration at a Distance: Changing Spatial Patterns of Scientific Collaboration within Europe. *Research Policy, 39*(5), 662–673.

Hoekman, J., Frenken, K., & Van Oort, F. (2009). The Geography of Collaborative Knowledge Production in Europe. *The Annals of Regional Science, 43*(3), 721–738.

Hoekman, J., Scherngell, T., Frenken, K., & Tijssen, R. (2013). Acquisition of European Research Funds and Its Effect on International Scientific Collaboration. *Journal of Economic Geography, 13*(1), 23–52.

Hollis, A. (2001). Co-Authorship and the Output of Academic Economists. *Labour Economics, 8*, 503–530.

Hong, W. (2008). Decline of the Center: The Decentralizing Process of Knowledge Transfer of Chinese Universities from 1985 to 2004. *Research Policy, 37*(4), 580–595.

Hotz, R. L. (1999, October 1). Mars Probe Lost Due to Simple Math Error. *Los Angeles Times*. Retrieved from http://articles.latimes.com/1999/oct/01/news/mn-17288

Hotz, R. L. (2015, August 10). How Many Scientists Does It Take to Write a Paper? Apparently, Thousands. *The Wall Street Journal*. Retrieved from http://www.wsj.com/articles/how-many-scientists-does-it-take-to-write-a-paper-apparently-thousands-1439169200

Hsiehchen, D., Espinoza, M., & Hsieh, A. (2015). Multinational Teams and Diseconomies of Scale in Collaborative Research. *Science Advances, 1*(8), e1500211.

Huang, H. W., & Zhang, S. L. (2000). College and University Mergers: Impact on Academic Libraries in China. *College & Research Libraries, 61*(2), 121–125.

Huang, M. H., Tang, M. C., & Chen, D. Z. (2011). Inequality of Publishing Performance and International Collaboration in Physics. *Journal of the American Society for Information Science and Technology, 62*(6), 1156–1165.

Huang, Z. (2015, November 10). Modern Talent Scout - Yuan Fang, Director of the Beijing Overseas Talents Center. *China Today*. Retrieved from http://www.chinatoday.com.cn/english/society/2015-11/10/content_708024.htm

Huber, F. (2012). Do Clusters Really Matter for Innovation Practices in Information Technology? Questioning the Significance of Technological Knowledge Spillovers. *Journal of Economic Geography, 12*(1), 107–126.

Hull, D. L. (1988). *Science as a Process: An Evolutionary Account of the Social and Conceptual Development of Science*. Chicago, IL: University of Chicago Press.

Human Genome Project Information Archive. (1990–2003). Retrieved From http://web.ornl.gov/sci/techresources/Human_Genome/index.shtml

Hunt, T. (Interviewee) (n.d.). *Do You Enjoy Collaboration*. Nobel Prize Inspiration Initiative [Interview's video podcast]. Retrieved from http://www.nobelprizeii.org/videos/do-you-enjoy-collaboration/

References 201

Hwang, K. (2008). International Collaboration in Multilayered Center-Periphery in the Globalization of Science and Technology. *Science, Technology, & Human Values, 33*(1), 101–133.

Hwang, K. (2012). Effects of the Language Barrier on Processes and Performance of International Scientific Collaboration, Collaborators' Participation, Organizational Integrity, and Interorganizational Relationships. *Science Communication, 35*(1), 3–31.

Hyde, J. K. (1988). Universities and Cities in Medieval Italy. In T. Bender (Ed.), *The University and the City: From Medieval Origins to the Present* (pp. 13–21). New York, NY: Oxford University Press.

Iaria, A., Schwarz, C., & Waldinger, F. (2018). Frontier Knowledge and Scientific Production: Evidence from the Collapse of International Science. *The Quarterly Journal of Economics, 133*(2), 927–991.

IDRC & State Science and Technology Commission People's Republic of China. (1998). *A Decade of Reform: Science & Technology Policy in China.* Ottawa: International Development Research Centre. Retrieved from https://www.idrc.ca/en/book/decade-reform-science-and-technology-policy-china

Ihde, A. J. (1961). The Karlsruhe Congress: A Centennial Retrospective. *Journal of Chemical Education, 38*(2), 83–86.

Ilakovac, V., Fister, K., Marusic, M., & Marusic, A. (2007). Reliability of Disclosure Forms of Authors' Contributions. *Canadian Medical Association Journal, 176*(1), 41–46.

Indiana University Center for Postsecondary Research. (2016). Carnegie Classifications 2015 Public Data File. Retrieved form http://carnegieclassifications.iu.edu/downloads/CCIHE2015-PublicDataFile.xlsx

Ingwersen, P., & Larsen, B. (2014). Influence of a Performance Indicator on Danish Research Production and Citation Impact 2000–12. *Scientometrics, 101*(2), 1325–1344.

Isabelle, D. A., & Heslop, L. A. (2011). Managing for Success in International Scientific Collaborations: Views from Canadian Government Senior Science Managers. *Science and Public Policy, 38*(5), 349.

Jacob, M., & Meek, V. L. (2013). Scientific Mobility and International Research Networks: Trends and Policy Tools for Promoting Research Excellence and Capacity Building. *Studies in Higher Education, 38*(3), 331–344.

Jakobson, L. (2007). China Aims High in Science and Technology: An Overview of the Challenges Ahead. In L. Jakobson (Ed.), *Innovation with Chinese Characteristics: High-Tech Research in China* (pp. 1–36). New York, NY: Palgrave Macmillan.

Jarvie, I. C., Milford, K., & Miller, D. W. (Eds.). (2006). *Karl Popper: Metaphysics and Epistemology*. Aldershot, UK: Ashgate Publishing.

Jaspers, K. (1959). *The Idea of the University*. London, UK: Owen.

Jeffrey, P. (2003). Smoothing the Waters Observations on the Process of Cross-Disciplinary Research Collaboration. *Social Studies of Science, 33*(4), 539–562.

Jeong, S., Choi, J. Y., & Kim, J. (2011). The Determinants of Research Collaboration Modes: Exploring the Effects of Research and Researcher Characteristics on Co-Authorship. *Scientometrics, 89*(3), 967–983.

Jing, Z. (2011, June 5). International Scientific Co-Op Urged. *China Daily*. Retrieved from http://europe.chinadaily.com.cn/china/2011-06/09/content_12667946.htm

Jirotka, M., Lee, C. P., & Olson, G. M. (2013). Supporting Scientific Collaboration: Methods, Tools and Concepts. *Computer Supported Cooperative Work, 22*(4–6), 667–715.

Johnson, D., & Grayson, K. (2005). Cognitive and Affective Trust in Service Relationships. *Journal of Business Research, 58*(4), 500–507.

Jones, B. F., Wuchty, S., & Uzzi, B. (2008). Multi-University Research Teams: Shifting Impact, Geography, and Stratification in Science. *Science, 322*(5905), 1259–1262.

Jonkers, K., & Cruz-Castro, L. (2013). Research upon Return: The Effect of International Mobility on Scientific Ties, Production and Impact. *Research Policy, 42*(8), 1366–1377.

Jonkers, K., & Tijssen, R. (2008). Chinese Researchers Returning Home: Impacts of International Mobility on Research Collaboration and Scientific Productivity. *Scientometrics*, 77(2), 309–333.

Jöns, H. (2009). 'Brain Circulation' and Transnational Knowledge Networks: Studying Long-Term Effects of Academic Mobility to Germany, 1954–2000. *Global Networks*, 9(3), 315–338.

Jöns, H., & Hoyler, M. (2013). Global Geographies of Higher Education: The Perspective of World University Rankings. *Geoforum*, 46, 45–59.

Jorgensen, R. (2007). Rewarding Collaboration [Editorial]. *The Plant Cell*, 19(10), 2967.

Joseph, K., Laband, D. N., & Patil, V. (2005). Author Order and Research Quality. *Southern Economic Journal*, 71(3), 545–555.

Josephson, P. R. (1997). *New Atlantis Revisited: Akademgorodok, the Siberian City of Science*. Princeton, NJ: Princeton University Press.

Jun, C. (2016, January 19). Innovation Contest Pushes Forward US-china Cooperation. *China Daily*. Retrieved from http://usa.chinadaily.com.cn/opinion/2016-01/19/content_23155992.htm

Kabo, F. W., Cotton-Nessler, N., Hwang, Y., Levenstein, M. C., & Owen-Smith, J. (2014). Proximity Effects on the Dynamics and Outcomes of Scientific Collaborations. *Research Policy*, 43(9), 1469–1485.

Kabo, F. W., Hwang, Y., Levenstein, M., & Owen-Smith, J. (2015). Shared Paths to the Lab: A Sociospatial Network Analysis of Collaboration. *Environment and Behavior*, 47(1), 57–84.

Kafouros, M., Wang, C., Piperopoulos, P., & Zhang, M. (2015). Academic Collaborations and Firm Innovation Performance in China: The Role of Region-Specific Institutions. *Research Policy*, 44(3), 803–817.

Kahn, S., & MacGarvie, M. (2011). The Effects of the Foreign Fulbright Program on Knowledge Creation in Science and Engineering. In J. Lerner & S. Stern (Eds.), *The Rate and Direction of Inventive Activity Revisited* (pp. 161–197). Chicago, IL: University of Chicago Press.

Kamalski, J., & Plume, A. (2013, September). *Comparative Benchmarking of European and US Research Collaboration and Researchers Mobility: A Report Prepared in Collaboration Between Science Europe and Elsevier's SciVal Analytics*. Science Europe, Elsevier. Retrieved from https://www.elsevier.com/research-intelligence/resource-library/comparative-benchmarking-of-european-and-us-research-collaboration-and-researcher-mobility

Karpagam, R., Gopalakrishnan, S., Babu, B. R., & Natarajan, M. (2012). Scientometric Analysis of Stem Cell Research: A Comparative Study of India and Other Countries. *Collnet Journal of Scientometrics and Information Management*, 6(2), 229–252.

Kato, M., & Ando, A. (2017). National Ties of International Scientific Collaboration and Researcher Mobility Found in Nature and Science. *Scientometrics*, 110(2), 673–694.

Katz, J. S., & Hicks, D. (1997). How Much Is A Collaboration Worth? A Calibrated Bibliometric Model. *Scientometrics*, 40(3), 541–554.

Katz, J. S., & Martin, B. R. (1997). What Is Research Collaboration? *Research Policy*, 26(1), 1–18.

Katz, M. L., & Shapiro, C. (1985). Network Externalities, Competition, and Compatibility. *The American Economic Review*, 75(3), 424–440.

Ke, W. (2013). A Fitness Model for Scholarly Impact Analysis. *Scientometrics*, 94(3), 981–998.

Kefalides, P. (1991, September). Proliferation of Research Parks Conceals Uneven Success Pattern. *The Scientist*. Retrieved from https://www.the-scientist.com/?articles.view/articleNo/12020/title/Proliferation-Of-Research-Parks-Conceals-Uneven-Success-Pattern/

Kenzer, M. S. (1992). Review [Review of the Book *the Geography of Science*, by H. Dorn]. *Isis*, 83(4), 634–635.

Khatib, F., DiMaio, F., Cooper, S., Kazmierczyk, M., Gilski, M., Krzywda, S., ... & Baker, D. (2011). Crystal Structure of a Monomeric Retroviral Protease Solved by Protein Folding Game Players. *Nature Structural and Molecular Biology*, 18(10), 1175.

Kilduff, M., & Tsai, W. (2007). *Social Networks and Organizations*. Thousand Oaks, CA: Sage.

Kim, M.-J. (1999). Korean International Co-Authorship in Science 1994–1996. *Journal of Information Science*, 25, 403–412.

King, D. A. (2004). The Scientific Impact of Nations. *Nature, 430*(6997), 311–316.
Kirat, T., & Lung, Y. (1999). Innovation and Proximity: Territories as Loci of Collective Learning Processes. *European Urban and Regional Studies, 6*(1), 27–38.
Klauder, C. Z., & Wise, H. C. (1929). *College Architecture in America and Its Part in the Development of the Campus*. New York, NY: C. Scribner's Sons.
Klein, J. T. (1990). *Interdisciplinarity: History, Theory, and Practice*. Detroit: Wayne state University Press.
Klein, J. T. (2004). Prospects for Transdisciplinarity. *Futures, 36*(4), 515–526.
Knapp, A. (2012, July 5). How Much Does It Cost to Find a Higgs Boson? *Forbes Online*. Retrieved from How Much Does it Cost to Find a Higgs Boson
Knight, D. M. (1976). *The Nature of Science: The History of Science in Western Culture since 1600*. London, UK: André Deutsch.
Knoben, J., & Oerlemans, L. A. (2006). Proximity and Inter-Organizational Collaboration: A Literature Review. *International Journal of Management Reviews, 8*(2), 71–89.
Koku, E., Nazer, N., & Wellman, B. (2001). Netting Scholars Online and Offline. *American Behavioral Scientist, 44*(10), 1752–1774.
Kossinets, G., & Watts, D. J. (2006). Empirical Analysis of an Evolving Social Network. *Science, 311* (5757), 88–90.
Kousha, K., & Thelwall, M. (2007). Google Scholar Citations and Google Web/URL Citations: A Multidiscipline Exploratory Analysis. *Journal of the American Society for Information Science and Technology, 57*(7), 1055–1065.
Kraemer, S. K. (2006). *Science and Technology Policy in the United States: Open Systems in Action*. New Brunswick, NJ: Rutgers University Press.
Kreimer, P. (2007). Relevancia Del Conocimiento Social En América Latina: De La Internacionalización "Neoliberal" a La División Internacional Del Trabajo Científico. *Perfiles Educativos, 28*, 84–101.
Kretschmer, H., Kretschmer, U., & Kretschmer, T. (2007). Reflection of Co-Authorship Networks in the Web: Web Hyperlinks versus Web Visibility Rates. *Scientometrics, 70*(2), 519–540.
Krige, J. (2003). The Politics of European Scientific Collaboration. In J. Krige & D. Pestre (Eds.), *Companion to Science in the Twentieth Century* (pp. 897–918). London, UK: Routledge.
Kronick, D. A. (2001). The Commerce of Letters: Networks And "Invisible Colleges" in Seventeenth-And Eighteenth-Century Europe. *The Library Quarterly: Information, Community, Policy, 71*(1), 28–43.
Kukliński A. (2001). The Role of Universities in Stimulating Regional Development and Educating Global Elites. *Higher Education in Europe, 26*(3), 437–445.
Kulczycki, E. (2017). Assessing Publications through a Bibliometric Indicator: The Case of Comprehensive Evaluation of Scientific Units in Poland. *Research Evaluation, 26*(1), 41–52.
Kullenberg, C., & Kasperowski, D. (2016). What Is Citizen science?–A Scientometric Meta-Analysis. *PLoS ONE, 11*(1), e0147152.
Kumar, S. (2015). Co-Authorship Networks: A Review of the Literature. *Aslib Journal of Information Management, 67*(1), 55–73.
Kumar, S., Rohani, V. A., & Ratnavelu, K. (2014). International Research Collaborations of ASEAN Nations in Economics, 1979–2010. *Scientometrics, 101*(1), 847–867.
Kuttim, M. (2016). The Role of Spatial and Non-Spatial Forms of Proximity in Knowledge Transfer: A Case of Technical University. *European Journal of Innovation Management, 19*(4), 468–491.
Kwiek, M. (2017). International Research Collaboration and International Research Orientation: Comparative Findings about European Academics. *Journal of Studies in International Education, 22*(2), 136–160.
Laband, D. N., & Tollison, R. D. (2000). Intellectual Collaboration. *Journal of Political Economy, 108*(3), 632–662.
Lambert, R. (2003). *Lambert Review of Business-University Collaboration: Final Report*. University of Illinois at Urbana-Champaign's Academy for Entrepreneurial Leadership Historical Research Reference in Entrepreneurship. Retrieved from https://ssrn.com/abstract=1509981

Lambright, W. H. (2000). Catalyzing Research Competitiveness: The Georgia Research Alliance. *Prometheus*, *18*(4), 357–372.

Landry, C. (2008). *The Creative City: A Toolkit for Urban Innovators* (2nd ed.). New Stroud: Comedia.

Landry, R., Traoré, N., & Godin, B. (1996). An Econometric Analysis of the Effect of Collaboration on Academic Research Productivity. *Higher Education*, *32*(3), 283–301.

Lank, E. (2006). *Collaborative Advantage. How Organizations Win by Working Together*. London, UK: Palgrave Macmillan.

Larivière, V., Desrochers, N., Macaluso, B., Mongeon, P., Paul-Hus, A., & Sugimoto, C. R. (2016). Contributorship and Division of Labor in Knowledge Production. *Social Studies of Science*, *46*(3), 417–435.

Larivière, V., Gingras, Y., Sugimoto, C. R., & Tsou, A. (2015). Team Size Matters: Collaboration and Scientific Impact since 1900. *Journal of the Association for Information Science and Technology*, *66*(7), 1323–1332.

Latour, B. (1987). *Science in Action: How to Follow Scientists and Engineers through Society*. Cambridge, MA: Harvard University Press.

Latour, B., & Woolgar, S. (1986). *Laboratory Life: The Construction of Scientific Facts*. Princeton, NJ: Princeton University Press.

Laudel, G. (2001). Collaboration, Creativity and Rewards: Why and How Scientists Collaborate. *International Journal of Technology Management*, *22*(7–8), 762–781.

Laudel, G. (2002). What Do We Measure by Co-Authorships? *Research Evaluation*, *11*(1), 3–15.

Lawani, S. M. (1980). *Quality, Collaboration and Citations in Cancer Research: A Bibliometric Study* (Doctoral Dissertation). Florida State University.

Lawani, S. M. (1986). Some Bibliometric Correlates of Quality in Scientific Research. *Scientometrics*, *9*(1–2), 13–25.

Lawton Smith, H. (2006). *Universities, Innovation and the Economy*. London, UK: Routledge.

Lazerson, M., & Lorenzoni, G. (1999). Resisting Organizational Inertia: The Evolution of Industrial Districts. *Journal of Management and Governance*, *3*(4), 361–377.

Leclerc, M., & Gagné, J. (1994). International Scientific Cooperation: The Continentalization of Science. *Scientometrics*, *31*(3), 261–292.

Lee, K. (2011). *University Architecture*. Shenyang, China: Liaoning Science & Technology Publishing House.

Lee, K., Brownstein, J. S., Mills, R. G., & Kohane, I. S. (2010). Does Collocation Inform the Impact of Collaboration? *PLoS ONE*, *5*(12), e14279.

Lee, S., & Bozeman, B. (2005). The Impact of Research Collaboration on Scientific Productivity. *Social Studies of Science*, *35*(5), 673–702.

Lei, X. P., Zhao, Z. Y., Zhang, X., Chen, D. Z., Huang, M. H., Zheng, J., ... & Zhao, Y. H. (2013). Technological Collaboration Patterns in Solar Cell Industry Based on Patent Inventors and Assignees Analysis. *Scientometrics*, *96*(2), 427–441.

Leicester, H. M. (1956). *The Historical Background of Chemistry*. New York, NY: John Wiley and Sons.

Leimu, R., & Koricheva, J. (2005). Does Scientific Collaboration Increase the Impact of Ecological Articles? *AIBS Bulletin*, *55*(5), 438–443.

Leonchuk, L., McGowen, L.C., & Gray, D.O. (2016). IUCRC Program Findings from the Center Structure Database [PDF Document]. Retrieved from https://projects.ncsu.edu/iucrc/Jan-Jun%2716/2014-2015%20CD%20Report%20Slides_standardized%20Final.pdf

Lessig, L. (2005). *Free Culture: The Nature and Future of Creativity*. New York, NY: Penguin.

Leta, J., & Chaimovich, H. (2002). Recognition and International Collaboration: The Brazilian Case. *Scientometrics*, *53*(3), 325–335.

Leverington, D. (2003). *Babylon to Voyager and Beyond: A History of Planetary Astronomy*. Cambridge, UK: Cambridge University Press.

Leydesdorff, L., & Park, H. W. (2017). Full and Fractional Counting in Bibliometric Networks. *Journal of Informetrics*, *11*(1), 117–120.

Leydesdorff, L., & Wagner, C. S. (2008). International Collaboration in Science and the Formation of a Core Group. *Journal of Informetrics*, *2*(4), 317–325.

Li, J., & Willett, P. (2009). Bibliometric Analysis of Chinese Research on Cyclization, MALDI-TOF, and Antibiotics. *Journal of Chemical Information and Modeling*, *50*(1), 22–29.

Liang, L., & Zhu, L. (2002). Major Factors Affecting China's Inter-Regional Research Collaboration: Regional Scientific Productivity and Geographical Proximity. *Scientometrics*, *55*(2), 287–316.

Libo, Z. (2015). A Scientometrics Study on Cooperation of Chinese S&T Research over the past Decade. *Journal of Intelligence*, *1*, 023.

Link, A. N., Siegel, D. S., & Wright, M. (Eds.). (2015). *The Chicago Handbook of University Technology Transfer and Academic Entrepreneurship*. Chicago, IL: University of Chicago Press.

Lintott, C., Schawinski, K., Bamford, S., Slosar, A., Land, K., Thomas, D., ... & Vandenberg, J. (2010). Galaxy Zoo 1: Data Release of Morphological Classifications for Nearly 900 000 Galaxies. *Monthly Notices of the Royal Astronomical Society*, *410*(1), 166–178.

Lisbon European Council. (2000, March 23 and 24). Presidency Conclusions. Retrieved from http://www.europarl.europa.eu/summits/lis1_en.htm

Liu, F. C., Simon, D. F., Sun, Y. T., & Cao, C. (2011). China's Innovation Policies: Evolution, Institutional Structure, and Trajectory. *Research Policy*, *40*(7), 917–931.

Liu, X., Bollen, J., Nelson, M. L., & Van De Sompel, H. (2005). Co-Authorship Networks in the Digital Library Research Community. *Information Processing & Management*, *41*(6), 1462–1480.

Livingstone, D. N. (2003). *Putting Science in Its Place: Geographies of Scientific Knowledge*. Chicago, IL: University of Chicago Press.

López, W. L., Silva, L. M., García-Cepero, M. C., Bustamante, M. C. A., & López, E. A. (2011). Retos Para La Colaboración Nacional E Internacional En La Psicología Latinoamericana: Un Análisis Del Sistema Redalyc, 2005–2007. *Estudos De Psicologia (Natal)*, *16*(1), 17–22.

Lorentzen, A. (2007). The Geography of Knowledge sourcing—A Case Study of Polish Manufacturing Enterprises. *European Planning Studies*, *15*(4), 467–486.

Lorentzen, A. (2008). Knowledge Networks in Local and Global Space. *Entrepreneurship and Regional Development*, *20*(6), 533–545.

Lorigo, L., & Pellacini, F. (2007). Frequency and Structure of Long Distance Scholarly Collaborations in a Physics Community. *Journal of the American Society for Information Science and Technology*, *58*(10), 1497–1502.

Lovelock, J. (2014, March 26). We Need Lone Scientists. *The Independent*. Retrieved from http://www.independent.co.uk/life-style/health-and-families/features/james-lovelock-we-need-lone-scientists-9215280.html

Luger, M. I, & Goldstein, H. A. (1991). *Technology in the Garden: Research Parks and Regional Economic Development*. Chapel Hill, NC: University of North Carolina Press.

Lundvall, B. Å. (1996). *The social dimension of the learning economy*. DRUID Working Papers 96-1, DRUID, Copenhagen Business School, Aalborg University.

Lundvall, B. Å. (2007). National Innovation Systems—Analytical Concept and Development Tool. *Industry and Innovation*, *14*(1), 95–119.

Luo, J., Chen, L. S., Duan, H. Z., Gong, Y. G., Hu, S., Ji, J., ... & Shao, C. G. (2016). TianQin: A Space-Borne Gravitational Wave Detector. *Classical and Quantum Gravity*, *33*(3), 035010.

Luo, J., Ordonez-Matamoros, G., & Kuhlmann, S. (2015). Aggregated Governance by R&D Evaluation Mechanism-Case Study of Chinese Academy of Sciences. *Asian Research Policy*, *6*(1), 56–72.

Luukkonen, T., & Nedeva, M. (2010). Towards Understanding Integration in Research and Research Policy. *Research Policy*, *39*(5), 674–686.

Luukkonen, T., Persson, O., & Sivertsen, G. (1992). Understanding Patterns of International Scientific Collaboration. *Science, Technology, & Human Values*, *17*(1), 101–126.

Luukkonen, T., Tijssen, R., Persson, O., & Sivertsen, G. (1993). The Measurement of International Scientific Collaboration. *Scientometrics, 28*(1), 15–36.

Lyons, E. E., Colglazier, E. W., Wagner, C. S., Börner, K., Dooley, D. M., Mote Jr., C. D., & Roco, M. C. (2016). How Collaborating in International Science Helps America. *Science & Diplomacy, 5*(2), 56–79.

Ma, F., Li, Y., & Chen, B. (2014). Study of the Collaboration in the Field of the Chinese Humanities and Social Sciences. *Scientometrics, 100*(2), 439–458.

Ma, H., Fang, C., Pang, B., & Wang, S. (2015). Structure of Chinese City Network as Driven by Technological Knowledge Flows. *Chinese Geographical Science, 25*(4), 498–510.

Ma, N., & Guan, J. (2005). An Exploratory Study on Collaboration Profiles of Chinese Publications in Molecular Biology. *Scientometrics, 65*(3), 343–355.

Machlup, F. (1979). Stocks and Flows of Knowledge. *Kyklos, 32*(1-2), 400–411.

Macías-Chapula, C. A. (2010). Influence of Local and Regional Publications in the Production of Public Health Research Papers in Latin America. *Scientometrics, 84*(3), 703–716.

Madsen, C. (2010). *Scientific Europe: Policies and Politics of the European Research Area*. Brentwood: Multi-Science Pub.

Maggioni, M. A., Nosvelli, M., & Uberti, T. E. (2007). Space versus Networks in the Geography of Innovation: A European Analysis. *Papers in Regional Science, 86*(3), 471–493.

Maglaughlin, K. L. & Sonnenwald, D. H. (2005). Factors that Impact Interdisciplinary Natural Science Research Collaboration in Academia. *Proceedings from International Society for Scientometrics and Informetrics (ISSI) 2005 Conference*. 24–25.

Mahon, D., & Niklas, R. (2016). The Evolution of a Foundation Program: Reflections on the Five Year Partnership between University College London and Nazarbayev University. In P. Blessinger (Ed.), *University Partnerships for Academic Programs and Professional Development* (pp. 93–109). Bingley, UK: Emerald Group Publishing Limited.

Maisonobe, M., Eckert, D., Grossetti, M., Jégou, L., & Milard, B. (2016). The World Network of Scientific Collaborations between Cities: Domestic or International Dynamics? *Journal of Informetrics, 10*(4), 1025–1036.

Maisonobe, M., Grossetti, M., Milard, B., Eckert, D., & Jégou, L. (2016). L'évolution Mondiale Des Réseaux De Collaborations Scientifiques Entre Villes: Des Échelles Multiples. *Revue Française De Sociologie, 57*(3), 417–441.

Marshall, A. (1890). *Principles of Economics*. London, UK: Macmillan.

Martin, B. R. (2016). R&D Policy Instruments–A Critical Review of What We Do and Don't Know. *Industry and Innovation, 23*(2), 157–176.

Marušić, A., Bošnjak, L., & Jerončić, A. (2011). A Systematic Review of Research on the Meaning, Ethics and Practices of Authorship across Scholarly Disciplines. *PLoS ONE, 6*(9), e23477.

Mashaal, M. (2006). *Bourbaki: A Secret Society of Mathematics*. Providence, RI: American Mathematical Society.

Massey, D. B, Quintas, P., & Wield, D. (1992). *High-Tech Fantasies: Science Parks in Society, Science, and Space*. London, UK: Routledge.

Mathiassen, L. (2002). Collaborative Practice Research. *Information Technology & People, 15*(4), 321–345.

Matthews, J. N. (2012). Chile Aims to Better Exploit Role as Telescope Host. *Physics Today, 65*(1), 20.

Matthiessen, C. W., Schwarz, A. W., & Find, S. (2010). World Cities of Scientific Knowledge: Systems, Networks and Potential Dynamics. An Analysis Based on Bibliometric Indicators. *Urban Studies, 47*(9), 1879–1897.

Mattsson, P., Sundberg, C. J., & Laget, P. (2011). Is Correspondence Reflected in the Author Position? A Bibliometric Study of the Relation between Corresponding Author and Byline Position. *Scientometrics, 87*(1), 99–105.

Maurseth, P. B., & Verspagen, B. (2002). Knowledge Spillovers in Europe: A Patent Citations Analysis. *The Scandinavian Journal of Economics, 104*(4), 531–545.

Mazloumian, A., Helbing, D., Lozano, S., Light, R. P., & Börner, K. (2013). Global Multi-Level Analysis of the 'Scientific Food Web'. *Scientific Reports*, *3*, 1167.
Mazumdar, M., Messinger, S., Finkelstein, D. M., Goldberg, J. D., Lindsell, C. J., Morton, S. C., ... Parker R. A. (2015). Evaluating Academic Scientists Collaborating in Team-Based Research: A Proposed Framework. *Academic Medicine: Journal of the Association of American Medical Colleges*, *90*(10), 1302–1308.
McCann, P. (2007). Sketching Out a Model of Innovation, Face-To-Face Interaction and Economic Geography. *Spatial Economic Analysis*, *2*(2), 117–134.
McCann, P. (2013). *Modern Urban and Regional Economics* (2nd ed.). Oxford, UK: Oxford University Press.
McElheny, V. K. (2010). *Drawing the Map of Life: Inside the Human Genome Project*. New York, NY: Basic Books.
McGovern, V. (2009, July 31). Perspective: How to Succeed in Big Science and Still Get Tenure. *Science Career Magazine*. DOI: 10.1126/science.caredit.a0900092
Meadows, A. J., & O'connor, J. G. (1971). Bibliographical Statistics as a Guide to Growth Points in Science. *Social Studies of Science*, *1*(1), 95–99.
Medoff, M. H. (2003). Collaboration and the Quality of Economics Research. *Labour Economics*, *10*, 597–608.
Meho, L. I. (2007). The Rise and Rise of Citation Analysis. *Physics World*, *20*(1), 32.
Melin, G., & Persson, O. (1996). Studying Research Collaboration Using Co-Authorships. *Scientometrics*, *36*(3), 363–377.
Mention, A. L. (2011). Co-Operation and Co-Opetition as Open Innovation Practices in the Service Sector: Which Influence on Innovation Novelty? *Technovation*, *31*(1), 44–53.
Merton, R. K. (1968). The Matthew Effect in Science. *Science*, *159*(3810), 56–63.
Merton, R. K. (1973). *The Sociology of Science: Theoretical and Empirical Investigations*. Chicago, IL: University of Chicago Press.
Merton, R. K. (1988). The Matthew Effect in Science, II: Cumulative Advantage and the Symbolism of Intellectual Property. *Isis*, *79*(4), 606–623.
Merton, R. K. & Zuckerman, H. (1973). Age, Aging, and Age Structure in Science. In R. K. Merton, *The Sociology of Science: Theoretical and Empirical Investigations* (pp. 497–559). Chicago, IL: University of Chicago Press.
Mervis, J., & Normile, D. (1998). North-South Relations: Lopsided Partnerships Give Way to Real Collaboration. *Science*, *279*, 1477.
Meskus, M., Marelli, L., & D'Agostino, G. (2018). Research Misconduct in the Age of Open Science: The Case of STAP Stem Cells. *Science as Culture*, *27*(1), 1–23.
Michael, A. E. (2016, October 19). It's Not Too Late to Save the Stacks. *The Chronicle of Higher Education*. Retrieved from https://www.chronicle.com/article/Its-Not-Too-Late-to-Save-the/238106
Migliaccio, A. R., & Philipsen, S. (2006). The Return of Romeo. Scientists' International Mobility and the Future of Research in Europe. *EMBO Reports*, *7*(11), 1067–1071.
Miller-Idriss, C., & Hanauer, E. (2011). Transnational Higher Education: Offshore Campuses in the Middle East. *Comparative Education*, *47*(2), 181–207.
Miller-Rushing, A., Primack, R., & Bonney, R. (2012). The History of Public Participation in Ecological Research. *Frontiers in Ecology and the Environment*, *10*(6), 285–290.
Mirskaya, E. Z. (1997). International Scientific Collaboration in the Post-Communist Countries: Modern Trends and Priorities. *Science and Public Policy*, *24*(5), 301–308.
Misra, J., Smith-Doerr, L., Dasgupta, N., Weaver, G., & Normanly, J. (2017). Collaboration and Gender Equity among Academic Scientists. *Social Sciences*, *6*(1), 1–25.
Mitchell, R. P. (2009, December 17). Where the Renaissance Still Lives. *The Harvard Gazette*. Retrieved from https://news.harvard.edu/gazette/story/2009/12/where-the-renaissance-still-lives/

Mok, K. (2005). Globalization and Educational Restructuring: University Merging and Changing Governance in China. *Higher Education, 50*(1), 57–88.
Mokyr, J. (1990). *The Lever of Riches: Technological Creativity and Economic Progress.* New York, NY: Oxford University Press.
Mokyr, J. (1994). Cardwell's Law and the Political Economy of Technological Progress. *Research Policy, 23*(5), 561–574.
Möller, T., Schmidt, M., & Hornbostel, S. (2016). Assessing the Effects of the German Excellence Initiative with Bibliometric Methods. *Scientometrics, 109*(3), 2217–2239.
Mongeon, P., & Larivière, V. (2015). Costly Collaborations: The Impact of Scientific Fraud on Co-Authors' Careers. *Journal of the Association for Information Science and Technology, 67*, 535–542.
Mongkhonvanit, J. (2014). *Coopetition for Regional Competitiveness: The Role of Academe in Knowledge-Based Industrial Clustering.* Singapore: Springer.
Monteiro, M., & Keating, E. (2009). Managing Misunderstandings: The Role of Language in Interdisciplinary Scientific Collaboration. *Science Communication, 31*(1), 6–28.
Morgan, K. (1997). The Learning Region: Institutions, Innovation and Regional Renewal. *Regional Studies, 41*(S1), 147–159.
Morgan, K. (2004). The Exaggerated Death of Geography: Learning, Proximity and Territorial Innovation Systems. *Journal of Economic Geography, 4*(1), 3–21.
Morillo, F. (2016). Public–Private Interactions Reflected through the Funding Acknowledgements. *Scientometrics, 108*(3), 1193–1204.
Moss, F. (2011). *The Sorcerers and Their Apprentices: How the Digital Magicians of the MIT Media Lab are Creating the Innovative Technologies that Will Transform Our Lives.* New York, NY: Crown Business.
Mowatt, G., Shirran, L., Grimshaw, J. M., Rennie, D., Flanagin, A., Yank, V., … Bero, L. A. (2002). Prevalence of Honorary and Ghost Authorship in Cochrane Reviews. *Jama, 287*(21), 2769–2771.
Mowery, D., & Sampat, B. (2005). Universities in National Innovation Systems. In J. Fagerberg, D. C. Mowery, & R. R. Nelson (Eds.), *The Oxford Handbook of Innovation* (pp. 209–239). Oxford: Oxford University Press.
Mullins, N.C. (1973). *Theory and Theory Groups in Contemporary American Sociology.* New York, NY: Harper and Row.
Muriithi, P., Horner, D., & Pemberton, L. (2013). Understanding Factors Influencing the Effect of Scientific Collaboration on Productivity in a Developing Country: Kenya. *Proceedings of the American Society for Information Science and Technology, 50*(1), 1–10.
Myrdal, G. (1957). *Economic Theory and Under-Developed Regions.* London, UK: G. Duckworth.
Nagpaul, P. (1999). Transnational Linkages of Indian Science: A Structural Analysis. *Scientometrics, 46*(1), 109–140.
Najwyższa Izba Kontroli. (2013). *Wdrażanie Innowacji Przez Szkoły Wyższe I Parki Technologiczne, Informacja O Wynikach Kontroli.* lbi-4101-08-00/2012. Warsaw, Poland: Najwyższa Izba Kontroli.
Narin, F., Stevens, K., & Whitlow, E. S. (1991). Scientific Co-Operation in Europe and the Citation of Multinationally Authored Papers. *Scientometrics, 21*(3), 313–323.
National Academies, Committee on Science, Engineering, and Public Policy, National Academy of Sciences, National Academy of Engineering, & Institute of Medicine. (2005). *Facilitating Interdisciplinary Research.* Washington, DC: National Academies Press.
National Science Foundation. (2006). *Investing in America's Future. Strategic Plan FY 2006–2011.* Arlington, VA: National Science Foundation. Retrieved from https://www.nsf.gov/pubs/2006/nsf0648/NSF-06-48.pdf
Naylor, S., & Ryan, J. R. (2010). *New Spaces of Exploration: Geographies of Discovery in the Twentieth Century.* London, UK: Tauris.
Neal, H. A., Smith, T. L., & McCormick, J. B. (2008). *Beyond Sputnik: US Science Policy in the Twenty-First Century.* Ann Arbor: University of Michigan Press.

Nedeva, M. (2013). Between the Global and the National: Organising European Science. *Research Policy, 42*(1), 220–230.

Nedeva, M., & Stampfer, M. (2012). From "Science in Europe" to "European Science". *Science, 336*(6084), 982–983.

Needham, J. (1954). *Science and Civilization in China. Vol. 1 Introductory Orientations.* Cambridge, UK: The Syndics of the Cambridge University Press.

Nekhamkin, I. (1965, June 11). "Science City" in Novosibirsk Solves Various Scientific and Technical Problems. *Ekonomicheskaya Gazeta (Economic Gazette)*, p. 7. (Joint Publication Research Service, Trans.). Washington. (Original work published in Moscow, 1965, May 12).

Nelson, R. R. (Ed.). (1993). *National Innovation Systems: A Comparative Analysis.* New York, NY: Oxford University Press.

Newman, M. E. (2001a). Clustering and Preferential Attachment in Growing Networks. *Physical Review E, 64*(2), 025102.

Newman, M. E. (2001b). The Structure of Scientific Collaboration Networks. *Proceedings of the National Academy of Sciences, 98*(2), 404–409.

Newman, M. E. (2004). Coauthorship Networks and Patterns of Scientific Collaboration. *Proceedings of the National Academy of Sciences, 101*(S 1), 5200–5205.

Nickelsen, K., & Krämer, F. (2016). Introduction: Cooperation and Competition in the Sciences. *NTM Zeitschrift Für Geschichte Der Wissenschaften, Technik Und Medizin, 24*(2), 119–123.

Nielsen, M. A. (2011). *Reinventing Discovery: The New Era of Networked Science.* Princeton, NJ: Princeton University Press.

Nomaler, Ö., Frenken, K., & Heimeriks, G. (2013). Do More Distant Collaborations Have More Citation Impact? *Journal of Informetrics, 7*(4), 966–971.

Nomaler, Ö., & Verspagen, B. (2016). River Deep, Mountain High: Of Long Run Knowledge Trajectories within and between Innovation Clusters. *Journal of Economic Geography, 16*(6), 1259–1278.

Nooteboom, B., Van Haverbeke, W., Duysters, G., Gilsing, V., & Van Den Oord, A. (2007). Optimal Cognitive Distance and Absorptive Capacity. *Research Policy, 36*(7), 1016–1034.

North, D. C. (1991). Institutions. *Journal of Economic Perspectives, 5*(1), 97–112.

Nowotny, H., Scott, P., & Gibbons, M. (2003). Introduction. 'Mode 2' Revisited: The New Production of Knowledge. *Minerva, 41*(3), 179–194.

Numprasertchai, S., & Igel, B. (2005). Managing Knowledge through Collaboration: Multiple Case Studies of Managing Research in University Laboratories in Thailand. *Technovation, 25*(10), 1173–1182.

O'Mara, M. P. (2005). *Cities of Knowledge: Cold War Science and the Search for the Next Silicon Valley.* Princeton, NJ: Princeton University Press.

O'Neil, C. (2016). *Weapons of Math Destruction: How Big Data Increases Inequality and Threatens Democracy.* New York, NY: Crown.

OECD. (2002). *Dynamising National Innovation Systems.* Paris, France: OECD Publishing.

OECD. (2007). *OECD Reviews of Innovation Policy. China. Synthesis Report.* Paris, France: OECD Publishing.

OECD. (2010). *Measuring Innovation: A New Perspective.* Paris, France: OECD Publishing.

OECD. (2015). *OECD Science, Technology and Industry Scoreboard 2015: Innovation for Growth and Society.* Paris, France: OECD Publishing.

Oinas P., & Lagendijk A. (2005). Toward Understanding Proximity, Distance and Diversity in Economic Interaction and Local Development. In A. Lagendijk & P. Oinas (Eds.), *Proximity, Distance and Diversity. Issues on Economic Interaction and Local Development* (pp. 307–333). Aldershot, UK: Ashgate.

Oldham, G. (2005, April 1). *International Scientific Collaboration: Policy Briefs, Science and Development Network.* Retrieved from www.scidev.net/dossiers/index.cfm?fuseaction=policybrief&dossier=13&policy=60

Olechnicka, A. (2013). Regional Cooperation or External Links? Spatial Proximity in Sicence-Bussiness Relations in Poland. In R. Capello, A. Olechnicka, & G. Gorzelak (Eds.), *Universities, Cities and Regions: Loci for Knowledge and Innovation Creation* (pp. 99–120). Oxon, UK: Routledge.

Olechnicka, A., & Ploszaj, A. (2010a). Mapping the Regional Science Performance. Evidence from Poland. *Collnet Journal of Scientometrics and Information Management, 4*(1), 21–27.

Olechnicka, A., & Ploszaj, A. (2010b). Spatial Aspects of Collaborative Networks in Science – Lessons from Poland, *Studia Regionalne I Lokalne*, 106–123. Special Issue 2010.

Olson, G. M., & Olson, J. S. (2000). Distance Matters. *Human-Computer Interaction, 15*(2), 139–178.

Olson, G. M, Zimmerman, A., & Bos, N. (2008). *Scientific Collaboration on the Internet*. Cambridge, MA: MIT Press.

Olson, J. S., & Olson, G. M. (2013). Working Together Apart: Collaboration over the Internet. *Synthesis Lectures on Human-Centered Informatics, 6*(5), 1–151.

Olson, J. S., Olson, G. M., & Cooney, D. (2008). Success Factors: Bridging Distance in Collaboration. In G. M. Olson, A. Zimmerman, & N. Bos (Eds.), *Scientific collaboration on the Internet*. Cambridge, MA: MIT Press.

Openshaw, S. (1983). *The Modifiable Areal Unit Problem*. Norwich, UK: Geo Books.

Ortega, J. L. (2014). Influence of Co-Authorship Networks in the Research Impact: Ego Network Analyses from Microsoft Academic Search. *Journal of Informetrics, 8*(3), 728–737.

Otlet, P. (1934). *Traité De Documentation: Le Livresur Le Livre, Théorie Etpratique*. Brussels: Editiones Mundaneum.

Ottati, G. D. (1994). Cooperation and Competition in the Industrial District as an Organization Model. *European Planning Studies, 2*(4), 463–483.

Otto, S. L. (2016). *The War on Science: Who's Waging It, Why It Matters, What We Can Do about It*. Minneapolis, MN: Milkweed Editions.

Owen-Smith, J. (2013). *Workplace Design, Collaboration, and Discovery*. Paper presented at the National Research Council Workshop on Institutional and Organizational Supports for Team Science. Washington, DC. Retrieved from http://sites.nationalacademies.org/DBASSE/

Paasi, A. (2015). "Hot Spots, Dark-Side Dots, Tin Pots": The Uneven Internationalism of the Global Academic Market. In P. Meusburger, D. Gregory, & L. Suarsana (Eds.), *Geographies of Knowledge and Power* (pp. 247–262). Dordrecht, The Netherlands: Springer.

Pachter, L. (2014, October 31). To Some a Citation Is Worth $3 per Year. Retrieved from https://liorpachter.wordpress.com/2014/10/31/to-some-a-citation-is-worth-3-per-year/

Palmer, C. L. (2001). *Work at the Boundaries of Science: Information and the Interdisciplinary Research Process*. Dordrecht, Netherlands: Kluwer Academic Publishers.

Pan, R. K., Kaski, K., & Fortunato, S. (2012). World Citation and Collaboration Networks: Uncovering the Role of Geography in Science. *Scientific Reports, 2*, 902.

Pan, R. K., Sinha, S., Kaski, K., & Saramäki, J. (2012). The Evolution of Interdisciplinarity in Physics Research. *Scientific Reports, 2*, 551.

Patel, N. (1973). Collaboration in the Professional Growth of American Sociology. *Social Science Information, 6*, 77–92.

Patuelli, R., Vaona, A., & Grimpe, C. (2010). The German East-West Divide in Knowledge Production: An Application to Nanomaterial Patenting. *Tijdschrift Voor Economische En Sociale Geografie, 101*(5), 568–582.

Paul-Hus, A., Desrochers, N., & Costas, R. (2016). Characterization, Description, and Considerations for the Use of Funding Acknowledgement Data in Web of Science. *Scientometrics, 108*(1), 167–182.

Paul-Hus, A., Mongeon, P., Sainte-Marie, M., & Larivière, V. (2017). The Sum of It All: Revealing Collaboration Patterns by Combining Authorship and Acknowledgements. *Journal of Informetrics, 11*(1), 80–87.

Pečlin, S., Južnič, P., Blagus, R., Sajko, M. Č., & Stare, J. (2012). Effects of International Collaboration and Status of Journal on Impact of Papers. *Scientometrics, 93*(3), 937–948.

Pepe, A. (2011). The Relationship between Acquaintanceship and Coauthorship in Scientific Collaboration Networks. *Journal of the American Society for Information Science and Technology*, 62(11), 2121–2132.
Peri, G. (2005). Determinants of Knowledge Flows and Their Effect on Innovation. *Review of Economics and Statistics*, 87(2), 308–322.
Perianes-Rodriguez, A., Waltman, L., & Van Eck, N. J. (2016). Constructing Bibliometric Networks: A Comparison between Full and Fractional Counting. *Journal of Informetrics*, 10(4), 1178–1195.
Persson, O., Glänzel, W., & Danell, R. (2004). Inflationary Bibliometric Values: The Role of Scientific Collaboration and the Need for Relative Indicators in Evaluative Studies. *Scientometrics*, 60(3), 421–432.
Petralia, S., Balland, P. A., & Rigby, D. L. (2016). Unveiling the Geography of Historical Patents in the United States from 1836 to 1975. *Scientific Data*, 3, 160074.
Pevsner, N. (1976). *A History of Building Types*. Princeton, NJ: Princeton University Press.
Phan, P. H., Siegel, D. S., & Wright, M. (2005). Science Parks and Incubators: Observations, Synthesis and Future Research. *Journal of Business Venturing*, 20(2), 165–182.
Picci, L. (2010). The Internationalization of Inventive Activity: A Gravity Model Using Patent Data. *Research Policy*, 39(8), 1070–1081.
Plotnikova, T., & Rake, B. (2014). Collaboration in Pharmaceutical Research: Exploration of Country-Level Determinants. *Scientometrics*, 98(2), 1173–1202.
Ponds, R. (2009). The Limits to Internationalization of Scientific Research Collaboration. *The Journal of Technology Transfer*, 34(1), 76–94.
Ponds, R., Van Oort, F., & Frenken, K. (2007). The Geographical and Institutional Proximity of Research Collaboration. *Papers in Regional Science*, 86(3), 423–443.
Ponomariov, B. L., & Boardman, P. C. (2010). Influencing Scientists' Collaboration and Productivity Patterns through New Institutions: University Research Centers and Scientific and Technical Human Capital. *Research Policy*, 39(5), 613–624.
Poo, M. M., & Wang, L. (2014). On CAS Reform and Pioneer Action Plan. *National Science Review*, 2(1), 1–12.
Porter, M. E. (1990). *The Competitive Advantage of Nations*. New York, NY: The Free Press.
Porter, M. E. (1998). Clusters and the New Economics of Competition. *Harvard Business Review*, 76(6), 77–90.
Porter, M. E. (2000). Location, Competition, and Economic Development: Local Clusters in a Global Economy. *Economic Development Quarterly*, 14(1), 15–34.
Powering CERN. (n.d.). Retrieved From https://home.cern/about/engineering/powering-cern
Idea ConsultiFQPPMI. (2014). *Study on Assessing the Contribution of the Framework Programmes to the Development of Human Research Capacity*. Brussels: European Commission. Retrieved from https://publications.europa.eu/en/publication-detail/-/publication/cd7726a9-17d0-4291-b6f9-60e832efcc83/language-en
Pratchett, T. (1993). *Men at Arms*. London, UK: Orion Publishing Group.
Pravdić, N., & Oluić-Vuković, V. (1986). Dual Approach to Multiple Authorship in the Study of Collaboration/Scientific Output Relationship. *Scientometrics*, 10(5-6), 259–280.
Presser, S. (1980). Collaboration and the Quality of Research. *Social Studies of Science*, 10(1), 95–101.
Price, D. J. De S. (1963). *Little Science, Big Science*. New York, NY: Columbia University Press.
Price, D. J. de S., & Beaver, D. (1966). Collaboration in an Invisible College. *American Psychologist*, 21(11), 1011.
Private funding for science. (2016). [Editorial]. *Nature Methods*, 13(7), 537. Retrieved from https://www.nature.com/articles/nmeth.3923
Proteins and Particles. (1999, October 16). *The Economist*, 84–85. Retrieved from https://www.economist.com/science-and-technology/2015/10/08/particle-biology
Qiu, J. (2014). International Collaboration in Science: A Chinese Perspective. *National Science Review*, 1(2), 318–321.

Qiu, J. (2015). International Collaboration and Science in China: A Western Perspective. *National Science Review, 2*(2), 241–245.
Rabellotti, R., Carabelli, A., & Hirsch, G. (2009). Italian Industrial Districts on the Move: Where are They Going? *European Planning Studies, 17*(1), 19–41.
Radosevic, S., & Yoruk, E. (2014). Are There Global Shifts in the World Science Base? Analysing the Catching up and Falling behind of World Regions. *Scientometrics, 101*(3), 1897–1924.
Rahm, D., & Luce, T. F. Jr. (1992). Issues in the Design of State Science-And Technology-Based Economic Development Programs: The Case of Pennsylvania's Ben Franklin Partnership. *Economic Development Quarterly, 6*(1), 41–51.
Rahm, E., & Thor, A. (2005). Citation Analysis of Database Publications. *ACM Sigmod Record, 34*(4), 48–53.
Ramanana-Rahary, S., Zitt, M., & Rousseau, R. (2009). Aggregation Properties of Relative Impact and Other Classical Indicators: Convexity Issues and the Yule-Simpson Paradox. *Scientometrics, 79*(2), 311–327.
Ravenstein, E. G. (1885). The Laws of Migration. *Journal of the Statistical Society of London, 48*(2), 167–235.
RE/MAX. (2015). *At Home in Europe*. Vienna, Austria: RE/MAX. Retrieved from http://www.at-home-in-europe.eu/
Rees, J., & Bradley, R. (1988). Research Policy and Review 24. State Science Policy and Economic Development in the United States: A Critical Perspective. *Environment and Planning A, 20*(8), 999–1012.
Reform of scientific research still needed despite Tu's Nobel. (2015, October 8). *China Daily*. Retrieved from http://usa.chinadaily.com.cn/epaper/2015-10/08/content_22132708.htm on 1. 03.2016+A24
Reilly, W. J. (1931). *The Law of Retail Gravitation*. New York, NY: Knickerbocker Press.
Reinkens, J. H. (1861). *Die Universität Zu Breslau Von Der Vereinigung Der Frankfurter Viadrina Mit Der Leopoldina. Festschrift Der Katholisch-Theologischen Facultät*. Breslau: Georg Philipp Aderholz.
Rennie, D., Yank, V., & Emanuel, L. (1997). When Authorship Fails: A Proposal to Make Contributors Accountable. *Jama, 278*(7), 579–585.
Resnik, D. B. (2005). *The Ethics of Science: An Introduction*. London: Routledge.
Richer, E. (2013). Bourbaki, Nicolas. In *Encyclopedia PlanetMath.org*. Retrieved from http://planetmath.org/bourbakinicolas
Riesenberg, D., & Lundberg, G. D. (1990). The Order of Authorship: Who's on First? *Jama, 264*(14), 1857–1857.
Rigby, D. L. (2015). Technological Relatedness and Knowledge Space: Entry and Exit of US Cities from Patent Classes. *Regional Studies, 49*(11), 1922–1937.
Ritala, P., Huizingh, E., Almpanopoulou, A., & Wijbenga, P. (2017). Tensions in R&D Networks: Implications for Knowledge Search and Integration. *Technological Forecasting and Social Change, 120*, 311–322.
Rivers, D., & Gray, D. O. (2013). Cooperative Research Centers as Small Business: Uncovering the Marketing and Recruiting Practices of University-Based Cooperative Research Centers. In C. Boardman, D. O. Gray, & D. Rivers (Eds.), *Cooperative Research Centers and Technical Innovation: Government Policies, Industry Strategies, and Organizational Dynamics* (pp. 175–198). New York, NY: Springer.
Rodriguez, M. A., & Pepe, A. (2008). On the Relationship between the Structural and Socio-academic Communities of a Coauthorship Network. *Journal of Informetrics, 2*(3), 195–201.
Rogers, E. M. (2003). *Diffusion of Innovations* (5th ed., Free Press trade pbk. ed.). New York, NY: Free Press.
Røsdal, T., Lekve, K., Scordato, L., Aanstad, S., & Piro, F. (2014). *Building Lasting Relationships: Evaluation of the Fulbright Norway Subsidy Scheme*. Oslo, Norway: Nordic Institute for Studies in Innovation, Research and Education (NIFU).

Rosenfield, P. L. (1992). The Potential of Transdisciplinary Research for Sustaining and Extending Linkages between the Health and Social Sciences. *Social Science & Medicine, 35*(11), 1343–1357.

Rossiter, M. W. (1993). The Matthew Matilda Effect in Science. *Social Studies of Science, 23*(2), 325–341.

Rothaermel, F. T., Agung, S. D., & Jiang, L. (2007). University Entrepreneurship: A Taxonomy of the Literature. *Industrial and Corporate Change, 16*(4), 691–791.

Rousseau, R. (2010). Comments on the Modified Collaborative Coefficient. *Scientometrics, 87*(1), 171–174.

The Royal Society. (2010, January). *New Frontiers in Science Diplomacy*. Policy document 01/10. London, UK: The Royal Society.

The Royal Society. (2011, March). *Knowledge, Networks and Nations: Global Scientific Collaboration in the 21st Century*. Policy document 03/11. London, UK: The Royal Society.

Rutten, R., & Boekema, F. (Eds.). (2007). *The Learning Region: Foundations, State-Of-The-Art, Future*. Cheltenham, UK: Edward Elgar.

Sailer, K., & McColloh, I. (2012). Social Networks and Spatial configuration—How Office Layouts Drive Social Interaction. *Social Networks, 34*(1), 47–58.

Sakakibara, M., & Cho, D. S. (2002). Cooperative R&D in Japan and Korea: A Comparison of Industrial Policy. *Research Policy, 31*, 673–692.

Salomon, J. J. (1977). Science Policy Studies and the Development of Science Policy. *Science, Technology and Society: A Cross-Disciplinary Perspective*. London, UK: SAGE.

Salter, L., & Hearn, A. (1996). *Outside the Lines: Issues in Interdisciplinary Research*. Montreal, Canada: McGill-Queen's Press.

Sánchez-Barrioluengo, M. (2014). 'Turning the Tables': Regions Shaping University Performance. *Regional Science, 1*(1), 276–285.

Sarsons, H. (2015, December 3). *Gender Differences in Recognition for Group Work*. Harvard University Working Paper. Retrieved from https://scholar.harvard.edu/sarsons/publications/note-gender-differences-recognition-group-work

Savanur, K., & Srikanth, R. (2010). Modified Collaborative Coefficient: A New Measure for Quantifying the Degree of Research Collaboration. *Scientometrics, 84*(2), 365–371.

Saxenian, A. (1994). *Regional Advantage: Culture and Competition in Silicon Valley and Route 128*. Cambridge, MA: Harvard University Press.

Saxenian, A. (2002). Brain Drain or Brain Circulation: How High- Skill Immigration Makes Everyone Better Off. *Brookings Review, 20*(1), 28–31.

Saxenian, A. (2005). From Brain Drain to Brain Circulation: Transnational Communities and Regional Upgrading in India and China. *Studies in Comparative International Development, 40*(2), 35–61.

Scellato, G., Franzoni, C., & Stephan, P. (2015). Migrant Scientists and International Networks. *Research Policy, 44*(1), 108–120.

Schamp, E. W., Rentmeister, B., & Lo, V. (2004). Dimensions of Proximity in Knowledge-Based Networks: The Cases of Investment Banking and Automobile Design. *European Planning Studies, 12*(5), 607–624.

Scherngell, T., & Barber, M. J. (2009). Spatial Interaction Modelling of Cross-Region R&D Collaborations: Empirical Evidence from the 5th EU Framework Programme. *Papers in Regional Science, 88*(3), 531–546.

Scherngell, T., & Hu, Y. (2011). Collaborative Knowledge Production in China: Regional Evidence from a Gravity Model Approach. *Regional Studies, 45*(6), 755–772.

Schiermeier, Q. (2016). Multibillion-Euro Innovation Hub Slammed by Auditors. *Nature, 532*, 291.

Schiff, L. (2002). *Developing Successful Models for Large-Scale, Collaborative Biomedical Research Projects*. Boston: Cure Project Educational Paper. Retrieved from www.bostoncure.org/downloads/collaborative-science.pdf

Schneider, J. W. (2009). An Outline of the Bibliometric Indicator Used for Performance-Based Funding of Research Institutions in Norway. *European Political Science, 8*(3), 364–378.

Schneider, J. W., Aagaard, K., & Bloch, C. W. (2016). What Happens When National Research Funding Is Linked to Differentiated Publication Counts? A Comparison of the Australian and Norwegian Publication-Based Funding Models. *Research Evaluation, 25*(3), 244–256.

Schott, T. (1993). World Science: Globalization of Institutions and Participation. *Science, Technology, & Human Values, 18*(2), 196–208.

Schott, T. (1998). Ties between Center and Periphery in the Scientific World-System: Accumulation of Rewards, Dominance and Self-Reliance in the Center. *Journal of World-Systems Research, 4*(2), 112–144.

Schrage, M. (1995). *No More Teams: Mastering the Dynamics of Creative Collaboration*. New York, NY: Currency and Doubleday.

Schubert, T., & Sooryamoorthy, R. (2010). Can the Centre–Periphery Model Explain Patterns of International Scientific Collaboration among Threshold and Industrialised Countries? the Case of South Africa and Germany. *Scientometrics, 83*(1), 181–203.

Schumpeter, J. A. (1942). *Capitalism, Socialism, and Democracy*. New York: Harper.

Schumpeter, J. A. (1947). The Creative Response in Economic History. *The Journal of Economic History, 7*(2), 149–159.

Science Europe. (2014). *Practical Guide to Three Approaches to Cross-Border Collaboration*. Brussels, Belgium: Science Europe.

Science-Metrix, Fraunhofer ISI, & Oxford Research. (2015). *Study on Network Analysis of the 7th Framework Programme Participation*. Brussels, Belgium: European Commission.

Sebestyén, T., Hau-Horváth, O., & Varga, A. (2017). How to Get from the Periphery into the Core? the Role of Geographical Location and Scientific Performance in Network Position in the Field of Neuroscience. *Letters in Spatial and Resource Sciences, 10*(3), 297–325.

Sebestyén, T., & Varga, A. (2013a). Research Productivity and the Quality of Interregional Knowledge Networks. *The Annals of Regional Science, 51*(1), 155–189.

Sebestyén, T., & Varga, A. (2013b). A Novel Comprehensive Index of Network Position and Node Characteristics in Knowledge Networks: Ego Network Quality. In T. Scherngell (Ed.), *The Geography of Networks and R&D Collaborations* (pp. 71–97). Cham, Switzerland: Springer.

Sedgwick, D. (2015, September 10). Automotive News China's BAIC Opens R&D Center in Silicon Valley. *Automotive News*. Retrieved from www.autonews.com

Sergescu, P. (1948). Mersenne L'animateur: 8 Septembre 1588-1 Er Septembre 1648. *Revue D'histoire Des Sciences Et De Leurs Applications, 2*(1), 5–12.

Shapin, S. (1988). The House of Experiment in Seventeenth-Century England. *Isis, 79*(3), 373–404.

Shapin, S. (1994). *A Social History of Truth*. Chicago, IL: University of Chicago Press.

Shea, W. R. (2003). *Designing Experiments & Games of Chance: The Unconventional Science of Blaise Pascal*. Canton, China: Science History Publications.

Shils, E. (1991). Reflections on Tradition, Centre and Periphery and the Universal Validity of Science: The Significance of the Life of S. Ramanujan. *Minerva, 29*(4), 393–419.

Shortland, M. (1993). Book Review [Review of the Book *the Geography of Science*, by H. Dorn]. *The British Journal for the History of Science, 26*(1), 130–132.

Shrum, W., Palackal, A., Dzorgbo, D. B., Mbatia, P., Schafer, M., & Miller, P. (2014). What Happened to the Internet? Scientific Communities in Three Low-Income Areas, 2000–2010. *Perspectives on Global Development and Technology, 13*(3), 301–331.

Sidone, O. J. G., Haddad, E. A., & Mena-Chalco, J. P. (2016). Scholarly Publication and Collaboration in Brazil: The Role of Geography. *Journal of the Association for Information Science and Technology, 68*(1), 243–258.

Simon, D. F. (2014). *Key Drivers Underlying China's International S&T Relations*. Presentation to PCAST, Washington. Retrieved from https://www.whitehouse.gov/sites/default/files/microsites/ostp/simon_denis.pdf.

References

Sivertsen, G. (2016). Publication-Based Funding: The Norwegian Model. In H. Daniel, M. Ochsner, & S. E. Hug (Eds.), *Research Assessment in the Humanities: Towards Criteria and Procedures* (pp. 79–90). New York, NY: Springer.

Sleeboom-Faulkner, M. (2013). Latent Science Collaboration: Strategies of Bioethical Capacity Building in Mainland China's Stem Cell World. *BioSocieties, 8*(1), 7–24.

Smith, A. (1776). *An Inquiry into the Wealth of Nations.* London, UK: Strahan and Cadell.

Smith, D. (2001). Collaborative Research: Policy and the Management of Knowledge Creation in UK Universities. *Higher Education Quarterly, 55*(2), 131–157.

Smith, P. H. (2006). Laboratories. In D. C. Lindberg, R. L. Numbers, & R. Porter (Eds.), *The Cambridge History of Science* (pp. 290–305). Vol. *3*. Cambridge: Cambridge University Press.

Sobel, D. (1996). *Longitude.* London, UK: Fourth Estate.

Somerville, H. (2013, November 20). China's Largest Retailer Opens Tech Lab in Palo Alto. *San Jose Mercury News.* Retrieved from www.mercurynews.com

Sonnenwald, D. H. (2003). Managing Cognitive and Affective Trust in the Conceptual R&D Organization. In M. Huotari & M. Iivonen (Eds.), *Trust in Knowledge Management and Systems in Organizations* (pp. 82–106). Hershey, PA: PA Idea Publishing.

Sonnenwald, D. H. (2007). Scientific Collaboration. *Annual Review of Information Science and Technology, 41*(1), 643–681.

Spencer, R. W. (2012). Open Innovation in the Eighteenth Century. *Research-Technology Management, 55*(4), 39–43.

Fraunhofer ISI Idea Consult SPRU. (2009). *The Impact of Collaboration on Europe's Scientific and Technological Performance. Final Report to the European Commission, DG Research.* Karlsruhe, Germany: Fraunhofer, Idea Consult, SPRU.

Stamboulis, Y. A. (2007). Towards a Systems Approach to Innovation Systems and Policy. *International Journal of Technology and Globalisation, 3*(1), 42–55.

State Council of the People's Republic of China. (2006). *The National Medium- and Long-Term Program for Science and Technology Development (2006–2020). An Outline.* Retrieved from https://www.itu.int/en/ITU-D/Cybersecurity/Documents/National_Strategies_Repository/China_2006.pdf

Steiner, I.D. (1972). *Group Processes and Productivity.* New York, NY: Academic Press.

Stephan, P. E. (2012). *How Economics Shapes Science.* Cambridge, MA: Harvard University Press.

Stephan, P. E., & Levin, S. G. (2001). Exceptional Contributions to US Science by the Foreign-Born and Foreign-Educated. *Population Research and Policy Review, 20*(1–2), 59–79.

Stephens, G. R., & Wikstrom, N. (2007). *American Intergovernmental Relations: A Fragmented Federal Policy.* New York, NY: Oxford University Press.

Stokes, D. E. (1997). *Pasteur's Quadrant: Basic Science and Technological Innovation.* Washington, DC: Brookings Institution Press.

Stokols, D., Harvey, R., Gress, J., Fuqua, J., & Phillips, K. (2005). In Vivo Studies of Transdisciplinary Scientific Collaboration: Lessons Learned and Implications for Active Living Research. *American Journal of Preventive Medicine, 28*(2), 202–213.

Stokols, D., Misra, S., Moser, R. P., Hall, K. L., & Taylor, B. K. (2008). The Ecology of Team Science: Understanding Contextual Influences on Transdisciplinary Collaboration. *American Journal of Preventive Medicine, 35*(2), S96–S115.

Stone, R. (2016). Global Tensions Rile Experimental University. *Science, 352*(6282), 136–137.

Storper, M., & Venables, A. J. (2004). Buzz: Face-To-Face Contact and the Urban Economy. *Journal of Economic Geography, 4*(4), 351–370.

Strange, K. (2008). Authorship: Why Not Just Toss a Coin? *American Journal of Physiology-Cell Physiology, 295*(3), C567–C570.

Strogatz, S. H. (2003). *Sync: The Emerging Science of Spontaneous Order.* New York, NY: Theia.

Su, H. N. (2017). Global Interdependence of Collaborative R&D-Typology and Association of International Co-Patenting. *Sustainability, 9*(4), 541.

Subramanyam, K. (1983). Bibliometric Studies of Research Collaboration: A Review. *Journal of Information Science*, 6(1), 33–38.

Sud, P., & Thelwall, M. (2016). Not All International Collaboration Is Beneficial: The Mendeley Readership and Citation Impact of Biochemical Research Collaboration. *Journal of the Association for Information Science and Technology*, 67(8), 1849–1857.

Sun, S., & Manson, S. M. (2011). Social Network Analysis of the Academic GIScience Community. *The Professional Geographer*, 63(1), 18–33.

Sun, Y., & Cao, C. (2014). Demystifying Central Government R&D Spending in China. *Science*, 345(6200), 1006–1008.

Sun, Y., & Cao, C. (2015). Intra-And Inter-Regional Research Collaboration across Organizational Boundaries: Evolving Patterns in China. *Technological Forecasting and Social Change*, 96, 215–231.

Sun, Y., & Liu, F. (2014). New Trends in Chinese Innovation Policies since 2009–A System Framework of Policy Analysis. *International Journal of Technology Management*, 65(1–4), 6–23.

Tahamtan, I., Afshar, A. S., & Ahamdzadeh, K. (2016). Factors Affecting Number of Citations: A Comprehensive Review of the Literature. *Scientometrics*, 107(3), 1195–1225.

Tai, Q., & Truex, R. (2015). Public Opinion Towards Return Migration: A Survey Experiment of Chinese Netizens. *China Quarterly*, 223, 770–786.

Tang, L., & Shapira, P. (2011). China–US Scientific Collaboration in Nanotechnology: Patterns and Dynamics. *Scientometrics*, 88(1). doi:10.1007/s11192-011-0376-z

Tang, L., & Shapira, P. (2012). Effects of International Collaboration and Knowledge Moderation on China's Nanotechnology Research Impacts. *Journal of Technology Management in China*, 7(1), 94–110.

Taylor, M. Z. (2016). *The Politics of Innovation: Why Some Countries are Better than Others at Science and Technology*. New York, NY: Oxford University Press.

Taylor, P. J., Hoyler, M., & Evans, D. M. (2008). A Geohistorical Study of 'The Rise of Modern Science': Mapping Scientific Practice through Urban Networks, 1500–1900. *Minerva*, 46(4), 391–410.

Terdiman, D. (2015, May 11). *Why Chinese Drone Giant DJI Is Opening A Silicon Valley R&D Lab*. Fast Company. Retrieved from https://www.fastcompany.com/3053220/why-chinese-drone-giant-dji-is-opening-a-silicon-valley-rd-lab

Thagard, P. (1997). Collaborative Knowledge. *Noûs*, 31, 242–261.

Thelen, B. A., & Thiet, R. K. (2008). Cultivating Connection: Incorporating Meaningful Citizen Science into Cape Cod National Seashore's Estuarine Research and Monitoring Programs. *Park Science*, 25(1), 74–80.

Thelwall, M., Haustein, S., Larivière, V., & Sugimoto, C. R. (2013). Do Altmetrics Work? Twitter and Ten Other Social Web Services. *PLoS ONE*, 8(5), e64841.

Thünen, J. H. von. (1826). *Der Isolierte Staat in Beziehung Auf Landwirtschaft Und Nationalökonomie*. Hamburg, Germany: Friedrich Perthes.

Tian, P. (2015). China's Diaspora Brings It Home. *Nature*, 7577(527), 68–71. Retrieved from http://www.nature.com/nature/journal/v527/n7577_supp/full/527S68a.html

Tocqueville, A. de. (2000). *Democracy in America*. (H. C. Mansfield & D. Winthrop, Trans). Chicago, IL: University of Chicago Press.

Todeschini, R., & Baccini, A. (2016). *Handbook of Bibliometric Indicators: Quantitative Tools for Studying and Evaluating Research*. Weinheim, Germany: Wiley-VCH.

Tödtling, F. (1994). The Uneven Landscape of Innovation Poles: Local Embeddedness and Global Networks. In A. Amin & N. Thrift (Eds.), *Globalization, Institutions, and Regional Development in Europe* (pp. 68–90). Oxford, UK: Oxford University Press.

Tödtling, F., & Trippl, M. (2005). One Size Fits All?: Towards a Differentiated Regional Innovation Policy Approach. *Research Policy*, 34(8), 1203–1219.

Toker, U., & Gray, D.O. (2008). Innovation Spaces: Workspace Planning and Innovation in U.S. University Research Centers. *Research Policy*, 37(2), 309–329.

References 217

Törnqvist, G. (2011). *The Geography of Creativity*. Cheltenham, UK: Edward Elgar.

Torre, A., & Gilly, J. P. (2000). On the Analytical Dimension of Proximity Dynamics. *Regional Studies*, 34(2), 169–180.

Torre, A., & Rallet, A. (2005). Proximity and Localization. *Regional Studies*, 39(1), 47–59.

Trachana, V. (2013). Austerity-Led Brain Drain Is Killing Greek Science: Lack of Funding and Recruitment Freezes are Driving Young Researchers Out of the Country. *Nature*, 496(7445), 271–272.

Traoré, N., & Landry, R. (1997). On the Determinants of Scientists' Collaboration. *Science Communication*, 19(2), 124–140.

Trippl, M., Sinozic, T., & Lawton Smith, H. (2015). The Role of Universities in Regional Development: Conceptual Models and Policy Institutions in the UK, Sweden and Austria. *European Planning Studies*, 23(9), 1722–1740.

Trott, P., & Hartmann, D. (2009). Why 'Open Innovation' Is Old Wine in New Bottles. *International Journal of Innovation Management*, 13(04), 715–736.

Tscharntke, T., Hochberg, M.E., Rand, T.A., Resh, V.H., & Krauss, J. (2007). Author Sequence and Credit for Contributions in Multiauthored Publications. *PLoS Biology*, 5(1), e18. doi:http://doi.org/10.1371/journal.pbio.0050018

Turekian, V. C., Macindoe, S., Copeland, D., Davis, L. S., Patman R. G., & Pozza, M. (2014). The Emergence of Science Diplomacy. In L. S. Davis (Ed.), *Science Diplomacy: New Day Or False Dawn?* (pp. 3–24). New Jersey: World Scientific Publishing.

Turner, P. V. (1984). *Campus: An American Planning Tradition*. New York, NY: Architectural History Foundation.

Turpin, T., Garrett-Jones, S., & Woolley, R. (2011). Cross-Sector Research Collaboration in Australia: The Cooperative Research Centres Program at the Crossroads. *Science and Public Policy*, 38(2), 87–98.

Twilley, N. (2016, February 11). Gravitational Waves Exist: The inside Story of How Scientists Finally Found Them. *The New Yorker*. Retrieved from https://www.newyorker.com/tech/elements/gravitational-waves-exist-heres-how-scientists-finally-found-them.

Uddin, S., Hossain, L., Abbasi, A., & Rasmussen, K. (2012). Trend and Efficiency Analysis of Co-Authorship Network. *Scientometrics*, 90(2), 687–699.

Ukrainski, K., Masso, J., & Kanep, H. (2014). Cooperation Patterns in Science within Europe: The Standpoint of Small Countries. *Scientometrics*, 99(3), 845–863.

Umlauf, F. (2016). *Structure and Dynamics of Policy Induced Networks in Systems of Innovation* (Doctoral dissertation). Universität Bremen, Bremen. Retrieved from https://d-nb.info/1111020760/34

UNESCO. (2015). *UNESCO Science Report: Towards 2030*. Paris, France: UNESCO.

University of Pittsburgh. (2006, February 8). *Summary investigative report on allegations of possible scientific misconduct on the part of Gerald P. Schatten, Ph.D*. Retrieved from http://hdl.handle.net/1813/11589

Uyarra, E. (2010). Conceptualizing the Regional Roles of Universities, Implications and Contradictions. *European Planning Studies*, 18(8), 1227–1246.

Van Noorden, R. (2014). Online Collaboration: Scientists and the Social Network. *Nature*, 512(7513), 126–129.

Van Raan, A. F. (2005). Measurement of Central Aspects of Scientific Research: Performance, Interdisciplinarity, Structure. *Measurement: Interdisciplinary Research and Perspectives*, 3(1), 1–19.

Van Rijnsoever, F. J., & Hessels, L. K. (2011). Factors Associated with Disciplinary and Interdisciplinary Research Collaboration. *Research Policy*, 40(3), 463–472.

Van Rijnsoever, F. J., Hessels, L. K., & Vandeberg, R. L. (2008). A Resource-Based View on the Interactions of University Researchers. *Research Policy*, 37(8), 1255–1266.

Vanni, T., Mesa-Frias, M., Sanchez-Garcia, R., Roesler, R., Schwartsmann, G., Goldani, M. Z., & Foss, A. M. (2014). International Scientific Collaboration in HIV and HPV: A Network Analysis. *PLoS ONE*, 9(3), e93376.

Vargas, A. O. (2009). Did Paul Kammerer Discover Epigenetic Inheritance? A Modern Look at the Controversial Midwife Toad Experiments. *Journal of Experimental Zoology Part B: Molecular and Developmental Evolution*, *312*(7), 667–678.

Vasileiadou, E. (2009). Stabilisation Operationalised: Using Time Series Analysis to Understand the Dynamics of Research Collaboration. *Journal of Informetrics*, *3*(1), 36–48.

Vasileiadou, E., & Vliegenthart, R. (2009). Research Productivity in the Era of the Internet Revisited. *Research Policy*, *38*(8), 1260–1268.

Velema, T. A. (2012). The Contingent Nature of Brain Gain and Brain Circulation: Their Foreign Context and the Impact of Return Scientists on the Scientific Community in Their Country of Origin. *Scientometrics*, *93*(3), 893–913.

Venkatraman, V. (2010, April 16),Conventions of Scientific Authorship, *Science*. Retrieved from http://www.sciencemag.org/careers/2010/04/conventions-scientific-authorship

Verburgh, A., Elen, J., & Lindblom-Ylänne, S. (2007). Investigating the Myth of the Relationship between Teaching and Research in Higher Education: A Review of Empirical Research. *Studies in Philosophy and Education*, *26*(5), 449–465.

Vest, C. M. (2007). *The American Research University from World War II to World Wide Web: Governments, the Private Sector, and the Emerging Meta-University*. Berkeley, CA: Center for Studies in Higher Education and University of California Press.

Vicens, Q., & Bourne, P. E. (2007). Ten Simple Rules for a Successful Collaboration. *PLOS Computational Biology*, *3*(3), e44.

Vidgen, R., Henneberg, S., & Naudé, P. (2007). What Sort of Community Is the European Conference on Information Systems? A Social Network Analysis 1993–2005. *European Journal of Information Systems*, *16*(1), 5–19.

Vinkler, P. (2008). Correlation between the Structure of Scientific Research, Scientometric Indicators and GDP in EU and non-EU Countries. *Scientometrics*, *74*(2), 237–254.

Visser, E. J., & Boschma, R. (2004). Learning in Districts: Novelty and Lock-In in a Regional Context. *European Planning Studies*, *12*(6), 793–808.

Vonortas, N. S. (1997). *Cooperation in Research and Development*. New York, NY: Springer Science+ Business Media.

Vonortas, N. S. (2013). Social Networks in R&D Program Evaluation. *The Journal of Technology Transfer*, *38*(5), 577–606.

Wagner, C. S. (2005). Six Case Studies of International Collaboration in Science. *Scientometrics*, *62*(1), 3–26.

Wagner, C. S. (2008). *The New Invisible College: Science for Development*. Washington, DC: Brookings Institution Press.

Wagner, C. S., & Leydesdorff, L. (2005). Network Structure, Self-Organization, and the Growth of International Collaboration in Science. *Research Policy*, *34*(10), 1608–1618.

Wagner, C. S., Park, H. W., & Leydesdorff, L. (2015). The Continuing Growth of Global Cooperation Networks in Research: A Conundrum for National Governments. *PLoS ONE*, *10*(7), e0131816.

Wagner-Döbler, R. (2001). Continuity and Discontinuity of Collaboration Behaviour since 1800—From a Bibliometric Point of View. *Scientometrics*, *52*(3), 503–517.

Wainwright, O. (2016, January 5). Step into Silicon Forest, Putin's Secret Weapon in the Global Tech Race. *The Guardian*. Retrieved from https://www.theguardian.com/artanddesign/2016/jan/05/silicon-forest-putin-secret-weapon-global-tech-race-siberia-russia

Wallace, M. L., Gingras, Y. & Duhon, R. (2009). A New Approach for Detecting Scientific Specialties from Raw Cocitation Networks. *Journal of the Association for Information Science and Technology*, *60*, 240–246.

Wallerstein, I. M. (2004). *World-Systems Analysis: An Introduction*. Durham, UK: Duke University Press.

Walley, K. (2007). Coopetition: An Introduction to the Subject and an Agenda for Research. *International Studies of Management & Organization*, *37*(2), 11–31.

Wallsten, S. (2004). Do Science Parks Generate Regional Economic Growth? an Empirical Analysis of Their Effects on Job Growth and Venture Capital. Working Paper 04-40. AEI-Brookings Joint Center for Regulatory Studies.

Walsh, J. P., & Maloney, N. G. (2007). Collaboration Structure, Communication Media, and Problems in Scientific Work Teams. *Journal of Computer-Mediated Communication, 12*(2), 712–732.

Waltman, L., Tijssen, R. J., & Van Eck, N. J. (2011). Globalisation of Science in Kilometres. *Journal of Informetrics, 5*(4), 574–582.

Wang, H., & Bao, Y. (2015). *Reverse Migration in Contemporary China: Returnees, Entrepreneurship and the Chinese Economy.* Houndmills, UK: Palgrave Macmillan.

Wang, J., & Shapira, P. (2015). Is There a Relationship between Research Sponsorship and Publication Impact? an Analysis of Funding Acknowledgments in Nanotechnology Papers. *PLoS ONE, 10*(2), e0117727.

Wanzenböck, I., Scherngell, T., & Brenner, T. (2014). Embeddedness of Regions in European Knowledge Networks: A Comparative Analysis of Inter-Regional R&D Collaborations, Co-Patents and Co-Publications. *The Annals of Regional Science, 53*(2), 337–368.

Ware, M., & Mabe, M. (2015, March). The STM Report. An Overview of Scientific and Scholarly Journal Publishing (4th Ed.). Retrieved from https://www.stm-assoc.org/2015_02_20_STM_Report_2015.pdf

Wasserman S., & Faust K. (2007). *Social Network Analysis: Methods and Applications.* New York, NY: Cambridge University Press.

Weaver, W. (1997). *A Legacy of Excellence: The Story of Villa I Tatti.* New York, NY: Harry N. Abrams.

Weigel, A. (2015). Amateur Ambition: How Athletic Programs Shape University Policy. *Arizona State University Sports & Entertainment Law Journal, 5*(1), 80–88.

Weiner, E. (2016). *The Geography of Genius: A Search for the World's Most Creative Places from Ancient Athens to Silicon Valley.* New York, NY: Simon & Schuster.

Welch, A. (2015). A New Epistemic Silk Road? the Chinese Knowledge Diaspora, and Its Implications for the Europe of Knowledge. *European Review, 23,* S95–S111.

Welch, A., & Hao, J. (2014). Hai Gui and Hai Dai: The Job-Seeking Experiences of High-Skilled Returnees to China. In Mok, K.-H. (Ed.), *Internationalization of Higher Education in East Asia: Trends of Student Mobility and Impact on Education Governance* (pp. 90–114). London, UK: Routledge.

Wessner, C. W. (2013). *Best Practices in State and Regional Innovation Initiatives: Competing in the 21st Century.* Washington, DC: National Academies Press. Retrieved from http://www.nap.edu/openbook.php?record_id=18364

Which country has the best brains? (2010, October 8). *BBC News Magazine.* Retrieved from http://www.bbc.co.uk/news/magazine-11500373

Whitley, R. (2000). *The Intellectual and Social Organization of the Sciences.* Oxford, UK: Oxford University Press.

Wiewel, W., & Perry, D. C. (2015). *Global Universities and Urban Development: Case Studies and Analysis.* Armonk, NY: M.E. Sharpe.

Williamson, O. E. (1991). Comparative Economic Organization: The Analysis of Discrete Structural Alternatives. *Administrative Science Quarterly, 36*(2), 269–296.

Wilsdon, J. (2007). China: The Next Science Superpower? *Engineering & Technology, 2*(3), 28–31.

Wilson, L. (1942). *The Academic Man: A Study in the Sociology of A Profession.* London, UK: Oxford University Press.

Wilson, S. M. (1999). *The Emperor's Giraffe and Other Stories of Cultures in Contact.* Boulder, CO: Westview Press.

Wissema, J. G. (2009). *Towards the Third Generation University: Managing the University in Transition.* Cheltenham: Edward Elgar Publishing.

Wolfe, A. J. (2013). *Competing with the Soviets: Science, Technology, and the State in Cold War America.* Baltimore, MD: Johns Hopkins University Press.

Woolfson, M. M. (2015). *Time and Age: Time Machines, Relativity, and Fossils.* London, UK: Imperial College Press.

Wootton, D. (2015). *The Invention of Science: A New History of Scientific Revolution.* London, UK: Allen Lane.

Wray, K. B. (2002). The Epistemic Significance of Collaborative Research. *Philosophy of Science, 69*(1), 150–168.

Wright, A. (2007). *Glut: Mastering Information through the Ages.* Washington, DC: Joseph Henry Press.

Wright, A. (2014). *Cataloging the World: Paul Otlet and the Birth of the Information Age.* Oxford University Press.

Wuchty, S., Jones, B. F., & Uzzi, B. (2007). The Increasing Dominance of Teams in Production of Knowledge. *Science, 316*(5827), 1036–1039.

Wulf, A. (2012). *Chasing Venus: The Race to Measure the Heavens.* New York, NY: Alfred A. Knopf.

Wulf, A. (2015). *The Invention of Nature: Alexander Von Humboldt's New World.* New York, NY: Alfred A. Knopf.

Wuyts, S., Colombo, M. G., Dutta, S., & Nooteboom, B. (2005). Empirical Tests of Optimal Cognitive Distance. *Journal of Economic Behavior & Organization, 58*(2), 277–302.

Xia, J., Harmon, J. L., Connolly, K. G., Donnelly, R. M., Anderson, M. R., & Howard, H. A. (2015). Who Publishes in "Predatory" Journals? *Journal of the Association for Information Science and Technology, 66*(7), 1406–1417.

Xian, W. (2015). A Quantitative Study of the Internationalization of the Academics and Research Productivity: Case Study of China. *Chinese Education & Society, 48*(4), 265–279.

Xinhua (2016a, February 14). Chinese Contribute to Detection of Gravitational Wave-Tsinghua Professor. *China Daily.* Retrieved from http://www.chinadaily.com.cn/china/2016-02/15/content_23480315.htm

Xinhua (2016b, February 15). China Plans More Gravitational Wave Research. *China Daily.* Retrieved from http://www.chinadaily.com.cn/china/2016-02/15/content_23480376.htm

Yingqi, C. (2016, February 17). Researchers Hope to Catch Next Big Wave. *China Daily.* Retrieved from http://europe.chinadaily.com.cn/china/2016-02/17/content_23515129.htm

Ynalvez, M. A., & Shrum, W. M. (2009). International Graduate Science Training and Scientific Collaboration. *International Sociology, 24*(6), 870–901.

Ynalvez, M. A., & Shrum, W. M. (2011). Professional Networks, Scientific Collaboration, and Publication Productivity in Resource-Constrained Research Institutions in a Developing Country. *Research Policy, 40*(2), 204–216.

Youtie, J., & Shapira P. (2008). Building an Innovation Hub: A Case Study of the Transformation of University Roles in Regional Technological and Economic Development. *Research Policy, 37*(8), 1188–1204.

Zanotto, S. R., Haeffner, C., & Guimarães, J. A. (2016). Unbalanced International Collaboration Affects Adversely the Usefulness of Countries' Scientific Output as Well as Their Technological and Social Impact. *Scientometrics, 109*(3), 1789.

Zha, Q. (2009). Diversification or Homogenization: How Governments and Markets Have Combined to (Re)Shape Chinese Higher Education in Its Recent Massification Process. *Higher Education, 58*(1), 41–58.

Zhai, L., Yan, X., Shibchurn, J., & Song, X. (2014). Evolutionary Analysis of International Collaboration Network of Chinese Scholars in Management Research. *Scientometrics, 98*(2), 1435–1454.

Zhang, Q., Perra, N., Gonçalves, B., Ciulla, F., & Vespignani, A. (2013). Characterizing Scientific Production and Consumption in Physics. *Scientific Reports, 3*, 1640.

Zheng, J., Zhao, Z. Y., Zhang, X., Chen, D. Z., & Huang, M. H. (2014). International Collaboration Development in Nanotechnology: A Perspective of Patent Network Analysis. *Scientometrics, 98*(1), 683–702.

Zhou, P., & Leydesdorff, L. (2006). The Emergence of China as a Leading Nation in Science. *Research Policy, 35*(1), 83–104.

Zhou, Y. (2015). The Rapid Rise of a Research Nation. *Nature, 528*, 170–173.

Žížalová, P. (2010). Geography of Knowledge-Based Collaboration in a Post-Communist Country: Specific Experience or Generalized Pattern? *European Planning Studies, 18*(5), 791–814.

Zucker, D. (2012). Developing Your Career in an Age of Team Science. *Journal of Investigative Medicine, 60*(5), 779–784.

Zweig, D., & Wang, H. (2013). Can China Bring Back the Best? the Communist Party Organizes China's Search for Talent. *The China Quarterly, 215*, 590–615.

Web sites

http://data.worldbank.org
http://english.cas.cn
https://urcmich.org
www.btaa.org
www.europeana.eu
www.global-innovation-initiative.org
www.kooperation-international.de
www.nobelprize.org
www.research-in-germany.de

Index

Académie Parisienne 32
Academy of Sciences: Chinese 74, 156–159, 161–162; French 30, 32; German 30; Hungarian 143; US National Academy 151, 169
acknowledgements 27, 44, 64, 66
Adams, Jonathan 28
Adams' age of research 28, 31
added value: European 143, 145; of collaboration 21–22, 109
ages of research *see* Adams Jonathan
Akademgorodok 21–22
altmetrics: types 64–65; advantages 64–65
Amsterdam 62, 98, 99
Antipolis, Sophia 5
article: collaborative 28, 34, 38, 74, 92, 97, 102–103, 126, 130, 157; per million inhabitants 14; in scientific journal 21, 23, 29, 35, 38, 57–59, 65, 78, 86, 89, 92–96, 101, 103, 106, 130, 135
ATLAS 58
Australia 14–15, 80, 87, 103–104, 162, 172–174
Austria 17, 79, 81, 87, 89, 104, 171
authorship (author): corresponding 103–104, 157; first 40, 57, 60, 157; *see also* first author bias; ghost 58; guest 58; gift 58; honorary 58, 140; hyper- 59, 104, 179; multi- 29, 34–35, 38, 60, 66; order 40, 58–59; standards 58; single/sole 27–29, 34, 38, 51, 174; subauthorship 43–44; *see also* co-authorship

Belgium 78–79, 81, 87, 104, 144, 149
bias: aggregation 178; first-author 59; disciplinary 119; spatial 119
bibliometrics: data sources 61–64; methods 66
big data 5

big science 9–10, 18, 26, 28, 33, 119, 136, 158–159, 164–165, 168
Bologna 24, 25, 98, 99
Bourbaki, Nicolas *also* Bourbaki's Theorem, Bourbaki group 27
Boyle Robert 8, 29, 30
brain: circulation 4, 152, 161–163; drain 103, 105, 151, 161–163; map 55
Bratislava 89
Brazil 81, 87, 100, 104, 142, 151, 153, 175
Brown University 175
Bush, Vannevar 135
business – as a collaboration partner 56, 123, 139, 148, 149, 167

Cambridge: city (UK) 5, 12, 24, 89, 98, 99, 117; city (USA) 5; University 23
Canada 15, 78–80, 87, 104, 142, 147, 149, 160
Cartan, Henri 27
Cardwell's Law 22–24, 26
Castells, Manuel 21, 25, 179
centrality – types 69–71, 100
centre-periphery: hierarchy 16; logic 3, 77, 102–106; model 102; pattern 77; relations 10, 103, 177, 182
Conseil Européen pour la Recherche Nucléaire (CERN) 9, 58, 89, 119, 136, 138, 159, 164, 165
Charpak, Georges 136
China 3, 15, 16, 17, 23, 74, 79, 80, 87, 92, 94, 96, 100, 104, 105, 133, 142, 151, 153, 154–163, 169, 170, 173, 175, 177, 181
citation: in-coming 16; out-going 16; as a collaboration measure 6, 38–39, 64–65, 77–78, 100–103, 128–129, 151
citizen science (*also* networked science, crowd science) 179–180, 184

Index

cluster 65, 89, 117, 121, 123–124, 127,128, 130, 132
co-affiliation 75, 105
co-authorship (co-author) 1, 6, 28, 34, 38–40, 45, 51, 52, 58, 59, 62, 64–69, 73, 74, 77–80, 84, 86, 88–96, 98–102, 104, 115, 118, 128, 130, 152, 155, 174, 179–180
coding: comprehensive 74; hierarchical 73–74
collaboration: interdisciplinary 50, 54, 56, 59, 108, 117, 159, 168; intersectoral 63, 116, 121, 123–125, 127; life-cycle 52–60; measures 66–72, 148; modes 43–44; network 34–35, 77, 92, 100, 103, 112, 114, 117–119, 130, 132, 156, 170, 174, 176–177; policy see policy; transdisciplinary 51
collaborative: advantage 107–109, 183; culture 145, 147–148; environment 20; turn 1–3, 28, 34–38, 39, 59, 106, 108, 135, 176, 178, 181
collaborator types 47
College for the Promoting of Physico-Mathematical Experimental Learning see Royal Society
college town 12, 15, 26
collocation 112–113, 116, 120, 126
Columbia University 175
communication 2,5, 11, 20, 31–33, 37, 41–42, 44, 49, 52–55, 61, 111, 113–116, 120, 165–168, 177–178, 184
Community of scholars (also: invisible college, Invisible College) 6, 11–13, 65, 135–136
competition 20, 22, 28, 30, 49, 52, 55, 121, 125–127, 136, 138, 157, 176, 184
conference/congress 33, 36–37, 40, 43–45, 57, 62, 65, 106, 112–113, 147, 158
Cooperative Research and Development Agreement (CRADA) 148–149
coopetition 30, 125–127, 184
coordination 41, 52, 54–56, 111, 120, 127, 138, 141, 145, 152, 156, 157, 166, 174, 179
core/centre 94, 102, 103, 105, 177
Cornell University 154, 175
costs: of collaboration 36, 46–49, 107, 110–114; coordination 111; transaction 111, 114, 178
counting (fractional, full/whole) 72–73, 97–98, 172, 174

creative class 19
cross-fertilisation 50, 121–122
crowd science see citizen science

Dartmouth College 175
Darwin, Charles 4, 28–29
discipline – specificity 51, 74
distance: as a barrier 33; changing nature of 36; functional 72; geographical collaboration (GCD) 71, 75; impact on collaboration 2, 61, 102, 106, 111–117, 129, 131; measures 75; network 70; organizational 56; vs proximity 2, 127–129, 177, 183–184
division of labour 38, 45–47, 65, 109

Einstein, Albert 10, 29
environment: collaborative/uncollaborative 155, 163, 164, 170; competitive 108, 125–126; international 14; local 110, 130; online 64; national 131, 177; natural 125; research/science/scientific 13, 108, 140, 166; regional 110, 122, 127; regulatory 164, 170; socioeconomic 132; working/workplace 11, 26, 112, 169
epistemic: responsibility 57; significance 121; validity 1, 107
Erdős, Paul 118
et al. 57–59
European Cooperation in Science and Technology (COST) 138
European Research Area 94, 137–145, 171, 181
European Southern Observatory see Very Large Telescope
European Union (EU) 1, 10, 15, 87, 89, 133, 137–138, 142, 144, 160, 166–167, 182

Feynman, Richard 40
Fogarty, John Edward 152
Fogarty International Center (FIC) 152
Framework Programme (Framework Programmes for Research and Technological Development) 64, 140–142
France 5, 15, 27, 49, 78–80, 87, 89, 103, 104, 122, 144, 160
Francis, Bacon 31
Fulbright, James William 151
Fulbright Program 151–152, 169

Garfield, Eugene 51, 62
geography of collaboration: driving factors 16–17; evolution 24; significance 1–7, 14, 22–24, 105–106, 176–178; theoretical framework 131
geolocalisation 61–62, 72, 74–76
Germany 14–16, 22–24, 33, 49, 78–80, 87, 89, 103–104, 106, 117, 122, 136, 144, 149, 151, 160, 165, 170, 171, 173
global pipelines 130–131
Goldilocks principle 117
gravity model 114–115, 120
growth: economic 18, 23; of collaboration 1–2, 18, 107–111, 131, 163, 180
guanxi 156

Harrison, John 134
Harvard University 10, 146, 175
helix: triple 121, 123–125, 127, 149; quadruple 124; quintuple 125
heterophily 112, 117
hierarchical structure 2, 5, 16, 102–103, 105, 119, 120, 156, 176, 177
homophily 112, 117
hub 25, 32, 92
hukou 162
Human Genome Project 23, 49, 120, 152, 159
humanities 10, 34, 35, 38, 39, 58, 66, 106, 143, 144, 168
Humboldt, Alexander 4
Humboldt Research Fellowship 170

India 17–18, 79–80, 87, 93, 104, 142, 149, 151, 153, 160, 169, 175
individual scientist (scholar) 29, 31, 38, 45–47, 49, 66, 69, 77, 108, 142, 164, 173 176, 178
industrial district 113, 121, 125, 127–128
Information and Communication Technologies (ICT): impact on scientific communication 36–37, 54, 166, 184
innovation 1, 11, 12, 19, 20, 23, 50, 61, 63, 105, 108–110, 117, 121–125, 127, 128, 132, 133, 135, 139, 141, 145, 148, 152–154, 156, 158–160, 164–167, 175
inspiration 20, 31, 40, 43–45, 50
interaction: difference from collaboration 41; influence of distance/proximity 113–115; face-to-face 20, 37, 54, 113, 178; via ICT 54; management of 168; measure 114–115; types of 127
internationalisation 77–91, 96, 100–101, 129, 178–180
Internet see Information and Communication Technologies (ICT)
Israel 23, 82, 87, 104, 175
Italy 10, 17–18, 24, 63, 79–80, 87, 89, 104, 128, 160, 172–173
Ivy League 147–148

Japan 15–16, 23, 49, 56, 80, 86–87, 93, 104, 140, 142, 144

knowledge: access to 49–50; broker 70; circulation/flows 45, 51, 65, 71, 89, 93, 103, 121–125, 129–130, 178, 181–183; creation/production 26, 35, 38, 40–42, 62, 65, 108–111, 121, 128, 139, 182; dissemination 31, 35–36; exchange 30–31; integration 50–51; network 100; procedural (know-how) 43; resource 24, 45–46, 70, 100, 117, 128, 136, 161; spillovers 122, 132; tacit 46, 51, 53, 127, 129; transfer 37, 43, 116, 139, 148–149, 158

laboratory (lab) 7–10, 12, 13, 26, 135, 151
language: barriers 54, 111; English 37, 54, 79; lingua franca/common language 37, 145
law: as a regulation 116, 170–171; as a principle 22–26, 32, 114, 118, 132, 180; intellectual property law 148, 156, 170–171, 180
Leibniz, Gottfried Wilhelm 28, 31
Leibniz University 149
Leibniz Association 168
Large Hadron Collider (LHC) 9, 48, 49, 143, 159
library: as a building (space) 7, 13; as an institution 10, 147; catalogue 5, 26
Linnaean taxonomy 5
Linnaeus Carl 5
Livingston David N. 4, 8, 18
local buzz 130–131
location 16, 21, 36, 48, 61, 65, 75, 106, 111, 118–120, 122, 127, 132, 151, 160, 176, 178, 180
Longitude Act 134
longue durée 22–26

management – role in collaboration 52, 54–55, 111, 139, 164, 168
Manhattan Project 9, 134
map (visual presentation): in geographical terms 54; of science 6, 86
Marie Skłodowska-Curie Actions (MSCA) 140
Matilda effect 59
Matthew effect 17, 59, 118, 132, 168
Mendeleev, Dmitrij 5, 33
Merton, Robert 59, 118, 125
metropolis 95–96
milieu: creative 12, 19–20; innovateur 123–124; institutional 137; local 128
Massachusetts Institute of Technology (MIT) 113, 153
mobility (academic/professional) 4, 63, 75, 103, 114, 130, 140–143, 145, 150–152, 164–165, 169, 170–171, 174
mode 1, mode 2 of knowledge production 108–110, 124, 131–132
multidisciplinary research 44, 50

National Institute of Health (NIH) 49, 152, 171
Nature – scientific journal 52, 58, 126, 179
New Invisible College 6, 135
Newton, Isaac 28, 114, 134
Nobel Prize laureates 11, 14–15, 35, 40, 48, 53, 59, 122, 136, 157, 179
node (in the network) 2, 69–71, 92–96, 106, 111–112, 114, 118, 129, 132

open innovation 108–109, 132, 148
Oxbridge 24
Oxford: city (UK) 5,12, 24, 89, 98–99; University 23

paper *see* article
Papin, Denis 29
Pasteur, Louis 7, 110
patent 35, 63, 65, 72, 85–87, 122, 124, 155, 170, 174
path: in the network 69–72; as a route 113
performance (research/scientific) 96, 100–103, 105, 108, 122, 130–131, 137, 168, 177; assessment/evaluation of 51, 59, 63, 111, 157, 164, 172–174
Philosophical Transactions - scientific journal 28, 30, 59
Physical Review Letters - scientific journal 35, 179

place: of scientific activity/of collaboration 4–26, 54, 97, 106, 111–114, 118–120, 162, 165, 177, 180, 182; of innovation 128; place-based 182–183; place-neutral 182–183; relation with space *see* space
Poland 15, 18, 22, 24, 79, 81, 87, 89, 100, 104, 150, 166, 172–173
policy: science 3, 17, 20, 133–175, 181–183; scientific collaboration 133–175; through science 133–135, 163
policymaker 107, 134, 138, 164, 173, 176
preferential attachment 112, 118, 120
Princeton University 175
project – research 28, 32, 39, 40, 42–44, 46, 50, 120, 122, 133, 138, 141, 143, 147, 153, 156–161, 171
proximity: cultural 112, 184; cognitive 112, 115, 117, 184; economic 54, 112, 184; functional 72; institutional 112, 115–117, 184; organisational 54, 112; social 53–54, 112, 184; spatial (physical) 2, 11, 21, 54, 95, 112–117, 131, 155, 177; technological 112, 184; non-spatial 115–117, 184; significance/importance 95, 112–117, 177
publish or perish 51–52, 105, 157, 164, 173, 176

R&D: centre/institution 160, 163, 167; collaboration 140, 164–165, 170.; employment 75; expenditure 75, 114, 136–137, 140, 146, 154, 156, 168; project 136; sector 122, 130, 148, 151
recognition 126, 154, 159, 176
region: R&D sector 129–131; as subnational entity 18, 19, 22, 24, 36, 61, 63, 67, 70, 75, 77, 86, 89–95, 100, 102, 106, 109, 116, 118, 120, 122–123, 127–128; learning 110, 121, 124, 128
regional development: policy 17, 22; relations with scientific collaboration 19, 107, 120–123, 125, 127–131
regional innovation system 12, 121–124, 128
regulations *see* law
relations: bilateral 67–68, 78–79, 92, 93, 142, 152, 153, 160, 164, 169; informal 44, 156; interpersonal 156; strength of 130
Republic of Letters 6, 31–33, 35, 76
research: applied 7, 110, 141, 158; basic 11, 110, 135, 144, 146, 175

research evaluation
research policy *see* science policy
returnee 130, 156, 158, 161–162, 170
Royal Society 30
Rubbia, Carlo 136
Russia 22, 81, 87, 101, 104, 106, 144, 149, 160, 175

Salomon, Jean-Jacques 134,163
science: infrastructure 5, 28, 48, 141, 143, 158, 165; park/town 18
Science Citation Index *see* Web of Science
science diplomacy 164–165
science evaluation: *see* performance evaluation
scientific: community 11, 31, 33, 35, 39, 47, 157; disciplines/fields 5, 34, 37, 40–41, 46, 49–51, 54, 57–58, 119, 141, 159, 160, 184; ethos 45, 54; frontier 49, 136, 138; journal 58; types (Wagner) 40, 119
scientific collaboration: definition 2–3, 41–42; types 42, 67, 119; geography 76–107; benefits/costs 2, 27, 47, 103, 108–109, 110–111, 116, 145, 169, 180; consequences 2, 47, 51, 122, 131, 181–182; effects/impact 38, 44, 72, 95, 100, 102, 106, 109, 111, 113, 119–123, 184; measures 66–72; weak/strong 41–44; modes 42–44; goals 41–43, 45, 54, 127, 137; limits 53,179–180; future 176, 178–184
Scientometrics – scientific journal 135
Scopus 62, 64–65, 78, 100, 150
Silicon Valley 5, 17, 20, 22, 109, 160
Singapore 14, 79, 82, 87, 99, 103–105
Skłodowska-Curie, Marie 15
South Korea 79, 80, 86–87, 93, 100, 104–105, 142, 144
space: common 116, 142; geographic 65, 178, 183; global 102; of ideas 65; mega-spaces 178; relation with place 3, 4–26; organizational 30; relation with scientific collaboration 3, 53, 66, 72, 111, 127, 178; shared office 169; virtual 120
spatial scientometrics – measures, methods 63, 64, 66–76, 131
spatial structure 1, 176, 179–180
specialisation 38, 42, 49, 59, 65, 126, 161, 176
spin-off, spin-out, start-up 12, 108, 109, 124

structural hole 129–130
student – as collaborator 11, 12, 29, 40, 126
Sweden 14, 23, 78, 71, 77, 89, 104, 150, 160
Switzerland 9, 14–16, 23, 78–81, 87, 89, 103–104, 119, 150, 165, 171, 175
synergy 38, 43, 109

Tallinn University of Technology 117
task: allocation/division 37, 42–44, 53, 160; specificity 41; types 42, 46
team 27–28, 31, 34–35, 42–44, 46–48, 50–51, 55–57, 66, 73, 113, 117, 119, 126, 142–143, 155, 157–158, 179, 184
teamwork *see* team
three Ts 19; *see also* creative class
Torricelli, Evangelista 30
trust 37, 44–47, 52–53, 55, 116, 143, 172, 178
truth-spot 8
turn *see* collaborative turn

Union of Soviet Socialist Republics (USSR) 16, 20, 21, 106
United Kingdom (UK) 9, 14, 15, 20, 78, 80, 87, 104, 122
United States (US, USA) 3, 11, 12, 14, 15, 20, 50, 55, 87, 104, 122, 133, 135, 145–154, 160, 163
university: campus 1, 5, 7, 11, 61, 72, 113, 153, 154, 168; entrepreneurial 110, 124; higher educational institution 116, 149, 154, 155, 158, 159, 162, 167, 176; rankings 16, 21, 24, 105, 126, 168; third mission (role) 12–13
University of Pennsylvania 175

van der Meer Simon 136
Venus – transit 32–33, 46
Very Large Telescope 165

Wagner, Caroline 119, 135, 137
weak ties 121, 129–130
Web of Science: as data source 15–16, 34–35, 38–39, 62–66, 74, 78–80, 92, 105–106; components (Social sciences Citation Index, Science Citation Index) 14, 34, 106
Weil, André 27

Yale University 175